Dictionary for

WRITERS
AND
READERS

David Grambs

To the memory of my father,
George Lorenzo Grambs, and
for my mother,
Myrtle Jane Wood Grambs

Portions of this book were previously published by McGraw-Hill, Inc., as *Words About Words* in 1984.

Grateful acknowledgment is made to the following for permission to reprint previously published material:
Fell Publishers, Inc.: Excerpts from *Al Kelly's Double Life* by Alexander Rose. Copyright © 1966 by Alexander Rose. Published by Frederick Fell Publishers, Inc., Hollywood, Florida. All rights reserved. Reprinted by permission.
Times Books, a division of Random House, Inc.: Excerpt from *The Writer's Lawyer* by Ronald L. Goldfarb and Gail E. Ross. Copyright © 1989 by Ronald L. Goldfarb and Gail E. Ross. Reprinted by permission of Times Books, a division of Random House, Inc.

Library of Congress Cataloging-in-Publication Data

The Random House dictionary for writers and readers / [edited by]
    David Grambs.
        p.   cm.
        "Portions of this book were previously published by McGraw-Hill as Words about words."
    ISBN 0-679-72860-0
    1. English language—Rhetoric—Dictionaries.   2. English language—Usage—Dictionaries.   3. Style, Literary—Dictionaries.   4. Authorship—Dictionaries.   I. Grambs, David. Words about words.   II. Random House (Firm)
PE1460.R28   1990
808'.042'03—dc20

Book design: Charlotte Staub
Manufactured in the United States of America

2 3 4 5 6 7 8 9

Random House, Inc., edition

The
Random House
Dictionary for
Writers and
Readers

The Random House

RANDOM HOUSE · NEW YORK

Contents

Acknowledgments

Dictionaries are usually produced by sizable staffs of editors and specialists. Because that was not the case with this book, I'm especially indebted to numerous people, almost all of them unremunerated, who gave a helping hand or offered useful suggestions.

Mac Havighurst provided pronunciations for some rare and forbidding words. Paul Schmidt checked foreign-language entries. For help with the supplementary Special Entries, I'm grateful to Donna Woolfolk Cross (propaganda devices), Jeffrey Grambs (journalistic attribution and evasion), Richard J. McSorley (newsroom headline jargon), David Myerson (libel), and Will Shortz (word-game words). Diane Giddis gave her invaluable scrutiny to all the special entries. The erudite Timothy Dickinson offered a dizzying number of suggestions; that I couldn't incorporate more of them is not only my loss but the reader's. Reinhold Aman, Robert K. Barnhart, Stuart Flexner, Charlton Laird, William Morris, and Joseph Shipley responded to particular queries. Thanks are also due to Jackie Abramowitz, Richard Bluestein, Lisa Frost, Gail Greene, Brian McKernan, Megan McKernan, the late Eugene Rachlis, and Jim Trupin. I'm especially indebted to *The New York Times* for quotations used in the book and to Madeline Kripke for many useful out-of-print books.

Cynthia Merman helped tremendously, and I owe her acquaintanceship to Glenn Cowley. For their help at the offices of Random House, I thank Joe Esposito, Bob Costello, Ellen Lichtenstein, and Chris Mohr. For its restfulness, scenic splendor, and running trails I'm grateful to my favorite working-vacation retreat, Mohonk Mountain House.

Introduction

The Random House Dictionary for Writers and Readers is a different kind of literary dictionary. Its focus is not so much literature, literary history, and belles lettres as it is the nuts and bolts of writing itself. Although many of the words defined are old, their use—or usefulness—today is emphasized. Besides including many terms not found in scholastic literary handbooks and even unabridged American and British dictionaries, the book differs from other literary references in two respects.

First, it is single-mindedly a glossary of terms related to prose and the devices of everyday speech, and hence does not include the numerous poetry (prosody) and classical drama terms commonly saturating other literary handbooks. Nor is this another lexicon of authors, works, or literary characters and periods with a history-of-English-literature slant. My intent has all along been simply to gather in one place words about words, terms of interest to the working writer and to any person who reads with a critical eye and likes to discuss the graces, tricks, and fine points involved in using the English language.

Second, it is a gallimaufry not only of traditional literary terms (allegory, metonymy, onomatopoeia, and the like) but also of hundreds of others related to language and writing: from journalism, linguistics, book reviewing, logic (and illogic), grammar, rhetoric, political speechwriting, editing and publishing, and to some extent advertising. (The highly technical terminology of phonetics is for the most part excluded, and this is not a book about graphology.) *The Random House Dictionary for Writers and Readers* also includes numerous distinctively British expressions and literary Latin and French borrowings as well as useful terms coined by writers and linguists that appear in no other dictionary.

This would seem to be an opportune time for publication of a lexicon focused on the craft of writing. Interest by Americans in the state of the language, and not a little concern about the way it is used, has perhaps never been greater than it is nowadays. If there was a groundbreaker for this period of fascination with words and writing, it was probably Edwin Newman's popular *Strictly Speaking*, a wry report on our native tongue's slippage published in the early 1970s and followed quickly by Newman's equally entertaining *A Civil Tongue*. Since then our bookstores seem always to be chock-full of books appealing to word and language lovers. Many newspapers now carry syndicated columns dealing with nettlesome usage questions—and replying to highly opinionated and nettled readers. If this is not the Age of William Safire, it is the Age of Concern About Our National Literacy. This book adds to the stream. But in being a kind of diagnostic reference (and, I hope, one always enjoyable to leaf through), it adds something usefully new and different.

Many terms here were found by hunting through dictionaries from A to Z, literally page by page: systematically chance discoveries. At other times I searched hopefully, quixotically: Is there a word for this literary mannerism, for that type of phrasing? Is there one for this journalistic device so often encountered in daily newspapers, for that rhetorical trick used by politicians?

The findings of such quests, I discovered, sometimes lay not in any dictionary but in the throwaway but often inspired coinages of lively writers and linguists. Lexicographers tend to frown upon so-called nonce words, those sometime coinages not fully accepted or legitimized by usage. This book unfrowningly welcomes to its pages numerous, and not always gravely serious, coinages pertaining to facets of writing (each identified as "———'s term for . . ."). I hope these will be useful, if not eternal—in most cases denoting something not denoted by any other term. Such coinages remind us that our language—and our language about language— can always profit from new terms that fill a specific need.

Pronunciations have been supplied where they seemed appropriate—that is, for words for which common sense might not be a safe bet. As other dictionaries show, this is a realm of many variants and of differing opinions (notably with Latin terms and in view of often differing British pronunciation), and I have been deliberately selective and simple here. For some of the more unfamiliar entries, a line or two about derivation has been added.

Two other decisions were made regarding format: not to number different meanings of a term and not to interpolate into definitions such labels as "rare," "obsolete," "archaic," and "slang." I am a little distrustful of lexical numbering and subnumbering, and would find my own numbers equally questionable. Labels, like numbered definitions, can certainly be helpful to a reader, but they can also be presumptuous, soon dated—or self-evident. It goes without saying (or labeling) that many of the words and phrases in this book are uncommon, a mite difficult, and not a part of everyday speech.

Two other features are central to the book's format, namely, illustrative quotations and twenty-four supplements, or "special entries," on different verbal topics separate from the general, alphabetical lexicon.

Words, even rare or difficult literary words, get lifeblood not from their mere presence in dictionaries but from actual usage in speech and writing. From the outset I felt that illustrative quotations from contemporary or recent writing were indispensable to the readability and richness of *The Random House Dictionary for Writers and Readers*; that is, quotations demonstrating (in almost all cases) an actual use of the term in question by a novelist, essayist, critic, journalist, or linguist. I wanted a broad, varied mix of modern citations, whether single sentences or brief passages, not only from scholars and grammarians but also from contemporary American and British fiction writers, and of course from journalists and book reviewers as well.

Not all entries are accompanied by quotations, but many of them are, and they come from both sides of the Atlantic. Thousands were collected, and final choices were often difficult, not to say agonizing. The citations help to bring some uncommon literary words to life and remind readers that these words not only can be profitably used but in fact are employed more than might be thought.

The special entry supplements cover areas of language-related nomenclature that, so far as I know, have received little attention in other language reference books, topics that invite, however cursorily, some measure of special treatment. A number of these special entries are thesauruslike addenda—lists of authorial adjectives, prose-descriptive adjectives, and publishing's ubiquitous blurb adjectives, for example—more usefully presented collectively. Others are meant as introductions to certain aspects of the English language, from the sly devices of propaganda and advertising to the lingo of word-gamers and the confusions of mixed metaphors. Two of the special entries, on fair use and libel, offer basic guidance on legal questions related to writing, and another provides a rather diverting "Fog Index" formula for assessing prose readability or density.

Even a reference meant to be comprehensive must be selective. No matter how rich and complete one tries to make a collection like this, there will always be regretted exclusions and lapses—

otherwise known as glaring omissions. Hundreds of "possibles" never made it into the final manuscript. Early in the project I expected to formulate an infallible rule of thumb regarding which term did and which did not belong between these two covers, but such a surefire axiom always eluded me. Lingering uncertainties about such yes-or-no rulings can be distressing, as can a sinking feeling that irresistible words will never stop turning up and a dictionary never finished. But deadlines, fortunately, have their purpose, and after a point there can be no more second thoughts, only second editions.

For a lexicographer it's heartening to recall that even Dr. Johnson tendered prefatory apologies regarding his dictionary. Like his, *The Random House Dictionary for Writers and Readers* "was written with little assistance of the learned, and without any patronage of the great; not in the soft obscurities of retirement, or under the shelter of academick bowers, but amidst inconvenience and distraction, in sickness and in sorrow." In my case, that is to say, without being Dr. Johnson, while holding down a full-time office job, and with a bit of phthisis at deadline time.

All in all, my most ardent hope is that you find this dictionary not merely helpful and reliable but also downright inviting to page through. And that it enhances—as merely discovering new terms can do—your awareness of the many subtleties in and motives behind writing both good and bad.

Pronunciation Key

add	lôrd	chest		
rāte	oil	get		
câre	pōͦol	joy		
	tŏͦok	kiln	oe	*French* jeu,
fäther	doubt	sing		soeur
bend	cup	ship	ü	*French* tu,
ēve	bûrn	thick		*German* über
sit	⎰ among	you	kh	*German* ich
īce	⎮ hasten	zh: pleasure	N	*French* son,
hot	ə⎨ possible			vin
cōde	⎮ melon			
	⎱ focus			

Parentheses around a symbol, as in **new** [*n(y)ōͦo*], mean that the sound may be pronounced or left out.

A single prime mark, ′, follows syllables that are given a primary or strong stress. A double mark, ″, follows syllables given a secondary or lighter stress.

Part I

THE RANDOM HOUSE DICTIONARY FOR WRITERS AND READERS

abbreviation *n.* The shortening of a word or phrase or use of only a few of its letters to represent the whole expression, whether by contraction, omission, use of initial letters only, or symbols; shortened or shorthand form of a word or phrase. *Adj.* abbreviated; *v.* abbreviate.

"Yellow Peril" Hadley swept through the school with the speed of a flu epidemic, and it must be said to his credit that Brinker took it well enough except when, in its inevitable abbreviation, people sometimes called him "Yellow" instead of "Peril."
—John Knowles, *A Separate Peace*

abecedarian *adj.* Pertaining to the alphabet, or alphabetically arranged; rudimentary; elementary. *N.* abecedarian.

Sisson's Synonyms, published by Prentice-Hall, and compiled by A. F. Sissons, is a contender in the abecedarian ranks. . . .
—Israel Shenker, *Harmless Drudges*

ab initio [*ab i·nish'ē·ō*] From the beginning: from the very start or outset.

That rather angry declaration of at least some respect for books; that distinctly wistful desire to write a book himself (to "tell it how it really is"—as if the poverty of that phrase did not *ab initio* castrate the wish it implied!). . . . —John Fowles, *The Ebony Tower*

ab irato [*ab i·rä' tō*] From an angry man: hence, not reasonable and possibly not to be taken too seriously.

abjective *n.* Newspaper jargon for a published apologetic correction to a previous error.

Abject because such notices are invariably apologies; *objection* because they're printed only in response to complaints from the injured parties; and *adjective* because they are meant to modify the original news report's effect. It should be noted, however, that as they are usually limited to two or three lines of small print hidden in the back section of the publication, *abjectives* rarely modify anything.
—Joel **Homer**, *Jargon*

à bouche ouverte [*ä bōōsh ōō·vert*] With open mouth: eagerly or uncritically; gullibly

ab ovo [*ab ō'vō*]   From the egg: from the very beginning, hence
completely and in great detail; thoroughly or voluminously.

abracadabra *n.*   Used as a magical word to forestall misfortune
or effect a miracle: supposedly magical or curative incantation;
overweening nonsense or jargon; gibberish.

> The error of all such unhappy viewers with alarm is in assuming that
> there is enough magic in pedagogy to teach "correct" English to the
> plain people. There is, in fact, far too little; even the fearsome abra-
> cadabra of Teachers College, Columbia, will never suffice for the
> purpose.   —H. L. Mencken, *The American Language*

absit invidia verbo [*äb'sit in·wid'ē·ə wer'bō*]   Let it be said without ill will: no offense intended.

absolute comparative   See AGENCY COMPARATIVE.

absolute superlative   See ABSOLUTE WORD.

absolute word   A word that, extreme or categorical in meaning, in
principle cannot be modified: specifically, an adjective or adverb not qualifiable by a "false" comparative or superlative,
e.g., "unique," "simultaneous," "eternally," "infinite." Also
ABSOLUTE SUPERLATIVE, FALSE COMPARATIVE, INCOMPARA-
BLE, INCOMPARABLE ABSOLUTE.

> Kael's . . . hyperenthusiasm has earned other critical comments.
> Some have said that her overuse of absolute superlatives is what one
> might expect from a critic unable to convince a reader by argument,
> allusion, or example; in short, her insensate praise reduces her re-
> views to meaninglessness.   —John English, *Criticizing the Critics*

abstract *n.*   A text summarizing the matter or principal points of
a book, article, record, or speech, esp. of an official or technical
document; abbreviated or concentrated version; condensation.
N. abstracter; *v.* abstract.

abstracted form   A word affix or element of a familiar expression
that is borrowed to form analogous words, to which it carries
an evident meaning or connotation, e.g., the suffix "-gate"
used to coin "Irangate" (from "Watergate") or "-aholic"
(from "alcoholic") in "workaholic." See also BOOSTED COIN-
AGE; PATTERNED FORM.

abstraction *n.*   The mental separating of common attributes or
qualities from distinct, individual objects or beings, oɪ of concepts from particular exemplars; word denotıng an ıdea or in-

tangible quality as opposed to something concrete. *Adj.* abstract; *adv.* abstractly.

> York Harding might write in graphic abstractions about the Third Force, but this was what it came down to—this was It.
> —Graham Greene, *The Quiet American*

abstract language Writing that is generalized, theoretical, or impersonal, typically with long Latinate words and often passive constructions (contrasted with concrete language).

> They don't hear—what worries a good many Americans when they get to work on discursive prose—that in a good many ways American-English is a significantly more abstract language than ours is. We say: "I want to book a seat." You say: "I want to make a reservation."
> —C. P. Snow, in *Writing in America*

abusage *n.* Improper or ungrammatical word usage; careless or irresponsible language; solecism.

> And it is around this fascinating vacuum that the American fetish for correctness, the agony over those droll Victorian antimacassars "usage" and "abusage," so resolutely assembles.
> —Richard Lanham, *Style*

acceptation *n.* The generally accepted meaning of a word, phrase, sentence, or concept.

accidence *n.* The part of grammar concerning inflections.

accidental pun See UNCONSCIOUS PUN.

accismus See special entry RHETORIC TERMS, p. 402.

accordion sentence Harry Shaw's term for a weak, snowballing sentence that is a sequence of tagged-on subordinate clauses, with each successive clause much like a hasty afterthought, e.g., "This is the man who goes to the club that is near the club that I couldn't join." Also DECAPITABLE SENTENCE.

accusative See special entry GRAMMAR ADJECTIVES, p. 398.

achthronym [*ak'thrō·nim''*] *n.* H. L. Mencken's term for an ethnic slur; ethnophaulism.

> The English have fewer strangers within their gates, and hence their native armamentarium is smaller, and not a few of the achthronyms . . . they use come from the United States.
> —H. L. Mencken, *The American Language*

acknowledgments See special entry PARTS OF A BOOK, p. 363.

A-copy *n.* Newspaper jargon for lazy, slipshod writing, esp. information from a public relations release passed off as newswriting. See also CANNED COPY.

à coups de dictionnaire [*ä cōo də dēk·syô·nâr*] With blows of a dictionary: with continual or incessant reference to the dictionary.

acrolect *n.* The most prestigious dialect in a creole, or mixed, language being closest to the standard international variety of the language (contrasted with basilect).

acronym *n.* A pronounceable word formed by initial letters or syllables from a series of words or compound term, e.g., "NATO," "radar." *Adj.* acronymic; *adv.* acronymically.

Honest acronyms emerge, either by pure chance or with a little discreet assistance, from genuinely preexisting phrases. Counterfeit acronyms, or retroacronyms, are formed by simply choosing some snappy or appropriate term and devising a phrase to which it can (falsely) be attributed.   —*Success With Words*

acrostic See special entry WORD-GAME WORDS, p. 394.

active title See special entry BOOK PUBLISHING TERMS, p. 361.

adage *n.* An often quoted saying.

The urge to be first with the facts on Wolfe appears to have reflected an authentic variation of the academic adage; for Halberstadt it was "scoop or perish." He may accomplish both.
                              —Eliot Fremont-Smith, *Village Voice*

adaptation See special entry BOOK PUBLISHING TERMS, p. 361.

ad baculum, a baculo [*ad bak'oŏ·ləm*] To the rod: appealing to or suggesting the use of force to settle the question, as when Joseph Stalin remarked about the pope's role in international politics, "How many [military] divisions does the pope have?"

Nevertheless, the decline of the German universities since 1932 testifies to the dangerous power of an argument *ad baculum,* not merely over the specific victim, but over everybody in the vicinity.
                              —David Hackett Fischer, *Historians' Fallacies*

ad captandum benevolentiam [*ad kap·tan'dəm ben"ə·vō·len'tē·əm*] With intent to win goodwill or favor.

ad captandum vulgus [*ad kap·tan'dəm vul'gəs*] With intent to take in the public: designed to court the crowd emotionally, even if using unsound reasoning, non sequiturs, etc.

ad crumenam [*ad kroŏ·mā'nəm*] To the purse: appealing to greed or to the hearer's pocket.

addendum *n.* Something added or to be added, as a subsequent comment, note, or insertion; appended supplement. *Pl.* addenda.

The public is probably not deceived about the quality of most of these books. If the question of quality is brought up, the answer is likely to be: no, they are not "literature." But there is an unexpressed addendum: and perhaps they are all the better for not being imaginative, for not being literature—they are not literature, they are reality, and *in a time like this* what we need is reality in large doses.
—Lionel Trilling, *The Liberal Imagination*

Addisonian termination The ending of a sentence with a preposition, as with "to," "of," or "with" (coined by critic Richard Hurd in reference to Joseph Addison).

adduce *v.* To bring up as a proof or an example; introduce for consideration or discussion; cite. *Adj.* adducible, adduceable.

. . . Sir Arthur Quiller Couch ("Q") . . . adduced the whole body of English literature in order to maintain that American literature was a provincial appendage and that its most distinguished *littérateurs* proved the primacy of the English language by being well within the mainstream of the English of England.
—Alistair Cooke, in *On Mencken*

ad hoc [*ad hok*] To this matter: for this specific instance or purpose; in this case; immediate; provisional.

Polly's motivating force was love; she wanted a world in which everybody loved everybody else whether they liked it or not, but she set this overflowing feminine cup in motion with a thoroughly masculine arsenal of charts, graphs, quorums, task forces, ad hocs, tunnel vision, and lists.   —Florence King, *When Sisterhood Was in Flower*

ad hominem [*ad hom'ə·nem''*] To the man: appealing to the sentiments or prejudices of the hearer or listener, rather than to his or her reason or intelligence; disparaging a person's character rather than his or her arguments; personal rather than substantive or ideological.

The Boss knew all about the so-called fallacy of the *argumentum ad hominem*. "It may be a fallacy," he said, "but it is shore-God useful.

If you use the right kind of *argumentum* you can always scare the *hominem* into a laundry bill he didn't expect."
—Robert Penn Warren, *All the King's Men*

ad ignorantiam [*ad" ig·nə·ran'shē·əm*]   To ignorance: depending for its effect on the hearer's not knowing something essential; arguing that something is true because it has not been proven false, or challenging another to disprove rather than endeavoring to prove.

ad infinitum   To infinity: without limit; endlessly or ceaselessly; forever.

Administrators *expedited, finalized, implemented, processed* ad infinitum, while social workers, already famed for euphemism, called their investigators *case workers*. . . .   —Mary Dohan, *Our Own Words*

ad judicium [*ad yōō·dik'ē·əm*]   To judgment: appealing to the common sense of mankind or to the judgment of the people.

ad-lib *v.*   To make an unprompted, extemporaneous remark; improvise. *Adj.* ad-lib; *adv.* ad-lib; *n.* ad-lib, ad-libber.

Myron Grunton, inspired, produced on the air one night completely ad lib the passage that found its way into the first Black Wing directive: "Germany once treated its Africans like a stern but loving stepfather, chastising them when necessary, often with death."
—Thomas Pynchon, *Gravity's Rainbow*

admass *n. British*   The populace that is easily influenced by publicity or advertising; the consumer public susceptible to mass-media persuasion. *Adj.* admass.

ad misericordiam [*ad mi·zer"ə·kôr'dē·əm*]   To compassion: appealing to a sense of pity or mercy; asking compassion.

ad nauseam   To the point of vomiting: to a sickening or wearisome degree; unrelievedly.

Henry Miller couldn't feel anything and dug graves for a living, William Burroughs was an exterminator, Carl Sandburg was a janitor, Faulkner had to run rum, and so on, ad nauseam.
—Robert Hendrickson, *The Literary Life*

adnomination [*ad·nom"ə·nā'shən*] *n.*   Punning; wordplay.

adolescent they   Roy H. Copperud's term for the use of the plural pronouns "they" or "their" with a singular verb, an ungrammatical but common practice in colloquial speech and writing, e.g., "Whoever does that will hurt their chances of passing English."

adoxography [*ad″ok·sog′rə·fē*] *n.* Good or ingenious writing on a trivial subject.

ad personam [*ad pər·sō′nəm*] To the person: appealing to the preferences, interests, or prejudices of another.

Mistaking lack of civility for vitality, she now substitutes for argument a protracted, obsessional invective—what amounts to a staff cinema critics' brand of *est.* Her favorite, most characteristic device of this kind is the *ad personam* physical (she might say, visceral) image: images, that is, of sexual conduct, deviance, impotence, masturbation; also of indigestion, elimination, excrement.
—Renata Adler, *The New York Review of Books*

ad populum [*ad pop′yə·ləm*] To the people: appealing to popular sentimental weaknesses rather than to facts or reasons.

ad rem [*ad rem*] To the matter: to the point; pertinent to the matter; straightforward.

Adam's introduction was a simple *ad rem* declaration of his personal identity. —Noah Jacobs, *Naming-Day in Eden*

ad unguem [*ad ung′gwem*] To the fingernail: with great precision; finely.

adverbial dressing gown Ernest Gowers's term for the clichéd accenting or modifying of a verb or adjective phrase with an adverb, e.g., "utterly refuse," "frightfully boring," "perfectly clear"; hackneyed intensive.

ad verbum To the word: word for word; literally; verbatim.

ad verecundiam [*ad ver″ə·koŏn′dē·əm*] To modesty: appealing to traditional values, reverence for authority, or sense of prestige; requiring an opponent to offend against decorum.

More common and more subtle forms of argument *ad verecundiam* appear in appeals to all the paraphernalia of pedantry. Among them are: 1. Appeals to pedantic words and phrases 2. Appeals to references 3. Appeals to quotations 4. Appeals to length 5. Appeals to detail and specificity 6. Appeals to mathematical symbols.
—David Hackett Fischer, *Historians' Fallacies*

adversaria *n.* Miscellaneous notes, comments, or passages; commonplace book.

adversary journalism   Investigative reporting that is unequivocal in its intent to oppose, expose, or cast suspicion on an institution, political figure, etc.; muckraking focused on a particular target.

To others in the field, the shift is a welcome evolution. They say some articles that pass as "investigative" journalism are "adversary" journalism in which charges of personal or institutional wrongdoing are based on suspicion rather than evidence.
                                    —Jonathan Friendly, *The New York Times*

adversative   See special entry GRAMMAR ADJECTIVES, p. 398.

advertorial *n.*   A paid-for statement, or informative advertisement, usually by a corporation or group of organizations, articulating or explaining a position or action to the public, and styled like an editorial; formal service or product-information advertisement, sometimes in the form of a magazine insert; a magazine's feature on goods, services, etc., for one of its advertisers.

advocacy advertising   Earnestly partisan or "personal" advertising, such as that defending a company's actions or pleading for the public's understanding.

advocacy journalism   Partisan, activist journalism, promulgating a cause, viewpoint, or crusade.

Additionally, he maintains, investigative reporting has been damaged by an upsurge in advocacy journalism masquerading as objective reportage.   —Selwyn Raab, *The New York Times*

adynaton   See special entry RHETORIC TERMS, p. 402.

aenos   See special entry RHETORIC TERMS, p. 402.

Aesopian language   Political double-talk or euphemism that has a special meaning to its advocates or initiates; a vocabulary of stock phrases, code words, and value judgments; dissembling or propagandistic jargon (from the early language of fable, in which chiefly slaves were conversant).

Soviet writers occasionally use Aesopian language, as writers did under the Czar, to convey forbidden thoughts in disguise. Defenders of the regime, while attacking those writers for the use of Aesopian language, are now couching their attacks in Aesopian language.
—Leon Lipson, quoted in Israel Shenker, *Words and Their Masters*

affectation *n.* Mannered or unnatural speech or writing, or adoption of a style unsuitable to the subject or occasion; a stylistic artifice or mannerism.

> . . . nor is there in the hall any affectation of language, nor that worn-out rhetoric which reminds you of a broken-winded barrel-organ playing *a che la morte,* bad enough in prose, but when set up in blank verse awful and shocking in its more than natural deformity. . . .
> —George Moore, *Confessions of a Young Man*

affective fallacy The fallacy of judging the worth of a literary work by its emotional effect on the reader.

affix-clipping *n.* The shifting or recombining of letters into new elements because of common pronunciation, e.g., "an apron" from "a napron" (distinguished from the hobson-jobson, which involves two languages); provection. Also METANALYSIS.

Afghanistanism *n.* Journalism that stresses remote stories or foreign news rather than more immediate, controversial, or local news.

à fond [*ä fôN*] To the bottom: thoroughly; fully.

a fortiori [*ä fôr″tē·ôr′ē*] From the stronger: with greater reason, or being logically a more obvious truth if a preceding assertion is true; by inference; all the more so.

> Marlow's interrupting voice also deepens our admiration for Conrad's narrative technique. That is, it is an artifice which intermittently calls attention to itself. So also, *a fortiori,* is the obtrusive and disjunctive surface treatment of Molly Bloom's maundering mind.
> —Annie Dillard, *Living by Fiction*

Africanism *n.* A word or expression deriving from African culture.

> For a long time, it was known that such individual words as *gumbo, goober, buckra, jazz, juba, voodoo* (or *hoodoo*), *okra, pojo* (a heron, made by folk etymology into "Po' Joe"), and possibly *chigger* were Africanisms.   —Albert Marckwardt, *American English*

after-wit *n.* See ESPRIT DE L'ESCALIER.

agency comparative Posing a comparison without indicating what the criterion or referent of the comparison is, esp. as a deliberate evasion in advertising, e.g., "Gives more relief" (than what?). Also ABSOLUTE COMPARATIVE, DANGLING COMPARATIVE, HANGING COMPARATIVE, UNFINISHED COMPARATIVE.

The incomplete or unrelated or "unqualified" comparative, also termed by the *New Yorker* the "agency comparative," has been the cause of considerable comment. In his famous essay on Sunkist oranges the late Leo Spitzer classed it as an "advertising elative," similar to *different*.   —Geoffrey Wagner, *On the Wisdom of Words*

agentless passive   See DIVINE PASSIVE.

agglutination *n.*   Compound-word formation from discrete word elements, or the creation of derivatives and inflections, by added affixes, e.g., "disestablishment" from "dis," "establish," and "ment." *Adj.* agglutinative, agglutinate; *v.* agglutinate.

agitprop [*aj'it·prop"*] *n.*   Political agitation and propaganda in literature, music, or art, esp. pro-Communist doctrinairism.

I wondered if I should try to climb on the Women's Lib bandwagon. First, I would have to change my name—Isabel Fairfax lacked the necessary agitprop crunch.
    —Florence King, *When Sisterhood Was in Flower*

aide-mémoire [*ād·mem·wâr*] *n.*   Memory-helper: document outlining or summarizing points of a communication, proposal, or agreement; memorandum; reminder; memory device or mnemonic.

Finny and I studied for it in the library Thursday afternoon; I went over vocabulary lists, and he wrote messages—je ne give a damn pas about le français, les filles en France ne wear pas les pantalons—and passed them with great seriousness to me, as *aide mémoire*.
    —John Knowles, *A Separate Peace*

à l'envoi [*ä läN·vwä*]   In emulation: in a spirit of emulation or rivalry.

allegory *n.*   The use of metaphoric, often schematic storytelling and characters for two levels of meaning, with that beneath the surface narrative expressing deeper human truths, whether with a spiritual or moral message or as a form of satire; a literary work whose characters, settings, and incidents have their own verisimilitude but also mask hidden, parallel significations; symbolic narrative. *Adj.* allegorical; *adv.* allegorically; *n.* allegorization, allegorist; *v.* allegorize.

Tolstoy describes her as a creature so sensitive that we wonder she can't speak. Now we see her lying at his feet, she bends her head back and gazes at him with her speaking eyes. The very suspicion of allegory destroys the validity of the scene.

—Joyce Cary, *Art and Reality*

alliteration *n.* Recurrence of stressed sounds in words near one another, usually of initial consonants. *Adj.* alliterative; *adv.* alliteratively; *v.* alliterate.

Even a writer who doesn't, as Chandler usually did, clean as he goes, would normally liquidate so languorous an alliterative lullaby long before the final draft. —Clive James, *First Reactions*

allocation *n.* Word arrangement considered in terms of a fixed, ordering principle (contrasted with collocation).

allocution *n.* Official exhortation; a formal address, esp. one that is authoritative and advisory. *Adj.* allocutive; *v.* allocute.

Semphill was sincerely delighted: the literary quality, the tops-i'-th'-turfy straightforwardness of the allocution gave him the keenest joy.

—Frederick William Rolfe (Frederick Baron Corvo),
Hadrian the Seventh

allonym *n.* Another person's name used as a pen name; a ghostwritten work. *Adj.* allonymous.

allusion *n.* A seemingly incidental but often significant reference, as to a writer, event, or figure from literature or mythology; passing or implicit mention. *Adj.* allusive; *adv.* allusively; *n.* allusiveness; *v.* allude.

I said that to tease Widmerpool, feeling pretty certain he had never read a line of Gogol, though he would rarely if ever admit to failure in recognizing an allusion, literary or otherwise.

—Anthony Powell, *The Soldier's Art*

alogism [*al′ə·jiz″əm*] *n.* An illogical statement.

alphabet soup Many initialisms or acronyms, esp. when referring to governmental and bureaucratic agencies; expression using letters or abbreviations rather than full words (coined by Al Smith regarding the New Deal).

In college I came under the influence of Ronald Sukenick, who introduced me to Symbolists and Surrealists, and my writing went from mopey death threats and Mad Magazine–level satire to wild and abrupt fragments bordering on alphabet soup.

—Richard Price, *The New York Times*

alphanumeric *adj.* Composed of both alphabetic letters and numbers (or, sometimes, special characters), e.g., "1-14," "9½ D," "R2D2."

alternade See special entry WORD-GAME WORDS, p. 394.

altiloquence, altiloquy [*al·til′ə·kwəns*] *n.* High-flown or pompous discourse. *Adj.* altiloquent.

ambages [*am·bā′jēz″*] *n.* A roundabout or deceptive manner of expression, or the posing of a riddle; circumlocutory quibble; indirect or cryptic ways or proceedings. *Adj.* ambagious; *adv.* ambagiously; *n.* ambagiousness.

Anyway, Puttermesser's golem—"infected by periphrasis, pleonasm and ambagious tautology," sidetracked by desire, one big dream of metaphysical fudge—must be destroyed.
— John Leonard, *The New York Times*

ambiguity *n.* The state or quality of having more than one possible meaning; unclear or unresolved sense; a double meaning or equivocal word or expression. *Adj.* ambiguous; *adv.* ambiguously; *n.* ambiguousness.

Disraeli had a standard reply unmatched for diplomatic ambiguity for people who sent him unsolicited manuscripts to read: "Many thanks; I shall lose no time in reading it."
— Robert Hendrickson, *The Literary Life*

ambiloquence, ambiloquy *n.* Competence in double-talk. *Adj.* ambiloquent, ambiloquous.

amblysia See special entry RHETORIC TERMS, p. 402.

amelioration *n.* See MELIORATION.

amende honorable [*ä·män dô·nô·rä·bl*(ə)] An honorable fine: a full and frank apology, however humiliating its admissions; formal acknowledgment of one's error or wrongdoing. *Pl.* amendes honorables.

" . . . I shall accept his invitation. I regard it as . . ."
"The *amende honorable,* sir?"
"I was going to say olive branch."
"Or olive branch. The two terms are virtually synonymous. The French phrase I would be inclined to consider perhaps slightly the more exact in the circumstances—carrying with it, as it does, the implication of remorse, of the desire to make restitution. But if you prefer the expression 'olive branch,' by all means employ it, sir."

"Thank you, Jeeves."

"Not at all, sir,"

"I suppose you know that you have made me completely forget what I was saying?"   —P. G. Wodehouse, *Thank You, Jeeves*

Americanism *n.*   A word or expression that originated in or is characteristic of the United States.

The agent who answered was Duane L. Traynor, who was naturally called "Pie" out of deference to Pie Traynor, baseball's greatest third baseman. (It was the kind of Americanism which appealed to Dasch, and thereafter he referred to Traynor by his nickname.)
    —Eugene Rachlis, *They Came to Kill*

amphibology, amphiboly *n.*   Grammatical ambiguity, òr a statement in which the placing of a word or phrase results in at least two possible meanings, e.g., "We'll engage them in battle hopefully after our reinforcements arrive"; sentence construction causing the reader uncertainty (contrasted with equivocation, or ambiguous use of a word); riddle. *Adj.* amphibological; *adv.* amphibologically. See also DILOGY, SQUINTING.

amphigory, amphigouri [*am'fə·gôr″ē*] *n.*   A verse or other literary piece with seeming sense but actually nonsensical; burlesque or parody in gibberish. *Adj.* amphigoric.

amplification *n.*   Expanding or developing a statement, argument, idea, or theme by providing more particulars, closer analysis, or possible conclusions; more extensive information or reasoning; additional comment; clarification. *V.* amplify.

Our newspapers bristle with phrases which have wandered inside their sentences, or which are not as they stand acceptable without some amplification.   —Basil Cottle, *The Plight of English*

ampollosity [*am″pə·los'i·tē*] *n.*   Turgid style; bombast.

ana *n.*   A collection of sayings by one person; variety of anecdotes, bits of information, or reminiscences characterizing a person, place, or event. *Pl.* ana, anas.

anachorism [*ə·nak'ə·riz″əm*] *n.*   Something out of place or inappropriate to a country; wrong action, scene, or character.

anachronism *n.*   A chronological error; a person, thing, word, or idiom inappropriate to the time of a literary work, esp. something placed or assumed too early; specific temporal or historical error. *Adj.* anachronistic, anachronic, anachronous, anachronical; *adv.* anachronistically, anachronically, anachronously. Also METACHRONISM.

Of course the deep south holds on by main strength to its regional expressions, just as it holds and treasures some other anachronisms, but no region can hold out for long against the highway, the high-tension line, and the national television.
— John Steinbeck, *Travels with Charley*

anacoluthon [*an"ə·kə·loō'thon"*] *n.* An abrupt syntactic shift in midsentence to another construction, sometimes for rhetorical effect, e.g., "Why don't I—but no, you should do it yourself"; change in train of thought or point of view. *Pl.* anacoluthons, anacolutha; *adj.* anacoluthic; *adv.* anacoluthically.

anadiplosis See special entry RHETORIC TERMS, p. 402.

anagoge, anagogy [*an'ə·gō"jē*] *n.* Spiritual or mystical literary interpretation of a word, passage, or text; scriptural exegesis, esp. with references to heaven or the hereafter. *Adj.* anagogic, anagogical; *adv.* anagogically.

anagram See special entry WORD-GAME WORDS, p. 394.

analects, analecta *n. pl.* Selected parts of a literary work or works; miscellaneous excerpts; literary gleanings. *Adj.* analectic.

analogism [*ə·nal'ə·jiz"əm*] *n.* Reasoning or arguing by analogy.

analogue, analog *n.* A word, story, or character that is parallel or similar to another; corresponding thing or point; verbal or literary counterpoint.

More, perhaps, than any other literary *genre,* the modern prose novel developed in a context of demeaning analogues: the children's tale, the *roman rose,* on the one hand; the immense spate of trash-fiction, erotic, melodramatic, or merely sentimental, on the other.
— George Steiner, *Language and Silence*

analogy *n.* A theoretical comparison or point-by-point correspondence between particulars of two different things, rather than a categorical likeness; resemblance in certain parallels; logical inference that if two things are alike in some respects, they will be alike in others. *Adj.* analogical, analogous; *adv.* analogously; *n.* analogousness; *v.* analogize.

She is also addicted to words like "larval" and "magma," and her analogies are often clinical. . . .

—Gore Vidal, *Matters of Fact and Fiction*

analphabet See special entry BOOKISH APPELLATIONS, p. 405.

analphabetic *adj.* Not alphabetic; illiterate.

We sent him the analysis and told him whether or not he really did have the right stuff in him to make a successful writer. All applicants, unless analphabetic, did. —Elizabeth Bishop, *The New Yorker*

ananym *n.* A pseudonym devised by spelling one's name backwards.

anaphora *n.* Repetition of a word or phrase in successive clauses, sentences, or paragraphs for rhetorical effect, e.g., "A sure man, a sure alternative, a sure vote!" *Adj.* anaphoral, anaphoric. Also EPANAPHORA.

The scorner of rhetoric is a formidable rhetorician under whose anaphoric blows the reader crumbles.

—George Steiner, *Times Literary Supplement*

anastrophe [ə·*nas'trə·fē*] *n.* Inversion of the usual order of words, or withholding of them, for rhetorical effect or emphasis, e.g., "came the day when," "into the store I went."

anathema *n.* An ecclesiastical pronouncement that damns, bans, or excommunicates the person so denounced; solemn curse or declaration of obloquy; unyielding condemnation; person or thing regarded as accursed, detestable, or to be excluded at all costs. *N.* anathematization; *v.* anathematize.

Confiscate! The mere word was anathema to him, and he stormed back and forth in excoriating condemnation, shaking a piercing finger of rebuke in the guilt-ridden faces of Colonel Cathcart, Colonel Korn and the poor battle-scarred captain with the submachine gun who commanded the M.P.s. —Joseph Heller, *Catch-22*

ancilla See special entry SCHOLARLY (BIBLIOGRAPHIC) TERMS, p. 400.

anecdota *n. pl.* Narratives that relate private or secret details of history; brief stories; gossip.

anecdote *n.* A brief, presumably interesting report of an experience or incident, esp. a humorous account reflecting human foibles; confidential tale or piece of gossip, or an unknown biographical or historical particular; digressive episode. *Adj.* anecdotal, anecdotic, anecdotical; *n.* anecdotist, anecdotalist.

> He joked with Baitsell about the formalities, laughed at the red ribbon attached to the will, told a couple of anecdotes about old Newport and Harry Lehr's will, and finally signed his name in a great, flourishing hand.   —Louis Auchincloss, *Powers of Attorney*

anent *prep.*   Concerning or regarding; about.

> The wings of the driver's Marlenesque nose shone, having shed or burned up their ration of powder, and she kept up an elegant monologue anent the local traffic, and smiled in profile, and pouted in profile, and beat her painted lashes in profile, while I prayed we would never get to that store, but we did.   —Vladimir Nabokov, *Lolita*

Anglicism *n.*   An English word or expression, esp. one used in a sentence in another language. See also BRITICISM.

> . . . Yourcenar is eminently "academic." She writes very careful literary French, studded with archaisms and occasional, and no doubt deliberate, Anglicisms.
> —John Weightman, *Times Literary Supplement*

Anglicist *n.*   A specialist or authority on the English language or English literature.

Anglicize *v.*   To adopt into English, often with a change in spelling or pronunciation; render in British English.

> He was a wanderer upon our shores, a Frenchman whose name had been anglicized to "Mr. Treete," who gave us lessons in his language.
> —John P. Marquand, *The Late George Apley*

Anglo-Saxonism *n.*   A word or idiom from Anglo-Saxon, or one similar to a word in Old English; word deemed inelegant or coarse, e.g., "swine."

animadversion *n.*   An unfavorable or censorious comment; critical disapproval; detraction. *V.* animadvert.

> But Gertrude Stein's animadversions and Hemingway's replies still lay well in the future during those latter days of 1926 when he had finished reading proofs and was eagerly awaiting the publication of *The Sun Also Rises*.   —Carlos Baker, *Hemingway*

annotation *n.*   An explanatory or critical note accompanying a text; gloss; authorial or scholarly comment. *Adj.* annotative, annotatory; *n.* annotator; *v.* annotate.

What do you expect me to do? Go into a monastery? Or spend the rest of my life keeping up your precious cult—editing and annotating and explaining you, until people get sick of the sound of your name?
—Christopher Isherwood, *The World in the Evening*

anonym *n.* A person remaining nameless; pseudonym; anonymous publication; idea, vagary, or phenomenon that has no term that precisely expresses it.

anonymuncule See special entry BOOKISH APPELLATIONS, p. 405.

antanaclasis *n.* A phrasing in which the topic or key word is repeated, sometimes with a different sense or connotation, for a play on words, e.g., "The business of America is business."

At first glance, Shirley Polykoff's slogan—"If I've only one life, let me live it as a blonde!"—seems like merely another example of a superficial and irritating rhetorical trope (*antanaclasis*) that now happens to be fashionable among advertising copy writers.
—Tom Wolfe, *Mauve Gloves & Madmen, Clutter & Vine*

antapology *n.* A reply to an apology.

anthimeria See special entry RHETORIC TERMS, p. 402.

anthorism *n.* A counterdefinition, or a delineation or description differing from that of an opponent.

anthropopathism [*an″thrə·pop′ə·thiz″əm*] *n.* See PATHETIC FALLACY.

anticlimax *n.* A descent from the important or dignified to the trivial or ridiculous, as in a sentence with a thoughtlessly arranged sequence of phrases; deflating effect; event, episode, etc. of less importance or interest than what precedes it. *Adj.* anticlimactic; *adv.* anticlimactically.

Unfortunately, what looks like a slow build-up turns out merely to preface a huge anti-climax: the bibliophile buys the book and that's that.
—David Montrose, *Times Literary Supplement*

antigram See special entry WORD-GAME WORDS, p. 394.

antilogy *n.* A contradiction in terms or an illogicality.

antinomy [*an·tin′ə·mē*] *n.* A contradiction between two statements or inferences that appear equally reasonable and valid, and hence an extreme form of paradox; an opposition of two laws or rules. *Adj.* antinomic, antinomical; *adv.* antinomically.

Other philosophers, though, take the antinomy very seriously—as an essential paradox of language. They are severely troubled that carefully expressed statements, analyzed by rigorous logic, should turn out to be nonsense.   —Peter Farb, *Word Play*

anti-novel *n.*   The French-influenced genre of modern fiction that rejects the realistic traditions of the novel, including plot or storytelling, straightforward narrative style, character motivation, and chronological sequence, in favor of experimental, often eclectic, impersonal, or surreal effects and sometimes innovative language. Also NOUVEAU ROMAN.

antiphrasis [*an·tif'rə·sis*] *n.*   Calling something its opposite for an ironic or satirical purpose e.g., the comment "How attractive!" on seeing something ugly; ironical antonymy. *Pl.* antiphrases; *adj.* antiphrastic; *adv.* antiphrastically.

anti-Saxonism *n.*   H. W. Fowler's term for love of or use of Latinate words in preference to simple, concrete (Anglo-Saxon) words, or an instance of this; abstract idiom.

antisyzygy [*an"ti·siz'ə·jē*] *n.*   See OXYMORON.

antithesis *n.*   The juxtaposing of contrasting words or ideas through parallel or balanced phrasing; rhetorical counterposing of opposites, as by asserting something and denying its contrary; the second or opposite element in an expressed contrast. *Pl.* antitheses; *adj.* antithetic, antithetical; *adv.* antithetically.

This poet ate his salad with his fingers, leaf by leaf, while talking to me about the antithesis of nature and art.
                                          —Sylvia Plath, *The Bell Jar*

antonomasia [*an·ton"ə·mā'zhə*] *n.*   Substitution of an epithet or nickname for a person's proper name, or of a proper name for a common noun, e.g., "Stan the Man," "a Caspar Milquetoast," "a Jezebel." Also CROSS-NAMING.

antonym *n.*   A word opposite in meaning to a given word. *Adj.* antonymous; *n.* antonymy.

The Greeks used caco- and dys- to manufacture the antonyms to eu- compounds   —Philip Howard, *Words Fail Me*

Aolist   See special entry BOOKISH APPELLATIONS, p. 405.

à outrance [*ä ōo·träns*] To excess: to the utmost; supremely; to the bitter end.

To force all intellectuals into the model of gullible left-wingers is procrusteanism *à outrance*.

    —Arthur M. Schlesinger, Jr., *The New York Times*

apaetesis See special entry RHETORIC TERMS, p. 402.

apagoge [*ap'ə·gō"jē*] *n.* A reductio ad absurdum argument, or demonstration of the impossibility of denying something; disproof of the opposing, contradictory case or argument. *Adj.* apagogic, apagogical; *adv.* apagogically.

aperçu *n.* A quick, penetrating insight; immediate impression, intuition, or estimate.

The program won an Emmy award in 1969, and its host, though frequently controversial for his acerbic aperçus, has earned the respect of conservatives and liberals alike.

    —Michiko Kakutani, *The New York Times*

aphasia *n.* The partial or total inability to speak or understand words, usually because of brain damage; impaired power of speech. *Adj.* aphasic; *n.* aphasiac, aphasic.

He was saved from having to reply by the intervention of an enormous, half-incoherent voice, like that of an ogre at the onset of aphasia, which now began to sing through loud-speakers with an intonation rather resembling Cecil Goldsmith's. . . .

    —Kingsley Amis, *Lucky Jim*

apheresis See BEHEADMENT under special entry WORD-GAME WORDS, p. 395.

aphorism *n.* A statement that succinctly frames a principle; a short, compelling observation or general truth. *Adj.* aphoristic, aphorismatic, aphorismic; *adv.* aphoristically; *n.* aphorist; *v.* aphorize.

In a section subtitled "The Art of Love," she remarks, with aphoristic felicity, "In real love you want the other person's good. In romantic love you want the other person."

    —Janet Flanner, *Janet Flanner's World*

apocope [*ə·pok'ə·pē*] *n.* The loss or omission of a letter, syllable, or sound at the end of a word, e.g., "goin' " for "going"; abbreviation. *Adj.* apocopic; *n.* apocopation; *v.* apocopate.

Thus "Don't say any more; you're making me cry so dreadfully," with which Gertie Lawrence; even on a recording, could wring our hearts, is apocopated into "Don't say any more," because Miss Taylor cannot cry.   —John Simon, *New York Magazine*

apocrisis   See special entry RHETORIC TERMS, p. 402.

apocrypha *n. pl.*   Writings, reports, etc., of doubtful authenticity or questionable authorship; tales wrongly attached to a person, time, topic, etc. *Adj.* apocryphal; *adv.* apocryphally; *n.* apocryph.

The stories are endless, infinitely familiar, traded by the faithful like baseball cards, fondled until they fray around the edges and blur into the apocryphal.   —Joan Didion, *Slouching Towards Bethlehem*

apodictic, apodictical, apodeictic *adj.*   Clearly demonstrable or provable; necessarily true; not disputable. *Adv.* apodictically.

I won't repeat verbatim what was said yesterday; you know as well as I do. I shall merely assert that the words you said, and the way you said them, make it apodictical that you knew the contents of that particular box of candy before Miss Mitchell removed the lid.
                                                —Rex Stout, *The Red Box*

apologetics *n.*   In theology, the field of scholarship defending the origins and faith of Christianity; earnest and systematic argument in defense of something; doctrinal validation or vindication.

I spent a month with the apologetics of Henry Kissinger, which is like playing Frisbee with a medicine ball that leaks.
                                      —John Leonard, *The New York Times*

apologia *n.*   A justification of a viewpoint or course of action, often as an explanatory response; defensive position paper; literary justification of one's motives, decisions, or actions in life.

Perhaps Mr. Avineri's greatest achievement is that his book succeeds in being an apologia for Zionism without ever sounding apologetic or surrendering intellectual probity.
                            —Werner J. Dannhauser, *The New York Times*

apologue *n.*   A didactic tale or fable, esp. an allegory having a moral; parable.

apology *n.*   A formal argument for or defense of an idea, action, philosophy, work, etc., as in the form of a critical rebuttal by an advocate or spokesperson; earnest case to justify something; an admission with regret of fault, error, wrongdoing, or discourtesy; excuse. *Adj.* apologetic; *adv.* apologetically; *n.* apologist; *v.* apologize.

Sometimes I would capitulate and apologize. My early apologies were sometimes sad and, for the moment, even sincere, though sometimes sincere with a kind of self-pity.

—Robert Penn Warren, *All the King's Men*

apomnemonysis   See special entry RHETORIC TERMS, p. 402.

apophasis   See special entry RHETORIC TERMS, p. 403.

aporia [ə·pôr′ē·ə] *n.*   Professing to be at a loss as to what to say, where to begin, or how to express something; talk about the inability to talk; true or feigned doubt or deliberation about an issue. *Pl.* aporias, aporiae.

The subjects are the horrors of family loving, love and sex, women's liberation, the aporias of good government, capitalism and socialism, tradition and its defiance, gentlemanliness and caddishness, and quite a few more.   —John Simon, *Paradigms Lost*

aposiopesis [ap″ə·sī″ə·pē′sis] *n.*   A conscious breaking off in the middle of a sentence because of emotion, a dramatic change in thought, or, sometimes, a shifting to understatement or irony. *Pl.* aposiopeses; *adj.* aposiopetic.

Had he halted during the delivery as if unable or unwilling to proceed (aposiopesis) and abandoned his original construction for another (anacoluthon) or feigned to conceal his real meaning (apophasis), his communication would have been irreparably disrupted.

—Noah Jacobs, *Naming-Day in Eden*

a posteriori [ä″ po·ster″ē·ôr′ē]   From what comes after: proceeding from effect back to cause, or reasoning from given facts to principles; pertaining to what can be known only through experience or facts; inductive or empirical (contrasted with a priori).

apostil, apostille [ə·pos′təl] *n.*   A note or comment in the margin; annotation.

apostrophe *n.*   Addressing an absent or imaginary person, as in a digression on stage or a rhetorical aside in an essay. *Adj.* apostrophic; *v.* apostrophize.

It is difficult to say whether what he wrote was essay or story, for it has elements of both, the essay strained by apostrophe and dramatic exhortation, the narrative presented for the most part discursively.

—Richard Ellmann, *James Joyce*

apothegm [*ap'ə·them″*] *n.* A pithy saying that is pointed or instructive in its wit. *Adj.* apothegmatic, apothegmatical; *adv.* apothegmatically.

Apothegms such as "Sociology is just philosophy masquerading as a science" cut them to the quick.
—Lincoln Barnett, *The Treasure of Our Tongue*

apparatus criticus See special entry SCHOLARLY (BIBLIOGRAPHIC) TERMS, p. 400.

appellation *n.* A name, designation, or title; distinguishing term; the act of naming or identifying. *Adj.* appellative; *adv.* appellatively; *n.* appellative.

"I feel awkward when people address me as Sir Alfred—I have always been known as Freddie, so Alfred is not a name I readily answer to. The title I keep in mothballs, rather like a dress uniform. But the appellation Professor is as comfortable to me as old clothes, for I've worn it most of my life." —A. J. Ayer, quoted in *The New Yorker*

applause line In speechwriting, a forceful, magniloquent, or climactic statement intended to prompt applause.

He made only two attempts to move the crowd with "applause lines," preferring to establish a sense of intimacy with the television viewer.
—William Safire, *The New York Times*

applesauce *n.* Insincere flattery or exaggerated or absurd opinion; hokum; bunk.

appositive See special entry GRAMMAR ADJECTIVES, p. 398.

a priori [*ä″ prē·ôr'ē*] From the previous: proceeding from cause to effect, or reasoning from a premise or assumption to its logical conclusion; deductive, or according to rational consequences, rather than from the facts of experience; preliminary or prior to examination; accepted without question or examination; arbitrary or presumptive (contrasted with a posteriori). *Adj.* aprioristic; *adv.* a priori, aprioristically; *n.* a priori, apriorist.

Sometimes she went even further by insisting he had had a crisis when he thought he had merely had a bad cabdriver, but when he accused her of a priori reasoning, she simply reminded him that he was a classic wunderkind and that all wunderkinder tend to deny they have mid-life crises. —Nora Ephron, *Scribble, Scribble*

à propos de bottes [*ä prō·pō də bôt*]   On the subject of boots: an expression used to change the subject.

Its analysis at that moment was in any case out of reach, because I realised that I had been left, at that moment, standing silently by Mrs. Wentworth, to whom I now explained, *à propos de bottes,* that I knew Barnby.   —Anthony Powell, *A Buyer's Market*

aptronym *n.*   A name befitting the occupation, role, or nature of a person or character, e.g., Squire Allworthy, Doctor Sawbones (coined by columnist P. Adams). Also LABEL NAME.

arbiter elegantiae (elegantiarum) [*är'bi·ter ā"lā·gän'tē·ī"* (*ā"lā·gän"tē·är'əm*)].   A judge of elegance or aesthetic taste; recognized discerning authority.

And in his role of *arbiter elegantia* [*sic*] Gore Vidal can write, without recourse to preposterous tableaux. . . .
                   —William F. Buckley, Jr., *The Governor Listeth*

archaism *n.*   Antiquated expression, diction, or style; out-of-date or old-fashioned word or phrase, often having some currency or literary usefulness, e.g., "perchance," "forsooth," "betwixt." *Adj.* archaic; archaistic; *adv.* archaically, archaistically; *n.* archaicism, archaist; *v.* archaize. See also MODERNISM.

A part of our reality is the unreality of archaic language about sex.
                   —Dwight Bolinger, *Language—The Loaded Weapon*

argle-bargle, argy-bargy *v. British*   To have a lively argument; wrangle. *N.* argle-bargle, argy-bargy.

argot *n.*   The special idiom used by a particular class or group, esp. an underworld jargon; distinctive parlance.

She smoked cigarettes one right after the other, and did not care who knew it; and she never was more than five minutes out of the office before she was talking in newspaper argot, not all of it quite accurate.
                   —John O'Hara, *Appointment in Samarra*

argument *n.*   A disagreement or debate; argumentation, or the process of expression and interchange in disputation; a course of reasoning to demonstrate a truth or a falsehood, or a reason given as a proof or a rebuttal; intended theme or rationale of a literary work; thrust; synopsis. *Adj.* argumentative, argumentive; *adv.* argumentatively, argumentively; *n.* argumentation, argumentativeness; *v.* argue. See also DONNÉE.

Frequently the apocalyptic argument can be distinguished by its na-
ïveté, revealed by its dogmatic acceptance of speculations as fact in
its rush to judgment, and by its quest for high drama.
                                            —Arthur Herzog, *The B.S. Factor*

aristarch See special entry BOOKISH APPELLATIONS, p. 405.

arrière-pensée *n.* an undisclosed intention or ulterior motive;
mental reservation or hesitation.

But the Perfect Reader, for whom all fine things are written, knows
no such delicate anguish. When he reads, it is without any *arrière
pensée,* any twingeing consciousness of self.
                                            —Christopher Morley, "The Perfect Reader"

articulate *adj.* Presented, in syllables or words, so as to be utter-
able or meaningful; intelligible; having the power of speech;
capable of or showing competence, clarity, or effectiveness of
expression. *Adv.* articulately; *n.* articulation, articulateness, articulator; *v.* articulate.

His long blond hair reached down his neck. He looked partly like a
jazz musician, partly like an eighteenth-century composer. He was
complicated, anguished, and absolutely articulate.
                                            —Anne Roiphe, *Torch Song*

aside *n.* An utterance in theatrical dialogue directed to the audience but supposedly not heard by other actors in their roles;
words spoken in low tones or confidentially; passing, private,
or covert comment; personal digression.

Mr. Wilson somehow packs his play with comic asides that cover
phenomena as varied as eskimos, U.F.O.s, Betty Grable, botany,
Columbia Records, and Karl Marx.
                                            —Frank Rich, *The New York Times*

asinus ad lyram See special entry BOOKISH APPELLATIONS,
p. 405.

aspersion *n.* A disparaging or slanderous comment, report, or
expression; calumny; slur. *Adj.* aspersive; *v.* asperse.

But whatever the fact here, the Americans were quickly aware of
every British aspersion upon their culture, whether in a book or in
one of the reviews.   —H. L. Mencken, *The American Language*

asphalia See special entry RHETORIC TERMS, p. 403.

assonance *n.* Resemblance of sound in words, or closeness or
correspondence of syllables with similar sounds and particu-

larly vowel sounds; vowel recurrence. *Adj.* assonant, assonantal, assonantic; *n.* assonant; *v.* assonate.

Dinted, dimpled, wimpled—his mind wandered down echoing corridors of assonance and alliteration ever further and further from the point. He was enamoured with the beauty of words.

—Aldous Huxley, *Crome Yellow*

asteism *n.* Ingeniously witty but civil mockery; sophisticated, genteel irony.

For a woman requires more than stolen glances, apprehensive sighs or the *parola ornata* of asteism (urbane wit) as tangible proof of man's devotion. —Noah Jacobs, *Naming-Day in Eden*

asyndeton [ə·*sin'di·ton''*] *n.* Omission of conjunctions between clauses, as for brevity or stylistic effect. *Adj.* asyndetic; *adv.* asyndetically.

Of all *Time*'s mannerisms, I find habitual asyndeton uniquely irritating; have we, for God's sake, not enough time to write "and"?
—Eric Partridge and John W. Clark,
British and American English Since 1900

atelic See IMPERFECTIVE under special entry GRAMMAR ADJECTIVES, p. 399.

athetize *v.* See OBELIZE.

atticism *n.* An elegantly concise turn of phrase or expression. *Adj.* attic.

Attic salt, Attic wit Classically dry or graceful wit.

attitudinize *v.* To assume or affect a point of view or pose, as reflected in the style or tone of a piece of writing; approach a subject tendentiously.

He is always conscious of his own despair; it is nearly a fault in him; the attitude sometimes verges on attitudinizing.
—Lionel Trilling, *The Liberal Imagination*

attribution *n.* Ascribing to or identification of as a source, or in journalism the explicit naming of one who discloses certain information; ascription of an unsigned or anonymous work to a particular person. *Adj.* attributional; *v.* attribute. See special entry JOURNALISTIC ATTRIBUTION AND EVASION, p. 378.

Nonattribution denies the reader a very essential fact—often *the* essential fact—the source of the information, of the idea, of the specu-

lation, of the proposal, of the supposition—even, sometimes, of the accusation.
                    —Floyd K. Baskette and Jack Z. Sissors, *The Art of Editing*

attributive See special entry GRAMMAR ADJECTIVES, p. 398.

au contraire To the contrary: quite the opposite.

Nor can it be said that they produce canvases of any greater interest than those to be found along Washington Square, or in the cold-water flats of New York's lower east side. There is, *au contraire,* more than a little truth to the contention that the east side has a certain edge over Montparnasse, and this in spite of the justly renowned Paris light.   —James Baldwin, *Notes of a Native Son*

auctorial *adj.* See AUTHORIAL.

au fait [*ō fā*] To the point: conversant with the facts; knowledgeable or well versed; expert.

au grand serieux [*ō gräN ser·yoe*] With great earnestness or, often, with undue gravity.

aulicism [*ôli·siz"əm*] *n.* A courtly expression.

au pied de la lettre [*ō pyā də lä let·r(ə)*] Precisely; to the letter.

She cut a slightly pathetic figure, as do all the people who, in this world, take the words of Scripture *au pied de la lettre.*
                    —Isak Dinesen, *Seven Gothic Tales*

aureate language Abstrusely Latinate coinages or diction. See also INKHORN WORD.

Save for the addition of some Latin "aureate" words—stylistic, artificial, and usually ephemeral borrowings like *diurne, palestral,* and *tenebrous*—plus a number of commercial and maritime terms from the Low Countries which continued to enter unobtrusively, the vocabulary had little notable increase. —Mary Dohan, *Our Own Words*

authorial *adj.* Of or concerning an author or the writer of a particular work. Also AUCTORIAL. See special entry AUTHORIAL ADJECTIVES, p. 373.

His obsession with grotesque and violent death is so persistent that after a while it begins to seem hostile, punitive—another form of authorial aggression.   —James Atlas, *The New York Times*

authorized biography See special entry BOOK PUBLISHING TERMS, p. 361.

autobiographical third Quentin Crisp's term for third-person prose style that is transparently autobiographical in tone, as in a self-conscious or egoistic novel.

Many writers have used the fictional first person; Mr. Mailer has invented the autobiographical third. It is an ingenious device but seems a little coy in so bold a man.

—Quentin Crisp, *How to Have a Life-Style*

autobiography *n.* The writing of one's own life story or experience; art or genre of self-biography; first-person account of one's own life. *Adj.* autobiographical; autobiographic; *adv.* autobiographically; *n.* autobiographer.

She still had a novel in mind, loosely autobiographical though really about the universal female experience, but had so far only mentally designed the book jacket. —Cyra McFadden, *The Serial*

autoclesis See special entry RHETORIC TERMS, p. 403.

autological *adj.* Self-descriptive, or being a word that exemplifies what it means, e.g., "English" is English, "polysyllabic" is polysyllabic (contrasted with heterological). *N.* autolog.

autologophag See LOGOPHAG under special entry BOOKISH APPELLATIONS, p. 406.

automatic writing Writing that is set down in a continuous, random way in an attempt to be a form of unconscious expression, sometimes for spiritualistic or telepathic purposes. Also SPIRIT WRITING.

His most famous contribution, besides the Compulsory Joy, was Automatic Writing—a theory of speed composition calculated, like psychoanalysis (another postwar toy), to surprise the subconscious and shake out the real stuff.

—Wilfrid Sheed, *The Good Word and Other Words*

autonymous *adj.* Naming or referring to oneself or itself.

autotelic [*ô″tō·tel′ik*] *adj.* Having in itself an end or excuse for being, as opposed to being didactic or utilitarian; created for its own sake.

Thadious Davis recognizes the Faulkner problem; Walter Taylor doesn't seem to know it exists. Neither really examines how Faulkner's parallel universe is at once autotelic and humanly compelling, a combination of visions which constitutes his greatness.

—Lachlan Mackinnon, *Times Literary Supplement*

auxesis See special entry RHETORIC TERMS, p. 403.

a verbis ad verbera [*ä wer'bēs äd wer'ber·ə*] From words to blows.

ax-grinder *n.* A carefully worded editorial that is seemingly objective but in fact is purposive and slanted; publicist or flack; one deemed too preoccupied with a given issue.

axiom *n.* A generally or universally accepted truth or incontestable principle; self-evident or fundamental propostion; verity. *Adj.* axiomatic; *adv.* axiomatically.

He recalled a slang axiom that never had any meaning in college days: "Don't buck the system; you're liable to gum the works."
—John O'Hara, *Appointment in Samarra*

B

babble *n.* Confused or meaningless utterance, or sound having no substance; rapid inarticulate or incoherent talk; cacophonous chatter. *N.* babbler; *v.* babble.

They were all talking at once, an exhilarated babble now and again mixed with humming: the strawberry street cry, a phrase of "Summertime." —Truman Capote, "The Muses Are Heard"

Babel *n.* A confused tumult of sounds, voices, or words; din of languages; verbal chaos.

The guest reclined, inert, upon a chair, while the room, confused in speech as though it were an apartment in Babel, tried to discourse to him of its divers tenantry. —O. Henry, "The Furnished Room"

babu English, baboo English Awkwardly earnest, often comically stilted English used by a foreigner, so called in derogation of the speech of native Bengali civil servants in imperial British India (from a Hindu word meaning "Mr." or "Esquire"). *N.* babuism.

Meanwhile there is the steady growth of a vocal and literate middle-class whose sons are trained at Oxford among our comfy liberalisms —and who find no jobs waiting for them when they come back here. The *babu* is growing in power, and the dull story is being repeated here as elsewhere. "Intellectual coolies of the world unite."
—Lawrence Durrell, *Mountolive*

baby talk The imperfect, garbled speech of infants and young children; improvised infantile talk often used by adults to communicate with children; awkward or dubious elementary idiom.

When a stranger addresses Charley in baby talk, Charley avoids him. For Charley is not a human; he's a dog, and he likes it that way.
—John Steinbeck, *Travels with Charley*

back-chat *n. British* Impudent repartee; comedian's patter; conversation.

There is certainly a lively fount of creation there, due partly to the mixed racial background, for half-remembered fragments of many old languages besides English are there for the picking up and may be passed around in merry back-chat among the semi-literate until their antecedents are quite lost. —C. M. Matthews, *Words Words Words*

back-formation *n.*   A word formed (by analogy with other words) by eliminating from an accepted word a seeming prefix or a suffix, that is, by assuming a "root" and thereby creating, say, a verb from a noun, e.g., "word-process" from "word-processor," "sunbathe" from "sun bather"; the process of forming such words.

But how about some discouragement for the verb *enthuse,* a back-formation from the noun *enthusiasm* that should never have been formed and should certainly not be backed?
                                                     —John Simon, *Paradigms Lost*

backgrounder *n.*   An unofficial governmental memorandum to explain or enlarge upon an action or policy, providing journalists with information that can be published without attribution; an interview with a single reporter, or a press conference, granting information on the record but with its source not revealed; press release.

Some backgrounders do provide valuable information to help explain a government decision or action. Some are silly.
                              —John Chancellor and Walter R. Mears, *The News Business*

backlist   See special entry BOOK PUBLISHING TERMS, p. 361.

back matter   See special entry PARTS OF A BOOK, p. 363.

back talk   Vociferous, balky disagreement, contradiction, or counterargument; impertinent contentiousness or retorts.

Until Image Words came along, "communication" meant "sharing" —but the communications division doesn't want any back talk. It wants to dish it out, not take it, so it "municates" instead.
                                                     —Arthur Herzog, *The B.S. Factor*

badinage [*bad″(ə)n·äzh′*] *n.*   Lighthearted, teasing talk; playful conversation; banter.

The movie is blatantly cartoonish, but that doesn't mean it isn't saying anything. I think we're meant to believe that its profane badinage and even its most exaggerated racial animosity have a deep, gritty truth in them, and that because it's a comedy it can go deeper than "serious" movies.   —Pauline Kael, *The New Yorker*

bad-mouth *v.*   To criticize or slur openly; engage in personal fault-finding. *N.* bad-mouther.

bafflegab *n.*   See GOBBLEDYGOOK.

bait-and-switch *adj.* Describing or pertaining to advertising that offers a product insincerely, with the true intention being to sell another, more expensive or profitable product.

Ads that deceive or claims that can't be backed are no-nos, and techniques such as "bait and switch" in which goods are offered to lure customers to buy higher-priced substitutes are also verboten.
—Bernice Kanner, *New York Daily News*

balderdash *n.* Nonsense.

Great spheroids of balderdash, how can you think about a doxy's tail when you're in the presence of a masterpiece?
—James Clavell, *Tai-Pan*

ballyhoo *n.* Overblown, sensationalized publicity or advertising; clamorous hype or propaganda. *V.* ballyhoo.

His companies began to have open stockholders' meetings, to bally-hoo service, the small investor could sit there all day hearing the bigwigs talk. —John Dos Passos, *The Big Money*

baloney *n.* Hollow and obvious nonsense; bunk.

This is not what they say. It's rather: "Our kind of baloney is better than your brand of baloney." A plague on both kinds of baloney.
—Saul Bellow, quoted in Israel Shenker, *Words and Their Masters*

banality *n.* An insipidly dull or obvious remark; dreary commonplace. *Adj.* banal; *adv.* banally.

At moments, in the bar afterwards, I let the rank maleness of my fellows blow through me, and try to think their wrinkled whiskery jowls, their acrid aromas, their urgent and bad-breathed banalities, into some kind of Stendhalian crystallization.
—John Updike, *A Month of Sundays*

banausic [bə·nôs'ik] *adj. Chiefly British* Utilitarian, functional, or mechanical, rather than inspired; smelling of the workshop; contrived.

Of course, it is part of the comedy of the evolution of the arts that each, as it emerges in the wake of some banausic innovation, is regarded as unworthy of the Muses' tutelage.
—Frederic Raphael, *The State of the Language*

bandwagon See special entry PROPAGANDA DEVICES, p. 380.

bank See special entry NEWSROOM HEADLINE JARGON, p. 385.

banner See special entry NEWSROOM HEADLINE JARGON, p. 385.

banter *n.*   Light and good-humored conversational chaffing or teasing; playful repartee. *Adj.* banteringly; *v.* banter.

As they wait for the starting time, they are jolly with each other and swap banter in the professional style of show people (I believe these preliminaries are called the warm-up).
                                                —Walker Percy, *The Moviegoer*

baragouin [*bä·rə·gwa*N'] *n.*   Outlandish, unintelligible speech.

I am tired of the plotting that gets nowhere. I am sick of signals and ciphers and secret meetings and such *baragouin*.
                                                —O. Henry, "Road of Destiny"

barb *n.*   A pointed, biting remark or observation. *Adj.* barbed.

She was furious at the woman for her preposterous statement, equally furious at Dick for having brought them there, for having become fuddled, for having untipped the capped barbs of his irony, for having come off humiliated.   —F. Scott Fitzgerald, *Tender Is the Night*

barbae tenus sapientes   See special entry BOOKISH APPELLATIONS, p. 405.

barbarism *n.*   A word or expression considered ill-conceived by usual language standards, such as a dubious coinage that is a hybrid of Greek and Latin elements or a crude, ill-adapted neologism, e.g., "complected" (rather than "complexioned"), "legalcy," or "suavitude."

On the other hand, some widely popular examples of sportspeak are barbarisms whose use should be a misdemeanor if not a capital offense.   —Red Smith, *The New York Times*

bardolatry *n.*   Excessive veneration of Shakespeare (from "Bard of Avon"). *N.* bardolater, bardolatrist.

"Bardolatry," Piper comments, "is a cult necessarily accompanied by votive images."   —Christopher Reid, *Times Literary Supplement*

barker   See special entry NEWSROOM HEADLINE JARGON, p. 385.

barnacular *n. British*   See GOBBLEDYGOOK.

Barnumism *n.*   Ostentatious, bombastic advertising; vulgar ballyhoo.

barratry *n.*   The stirring up of quarrels or provoking of lawsuits; inciting contention or litigation. *Adj.* barratrous; *adv.* barratrously; *n.* barrator, barrater, barretor.

The Fake Factor . . . can be found . . . in the folderol of the futurists; in the foofaraw of the faddists; in the barratry of book reviews. . . .
—Arthur Herzog, *The B.S. Factor*

bas bleu [*bä blœ*] See BLUESTOCKING.

Basic English (British American Scientific International Commercial) An 850-word basic English vocabulary formulated by C. K. Ogden in the 1920s: 600 nouns, 150 adjectives, and 16 verbs among 100 "structural" words.

And Orwell was to have a passing phase of interest in Basic English, seen as a rival to Esperanto but to serve the same great pacific purpose.
—Bernard Crick, *George Orwell*

basilect [*bas'ə·lekt"*] *n.* The least prestigious, nonstandard dialect of a creole, or mixed, language (contrasted with acrolect).

bastard title See HALF TITLE under special entry PARTS OF A BOOK, p. 364.

bastardization *n.* See CORRUPTION.

bathos *n.* Intrusive triteness or deflation that catches by surprise; inadvertent and ludicrous anticlimax; insincere, strained pathos. *Adj.* bathetic; *adv.* bathetically.

Yet her peroration spoils the effect by rhetorical overreach: "The color is black, the material is leather, the seduction is beauty, the justification is honesty, the aim is ecstasy, the fantasy is death." That slips into bathos because the freight is too heavy. . . .
—David Bromwick, *The New York Times*

battered ornament H. W. Fowler's term for any of various pretty or uncommon types of words resorted to to dress up prose, including old catch-phrases, jocular archaisms, foreign idioms, needless synonyms (elegant variations), and genteel, overused metaphors.

battology *n.* Needless and tiresome verbal repetition. *Adj.* battological; *v.* battologize.

bavardage [*bav"ər·däzh'*] *n.* Small talk or chitchat; idle chatter.

Given these sombre facts, there would be something hateful about the lightness of Sollers's treatment of them, mere *bavardage* one might say, were it not for his outstanding intelligence.
—Stephen Romer, *Times Literary Supplement*

bawdry *n.* Coarsely suggestive or obscene sexual language; ribaldry.

Miller stands under his Paris street-lamp, defiantly but genially drunk,
trolling his catch mixed of beauty and banality and recurrent bawdry
—a little pathetic because he thinks he is a discoverer and doesn't
realize that he is only a tourist on a well-marked tour.
                                    —Stanley Kauffmann, in *The Critic As Artist*

BBC English, BBC vowels   Cultured British speech; received pronunciation.

The obvious therapy is not only to normalize jargons but to imitate
them, parody them, and translate them one into another. America
possesses no central normative prose style considered that of an educated man, no BBC English.   —Richard Lanham, *Style*

bdelygmia   See special entry RHETORIC TERMS, p. 403.

begged question   See QUESTION-BEGGING.

behabitive *n.*   J. L. Austin's term for any of the everyday, for the
most part purely social or polite greetings or responses exchanged by people, e.g., "How do you do?"; a protocol civility.

beheadment   See special entry WORD-GAME WORDS, p. 395.

bel esprit   See special entry BOOKISH APPELLATIONS, p. 405.

belles lettres   Fine or imaginative, usually sophisticated, writing
that, however limited its general appeal, is an aesthetic end in
itself, including poetry, drama, light essays, and literary criticism. *Adj.* belletristic, bellettristic; *n.* belletrism, belles-
lettrism, belletrist, belle-lettrist.

The fear, as in literary criticism, is that one will lapse, or will be
accused of lapsing, back into the old belle-lettristic mode, than which
it is rightly felt that nothing could be more deadly—though other
things can be as bad.
                                    —Michael Tanner, in *The State of the Language*

ben trovato   Well thought up: describing a notion or anecdote that
is untrue but appropriate or memorable; feicitous or well con-
ceived (from the Italian *Si non e vero e ben trovato,* "Not true
but well put"). *N.* ben trovato. See also RECEIVED IDEA,
THOUGHT-CLICHÉ.

The type of *ben trovato,* or aptly made-up story, includes Galileo's
experiment of dropping weights from the Leaning Tower of Pisa,
Newton's observing the fall of an apple . . . and the remark "Let
them eat cake," attributed to Marie Antoinette.
                                    —Jacques Barzun, *The Modern Researcher*

Bernstein's Second Law   Theodore Bernstein's dictum (from *The Careful Writer*) regarding word usage and meaning: "Bad words tend to drive out good ones, and when they do, the good ones never appreciate in value, but most often lose in value, whereas the bad words may remain or get better." (Bad words are "secondary meanings that diverge from the true or primary meanings of words, and that come into use because of ignorance, confusion, faddishness, or the importunities of slang.")

bestseller   See special entry BOOK PUBLISHING TERMS, p. 361.

bible *n*.   Any book considered authoritative or indispensable on a particular subject or subjects; unrivaled reference book or guidebook; vade mecum.

The Hashbury hippies made a kind of bible out of Robert Heinlein's *Stranger in a Strange Land*; Leary and the Airplane grokked sister lovers and water brothers, and in time maybe others.
                                —Michael Crichton, in *The Critic as Artist*

biblia abiblia   Books that are no books: books of no human interest or worthless as literature.

bibliobibuli   See special entry BOOKISH APPELLATIONS, p. 405.

biblioclast   See special entry BOOKISH APPELLATIONS, p. 405.

bibliography *n*.   The study or historical cataloguing of books and writings, including dates, places of publication, description of editions, etc., or a volume containing such information; textual scholarship; listing of writings, or of sources of information in print, dealing with a particular subject, period, or author, often with descriptive notes; in a particular book, a list of works consulted by the author. *Adj*. bibliographic, bibliographical; *adv*. bibliographically; *n*. bibliograph, bibliographer.

bibliolater, biblioatrist   See special entry BOOKISH APPELLATIONS, p. 405.

bibliophile   See special entry BOOKISH APPELLATIONS, p. 405.

bibliotaph   See special entry BOOKISH APPELLATIONS, p. 405.

bidialectalism, bidialectism *n*.   The use of two dialects within a language, that is, of a familiar, informal mode of speech at home or among friends and of another, more proper idiom in social or professional situations. *Adv.* bidialectal; *adv.* bidialectally.

big lie (the)   Untruth on a large, shameless scale, such as a bold falsehood generated and propagated by an unscrupulous government when a less monumental lie might be less believable propaganda; deceit on a grand scale.

> There has been going about what *Editor & Publisher,* the frightened handmaiden of the newspaper industry, calls a Big Lie, to the effect that retail sales held up during the blackout better than anybody could have expected; the Big Lie is a product, *E.&P.* thinks, of a cabal of salesmen of television and radio time.   —A. J. Liebling, *The Press*

big word   A word that is long, technical, or unfamiliar, esp. an abstraction. See also SESQUIPEDALIAN.

> Hank here is the one who knows the big words. Come on, Hank, let's have some jawbreakers!   —Peter De Vries, *The Cat's Pajamas*

bikini head   See special entry NEWSROOM HEADLINE JARGON, p. 386.

Bildungsroman [*bil'doŏngs·rō·män''*] *n.*   A novel about a person's spiritual or psychological maturation in life. *Pl.* Bildungsromane, Bildungsromans. Also ERZIEHUNGSROMAN.

> It was the last daylight hour of a December afternoon more than twenty years ago—I was twenty-three, writing and publishing my first short stories, and like many a *Bildungsroman* hero before me, already contemplating my own massive *Bildungsroman*—when I arrived at his hideaway to meet the great man.
>   —Philip Roth, *The Ghost Writer*

bilge *n.*   Stale or worthless verbiage; nonsense.

> "I thought you would be surprised. Yes, that is what a bloke called Ivor Llewellyn is paying him—fifteen hundred dollars a week. Have you ever read any of Ambrose's bilge?"
>   —P. G. Wodehouse, *The Luck of the Bodkins*

bilingual *adj.*   Expressed in or involving two languages; using or versed in two languages, esp. with fluency in each; diglot. *Adv.* bilingually; *n.* bilingualism.

billingsgate *n.*   Coarse, scolding, or abusive language; scurrilous rant (from the language of fishmongers at the so-named market on the London waterfront).

Beginning gently enough with the silky admonition "Fortified Area—Stay Off," the tone changes abruptly to a sinister "Communicable Diseases—Proceed at Your Own Risk." Should this prove inadequate, and it always does, the next two hundred feet are devoted to some choice billingsgate culled from Restoration plays, calculated to make a mule skinner flush to the roots of his hair.

    —S. J. Perelman, "You Should Live So, Walden Pond"

binder line See special entry NEWSROOM HEADLINE JARGON, p. 386.

biographical fallacy The fallacy of interpreting an author's work on the basis of his known life experience.

There is no need to be afraid of the biographical fallacy: even if we knew nothing about Chandler's life, it would still be evident that a fantasy is being worked out.   —Clive James, *First Reactions*

biverbal *adj.* Involving two words; equivocal or punning.

blab *v.* To speak heedlessly or tactlessly and thereby disclose something confidential or secret; chatter; gossip. *N.* blab.

black-and-white fallacy See FALSE DILEMMA.

blacksmith *n.* Newspaper jargon for a perfunctory, inferior reporter who only "pounds out" news stories.

blague [*bläg*] *n.* Boastful claptrap or nonsense; bunk. *V.* blague.

A razzamatazz society; vogue was everything. Time of the can-can, the courtisane, and the *blague*, that form of wit so different from the bon mot or the jeu d'esprit. The idea was to laugh at everything.

    —Eleanor Clark, *The Oysters of Locmariaquer*

blah *n.* Worthless, wearisome chatter or nonsense; drivel.

. . . a lot of Mr. Wilson's very witty book which is full of malice as well as ideas, is a defence of the view that malice is not alien to the passions for truth, integrity, and the affections: a lot of blah and stupidity has to be cauterized.   —V. S. Pritchett, *The Tale Bearers*

blanket head See BINDER LINE under special entry NEWSROOM HEADLINE JARGON, p. 386.

blanket term A general, broadly inclusive word or classification, e.g., "area," "development."

So, like "dysfunction," "deviance" is a blanket term useful as camouflage for sniping at all non-conformists in the name of science, tarring Socrates or Spinoza with the same brush as Al Capone and Jack the Ripper.   —Stanislav Andreski, *Social Sciences as Sorcery*

blankety-blank *adj.*   Damned, or execrable in words too strong to utter: used as a euphemism for a profanity or profanities.

blarney *n.*   Smooth cajolery or flattery; sweet talk; persuasive nonsense.

But it is plain to most noncreative readers that the myth does not work at all in Joyce's creation and were it not for his glorious blarney and fine naturalistic gifts, the book's classical structure alone could not have supported the novel.
—Gore Vidal, *Matters of Fact and Fiction*

blasphemy *n.*   Language or an expression that flouts the name of God or religious sensibilities; irreverence or cursing; an offensively impious expression. *Adj.* blasphemous; *adv.* blasphemously; *n.* blasphemer; *v.* blaspheme.

He was quite aware that a number of the men saying their prayers were also watching him closely with murder in their eyes, and it seemed to stimulate him to fresh feats of imaginative blasphemy.
—Katherine Anne Porter, *Ship of Fools*

blather *n.*   Long-winded, heedless talk; foolish verbiage. *N.* blatherskite; *v.* blather.

[James] Bond, Reagan blathers on, is "fearless, skilled, courageous, and the other thing: he always gets his girl." The next thing you know, Ron will be telling it to the marines.
—J. Hoberman, *Village Voice*

blend word   A word created by melding two words into one. Also BRUNCH WORD, CENTAUR WORD, PORTMANTEAU WORD, TELESCOPE WORD.

Time magazine and theatrical columnists are well known for the technique of intentionally combining two words to form the new blend: *slanguage, sextraordinary,* and *alcoholidays.*
—Peter Farb, *Word Play*

blether *n. British*   Voluble nonsense; blather.

blind advertisement   An advertisement in which the advertiser's name is not given.

blind attribution   Reporting in which sources of information or statements are not specifically or personally identified, or such a source.

The essence of the reform, then, will not be the jailing of more editors —which would please too many authors. It will be the editor's involvement in what used to get by as "blind attributions"—sources, subjects, and spokespeople who, unidentified, could so easily turn out to be nefarious liars, composite characters, and out-and-out fictions.   —Arthur Plotnik, *The Elements of Editing*

blind lead   A news story opening sentence or paragraph that does not name the person who is the subject of the story (disclosed in the second paragraph), e.g., "An unemployed copywriter spent most of yesterday sitting atop a highway billboard."

blockbuster   See special entry BOOK PUBLISHING TERMS, p. 361.

bloomer *n. British*   A social or verbal blunder; boner.

"I say, Monty," he said at length, his voice proceeding hollowly from the bathroom, "I don't quite know how to break it to you, but I'm afraid I've made—with the best intentions—something of a bloomer."   —P. G. Wodehouse, *The Luck of the Bodkins*

blooper *n.*   A slip of the tongue, esp. a conspicuous, embarrassing verbal error.

A blooper is worse than a goof, more adult than a boo-boo, not as serious as a blunder, equivalent to a gaffe.
                —William Safire, *The New Language of Politics*

bloviate *v.*   To orate verbosely and windily; hold forth bumptiously. *N.* bloviation.

The major characters of our time march, prance, bloviate, and sometimes sorrow in its pages as one of the decade's great editors makes them come alive.   —Theodore H. White (*blurb*)

blue-pencil *v.*   To correct or edit writing, as by changing or deleting; cross out; censor. *N.* blue pencil, blue penciler.

You spend hours evolving a phrase, a nuance, and slash goes the blue pencil. I tell you, it's enough to make a chap give up writing.
                —S. J. Perelman, *The Last Laugh*

bluestocking *n.*   A learned, literary woman; female intellectual or pedant. Also BAS BLEU, FEMME SAVANT.

The most unfeminine thing a girl could do, in her opinion, was become a "bluestocking," as she called female intellectuals, so when it developed that I loved to read, she set out to separate me from books with every weapon in her arsenal.
                —Florence King, *When Sisterhood Was in Flower*

blurb *n.*   A brief commendatory comment, such as an endorsing quote on a book jacket; puff; publisher's brief explanatory or laudatory phrase, like a subtitle, beneath the title of a book or book advertisement. *V.* blurb   See special entry BLURB ADJECTIVES, p. 370.

The voice is that of a generous soul . . . so ready to blurb young writers' books that for years (as he agrees) it was impossible to tell whether or not the praise in his blurbs was serious.
—Edward Hoagland, *The New York Times*

bluster *n.*   Windy, swaggering speech that attempts to be boastful or threatening or both; bumptious talk; egotistical cant. *Adj.* blustering, blusterous, blustery; *adv.* blusteringly, blusterously; *v.* bluster.

We were shown through the house. It was empty and echoed our footsteps, Father's blustering words, and Mr. Hansom's enthusiastic, pale words.   —Joyce Carol Oates, *Expensive People*

Boanerges   See special entry BOOKISH APPELLATIONS, p. 405.

Boeotian   See special entry BOOKISH APPELLATIONS, p. 405.

bogus titles   See COINED TITLES.

boilerplate *n.*   Standard, stereotypical news stories, features, etc., syndicated to newspapers; ready-to-print copy; pedestrian or hackneyed writing (from the printer's matrix or plate form). *Adj.* boilerplate.

In newspaper jargon, you might call all this the boiler plate of the novel—durable informative matter set up in stereotype and sold to country newspapers as filler to eke out a scarcity of local news, i.e., of "plot." And the novel, like newspaper boiler plate, contains not only a miscellany of odd facts but household hints and how-to-do-it instructions (you can learn how to make strawberry jam from *Anna Karenina* and how to reap a field and hunt ducks).
—Mary McCarthy, *On the Contrary*

Boloism *n.*   Pacifist or defeatist propagandizing as an underground cause, as in activities or literature favoring an enemy country (from Bolo Pasha, executed for treason in France in 1918).

bombast *n.*   Inflated, pretentious language; self-important speech or writing; fustian. *Adj.* bombastic; *adv.* bombastically.

He spoke in long sentences, Proustian he may have thought—actually Germanic, and filled with incredible bombast. "On balance, I should not venture to assay the merit of the tendency without more mature consideration,'' he was saying.   —Saul Bellow, *Herzog*

Bombastes Furioso   See special entry BOOKISH APPELLATIONS, p. 405.

bomfog *n*.   Saccharinely lofty or bombastic oratory; pious rhetoric; a glittering generality (from Nelson Rockefeller's many "Brotherhood of Man Under the Fatherhood of God" campaign speeches).

"Shorthand for all the false generic terms and expressions that define women as non-human, BOMFOG, in the words of the author Eve Merriam, 'continues to engulf our language and distort our thinking.' "
—Casey Miller and Kate Swift, *The Handbook of Nonsexist Writing*

boner *n*.   A ludicrous mistake in fact or slip of the tongue; a blunder in language, such as a malapropism, comical coinage, or inadvertent double meaning.

Not many years ago, it was a popular sport to collect and publish silly mistakes made by schoolchildren in their compositions. Many books of these so-called boners were printed for the delectation of grownups who laughed and chuckled.
—Richard Mitchell, *Less Than Words Can Say*

bon mot   A clever, well-phrased observation or remark; witticism. *Pl*. bons mots, bon mots.

The literary Jews also sprinkled their prose with Yiddish bon mots in lieu of the Latin that the Southerners favored.
—Richard Kostelanetz, *Literary Politics in America*

boobe-myseh, bobbe-myseh, bubba-meiseh [*bub′e·mī   sə*] *n*. *Yiddish*   An old wives' tale; nonsense or untruth.

I was hoping the cat would get his tongue as well as the rest of him. But you blew it with the bubba-meiseh about Daniel Mariana Trench.
—S. J. Perelman, *The Last Laugh*

bookburner *n*.   A self-appointed judge of what people may or may not read; censorious antiintellectual.

bookchat *n*.   The interchange or idiom of book critics or publishing professionals; literary conversation, esp. that which is fatuously inbred and genteel.

"Mulligan Stew" is full of Joyce . . . and of Nabokov, Flaubert . . . various Latin Americans, everybody else I haven't mentioned, plus the rest of us—the entire service class of careerist bookchat.   —John Leonard, *The New York Times*

bookish *adj.* Of or relating to books; showing or reflecting knowledge of books rather than practical experience; fond of books; literary or scholarly; erudite; pedantic. *Adv.* bookishly; *n.* bookishness.

The grateful savants had accepted, and they were spending the rest of their lives reading fifteenth-hand opinions, taking pleasant naps, and drooling out to yawning students the anemic and wordy bookishness which they called learning.   —Sinclair Lewis, *Elmer Gantry*

bookworm *n.* A zealous, continual reader of books, esp. an absorbed or diligent student or scholar.

We are not so much concerned, Mr. Humbird, with having our students become bookworms or be able to reel off all the capitals of Europe which nobody knows anyway, or learn by heart the dates of forgotten battles.   —Vladimir Nabokov, *Lolita*

boosted coinage William Safire's term for a newly introduced word or phrase that is modeled on a familiar expression, e.g., "bamboo curtain" (from "iron curtain"), "narrowcasting" (from "broadcasting"), "truly greedy" (from "truly needy"). See also ABSTRACTED FORM, PATTERNED FORM.

boosterism *n.* The activities or language of enthusiastic supporters, esp. in matters of local or regional pride; the buoyantly exaggerated manner of expression long characteristic of Americans; an idiom of optimism or boastfulness typified by confusion of the present and future tenses; "positive" hyperbole; puffery.

Under the lead of a progressive minister, Dick and other young people of Boyd City grapple with the issues of "how to apply Christ's teachings in our town" and find a solution in "civic Christianity" and "municipal virtue"—a kind of hybrid of boosterism and religion.
                          —Jerry Griswold, *The New York Times*

borborology [*bôr″bə·rol′ə·jē*] *n.* Gross language; filthy talk.

borborygmite See special entry BOOKISH APPELLATIONS, p. 405.

borrowing *n.* A foreign word or phrase used in English, esp. an expression in some way naturalized in spelling and/or pronunciation. Also DOMESTICATED WORD, LOAN-WORD, NATURALIZED WORD.

In general the German borrowings have been nouns, but it is of some interest to observe such interjections as *nix, ouch,* and *phooey*— some of which could also have been Yiddish—among them, and it has been assumed that *hurrah* was an early importation from the German as well.　　—Albert H. Marckwardt, *American English*

bosh *n.* Stupid talk or opinions; nonsense.

bos in lingua [*bōs in ling'gwə*] An ox on the tongue: a weighty reason for silence.

boss word *British* An impressive-sounding vogue word favored by the managerial class; white-collar buzzword. Also GLAMOUR WORD.

Boswell *n.* One who continually records the activities and conversation of a notable person; devoted biographer. *Adj.* Boswellian; *v.* Boswellize.

bowdlerization [*bōd″lə·ri·zā'shən*] *n.* The altering, rewording, or striking out of parts of a literary work out of a sense of propriety or prudery, often with euphemistic paraphrases; moralistic censorship; prudishly modified version of a book. *N.* bowdlerism; *v.* bowdlerize. Also EXPURGATION.

It now develops that even before it was submitted to the publisher, Dreiser's work was greatly censored—indeed, bowdlerized—by his wife, "Jug," and a good friend, newspaperman Arthur Henry.
　　—Ray Walters, *The New York Times*

brachylogy [*bra·kil'ə·jē*] *n.* Condensed expression, or an instance of this; ellipsis; laconic speech.

braggadocio [*brag″ə·dō'shē·ō*] *n.* Bumptious bragging or self-inflation; boastful language. *Adj.* braggadocian.

. . . the fancy lingoes of psychiatry, pedagogy, welfare, and big business—these are the twentieth-century equivalents of "tall talk," sharing in the windiness of the nineteenth-century variety, but, unlike it, incredibly dull and vapid. The hyperbole, grotesquery, and braggadocio survive only in American slang.
　　—Thomas Pyles, *Words and Ways of American English*

brand-name author See special entry BOOK PUBLISHING TERMS, p. 361.

breaking Priscian's head Breaking a grammatical rule (from Priscianus of Caesarea, authoritative sixth-century Latin grammarian revered throughout the Middle Ages).

breakover *n.*   See RUNOVER.

breathseller   See special entry BOOKISH APPELLATIONS, p. 405.

breedbate   See MAKEBATE.

breviloquy [*bre·vil'ə·kwē*] *n.*   See PARCILOQUY.

brickbat *n.*   An express criticism or insult.

> Wagner is, for the moment, the fair-haired boy of all the papers he
> rescued from limbo, and I am waiting anxiously to see which of them
> will break the truce of gratitude and hurl the first brickbat; almost all
> of them were sharply critical of him before the blackout.
> > —A. J. Liebling, *The Press*

brief *n.*   An instructive, often preliminary summary or abstract,
such as a concise recapitulation of relevant facts and prece-
dents in a legal case; expressed argument, contention, or case,
esp. an explicit defense. *V.* brief.

> Simon's brief for insisting on "films" instead of "movies" reminds
> one of two monks chaffering over the word "consubstantiation"—no
> mean issue in its day.
> > —Wilfrid Sheed, *The Good Word and Other Words*

bright *n.*   A brief, light, or humorous anecdotal news item, often
appearing at the bottom of a newspaper column.

Briticism, Britishism *n.*   A word, phrase, or pronunciation common to Great Britain but not in American usage, e.g., "boot"
(trunk), "lift" (elevator); a feature of British English. See also
ANGLICISM.

> The average American's dislike for Briticisms has been intensified by
> the imitation of British usage by some Americans, who have affected
> both British pronunciations and British words.
> > —Porter Perrin, *An Index to English*

broadside *n.*   A verbal attack or denunciation, esp. in a publication; adverse critique; tirade.

> Constantine Curran, who was now editing *St. Stephen's*, the Univer-
> sity College magazine, asked Joyce to send him something he could
> not market elsewhere, but was staggered when Joyce disingenuously
> submitted a new and scabrous broadside, "The Holy Office."
> > —Richard Ellmann, *James Joyce*

broken head   See special entry NEWSROOM HEADLINE JARGON, p.
386.

bromide *n.* A tritely typical and tiresome observation or remark; soporific platitude. *Adj.* bromidic; *adv.* bromidically.

The story goes that Pinocchio's nose got longer with each lie he told. I wonder if it might also get swaybacked under the weight of bromide, and if this might account for the odd, pendulous construction of the nose of Richard Nixon. —Herbert Gold, *Newsweek*

brunch word See BLEND WORD.

brutum fulmen [*broŏt'əm foŏl'mən*] Failed thunderbolt: empty noise or idle threat. *Pl.* bruta fulmina.

bull *n.* Exaggerated, self-serving, or mendacious talk; ridiculous nonsense.

There is an unconscionable quantity of bull—to put it as decorously as possible—poured and plastered all over what [Hemingway] writes about bullfights. By bull I mean juvenile romantic gushing and sentimentalizing of simple facts. —Max Eastman, *The New Republic*

bull *n.* A verbal blunder. See also special entry IRISH BULLS, p. 392.

bully pulpit Use of high office, power in media, or similar station to exhort or moralize to the people, as in the case of the presidency or an influential, prestigious newspaper. See also JAW-BONE.

And Moyers, unlike most newscasters, has something to say; he has abiding beliefs about what is right and wrong. And the CBS *Evening News* is, as they say, a bully pulpit.
—James Traub, *United Mainliner*

bumblery *n.* See GOBBLEDYGOOK.

bumf, bumph *n. British* Dreary official documents or paperwork; trashy magazines or novels (from "bum-fodder," or toilet paper).

I'm up to my arse in bumph and don't expect I shall be able to spare you more than a minute or two for waffling.
—Anthony Powell, *The Soldier's Art*

bumping heads See special entry NEWSROOM HEADLINE JARGON, p. 386.

bunk, bunkum, buncombe *n.* Foolish or hypocritical talk, esp. public or political cant; hollow nonsense or rhetoric.

Only the other day we read in the newspapers some bunkum about a middle-aged morals offender who pleaded guilty to the violation of the Mann act and to transporting a nine-year-old girl across state lines for immoral purposes, whatever these are.
—Vladimir Nabokov, *Lolita*

bureaucrap *n. British*   See GOBBLEDYGOOK.

bureaucratese *n.*   See GOBBLEDYGOOK.

buried metaphor   See IMPLIED METAPHOR.

buried offer   A deliberately understated consumer offer in the text of an advertisement, often made inexplicit or obscure so that the reader will mistakenly interpret it as an offer to receive something free of charge.

buried story   A news story relegated to the back pages (or end of a broadcast) or given minor play, esp. one considered to merit better coverage.

Buried Whom   James Thurber's term for the problematical placing of a correct "whom" in a tortuously complicated sentence.

The Buried Whom, as it is called, forms a special problem. This is where the word occurs deep in a sentence. For a ready example, take the common expression: "He did not know whether he knew her or not because he had not heard whom the other had said she was until too late to see her." The simplest way out of this is to abandon the "whom" altogether and substitute "where" (a reading of the sentence that way will show how much better it is). Unfortunately, it is only in rare cases that "where" can be used in place of "whom." Nothing could be more flagrantly bad, for instance, than to say "Where are you?" in demanding a person's identity. The only conceivable answer is, "Here I am," which would give no hint at all as to whom the person was. . . .
—James Thurber, *The Owl in the Attic*

burlesque *n.*   A broadly comic literary or dramatic work that, less mordant than satire, ridicules through exaggerated, often good-natured imitation, esp. a mock low-style treatment of a serious or elevated theme or of minor faults; mockery through ludicrous plot and caricature; broad takeoff. *V.* burlesque.

She was convinced I spent too much time on my *New Yorker* efforts, and so one night I grimly set the alarm clock to ring in forty-five minutes and began writing a piece about a little man going round and round and round in a revolving door, attracting crowds and the police, setting a world's record for this endurance event, winning fame and fortune. This burlesque of Channel swimming and the like ran to fewer than a thousand words, and was instantly bought by the *New Yorker*. —James Thurber, *The Years with Ross*

bushwa, bushwah [*boōsh'wä*] *n.* Baloney; bull.

And as she lay stretched on the sand, and the hot oil of popcorn and sharpness of mustard came in puffs, with crackling, from the stands of Silver Beach, she kept answering Simon, whom I couldn't hear—he was on his side next to her in his red trunks—"Oh, fooey, no. What bushwah! Love, shmuv!"
—Saul Bellow, *The Adventures of Augie March*

business English See COMMERCIALESE.

buzzphrase *n.* A trendy, jargonlike technical or pseudotechnical idiom, often having an abbreviated or slangy flavor.

buzzword *n.* A vogue term with a catchy or seemingly impressive cachet, esp. one from the jargon of technology, business, or government.

The phrase is everywhere. . . . It is, in part, modish nonsense following a direct linguistic line from such buzzwords as "buzzword," "synergy" and "stonewall." —Sam Vaughan, *The New York Times*

byline *n.* A line at the head of an article, story, or column giving the writer's name. *N.* byliner; *v.* byline.

The general feeling I got from the file of old *Journals* was the one I now experience when I read an accumulation of several days' *Journal-Americans*—that of entering a self-contained world which has little relevance to the one outside but which has its own constants: gossip, xenophobia, the movies, and a continual Byzantine-palace struggle for precedence among byliners. —A. J. Liebling, *The Press*

byname *n. British* A secondary name, such as a surname; sobriquet; nickname.

byword *n.* A common saying or proverb, or a much-used word or phrase; widely familiar term; epithet; something or somebody personifying a type, quality, or the like; exemplar or paragon.

This, I did not need telling, was Anthony Blanche, the "aesthete" *par excellence*, a byword of iniquity from Cherwell Edge to Somerville, a young man who seemed to me, then, fresh from the sombre company of the College Essay Society, ageless as a lizard, as foreign as a Martian. —Evelyn Waugh, *Brideshead Revisited*

C

cablese *n.* Language shortened like that of a cablegram or tele-
gram, typically by omitting conjunctions, articles, and unnecessary pronouns and by using abbreviations; expeditiously
functional, shorthand English; elliptical style. Also TELE-
GRAPHESE, TELEGRAPH STYLE.

On February 8th, a reporter sent Rossellini his New York editors'
five pages of cables, in cablese jargon, deploring the unfavorable
American attitude toward Bergman, which could be counteracted if
permission given us to take human-interest photos of the new family
soonestly, as you know how American public reacts to baby pix.
　　　　　　　　　　　　—Janet Flanner, *Janet Flanner's World*

cacemphaton [*ka·kem'fə·tən*] *n.* A harsh-sounding word or
expression.

cacoëthes carpendi [*kak"ō·ē'thēz kär·pen'dē*] A mania for fault-
finding; nitpicking.

cacoëthes loquendi [*kak"ō·ē'thēz lô·kwen'dē*] A mania for talking;
compulsive chatter.

cacoëthes scribendi [*kak"ō·ē'thēz skrē·ben'dē*] The compulsion to
write; scribbler's itch.

He didn't want to be disturbed in his writing, or the meditations
incidental to his writing. Time and again, Mrs. Thing—I never found
out her name—had to drag him downstairs by the scruff of his neck
to his supper, he was that taken up by his work, you wouldn't believe.
Poor devil! I don't expect he's ever heard of *cacoethes scribendi*, but
he's got it pretty badly.　　　　　　—Cyril Hare, *Suicide Excepted*

cacograph See special entry, BOOKISH APPELLATIONS, p. 405.

cacology *n.* Bad pronunciation; impropriety of wording or unacceptable diction.

cacophemism *n.* Discrediting or speaking harshly of something,
esp. superstitious derogation to ward off bad luck. See also
CLEDONISM.

cacophony *n.* Disagreeable or jarring sound; aural infelicity; discordance; babble or tumult. *Adj.* cacophonous; *adv.* cacophonously.

> And always with an air of vast importance, always in vexed and formidable sentences, always in the longest words possible, always in the most cacophonous English that even a professor ever wrote.
> —H. L. Mencken, *Prejudices: First Series*

cacozelia [*kak″ə·zē′lē·ə*] *n.* Studied affectation in diction or style, as in a speech filled with pedantic Latinisms and inkhorn words; ludicrous or dubious imitation in literary composition; misdirected zeal in writing.

cadence *n.* Measured flow or beat in sound or rhythm, as in a line of verse or prose; particular or characteristic pattern or modulation of phrasing in language.

> Sounds have authors . . . I'm led through the village of a Stendhal novel as though walking in time to the cadence of his phrases.
> —David Sudnow, *Talk's Body*

cadit quaestio [*käd″it kwī′stē·ō*] The investigation drops: the argument or case collapses; that dispenses with the issue.

calembour *n.* A pun.

calepin [*kal′ə·pin″*] *n.* A dictionary, esp. a polyglot dictionary.

calque [*kalk*] *n.* An imitative borrowing in language, or a word modeled on an aspect or range of meaning of a particular word in another language, e.g., the English measurement "foot" from the Latin "pes." Also LOAN-TRANSLATION.

> The chapter is full of loanwords, calques, neologisms, as well as curious learning: as we are as far away from the down-to-earth broodings of Bloom as it is possible to imagine.
> —Anthony Burgess, *Joysprick*

calumny *n.* A deliberate or malicious false statement injurious to another's reputation; defamatory report or accusation; slander. *Adj.* calumnious, calumniatory; *adv.* calumniously; *n.* calumniator; *v.* calumniate.

Canadianism *n.* An expression peculiar to Canadian usage, e.g., "on pogey" (on the dole), "chimo" (to your health), "slacking" (being idle or goldbricking), and "hydro" (electricity service).

canard [kə·närd'] *n.* A groundless and hence false report, esp. one deliberately fabricated and spread; specious anecdote; rumor or hoax.

Since prudent Veen preferred killing his man in Europe (decrepit but indestructible Gamaliel was said to be doing his best to forbid duels in the Western Hemisphere—a canard or an idealistic President's instant-coffee caprice, for nothing was to come of it after all), Demon rented the fastest petroloplane available, overtook the Baron (looking very fit) in Nice, saw him enter Gunter's Bookshop, went in after him, and in the presence of the imperturbable and rather bored English shopkeeper, backslapped the astonished Baron across the face with a lavender glove. —Vladimir Nabokov, *Ada*

candyfloss *n.* *British* (cotton candy) Flimsy, shallow, saccharine, or merely cosmetic ideas or proposals. See also FLUFF.

canned copy Information or prepared releases sent to news media by publicists or press agents; public-relations writing. See also A-COPY.

cannibalism *n.* H. W. Fowler's term for the oversight of omitting one of two like words that fall adjacent, most commonly a "that" or a preposition such as "to" or "in," e.g., "She has to learn what this relates to (to) make any headway." Also DOUBLE DUTY.

cant *n.* Language that is hypocritical or wearisomely hollow and predictable, such as stereotypical political jargon, repetitious promotional claims, or pious religious clichés; transparent, rote idiom or stock phrases; whining, singsong speech, such as that used by importuning beggars; argot of a group or lower social class. *Adj.* canting; *v.* cant.

But the official language of the United States is now cant. As I said at the beginning, the condition of the *real* language is critical. —Jean Stafford, *Saturday Review*

cantilevered verb Theodore Bernstein's term for a verb that, customarily requiring a preposition or an object, comes to be used intransitively, e.g., "he communicates," "she copes," "they publish."

Psychoanalysis, of course, uses cantilevered verbs as a kind of shorthand; analysts will say that a patient *identifies* or *relates* or does not *adjust*. Laymen tend to pick up this kind of jargon and, whether useful or not, it becomes popular. —Theodore Bernstein, *The Careful Writer*

capping *n.* See SIGNIFYING.

captation *n.* An attempt to obtain applause or recognition; making an ad captandum speech.

caption See CUTLINE under special entry NEWSROOM HEADLINE JARGON, p. 386.

captious *adj.* Intended to confuse or artfully entangle in argument; deceptive or sophistical; marked by or intent on mean or petty objections; hypercritical; carping. *Adv.* captiously; *n.* captiousness.

But the curious fact is that no two Structural Linguists define it the same way—a fact that has led some captious critics to remark that their contempt for writing doubtless stems from their inability to write.   —Lincoln Barnett, *The Treasure of Our Tongue*

carcinomenclature *n.* See GOBBLEDYGOOK.

card-stacking See special entry PROPAGANDA DEVICES, p. 380.

caricature *n.* Exaggerated, distorted, or oversimplified representation of somebody or something, as by accenting certain qualities or traits, whether intentionally for ludicrous effect or unintentionally, as in a too broadly or shallowly depicted fictional character; gross or reductive imitation. *Adj.* caricaturable, caricatural; *n.* caricaturist; *v.* caricature.

As always with Macaulay, the portrait was exaggerated—a caricature rather than a portrait—but, alas, caricatures usually include more than a grain of truth.   —J. H. Plumb, *The New York Times*

carriwitchet [*kar″ə·wich′it*] *n.* An absurd, riddling question, somewhat of a hoax; teasing quibble; pun.

casuistry *n.* The determining of right and wrong in matters of conduct or conscience, or the applying of principles of ethics, particularly in instances that are complex or ambiguous; false, deceptive reasoning about law or morals; sophistical persuasion. *Adj.* casuistic, casuistical; *adv.* casuistically.

After you strip this prose of its casuistic caveats, distinctions, and reservations, there still remains the "needs to be taken as seriously, as studiously"; there remains that "structural" identity that, at least for this high-culture illiterate, means flagrant gilding by association.
                              —John Simon, *Reverse Angle*

catachresis [*kat″ə·krē′sis*] *n.* Misuse of a word, as from confusing it with another word, straining its meaning, or creating a mixed (often paradoxical) metaphor; a forced figure of speech; mistaken terminology; the erroneous modification of an unfamiliar word resulting in a so-called folk etymology. *Adj*. catachrestic; *adv*. catachrestically.

It is, further, seldom shown how catachresis turns into metaphor (e.g., Latin is Greek to me).
　　　　　　　　　　　　　　—Geoffrey Wagner, *On the Wisdom of Words*

catacosmesis　See special entry RHETORIC TERMS, p. 403.

catalogue, catalog　*n*.　A listing or enumerating of things, qualities, or cultural artifacts; orderly arranging; recitation. *Adj*. catalogic; *n*. cataloguer, cataloger; *v*. catalogue, catalog.

Instead of a catalogue of ships, Fleming gives us a catalogue of clothes, toilet accessories, or background material about some exotic place or some arcane field of knowledge.
　　　　　　　　　　　　　　—George Grella, in *The Critic as Artist*

catalogue raisonné　See special entry SCHOLARLY (BIBLIO-GRAPHIC) TERMS, p. 400.

catarolysis [*kat″ə·rol′i·sis*]　*n*.　Cursing to let off steam. See also LALOCHEZIA.

catchfools　*n*.　Words that, similar in spelling, are commonly confused or misspelled, such as "euphemism" and "euphuism," "deprecate" and "depreciate." Also DANGEROUS PAIRS, PAIRS AND SNARES.

catchline　*n*.　A pithy or provocative phrase or sentence used as an attention-getting heading or signature; advertising tagline; slogan.

Smart as she was you had to watch her for terrible breaks once and a while, like the time she was going to run a broadside on the new lipstick. Her catchline *For Sheeny Lips* would have sunk us. I killed it at the printers just in time.　　—Christopher Morley, *Kitty Foyle*

catchpenny　*adj*. *Chiefly British*　Describing a book or publication existing solely for the ignorant or unwary; popular but superficial; ready-made or trite; cheap. N. catchpenny.

Most officials write grammatically correct English. Their style is untainted by the silly jargon of commercialese, the catchpenny tricks of the worse sort of journalism, the more nebulous nebulosities of politicians, or the recondite abstractions of Greek or Latin origin in which

men of science, philosophers and economists too often wrap their
thoughts. —Sir Ernest Gowers, *Plain Words*

catchphrase A common or appealing phrase in popular, often un-
thinking usage; watchword or slogan.

... American style ... overworks its catchphrases until they become not merely meaningless playtalk, like English catchphrases, but
sickening, like overworked popular songs.
—Raymond Chandler, *Raymond Chandler Speaking*

catchword *n.* A word associated with a particular person or thing
or crystallizing an issue; identifying slogan; in printing, a guide-
word at the top of a page, as in a dictionary, to indicate the first
or last word on that page; a striking, catchy, attention-getting
word heading an advertisement.

As he turned away, I saw the *Daily Wire* sticking out of his shabby
pocket. He bade me farewell in quite a blaze of catchwords, and went
stumping up the road.
—G. K. Chesterton, in *The Man Who Was Chesterton*

catechism *n.* Oral indoctrination, or a handbook summarizing religious tenets in instructional form; manual or summary or a
doctrine in formal question-and-answer form, or a formal interrogation, used as a test, with certain expected, correct answers.
Adj. catechismal, catechistic; *adv.* catechistically; *n.* catechi-
zation, catechist, catechizer, catechumen; *v.* catechize.

I used to be invited to Weissenkorns' for supper and put through a
catechism on Philadelphia, about which I knew nothing.
—Christopher Morley, *Kitty Foyle*

caudle lecture See CURTAIN LECTURE

causative See special entry GRAMMAR ADJECTIVES, p. 398.

causerie [*kō″·zə·rē′*] *n.* A light and informal conversation; brief,
conversational essay; casual, familiar writing. *N.* causeur.

My father never spoke on the wireless, never had any other preparation for criticism than his own wide reading and genial tastes and
never attended a literary congress. He wrote biography, essays,
book-reviews, *causeries*, verse (Gilbertian, Tennysonian and in the
manner of Austin Dobson); he read manuscripts for publishers, edited
new editions of standard works and always replied ungrudgingly and
at length to all who applied to him for advice.
—Evelyn Waugh, *A Little Learning*

caveat *n.*   A cautionary notice or warning relevant to an action or matter; explanatory qualification or reservation to be borne in mind; apology or excuse.

In the meantime, teachers of writing may safely settle for traditional grammar, if they take to heart these caveats: (1) Grammar is conceptual, and has limited value in teaching very young children. (2) The objective of teaching grammar at any level is working knowledge, not exhaustive knowledge. (3) Grammar is not utterly prescriptive in good writing.   —Clifton Fadiman and James Howard, *Empty Pages*

cénacle [*sā·näk·l(ə)*] *n.*   A literary or ideological group; artists' coterie. See also CONVERSAZIONE.

Synge had begun to write his plays; Lady Gregory at the age of fifty had revealed an unexpected skill at peasant comedy; George Russell, talented himself, was hospitably encouraging a *cénacle* that included Padraic Colum, "Seumas O'Sullivan," and other writers who, if they were minor, were young and lively.
                                    —Richard Ellmann, *James Joyce*

censorship *n.*   Suppression of literature considered objectionable, esp. for moral, political, or religious reasons. *Adj.* censorious; *adv.* censoriously; *n.* censor; *v.* censor.

I glanced at an ancient baroque door and asked him about censorship on television. He giggled happily. "Oh it is wonderful! It is the wildest, silliest little game! The censors take out what they think the people think the censors think they should be taking out."
                                    —Chandler Brossard, *The Spanish Scene*

centaur word   See BLEND WORD.

cento [*sen'tō*] *n.*   A literary work composed of patches from other works; patchwork; pastiche.

ceteris paribus, caeteris paribus [*kā'tə·ris par'i·bəs*]   All other things being equal or remaining unchanged.

chaff *n.*   Light, good-natured talk or teasing; banter. *Adj.* chaffing; *adv.* chaffingly; *v.* chaff.

The Dutch commercial travelers condoling or congratulating with one another in measured tones on the current market would give place to a group of French *permissionaires* exchanging rapid chaff on the exploits of their leave, in an esoteric jargon of considerable gaiety. . . .
                                    —Margaret Schlauch, *The Gift of Language*

chapbook *n.* A small, inexpensive book or pamphlet peddled by hawkers (formerly one sold by chapmen, containing ballads, rhymes, tales, etc.).

character assassination A slanderous propaganda campaign to disgrace a public figure, esp. in politics; concerted or opportunistic defamation.

characterization *n.* Portrayal or description so as to distinguish; the creation and representation of characters in fiction; delineation; the use in journalism of descriptive or categorical words as modifiers, sometimes irrelevantly (physical value judgments) and sometimes prejudicially (subtly moralistic or pejorative words). *Adj.* characterizable; *v.* characterize.

Characterization, too, can border on opinion, and should be excluded from the news columns. A paragraph about the President's news conference contained this sentence: "The ambiguity of his replies sent some men away convinced that the major policy change was indeed in prospect, but the White House later took pains to explain that this was not the case." Strike out the words "the ambiguity of" and you retain the same meaning without the editorial flavor.
—Theodore Bernstein, *Watch Your Language*

character sketch A brief descriptive portrait in writing of an individual, usually with close observation of his or her distinctive traits.

In 1928 a private press published her character sketch of the Sapphic poetess Renée Vivien, born Pauline Tarn, in London, of an English father and an American mother, a fragile neurotic figure who spent most of her short, self-destructive life in Paris, maintained in mysterious semi-Oriental elegance and living on spiced foods and alcohol in a garden apartment by chance next to Colette's, near the Bois de Boulogne. —Janet Flanner, *Janet Flanner's World*

charade See special entry WORD-GAME WORDS, p. 395.

charientism [*kar'ē·ən·tiz"əm*] *n.* A gracefully veiled insult, so phrased that the target must take it as unintended, and hence a form of irony.

charitable word See special entry WORD-GAME WORDS, p. 395.

chat *v.* To talk informally or casually; converse; make small talk. *N.* chat

She sipped her sherry (her second glass) and listened anxiously to Hugh's muffled cries, and dutifully to animated chat about local poli-

tics, and Councilor Biggs-Anderson (a local Tory villain) and the
gravel pit, and the principle of the thing, and conservation.
                              —Margaret Drabble. *The Realms of Gold*

chatter *n.* Rapid and idle or trivial talk; heedlessly incessant or
foolish utterance or conversation; prattle. *V.* chatter.

I listened to the sound of the wheels carrying on their endless conversation with the tracks. At first their rapid chatter sounded like nothing
but metallic and monotonous double-talk. But later, as my ear became accustomed to their language, I realized that they were asking
each other, over and over again, What Makes Sammy Run? What
Makes Sammy run what makes sammy run what makes sammy run-
whatmakessammyrun . . .
                              —Budd Schulberg, *What Makes Sammy Run?*

cheap originality H. W. and F. G. Fowler's term for a writer's ill-
advised avoiding of a trite phrase by inverting or otherwise
tampering with it, e.g., changing "wear and tear" to "tear and
wear."

checkbook journalism Payment to people, esp. prominent people
for exclusive profiles or interviews.

And all in all, the entire episode has made me change my point of
view on checkbook journalism. I used to think it was a mistake to pay
anyone for a story. I used to think it made it impossible for serious
journalists to cover events. I used to think it would mean that news
stories would begin to go to the highest bidder. Now I think the
networks should pay everyone. Hard news sources, soft news
sources, everyone. It will serve to remind us that, at this point at
least, there is no reason to confuse television news with journalism.
                              —Nora Ephron, *Scribble Scribble*

chee-chee *n.* Mincing English; decadently affected, elaborative
idiom (used disparagingly in reference to the English speech of
Eurasians or East Indians; from Hindu word for dirt). Also CHI-
CHI.

chef d'oeuvre [*shā doe·vr(ə)*]   A masterpiece.

Certainly, I have read my last word. Print can hold for me now
nothing but anticlimaxes. *It*, the chef d'oeuvre of Madame Elinor
Glyn, has come into my life. And Sherman's coming into Atlanta is
but a sneaking, tiptoe performance in comparison.
                              —Dorothy Parker, *The Portable Dorothy Parker*

chestnut *n.* An old, too familiar or too often repeated joke, story, work, etc.

cheval de bataille [*shə·väl də bä·tī*] War-horse: one's favorite subject or argument, often to a tiresome degree; hobbyhorse.

cheville [*shə·vē*] *n.* An unnecessary word added to round off a sentence or complete a line of verse.

> . . . and I have never been able to read with any very thorough sense of pleasure even the opening lines of "Rolls," that splendid lyrical outburst. What I remember of it now are those two odious *chevilles* —*marchait et respirait,* and *Astarté fille de l'onde amère.* . . .
> —George Moore, *Confessions of a Young Man*

chiasmus [*kī·az′məs*] *n.* The inverting of the second or latter of two phrases that would otherwise be parallel in form, e.g., "I like the idea; its execution, I don't." *Pl.* chiasmi; *adj.* chiastic.

> John Henry Newman, in his *Apologia pro vita sua* (1864), used chiasmic [*sic*] or inverted parallel structure for strong emphasis: "I have changed in many things: in this I have not."
> —*Encyclopaedia Britannica*

chi-chi *n.* See CHEE-CHEE.

chin-chin *n.* Polite or ceremonious speech; casual or idle chat; also used as expression of goodwill or farewell. *V.* chin-chin.

chitchat *n.* Casual, familiar talk; conversation. *V.* chitchat.

> It was one of those intimate late-night pauses—we had been drinking for two hours and had passed the point of drunken chitchat.
> —Paul Theroux, *The Consul's File*

Choctaw *n.* Odd and incomprehensible language; jargon or gibberish.

chop-logic *n.* Absurdly convoluted, sophistical, or illogical argumentation; glib and specious reasoning; person who uses such logic. *Adj.* choplogic, choplogical. Also LOGIC-CHOPPING.

> You're covetous, a virgin liar, false as marcasites; you furtively steal my pesetas for cognac, bite my back, neck, arms, and offer me daily chop-logic, and I despise all of your defects.
> —Edward Dahlberg, *The Olive of Minerva*

chrestomathy [*kre·stom′ə·thē*] *n.* A book of selected passages for foreign-language study; miscellany of an author's writings. *Adj.* chrestomathic.

chronicle *n.* A chronological record of events or facts, esp. a historical narrative or register without interpretation or comment; account; story. *N.* chronicler; *v.* chronicle.

The Franks, as a family, came to an end, and, fittingly enough, thought the diarist, so did her chronicle of their effort to go sensibly on as themselves, in spite of everything.

—Philip Roth, *The Ghost Writer*

chronique scandaleuse [*krô·nēk skän·dä·loez*] A history or account that deals with the intimate lives, love affairs, intrigues, etc., of the great and famous, esp. a personal or eyewitness account; stew of sordid gossip.

You have done nothing, of late, worthy to be recorded in the *chronique scandeleuse* of Nepenthe.   —Norman Douglas, *South Wind*

chronogram   See special entry WORD-GAME WORDS, p. 395.

circular reasoning   See QUESTION-BEGGING.

circumbendibus *n.* A roundabout process or story; circumlocution. *Pl.* circumbendibuses.

circumlocution *n.* Wordy and indirect language, sometimes as an evasion; roundabout verbosity; an instance of wordiness. *Adj.* circumlocutional, circumlocutionary, circumlocutory; *n.* circumlocutionist. See also CIRCUMBENDIBUS, PERIPHRASIS.

Henry James, in his later fiction, tried to make his characters and prose so refined in subtlety that his paragraphs are often monuments of circumlocution. Edith Wharton recalled James's trying to ask an old man the directions to the King's Road at Windsor: "My good man, if you'll be good enough to come here, please; a little nearer— so," and as the old man came up: "My friend, to put it to you in two words, this lady and I have just arrived here from *Slough*; that is to say, to be more strictly accurate, we have recently *passed through* Slough on our way here, having actually motored to Windsor from Rye, which was our point of departure; and the darkness having overtaken us, we should be much obliged if you would tell us where we now are in relation, say, to the High Street, which, as you of course know, leads to the Castle after leaving on the left hand the turn down to the railroad station."

—Robert Morsberger, *Commonsense Grammar and Style*

circus makeup   See special entry NEWSROOM HEADLINE JARGON, p. 386.

citation *n.* The mentioning or quoting of a source, author, or passage, or a reference to another authority; itemization, as of supportive facts or documents; verbatim quotation from another person or work to illustrate or support; reference. *Adj.* citational, citatory; *n.* citer; *v.* cite.

"When enough citations come in from cultivated writers, passed by trained copy editors," the lexicographer replied, "the 'mistake' becomes the spelling."   —William Safire, *What's the Good Word?*

clang association See KLANG ASSOCIATION.

claptrap *n.* Something showy or meretricious introduced to win applause, as an emotional speech or specious argument; vain blather; nonsense. *Adj.* claptrap.

To be sure, in the role of historian Ford delivered himself of turgid discussions on the Provençal past, replete with names, dates, and sociological claptrap.   —James Lord, *The American Scholar*

classicism *n.* A classical Greek or Roman word or idiom in English, or a term or coinage based on or similar to one from one of the classical languages; classical scholarship; mode or aesthetic ideology based on or allegedly derived from a "classic" epoch. *Adj.* classical, classicistic; *n.* classicist; *v.* classicize.

This artificial facility found vent in his renderings of the Rubaiyat. "Saprous bones," "somatick atoms" and "aimaterose heart" seem legitimate classicisms; but "methystine lake" requires some explanation as a term for drunkeness.
    —Shane Leslie, Introduction to *Hadrian the Seventh*

claver See QUIDNUNC under special entry BOOKISH APPELLATIONS, p. 407.

clean copy See FAIR COPY under special entry BOOK PUBLISHING TERMS, p. 361.

cledonism [*klē'də·niz"əm*] *n.* The eschewing of unlucky words, or the use of euphemism to ward off misfortune; superstitious circumlocution. See also CACOPHEMISM.

clench *n.* A pun; a statement that settles or wins an argument.

cliché *n.* An expression so overused as to be trite, such as a hackneyed idiom or dead metaphor; stereotyped, overworked idea; evident commonplace. *Adj.* cliché, clichéd.

The language is a double-depressant of numbing, cliché-ridden prose that ranges from Lady Bountiful pitter-patter to tearoom philosophizing.   —Colman McCarthy, *The Washington Post*

climax *n.*   The arranging of ideas, statements, or episodes for forceful effect; cogent, cumulative development; final statement or incident in a thematic sequence; momentous or dramatic high point. *Adj.* climactic, climactical; *adv.* climactically; *v.* climax.

> Literary suffering is always tailored. It accustoms us to the idea that difficulty and the courage to meet it come only at the right moment in the plot—here the crisis, there the climax.
>
> —Jack Beatty, *The New Republic*

clincher *n.*   A decisive or telling fact, argument, or comment; most crucial or pivotal aspect or feature.

> We are told that a president must communicate with the people, that those who govern must take the people into their confidence, that there must—this is the clincher—there must be an ongoing dialogue.
>
> —Edwin Newman, *Strictly Speaking*

clinquant [*kling'kənt*] n.   Showy but valueless writing or literary effects; artistic tinsel. *Adj.* clinquant.

clipped word, clipped form   A shortened form of a word as is common in informal speech, news headlines, and advertising, e.g., "cab," "flu," "veggies." Also CURTAILED WORD, STUMP WORD.

clishmaclaver [*klish"mə·klā'vər*] *n. Scottish*   Chatter, gossip.

cloaked attribution   See special entry JOURNALISTIC ATTRIBUTION AND EVASION, p. 379.

close punctuation, closed punctuation   A style of liberal, frequent punctuation in copy, above all using commas freely (contrasted with open punctuation).

clou [*klōō*] *n.*   A major point of interest or chief focus; central idea.

cock *n. British*   Poppycock; nonsense.

cock-and-bull story   A story or explanation obviously concocted and not to be believed.

> Did Ladlehaus think he was a fool? There were his dates plain as day right there on his tombstone. Dead eleven years. Now how did the fellow expect him to believe a cock-and-bull story like that?
>
> —Stanley Elkin, *The Living End*

coda *n.* A concluding part of a literary work, often as a set piece that rounds out or brings together; culminating passage; peroration.

The message was the same each time—learn to love thyself—and was usually tacked on as abruptly and tearfully as those codas that once concluded episodes of "Father Knows Best."
—Frank Rich, *The New York Times*

code word A code name; a word with a covert meaning, such as a sociological generality or a euphemism with an inexplicit but unmistakable signification to certain people, e.g., the Marxist term "rootless cosmopolite" for Jew; word of menace; shibboleth.

He noticed it in her friends, too—that nearly manic combing of the hair, the chewing gum and talk about music. They disparaged everything, and their talk was full of clichés and code words.
—Ann Beattie, *Falling in Place*

codex See special entry SCHOLARLY (BIBLIOGRAPHIC) TERMS, p. 401.

codswallop [*kodz'wol"əp*] *n. British* Baloney or hot air; gammon or humbug.

Genes, Mind, and Culture is written in the prose style and with the literary manners which have earned sociology the amused contempt of scholars throughout the world and which are the despair of the many serious and highly literate sociologists who object to their subject's being thought of as so much codswallop.
—P. B. Medawar, *The New York Review of Books*

coffee-table book See special entry BOOK PUBLISHING TERMS, p. 361.

cognate *adj.* Related or having common ancestry, as two words having the same derivation; descended from the same verbal root; intrinsically similar. *N.* cognate, cognateness.

The vulgarity of a lot of writing about food is cognate with the vulgarity of a lot of writing about sex.
—Anthony Burgess, *The New York Times*

cognomen *n.* A surname or family name; any name, esp. a nickname or epithet. *Pl.* cognomens, cognomina; *adj.* cognominal.

Had Napoleon borne the cognomen Klotz or had George Washington sustained the appellation Izod Flopson, those unamiable names would now be uttered with reverence.
—Noah Jacobs, *Naming-Day in Eden*

cognoscenti [*kon"yə·shen'tē*] *n. pl.*   Individuals having authoritative knowledge of a field or subject, esp. in the arts; informed or expert specialists. *Sing.* cognoscente.

Some of the illustrations will be revelations even to the *cognoscenti.* The soaring drama of the Galleria Vittorio Emanuele II, Milan, for example, in an extraordinary fish-eye photo.
> —J. Mordaunt Crook, *Times Literary Supplement*

coherence *n.*   Order and sense in expression, or ease and interrelationship in arrangement of thoughts or parts of a sentence; logical consistency or clarity of syntax. *Adj.* coherent; *adv.* coherently; *v.* cohere.

Every man in the chapel hoped that when his hour came he, too, would be eulogized, which is to say forgiven, and that all of his lapses, greeds, errors, and strayings from the truth would be invested with coherence and looked upon with charity.
> —James Baldwin, *Notes of a Native Son*

coinage *n.*   The creating of words or expressions; a made-up or newly introduced term, e.g., "Kodak." *N.* coiner; *v.* coin.

The language of Riddley Walker is a tissue of lyric bursts, suggestive garbling . . . and numberless crude but lively coinages (sex becomes "doing the juicy").   —Benjamin DeMott, *The New York Times*

coined titles   Theodore Bernstein's term for identifying words or descriptive nouns, often questionable as attributives and awkwardly strung together, used before a person's name, esp. in newspaper writing, e.g., "West 135th Street scrubwoman and subway rider Anna Thompson. . . ." Also BOGUS TITLES, FALSE TITLES.

collage *n.*   A work of art that is a mixture of varied elements, such as a novel that is a hodgepodge of quotations, allusions, verses, etc.; mixture of different elements.

The use of narrative collage, then, enables a writer to recreate, if he wishes, a world shattered, and perhaps senseless, and certainly strange.   —Annie Dillard, *Living by Fiction*

collate   See special entry SCHOLARLY (BIBLIOGRAPHIC) TERMS, p. 401.

collectanea [*kol"ek·tā'nē·ə*] *n.*   Collected writings of an author or authors; selected literary excerpts.

Pickering not only depended upon his own collectanea for its substance; he made drafts upon Witherspoon, and got a great deal of material from the denunciations of Americanisms in the British reviews of the time.   —H. L. Mencken, *The American Language*

collective   See special entry GRAMMAR ADJECTIVES, p. 398.

collingual *adj.*   Using the same language or jargon.

collocation *n.*   The combining or pairing of words, esp. when notably different; verbal arrangement considered in terms of the words' reference to each other (contrasted with allocation). *Adj.* collocative; *v.* collocate. See also SYNTAGMATIC.

Seldom have brief sentences by a famous author been compounded of more drooping English . . . as if a true aphorist dealt in such verbal collocations as "precisely," and "but on the contrary," and "using one's intelligence," or needed to use italics for emphasis.
          —Geoffrey Grigson, *Times Literary Supplement*

colloquial *adj.*   Describing words or expressions common to language as it is spoken or to writing intended to be naturally conversational in effect; informal, rather than elevated; involving or characteristic of conversation. *Adv.* colloquially; *n.* colloquiality, colloquialness, colloquialist; *v.* colloquialize.

My father, who had not memorized any St. Augustine, but, after eleven years in college, had memorized some Horace, responded in Latin: *"Adhuc sub judice lis est,"* which means "The proceedings are still in front of the judge" or, more colloquially, "The jury's still out on that."   —David Black, *Like Father*

colloquialism *n.*   Spoken or conversational expression; familiar or informal English that falls between standard English and slang; everyday speech; an informal word or expression, or (loosely) a local or dialectical usage.

"I had to learn American just like a foreign language. To learn it I had to study and analyze it. As a result, when I use slang, colloquialisms, snide talk or any kind of off-beat language I do it deliberately."   —Raymond Chandler, *Raymond Chandler Speaking*

colloquy [*kol'ə·kwē*] *n.*   A conversation or dialogue; serious or formal conference. *V.* colloquize.

As Tilney approached, Judge Caulkins greeted him with the fulsomeness of one anxious to escape an embarrassing colloquy.
          —Louis Auchincloss, *Powers of Attorney*

colonialism *n.*   A colonial word or phrase, such as one used by a Australian or New Zealander; provincial idiom.

colophon   See special entry PARTS OF A BOOK, p. 363.

colporteur   See special entry BOOKISH APPELLATIONS, p. 406.

comma chaser   A copy editor.

comma splice   Improper use of a comma, above all between clauses requiring either a conjunction or a full stop (semicolon, colon, or period). Also COMMA BLUNDER, COMMA FAULT.

Mr. Mudrick is rude, contentious, incorrigible, comma spliced, headlong, raunchy, scornful and know-it-all.
—John Leonard, *The New York Times*

commatic [*kə·mat'ik*] *adj.*   In short stanzas, phrases, or sentences; pertaining to commas. *N.* commatism.

commentary *n.*   A report or treatise explaining or annotating a text; accompanying interpretation or gloss; an informal presentation of notes or observations relevant to something; something that tellingly reflects or exemplifies a situation, truth, etc., and thus serves as a comment or revelation. *Pl.* a narrative historical record related as a personal memoir. *Adj.* commentarial.

The book—I quote—is to be in essence the history of a political movement. It will consist partly of a hitherto unpublished nineteenth-century memoir and partly of an informed commentary by a modern expert on the movement and its development over the years.
—Eric Ambler, *The Care of Time*

commercialese *n.*   The formal and formulaic jargon of business communication, characterized by use of "we," stock phrases suggesting expeditious courtesy ("as per," "duly noted," "are in receipt of," "thanking you in advance"), a tone of circumspect or obsequious acknowledgment, and a certain emphasis on matters of "have," "are," and "will." Also BUSINESS ENGLISH, OFFICESE.

The other reason for which commercialese concerns us here is that, by its very nature, it tends to add the malefic influence of sloppy ineptitude to that of the colourlessness, chilliness and verbosity of officialese and to that of the slick approximations and story-at-any-price subterfuges of journalese.
—Eric Partridge and John W. Clark,
British and American English Since 1900

commercial fiction   See special entry BOOK PUBLISHING TERMS, p. 361.

commonplace *n.*   An obvious or trite comment or opinion; routine, unremarkable observation.

> When he first noticed me he tried to flummox me by addressing me in Latin, but I was equal to that dodge, and after a few commonplaces we changed to English.   —Robertson Davies, *Fifth Business*

commonplace book   A personal notebook for recording literary passages, quotations, special thoughts, memories, etc.

> In any case, Trapnel's was still an unexplored period. Gwinnett added another item. "Did you know he kept a *Commonplace Book* during his last years?"   —Anthony Powell, *Temporary Kings*

commoratio   See special entry RHETORIC TERMS p. 403.

communiqué *n.*   An official announcement or bulletin, usually addressed to the media or other official bodies rather than the public.

> The communiqué contained—here you proceed at your own risk and probably would be well advised to have a companion—friendly and cooperative relations, harmonious relations, constructive relations, cooperative relations, the totality of varied relationships, a close and mutually beneficial relationship based on the principle of equality (it's only the beginning folks, only the beginning), a common determination, an enhanced scope for creativity, the maintenance of peace and the evolution of a stable international order. . . . The Tokyo communiqué somehow left out resolute action, which governments often promise to take at the end of meaningless meetings.
>   —Edwin Newman, *A Civil Tongue*

company terms   See VENEREAL NOUN.

compendium *n.*   A résumé of a written work, text, or area of inquiry; brief but comprehensive summary; collection or inventory. *Adj.* compendious; *adv.* compendiously; *n.* compendiousness.

> We—whoever "we" are—might define the compulsion as a pleasurable urge to express through verbal imagery a compendium of certain inexplicably correlated vagaries observed by him in mental patients, on and off, since his first year at Chose.   —Vladimir Nabokov, *Ada*

composite *n.* An article or news story citing one source that is actually taken from several people who have provided information; a literary character drawn from several people in real life; eclectic fictional work.

"Motor City Blue" turned out to be a competent composite—and the word is used advisedly—of the stereotypes of the hard-boiled species.   —Newgate Callendar, *The New York Times*

comprobatio See special entry RHETORIC TERMS, p. 403.

comstock See special entry BOOKISH APPELLATIONS, p. 406.

Comstockery *n.* Zealous censorship of books or art because of supposed immorality or salaciousness; literary prudery.

conceit *n.* An elaborated metaphor, fanciful analogy, or cleverly evocative turn of expression, sometimes one that is affected or strained; intellectual whimsy; stylistic artifice. Also CONCETTO.

Devoid of inspiration, I found that nothing would come, and although I sat there for half an hour while my mind fiddled with half-jelled ideas and nebulous conceits, I refused to let myself panic at my stagnation; after all, I reasoned, I had barely settled into these strange surroundings.   —William Styron, *Sophie's Choice*

concettism [kən·chet′iz·əm] Love of or use of literary conceits, intellectual analogies, or erudite comparisons; stylistic artifice.

concetto *n.* See CONCEIT.

concinnity [kən·sin′i·tē] *n.* Skill and harmony, esp. of style, in a literary work; elegant arrangement. *Adj.* concinnous, concinnate; *v.* concinnate.

concordance *n.* An alphabetical listing of the words used by a writer or occurring in a text, with references for the reader to the relevant passages; index of terminology and frequency of usage.

concrete language Writing that is simple and direct or that is metaphorically vivid, in either case using simple diction and syntax rather than being lofty, abstract cerebration; immediate, accessible, down-to-earth prose (contrasted with abstract language).

It takes some sophistication even to talk about easily separable words and come up with definitions or synonyms. Most people eventually learn to manage this with concrete nouns, but even individual words, the more abstract and relational they become, get progressively harder to talk about (can you define the preposition *from*?). . . .

　　　　　　　　—Dwight Bolinger, *The State of Language*

condensation *n.* The reducing of a book's or other literary work's size to fewer words by omitting its less important parts without affecting its overall purport, story, etc.; shortened or compressed version of a written work or speech. *Adj.* condensed; *adv.* condensedly; *v.* condense.

His one-volume history of the Army Air Force in World War Two was supposed to be a readable condensation of the twenty-seven-volume *Official History of the Army Air Force in World War Two.*

　　　　　　　　—Kurt Vonnegut, Jr., *Slaughterhouse-Five*

confabulate *v.* To talk together or converse informally; chat. *Adj.* confabular, confabulatory; *n.* confabulation.

confession *n.* Admission or acknowledgment, esp. of personal sin, wrongdoing, responsibility, etc.; a public disclosure of one's misconduct or fault in a matter; declaration of faith or love; candid, often soul-searching or remorseful memoir or autobiographical discourse. *Pl.* a spiritual autobiography or book of frank reminiscences or revelations. *Adj.* confessional; *adv.* confessionally; *n.* confessionalism; *v.* confess.

I'm catching her up on the details only to make a point about bad confessional writers (the *Voice* is full of them): they've got their eye on the effect they're making, not on the experience they're describing. Far too often they confess something only to make us admire their anguish, their courage, their honesty; or they squeeze a little bit of experience until it's dry, hoping to make it yield up some grand historical truth.

　　　　　　　　—David Denby, *The New Republic*

conflation *n.* A combining or blending of two or more versions of a text; confusion or mixing up. *Adj.* conflate; *v.* conflate.

Big, heavy, textbooky. . . . They aim to take in a typical freshman, gawky and clueless, process him cover to cover, and turn out a conflation of Walter Pater and George Orwell.

　　　　　　　　—Richard Lanham, *Style*

conjunctive See special entry GRAMMAR ADJECTIVES, p. 398.

connotation *n.* The conveying of verbal meaning with or apart from a word's more evident, denotative meaning; implicit, associative sense of a word beyond its primary or literal meaning;

affective or emotional purport of a term or expression; implication. *Adj.* connotational, connotative; *adv.* connotatively; *v.* connote.

Of course, the mere name of my mother has no special connotation, no significance, but the woman herself was the vague consoling spirit behind the terrible seasons of this life when unlikely accidents, tabloid adventures, shocking episodes, surrounded a solitary and wistful heart.   —John Hawkes, *Second Skin*

consensus gentium fallacy [*kən·sen'səs gen'tē·əm*]   The fallacy of arguing that an idea is true because most people believe it or because it has been said throughout history (from the Latin for "common opinion of the nations").

conspectus See special entry SCHOLARLY (BIBLIOGRAPHIC) TERMS, p. 401.

constructio ad sensum [*kən·struk'tē·ō ad sen'səm*]   Construction according to sense, or framing a sentence from word sense rather than by adhering to standard grammar; intuitive syntax. Also SYNESIS.

conte [*kôNt*] *n.*   A tale or short narrative, esp. one relating an adventure; concisely styled, rigorously crafted and plotted short story; long short story. See also NOVELLA, RÉCIT.

contraction *n.*   The shortening of a word or phrase by omitting a letter or letters, esp. within the word, and a curtailment reflected in its pronunciation; an internally truncated word or phrase, with the omitted letter or letters usually indicated by an apostrophe. *Adj.* contractional, contractive; *v.* contract.

The word that excited Swift to greatest fury was *mob,* a vulgar contraction of *mobile vulgus.*   —Ernest Gowers, *Plain Words*

contrapuntal phrases   William Safire's term for the well-turned pairing of complementary phrases, one of them using substitute words or an inversion, for a ringing, aphoristic, or oratorical effect, e.g., "Never refrain from having hope, but never find hope in refrains."

contumely [*kon't(y)ōō·m(ə)lē*] *n.*   Rude, abrasive insult in speech or writing, vituperation or scornful candor.

The undergirding reason for all the anger and contumely was that the nation's critics saw in the philosophical stance of Webster III a betrayal of trust, an abdication of responsibility for the treasure of our tongue.   —Lincoln Barnett, *The Treasure of Our Tongue*

conundrum *n.* A riddle involving disparate things and whose answer involves a pun; problem or perplexing phenomenon; quizzical matter.

It's the social reformers and novelists who create these artificial conundrums; they want to see their rotten literature; they want to make us forget that the only interesting and important part of the business is what nobody talks or writes about.

    —Norman Douglas, *South Wind*

conversazione [*kon″vər·sät·syō′nē*] *n.* A social gathering or meeting for discussion of the arts, literature, a science, etc. *Pl.* conversaziones, conversazioni. See also CÉNACLE.

coordinate See special entry GRAMMAR ADJECTIVES, p. 398.

copulative See special entry GRAMMAR ADJECTIVES, p. 398.

copy *n.* Matter to be printed, esp. text for a newspaper or for publicity; wordage at hand; promotional writing; newsworthiness, such as the activities of a celebrity; suitable news material.

A reporter for one press association interviewed Gerda Melind and found that she had had premonitions. Under these circumstances, women with premonitions make good newspaper copy even if their recollections are not verifiable.

    —Eugene Rachlis, *They Came to Kill*

copybook *adj.* Commonplace or conventional; tritely standard; stock.

"A straight copybook honey-trap, that's what we were aiming for," Connie sang, very loud indeed. "Your real old-fashioned burn. A big operator might laugh it off, but not Brother Kirov, least of all if he was on Karla's books."   —John le Carré, *Smiley's People*

copy editing The reading and correcting of manuscripts before setting of type, usually entailing attention to grammar, spelling, punctuation, style and format consistency, and factual particulars such as names and places mentioned. *N.* copy editor; *v.* copy edit. Also COPY READING.

copyline *n. British* An advertising slogan.

The consumer goods with which such couples furnish and try to define their lives are tellingly described in a voice that sometimes carries

a slight, stagey echo of the sales copyline; Norma Jean's electric organ has "a pecan-look finish and eighteen preset chords with optional flute, violin, trumpet and banjo accompaniments."
—Carol Rumens, *Times Literary Supplement*

copy reading See COPY EDITING.

copyright page See special entry PARTS OF A BOOK, p. 363.

copy slant The style or manner of persuasion used in advertising to present a selling point.

copywriting *n.* The writing of promotional, public relations, or advertising copy. *N.* copywriter.

The narrator's admission that he is using the language of the advertising copy-writer is a revealing one, and he resorts, later, to the same jargon: "The Aston-Martin started with a deep, healthy roar."
—David Lodge, *Language of Fiction*

corn *n.* Literature or drama that is mawkishly old-fashioned or sentimental; obvious and embarrassing melodrama; saccharine writing. *Adj.* corny; *adv.* cornily; *n.* corniness.

The inhabitants of Holcomb, Kansas, do not on any page engage in the subtle and economical dialogue Mr. Capote ascribes to the characters in his novels. They speak the words which reporters hear when they interview the participants in prodigious events, and listen to with embarrassed ears. The stuff is corny, yet not just corny. The corn is celestial.   —Rebecca West, "A Grave and Reverend Book"

Cornish-Morris Law of That and Which George Cornish and William Morris's term for the editorial compulsion to change a "that" or a "which" in a sentence: "If the author writes 'which,' the copy editor changes it to 'that'—and vice versa." See also WHICH-MIRE.

corollary *n.* An assertion or proposition that follows implicitly, with little or no proof, from a given statement; an immediate deduction or inference; natural consequence, parallel, or accompaniment. *Adj.* corollary.

"If this book doesn't make you angry, it wasn't worth writing." As any logician can tell you, the corollary of the above quotation is not necessarily true, that is, if the book does make you angry, it does not necessarily follow that it was worth writing.
—Laurence Urdang, *Verbatim*

correlative See special entry GRAMMAR ADJECTIVES, p. 398.

corrigendum See special entry SCHOLARLY (BIBLIOGRAPHIC) TERMS, p. 401.

corruption *n.* Change of an unfamiliar term or form to one more familiar, or departure from correct or standard word use; debased or unorthodox word form; perverted wording of a text or document. *Adj.* corrupt; *v.* corrupt. Also BASTARDIZATION.

His voice was polite again; he even chuckled. "After the first shock of seeing the Scrolls destroyed, we realized you'd actually given us a unique opportunity. All the texts are corrupt, you know, even these —copies of copies of copies, full of *errata* and *lacunae*—but we never could agree on a common reading, and of course the old Scrolls acquired a great spurious authority for sentimental reasons, even though they contradict each other and themselves."

—John Barth, *Giles Goat-Boy*

counteradvertising *n.* Advertising that refutes the message of other, adversary advertising.

counterblast *n. British* A violent action or demonstration; forceful declaration or retort.

counterword *n.* A word used so inexactly or excessively as to be vapid, esp. an overused and hence vague term of approval or disapproval in colloquial speech or advertising, e.g., "wonderful," "fantastic"; trite evaluative adjective.

Fortunately, counterwords and counterphrases collapse eventually of the weight put upon them. —Mary Dohan, *Our Own Words*

coup de plume [*kōo də plüm*] Stroke of the pen: a literary attack.

coup d'essai [*kōo de·sā*] Trial stroke: a trial or warm-up piece; an effort serving as practice; first attempt.

court holy water, court holy bread Fair but insincere words; empty verbiage; flattery.

covering word A general, abstract word so broad in meaning as to cover a variety of senses; cautiously vague abstraction; catchall term, e.g., "implementation," "facility," "arrangement." Also OMNIBUS WORD.

cracking *n.* See SIGNIFYING.

cradle books See INCUNABULA.

crambe repetita [*kräm'bā rep"i·tē'tə*] Warmed-over cabbage: annoying repetition or a tiresome, harped-on old story.

crap *n.*   Worthless or contemptible talk or content, whether unconvincing or deceitfully exaggerated; rubbish; bunk. *Adj.* crappy.

> If you really want to hear about it, the first thing you'll probably want to know is where I was born, and what my lousy childhood was like, and how my parents were occupied and all before they had me, and all that David Copperfield kind of crap, but I don't feel like going into it, if you want to know the truth.
>
> —J. D. Salinger, *The Catcher in the Rye*

craven conditional   William Safire's term for the use of politely cautious or periphrastic subjunctives or catchphrases, e.g., constant resort to "on the one hand," "on the other hand."

> Many academics, diplomats, and television commentators share a favored locution that can be described as "the craven conditional"— the weak-kneed, pompously deferential "it would seem" or "I would say."   —William Safire, *What's the Good Word?*

credo *n.*   A statement of belief, faith, or doctrine; a religious, social, political, or artistic principle or body of principles; dictum.

creole *n.*   A mixed but prevailing pidgin, as in Haiti, that grows out of a melding of differing dominant and subject cultures, usually with a grafting of the dominant vocabulary onto the subject grammar. *Adj.* creolization; *v.* creolize.

> A social superior asserts his condescension toward a subordinate by beginning a conversation in the creole; the subordinate, however, tries to enhance his dignity by responding in the official language.
>
> —Peter Farb, *Word Play*

crib *n.*   A student's illicit line-by-line translation of a particular foreign-language text or work, or a printed résumé or explication of a literary text; makeshift trot; a booklet, notes, or list of answers used for academic cheating. *V.* crib. Also PONY.

cri de coeur [*krē də koer*]   Cry from the heart: an ardent, impassioned declaration, appeal, or lament; outpouring. *Pl.* cris de coeur, cris du coeur.

> . . . "The Men's Club" might at first glance seem to be part of an antifeminist backlash. . . . As an ostensible *cri de coeur* from a small herd of male chauvinist pigs, it will thrive upon the outrage it provokes and the rueful yearnings it indulges.
>
> —Robert Towers, *The New York Times*

cri de guerre [*krē də ger*]   War cry: a martial motto or slogan, as used on a heraldic device; rallying cry.

crinoline head   See DEADHEAD under special entry NEWSROOM HEADLINE JARGON, p. 386.

criticaster *n.*   An incompetent or inferior critic.

Fitzedward Hall is not far from the truth when he rails against "vernacular philology" in the hands of "criticasters" like White, accusing them of ipsedixitism and a disregard for calm statement or argument.
—Dennis E. Barron, *Grammar and Good Taste*

critique *n.*   A critical appraisal or commentary, esp. of a literary work; an acute review or evaluation, generally with respect to an understood standard or interested public; report. *V.* critique.

The *New Yorker* recently observed, in a memorial note about the late Wolcott Gibbs, that if his written editorial opinions "could be released to the world (as they most assuredly can't be), they would make probably a funnier and sounder critique of creative writing in the late twenties and early thirties than has ever been assembled."
—John Fischer, in *Writing in America*

croaker   See special entry WORD-GAME WORDS, p. 395.

crossline   See special entry NEWSROOM HEADLINE JARGON, p. 386.

cross-naming *n.*   See ANTONOMASIA.

cross questions and crooked answers *British*   A parlor game calling for ludicrous replies to simple questions; hence, hedging or evasion.

cross-statement *n.*   Thomas Whissen's term for a somewhat deceptively simple statement that wickedly retracts or undercuts at its end what it conveys at the beginning, catching the reader off guard, and hence a form of ironic phrasing, e.g., "He accepts apologies as well as he makes them," "He was as eager to get out of debt as he was to get in"; witticism with a barbed twist.

cross-talk *n. British*   Rapid interchange or repartee; fast dialogue between two comedians.

The second justification for a judge's question is that he may know the answer himself but it is his duty to ask a question if he thinks that

any of the jury may not share his knowledge. In much the same way
a cross-talk comedian who has been asked a question repeats it for
the benefit of those members of the audience who are hard of hearing
or slow on the uptake.   —G. L. Brook, *Varieties of English*

crusade *n.* A journalistic focus on a cause or an abuse, such as a
needed political corruption or governmental measure; purposive, editorialized, civic-minded reporting. *N.* crusader; *v.* crusade.

The truth is that this crusading business is one of the worst curses of
journalism, and perhaps the main enemy of that fairness and accuracy
and intelligent purpose which should mark the self-respecting newspaper. It trades upon one of the sorriest weaknesses of man—the
desire to see the other fellow jump. It is at the heart of that Puritanical
frenzy, that obscene psychic sadism, which is our national vice. No
newspaper, carrying on a crusade against a man, ever does it fairly
and decently; not many of them even make the pretense.
                           —H. L. Mencken, *A Gang of Pecksniffs*

crux criticorum [*krŏŏks' kri·ti·kôr'əm*] Cross for critics: a riddle
or puzzle for the critics.

cui bono [*kwē' bō'nō*] To whose benefit; to what end or for what
good (more strictly, "who [behind it all] stands to gain from
this): referring to questionable information or scholarship.

Who is lurking in the shadows to presuade the Ford salesman to do
less than his best to convince a customer to buy a Ford? *Cui bono?*
                    —William F. Buckley, Jr., *The Governor Listeth*

curiosa *n.* Literature on unusual subjects; esp. erotic books or
pamphlets concerning homosexual behavior or sexual deviation.

Mr. Deacon was not above marketing the odd volume of *curiosa*—
eroticism preferably confined to the male sex—but did not care to be
bothered with the sale of more humdrum literary works.
                           —Anthony Powell, *Temporary Kings*

curiosa felicitas Agreeable style due to care; apt and elegant ex-
pressism; studied felicity.

curlicism *n.* Literary indecency (from Edmund Curll, detested
eighteenth-century hack publisher and pornographer).

currente calamo [*kə·ren'tē kal'ə·mō*] With a running pen: fluidly
or offhand.

I turn to an earlier, and rather different, anthology, *The Faber Book
of Aphorisms*, edited by W. H. Auden and Louis Kronenberger . . . ,

to show how these two editors took their aphorisms from the considered and the unconsidered (if unconsidered is quite the word),
currente calamo.   —Geoffrey Grigson, *Times Literary Supplement*

curse *n.*   A calling on God or the supernatural to visit evil or harm
on somebody or something, or the evil or ill fate thus invoked;
bane, scourge, or misfortune; person or thing accursed or re-
viled; oath or expression of censure or execration; uttered obscenity or profanity; taboo word. *Adj.* cursed, curst; *v.* curse.

Wash Williams began telling the story of his married life with the tall
blonde girl with blue eyes whom he had met when he was a young
operator at Dayton, Ohio. Here and there his story was touched with
moments of beauty intermingled with strings of vile curses.
—Sherwood Anderson, *Winesburg, Ohio*

cursus *n.*   The cadence or rhythm of prose; stylistic movement or
flow.

curtailed word   See CLIPPED WORD.

curtailment   See special entry WORD-GAME WORDS, p. 395.

curtain lecture   A wife's querulous or censorious lecture to her
husband in bed or in private. Also CAUDLE LECTURE. See also
PILLOW TALK.

cut-and-paste *adj.*   Fashioned by assembling brief items, varied
excerpts, bits and pieces of journalism, etc.; involving reor-
ganization or rearrangement; piecemeal; haphazard. Also
SCISSORS-AND-PASTE.

As a result this book is not a hurried scissors-and-paste job, but a
carefully researched volume about a man who is a more intriguing
mixture of contradictions than meets the eye.
—Caroline Seebohm, *The New York Times*

cut and thrust *Chiefly British*   Lively argument or repartee.

cutline   See special entry NEWSROOM HEADLINE JARGON, p. 386.

cutting *n. British*   A newspaper clipping.

Then something else: the fact that, in (silly) terms of having your
name in the papers, I've always gone down rather than up for my
men. I'd known for some time that that wasn't healthy. As if it wasn't
enough to give my delightful body-and-soul to them, but there had to
be the press cuttings as well.   —John Fowles, *Daniel Martin*

D

daedal [*dēd'əl*] *adj.* Ingeniously contrived or intricate; skillfully and artistically crafted; abounding or adorned with many and various things.

damp squib *British* Something that is ineffective or that falls flat, such as a lame attempt at humor.

dangerous pairs See CATCHFOOLS.

dangerous sense C. S. Lewis's term for a word's current, modern meaning that can be misapplied to the word's use in older literature, written when it had a different sense, e.g., "philosophy" (originally meant science).

> In examining a word I shall often have to distinguish one of its meanings as its *dangerous sense*. . . . When the *dangerous sense* is a sense which did not exist at all in the age when our author wrote, it is less dangerous. —C. S. Lewis, *Studies in Words*

dangler *n.* A misplaced modifier or dependent segment of a sentence that often suggests an unintended or jarringly humorous meaning because of its isolation from what it properly refers to, e.g., "Sprinting ahead, the cave was soon only yards away"; phrase or clause separated from its antecedent; unattached modifier or participle. Also DANGLING MODIFIER.

> Strictly speaking, as Jespersen notes, *strictly speaking* is always a loose participle—perhaps if Newman had known anything at all about grammar he would have avoided that "dangler" for the title of his first book. —Jim Quinn, *American Tongue and Cheek*

dangling comparative See AGENCY COMPARATIVE.

dangling modifier See DANGLER.

dative See special entry GRAMMAR ADJECTIVES, p. 399.

deadhead See special entry NEWSROOM HEADLINE JARGON, p. 386.

dead metaphor A metaphor so shopworn that it has lost its original figurative force and become flat and clichéd, e.g., "green with envy."

It must be remembered that in speech and everyday prose the commonest metaphors are the dead ones, dull at best and mixed at worst.
—Basil Cottle, *The Plight of English*

deadwood *n.* Useless or expendable words that add nothing to clarity or meaning; verbiage; redundancy. See also VERBALISM.

"Overly specific" is inferior to "over-specific," as "inside of her" is to "inside her"; deadwood is always undesirable.
—John Simon, *Paradigms Lost*

debutante deviation John Opdyke's term for a mannered and incorrect use or overuse of the word "so" (to mean "so much"), e.g., "I so liked your performance," "I love him so."

decapitable sentence See ACCORDION SENTENCE.

decapitation See BEHEADMENT under special entry WORD-GAME WORDS, p. 395.

deck See BANK under special entry NEWSROOM HEADLINE JARGON, p. 385.

deck head See STEP HEAD under special entry NEWSROOM HEADLINE JARGON, p. 386.

declamation *n.* Utterance or expression as an exercise in rhetorical speech; recitation or elocution; vociferous or magniloquent oratory; a rhetorical speech or harangue. *Adj.* declamatory; *n.* declaimer; *v.* declaim.

He declaimed, and his declamatory style was modeled partly on the Shakespeareans of his youth, partly on the bombast and singsong of prize-ring announcements and partly on the style of the vanished horsecar and trolley-car conductors who had made an incantation of the place names along their routes.
—John Cheever, *The Wapshot Chronicle*

declarative See special entry GRAMMAR ADJECTIVES, p. 399.

dedication See special entry PARTS OF A BOOK, p. 363.

defective See special entry GRAMMAR ADJECTIVES, p. 399.

definiendum [*di·fin″ē·en′dəm*] *n.* A term or expression being defined. *Pl.* definienda.

definiens [*di·fin′ē·enz″*] *n.* The word or words constituting the definition of a word. *Pl.* definientia.

definition *n.* A statement of the specific meaning or meanings of a word, expression, or thing, as in a dictionary; formulating, categorical description of something; clarification; determining visibility, limits, or properties of something. *Adj.* definitional; *adv.* definitionally; *v.* define.

It is fairly obvious that a satisfactory definition of "civil rights" does not exist. Perhaps it is time one were formulated. It would be good to have one that is a definition and not a slogan.
— Mario Pei, *Words in Sheep's Clothing*

definitive *adj.* Serving to define, specify, or differentiate; final and decisive, or markedly conclusive; authoritatively true, representative, or comprehensive, as a biography having current distinction; unsurpassedly reliable.

Most nonfiction writers have a definitiveness complex. They feel that their article must be the last word and the most comprehensive word. It's a commendable impulse, but there is no definitive article. What you think is definitive today will turn undefinitive by tomorrow, and the writer who doggedly pursues every last fact will find himself pursuing the rainbow and never settling down to write.
— William Zinsser, *On Writing Well*

degender *v.* To delete or change reference to gender to obviate sexism, as with male pronouns used generically.

deictic [*dīk'tik*] *adj.* Proving directly; indicating or pointing to specifically, such as the pronouns "that" and "those"; demonstrative; conspicuous or notable.

Today the rupture of orthographic rules in order to acquire a unique image is largely the preserve of trademarks, which thus attempt to be "deictic". . . .   — Geoffrey Wagner, *On the Wisdom of Words*

deipnosophy [*dīp·nos'ə·fē*] *n.* See TABLE TALK.

delenda [*di·len'də*] *n. pl.* Things to be deleted. *Sing.* delendum.

deletion *n.* The crossing out or removing of a word or words; word or passage taken out. *V.* delete.

A quarter of a century later we might have had Mr. Truman saying, "I'll tell you one thing. If I do, the Cardinals will have a (expletive deleted) good team," a device that puts the burden of supplying the profanity on the reader but does nothing to reduce the no-nonsense impression the curser (or precurser, really) seeks to give.
— Edwin Newman, *Strictly Speaking*

Delphic utterance An oracular statement the interpretation of which is obscure or ambiguous; equivocal prophecy or answer.

But with respect to the future consequences of the space program, they might as well have hired a gypsy to study the palm of Werner von Braun or invited an astrologer to contribute a paper to their project. Their conclusions about the space program are either tenuous in the extreme, or truistic, or else Delphic utterances of the sort which confidently predict with considerable semantical confusion that maybe X will happen, or maybe it won't.
—David Hackett Fischer, *Historians' Fallacies*

demagoguery, demagogy, demagogism *n.* The practices or language of a leader who, avid for power, appeals to popular emotions and prejudices and makes false claims and promises; impassioned, duplicitous cant; opportunistic rhetoric. *Adj.* demagogic, demagogical; *adv.* demagogically; *n.* demagogue, demagog.

Since obsessions dragoon our energy by endless repetitive contemplations of guilt we can neither measure nor forget, political power of the most frightening sort was obviously waiting for the first demagogue who would smash the obsession and free the white man of his guilt.   —Norman Mailer, *Miami and the Siege of Chicago*

démarche [*dā·märsh'*] *n.* A diplomatic maneuver (or countermaneuver), tactic, or response, such as a formal positional statement presented to another government orally or in writing; any presentation of a viewpoint to a public official.

démenti [*dā·mäN·tē*] *n.* Official or formal denial of a rumor or allegation, as in diplomacy.

"We're killing this story," he said. "Go round to the Press Bureau and have Benito issue an official *dementi* before four o'clock. See it's posted in the hotel and in the wireless station. And put it about among the boys that the story's dead."   —Evelyn Waugh, *Scoop*

demonstrative See special entry GRAMMAR ADJECTIVES, p. 399.

demotic *adj.* Of or pertaining to the common people; like or characteristic of popular speech; vernacular.

The book was to have been an original, racy English picaresque novel, a mixture of Petronius, Harriette Wilson and *Lazarillo de Tormes*. A crisp astringent picture of English harlotry, nearly all dialogue, some of it in rhyming slang and Soho English, the rest in the genteel demotic speech of furnished flatlets off the Tottenham Court Road.   —Cyril Connolly, *The Rock Pool*

denotation *n.*   The primary, explicit meaning of a word or what it represents, or its shared sense among most speakers of a language, as opposed to connotation; literal meaning; term that specifies, signifies, or names. *Adj.* denotative, denotive; *adv.* denotatively; *n.* denotativeness, denotement.

dentiloquist   See special entry BOOKISH APPELLATIONS, p. 406.

de omnibus rebus et quibusdam aliis [*dā om'nə·boŏs rāboŏs et kwi·boŏs'däm ä'li·ēs*]   About everything and a few things besides: a remark about books that are rambling and wordy.

de profundis [*dā prō·foŏn'dis*]   Out of the depths: an expression of profound sorrow or misery; agonized plaint or lament. *Adj.* de profundis; *adv.* de profundis.

The chief requisite of Academese is the rumble *de profundis,* as I discovered a few years ago when I assisted in compiling the findings produced by one of those portentous projects on "The National Purpose" which the big foundations like to put their money into from time to time.   —Lincoln Barnett, *The Treasure of Our Tongue*

derivation *n.*   The ascertaining of the origin of a word or phrase, or the tracing of a word form or inflection to a root or base word; an etymology. *Adv.* derivational.

I believe there are objects in nature—namely, fossils—which occur in layers, and which some half-rational fantasts insist derive from animals, the bottom ones more ancient than the top. The same, I think, with word derivations—arguments straining back to Sanskrit or Indo-European. I have never seen a word derive.
                                        —Renata Adler, *Speedboat*

derivative *adj.*   Derived, or not original; borrowed or adapted from or modeled on another source, such as a book (usu. a novel) unimaginatively similar to a previous one; copied or secondhand; involving linguistic derivation; traceable to another, older word through etymological investigation. *Adv.* derivatively; *n.* derivation, derivative, derivate, derivativeness; *v.* derive.

derogatory, derogative *adj.*   Expressing unfavorable criticism or low opinion; detracting; belittling. *Adv.* derogatorily; *n.* derogation; *v.* derogate.

The patient all this while continued slouching and hunching about the room, poking into corners and picking up and fingering objects for derogatory comment.   —Peter De Vries, *Madder Music*

descant *n.* A commenting or discussing at length, esp. with great interest or fervor. *V.* descant.

description *n.* The act or method of verbal depiction of somebody or something, or discourse presenting a mental or sensory recreation of something actual, experienced, or imagined; literal or metaphorical rendering of the form or nature of somebody or something; likeness or sketch; sort or type. *Adj.* descriptive; *adv.* descriptively; *n.* descriptive, descriptiveness; *v.* describe.

Of course this novice's report lacked whoop and crash and lurid description, and therefore wanted the true ring; but its antique wording was quaint and sweet and simple, and full of the fragrances and flavors of the time, and these little merits made up in a measure for its more important lacks.
—Mark Twain, *A Connecticut Yankee in King Arthur's Court*

descriptive *adj.* Describing from an objective, factual standpoint rather than with historical or comparative judgment, as in an analysis of language or usage intended to be informative and not evaluative; marked by or showing observation of actual usage, as contrasted with a prescriptive (or proscriptive) attitude growing out of a concern for orthodox grammar or correctness.

descriptor *n.* A word or expression that describes or identifies.

desultory *adj.* Lacking plan or purpose and rambling from one subject to another; unfocused and not cohesive; haphazard; random. *Adv.* desultorily; *n.* desultoriness.

But Miss Jaffe's execution of the idea is disappointingly desultory.
—Annie Gottlieb, *The New York Times*

determinative See special entry GRAMMAR ADJECTIVES, p. 399.

detraction *n.* An instance of or work belittling or attacking the reputation of somebody or something, esp. through malicious criticism or misrepresentation; disparagement. *Adj.* detractive, detractory; *adv.* detractively.

He knew what was said about her; for, popular as she was, there had always been a faint undercurrent of detraction.
—Edith Wharton, "The Other Two"

devil *n. British* An author's subordinate hired to assist with the writing of a book, often without credit or pay; printer's apprentice; any assistant. *V.* devil.

In his early days, when in low water, Salvidge had done some devilling, when St John Clarke was without a secretary collecting French Revolution material for *Dust Thou Art*.
— Anthony Powell, *Hearing Secret Harmonies*

devil's mass Indiscriminate cursing.

diacritic, diacritical mark *n.* A distinguishing mark given to a character or letter to indicate stress or pronunciation, such as a superscribed accent; phonetic sign. *Adj.* diacritic, diacritical.

The "etymons," as he called them, were the root terms for *Pass* and *Fail*, but inflected with prefixes, infixes, suffixes, and diacritical marks to such an extent, and so variously from fragment to fragment, that conflicting interpretations, in his opinion, could be said to figure the intellectual biography of studentdom, as had been amply demonstrated in a wealth of what he called *Geistesgeschichten*. . . .
— John Barth, *Giles Goat-Boy*

diagram *v.* To make a labeled scheme of lines to clarify the syntax of a sentence, with subordinate phrases and clauses represented along angled lines appended to the main, subject-predicate line. *Adj.* diagrammable, diagrammatic, diagrammatical; *adv.* diagrammatically; *n.* diagram.

Girls pin notes under their skirts which they modestly lower when a proctor comes along. They hide answers in their brassieres. Some of the boys come with sentences diagrammed on their palms and definitions printed all the way up their arms.
— Bernard Malamud, *A New Life*

dialect *n.* A special or regional strain of a language, usually oral in its dissemination, that is distinctive in its idiom, pronunciation, or grammar and is often one of several varieties of a common tongue; the language peculiar to a social class, foreign-born group, or the like; idiosyncratic or nonstandard speech. *Adj.* dialectal; *adv.* dialectically.

It was a hard school. One could not learn geography very well through the medium of strange dialects, from dark minds that mingled fact and fable and that measured distances by "sleeps" that varied according to the difficulty of the going.
— Jack London, "Lost Face"

dialectic *n.* The seeking or investigation of truth through reasoning and intellectual discussion, esp. by exposing false beliefs and contradictions in an opposing argument; a method of argumentation or exposition that considers opposing ideas or options to reach a rational solution; the Hegelian critical theory of the progress and resolution of ideas from thesis and antithesis to synthesis; an intellectual exchange or focused dialogue. *Pl.* a "continuing conversation" or discursive technique for resolving conflict. *Adj.* dialectic, dialectical; *adv.* dialectically; *n.* dialectician, dialecticism.

The spirit of dialectic and theory sat lightly upon the young men in Philadelphia—half of them were under forty; they wanted to get things done.   —Stuart Chase, *The Tyranny of Words*

diallage   See special entry RHETORIC TERMS, p. 403.

diallelon [*dī″ə·lē′lon*] *n.*   A circular definition.

dialogue *n.*   Conversation between two or more people, or the literary representation of direct speech; quoted utterance; a work written entirely in the form of a colloquy, esp. in philosophy; an exchange of ideas or opinions. *Adj.* dialogic, dialogical; *adv.* dialogically. See special entry DIALOGUE VERBS, p. 376.

He was for long thought to write very bad English, and indeed he gave you the impression of writing with the stub of a blunt pencil; his style was laboured, an uneasy mixture of the classical and the slangy, and his dialogue was such as could never have issued from the mouth of a human being.   —W. Somerset Maugham, *Cakes and Ale*

dialogue des sourds [*dē·ä·lôg dā sŌŌr*]   Dialogue of the deaf: a discussion in which the participants pay no attention to one another's argument.

dialysis   See special entry RHETORIC TERMS, p. 403.

diaskeuast   See special entry BOOKISH APPELLATIONS, p. 406.

diasyrm   See special entry RHETORIC TERMS, p. 403.

diatribe *n.*   An abusive, often prolonged attack or denunciation; acrimonious harangue or critique.

Without polemic, dialectic or diatribe, she has conveyed more clearly than anyone I've ever read before what it was like to be a girl in the 50's, when one had a chance to grow up quietly and gradually.
     —Susan Bolotin, *The New York Times*

diatyposis   See special entry RHETORIC TERMS, p. 403.

dichaeologia   See special entry RHETORIC TERMS, p. 403.

dichotomy *n.*   A division or counterposing into two groups or positions, usually contradictory or mutually exclusive; a specified, vis-à-vis contrast. *Adj.* dichotomous; *adv.* dichotomously; *n.* dichotomousness, dichotomist; *v.* dichotomize.

I submit to you staffers that the solution establishes itself before our very eyes: namely, that an *absolute*—in any particular field—must be presented as a *dichotomy!* Yes, if one mother company, such as our Vanity, could confront the public with a pure dichotomy, in any particular product, it would gain virtual monopoly there. Yes, and *we* will present such a dichotomy.
                                                —Terry Southern, *The Magic Christian*

diction *n.*   Choice of words with respect to clarity, variety, taste, etc.; aptness of vocabulary and phrasing; correctness of pronunciation; enunciation. *Adj.* dictional; *adv.* dictionally.

It is destructive enough to the novel's texture to hear this "historical" Arthur speak in the diction of a mod Labor candidate or an American president standing for re-election.
                                                —Alan Cheuse, *The New York Times*

dictionary *n.*   An alphabetical reference book defining words or topics, esp. a work giving the meaning of words in one language or two; a special or general reference to terminology; lexicon; accepted vocabulary.

She didn't use those words the way women usually do, conscious they're making you think they're talking like men, but having to get a running start for every word not considered fit for ladies or dictionaries.   —Budd Schulberg, *What Makes Sammy Run?*

dictum *n.*   An authoritative pronouncement or principle; precept or credo; a popular saying; maxim.

Eighteenth-century grammars might have been more uniform had there been an agreed-upon standard of linguistic propriety, but, with a nod to the dictum of Horace establishing usage as arbiter, each codifier elected his own authorities.
                                                —Edward Finegan, *Attitudes Toward English Usage*

dictum de dicto   Saying from a saying: a secondhand report; hearsay.

didactic *adj.*   Demonstrating intent to teach or edify; purposively instructive or informative; excessively earnest or pedantic, esp.

ın a narrow, self-righteous way; moralistic. *Adv*. didactically; *n*. didact, didacticism, didactics.

One is literally fabulous. The other makes use of a dry, rather didactic style in which the detail is as precisely observed as if the author were writing a manual for the construction of a solar heating unit.

—Gore Vidal, *Matters of Fact and Fiction*

digest *n*. A collection, condensation, or summary of information, such as a compilation of technical reports or literary pieces; periodical containing selected excerpts or articles from other publications. *V*. digest.

diglossia *n*. The coexisting of two different but relatively standardized, native varieties of speech in an environment or community, usually differentiated in formality or social prestige. *Adj*. diglossic.

After some improvement in the national situation with regard to racial inequality, the television networks hired former Black basketball stars on their sportscasting teams and thereby probably inadvertently produced a diglossic situation in which one sportscaster is, even when unseen, obviously white, while the other, who is usually assigned the job of giving background commentary and who handles the halftime interviews, etc., is just as obviously Black.

—J. L. Dillard, *All-American English*

digraph *n*. Two letters representing one speech sound, as the "ai" in "bait."

digression *n*. A turning aside or straying from the main discourse or topic; departure from the theme; excursive passage. *Adj*. digressive, digressional, digressionary; *adv*. digressively; *v*. digress.

He got a *D* plus because they kept yelling "Digression!" at him all the time. For instance, he made this speech about this farm his father bought in Vermont. They kept yelling "Digression!" at him the whole time he was making it, and this teacher, Mr. Vinson, gave him an *F* on it because he hadn't told what kind of animals and vegetables and stuff grew on the farm and all.

—J. D. Salinger, *The Catcher in the Rye*

dilogy *n*. Equivocal expression (not due to syntax) in which there are two apparent meanings but only one of them ostensibly intended, e.g., "Friends—I know you too well to call you Ladies and Gentlemen . . ."; repetition of a word or phrase. See also AMPHIBOLOGY, DELPHIC UTTERANCE, EQUIVOQUE.

diminutive *n.*   A word or word element indicating (often by addition of a suffix) small size or familiarly lovable, pitiable, or
dismissible qualities, sometimes condescendingly. *Adv.* diminutive. See also HYPOCORISTIC.

My grandmother, too, used to put other people's ailments into the
diminutive; strokelets were what her friends had. Aldo said he was
bored to tearsies by my grandmother's diminutives.
                                                      —Renata Adler, *Speedboat*

dingbat *n.*   An ornamental piece of type used on a page, such as
an asterisk or bullet. Also FLUBDUB.

The compulsive editor, when checking the specs on an article, can't
help checking also for such items as initial capital and closing dingbat,
if they are used routinely. These decorative items have a way of being
forgotten by the first editor of the manuscript—unless that editor,
too, is functionally compulsive and puts them in immediately.
                                    —Arthur Plotnik, *The Elements of Editing*

dingbatted maledicta   Reinhold Aman's term for typographical
symbols or punctuation marks to represent obscene language.

I don't recall ever having seen such dingbatted maledicta, or symbolic
euphemisms, in any German, Dutch, Afrikaans, Norwegian, Danish,
Swedish, Icelandic, Yiddish, French, Italian, Spanish, Portuguese, or
Romanian publication. Are such dingbats used in foreign-language
publications to represent offensive words? And if not, how *do* other
languages defuse maledicta other than by d—mb dashes or a*inine
asterisks?   —Reinhold Aman, *Maledicta*

direct discourse   The language of any person or literary character
quoted, as in a conversation or in fictional dialogue; verbatim
utterance (contrasted with indirect discourse).

disambiguate *v. Chiefly British*   To eliminate ambiguity from; decipher. *N.* disambiguation.

Clearly our efforts to "disambiguate" texts can themselves prove
disconcertingly ambiguous, even if they're not all actually as undis-
ambiguable as Kermode believes . . . *Hamlet* to be.
                      —Valentine Cunningham, *Times Literary Supplement*

disclaimer *n.*   A specific denial or disavowal, esp. an explicit public statement of nonresponsibility or nonaffiliation; protective
explanation; waiver. *Adj.* disclamatory; *v.* disclaim.

She turns on "Heated Topics," a feminist talk show so controversial
that it begins with a viewer-discretion warning and ends with a disclaimer.   —Mary Cantwell, *The New York Times*

discourse *n.* Verbal expression or interchange of ideas; discussion or conversation; a formal address or paper on a subject. *Adj.* discoursive; *adv.* discoursively; *n.* discoursiveness; *v.* discourse.

He is not so amused, however, at the disclosure of my having temporarily "lost" my papers in the forest. He gives me a discourse on carelessness. It is a short discourse but it weighs about four tons.
—Tom Robbins, *Another Roadside Attraction*

discursive *adj.* Covering a range of topics or discoursing freely and broadly, moving from subject to subject; characterized by rational analysis rather than intuition. *Adv.* discursively; *n.* discursiveness.

He published some of the best reporting—of an unofficial and personal kind—that was written about the war, and he elicited from Augustus John his delightful discursive memoirs, in which history is unimportant and chronology does not exist.
—Edmund Wilson, *Classics and Commercials*

disedification *n.* Flouting the morals or piety of (a group or readership); offending religious feelings. *V.* disedify.

You don't have to love Bob Silvers to love his magazine. A modicum of disedification goes with the territory. To paraphrase Leo Durocher, nice editors finish last. —Philip Nobile, *Intellectual Skywriting*

disinformation *n.* False or misleading information or documentation contrived to deceive or subvert, esp. deliberate fabrication by an intelligence agency. *V.* disinform.

If I say the US is intervening in El Salvador to help a gang of nun-raping cutthroats with no popular support, I may be misinformed, or I may be disinformed. —Alexander Cockburn, *Village Voice*

disjecta membra [*dis·jek″tə mem′brə*] Scattered members: disjointed quotations or fragments; verbal bits and pieces.

The man burst into a hearty laugh. "They might be useful to me as relics of my adventure," said he, "but beyond that I can hardly see what use the *disjecta membra* of my late acquaintance are going to be to me. . . ."
—Arthur Conan Doyle, "The Adventure of the Blue Carbuncle"

disjunctive See special entry GRAMMAR ADJECTIVES, p. 399.

disparagement *n.* The expression of low opinion; regarding or portraying unfavorably so as to lower in esteem; discredit or belittlement of one's dignity. *Adj.* disparaging; *adv.* disparagingly; *v.* disparage.

Some years ago, Edna Ferber wrote a book about a very tiny group of very rich Texans. Her description was accurate, so far as my knowledge extends, but the emphasis was one of disparagement.
—John Steinbeck, *Travels with Charley*

disquisition *n.*   A formal or academic discussion of or inquiry into a subject; treatise or dissertation. *Adj.* disquisitional.

He spoke as if all that he said were in every idea and in every syllable final, finished, perfected beyond disquisition long before he was born; and truth and eternity dwelt like clearest water in the rhythms of his language and in the contours of his voice; his voice accepted and bore this language like the bed of a brook.
—James Agee, *A Death in the Family*

dissertation *n.*   A formal and extensive treatment of a subject, such as an academic thesis; treatise; earnest presentation of one's opinion; discourse; explanation. *Adj.* dissertational, dissertative; *n.* dissertator; *v.* dissert.

As the local landlady Signora Maura shows the young couple about the house they have just rented from her, she distracts their attention from the walls with a long dissertation on the gas meter.
—Gore Vidal, *Matters of Fact and Fiction*

dissonance *n.*   Disharmony or discordance of sound, as by incongruity or harshness in choice or combination of words. *Adj.* dissonant; *adv.* dissonantly.

distributive   See special entry GRAMMAR ADJECTIVES, p. 399.

dithyramb *n.*   A verse form of Greek origin; impassioned work or prose passage extolling something, often in poetic or impressionistic language; exalting tribute, sometimes excessive or mawkish; paean. *Adj.* dithyrambic; *adv.* dithyrambically.

All of us not actually illiterate or imbecile feel that something is wrong when a writer attempts to compel his readers' feelings by the exploitation of early deaths, handsome sinners with lunatic wives, and ecstatic dithyrambs.   —Rebecca West, *Rebecca West: A Celebration*

dittography *n.*   In writing or printing, the unintentional repetition of letters or words. *N.* dittograph. See also HAPLOGRAPH.

In my next "paragraph" I contrived, quite aptly, to introduce some five or six quotations from verses of Praed which J.F. had not read to us. I awaited the result with curiosity. My "paragraph" was returned to me with the comment in J.F.'s writing: "*A mere orgy of dittography.*"   —Evelyn Waugh, *A Little Learning*

Divine Passive   Richard Mitchell's term for the stilted use of passive verbs in pretentiously officious or ponderous language, e.g., "it has been found that," "is clearly indicated by." Also AGENTLESS PASSIVE.

Among the better class of Grammarians, that construction is known as the Divine Passive. It intends to suggest that neither the writer nor anyone else through whose head you might like to hammer a blunt wooden spike can be held accountable for anything in any way.   —Richard Mitchell, *Less Than Words Can Say*

dixit *n.*   See IPSE DIXIT.

D-notice *n. British*   In England, an official governmental request to news editors not to publish stories on certain subjects for reasons of national security.

docta ignorantia [*dok'tə ig"nō·rän'tē·ə*]   Learned ignorance.

doctrinaire *adj.*   Characterized by impractical, abstract doctrine or speculative opinion and thus narrow in point of view; rigidly theoretical or parochial, without flexibility or regard to circumstances; stubbornly doctrinal. *Adv.* doctrinarily; *n.* doctrinairism, doctrinaire, doctrinairian.

But there is, for me, a certain softness in her argument, based as it is on a diagnosis of psychology that is both excessively doctrinaire in its remedy and equivocal.   —Susan Sontag, *Against Interpretation*

documentation *n.*   The use or citing of documents or specific sources as references or substantiating evidence, or the documents thus supplied; printed authenticating information; historical or objective data, such as footnotes, bibliographies, and appendices; the instruction booklet or manual that accompanies computer programs. *Adj.* documentational; *v.* document.

The documentation of Augustus Walmer is slight. There is a journal kept fitfully during his early years on the islands. There are the letters to his agent in which he discussed the day-to-day matters of running his estate while he was on the mainland. There are letters written to Amelia Pontefract over the long years of their friendship and his rancorous correspondence with the Duchy over the terms of his lease. That is all.   —Ann Schlee, *The Proprietor*

dogmatic *adj.*   Assertively doctrinal, or promulgating a strong belief or viewpoint as if it were fact; showing firm and forceful opinion; unyieldingly certain or prescriptive; narrow and magisterial. *Adj.* dogmatical; *adv.* dogmatically; *n.* dogma, dogmatism, dogmatist, dogmaticism; *v.* dogmatize.

> For ten minutes Challee tried to get Bird to withdraw the word "sick." The young doctor was upset. He became querulous and dogmatic, and threw up clouds of terminology.
> —Herman Wouk, *The Caine Mutiny*

dolichologia [*dol″i·kə·lō′jē·ə*] *n. British*   See GOBBLEDYGOOK.

dolus bonus [*dōl′əs bō′nəs*]   Good deceit: in Roman and civil law, permissible bargaining and cunning in selling, as in the case of a merchant's overpraising of his products.

dolus malus [*dōl′əs mäl′əs*]   Evil deceit: in Roman and civil law, unlawful deceit or misrepresentation growing out of evil intent or malice; fraud.

domesticated word   See BORROWING.

donnée [*dō·nā′*] *n.*   A given (idea): the "bestowed" assumption upon which a literary work proceeds, or its fundamental elements; artistic premise. See also ARGUMENT, TENDENZ.

> Even less likely is this book's *donnée*, which would have baseball serve as a grand metaphor for American culture ("Holy cow!" as Phil Rizzuto would say).   —Daniel Okrent, *The New York Times*

donnish *adj. Chiefly British*   Characteristic of a university professor or don; pedantically erudite; remote from worldly concerns. *Adv.* donnishly; *n.* donnishness.

> Crace sent a formal reference from Eton, with a tinge of donnish sarcasm in it: "I do not know at all what is required by the authorities for candidates in the Indian police. I send a formal certificate which is probably all that is necessary."   —Bernard Crick, *George Orwell*

dontopedalogy *n.*   Prince Philip's (Duke of Edinburgh) term for verbal bumbling or foot-in-mouth disease.

dope story   A summary-information news article that attempts to clarify a news event through evaluative and interpretive analysis; story published under a journalist's byline that was actually leaked or fed to him or her to a political or public-opinion end, and hence a planted scoop or media trial balloon.

double borrowing   A coming into usage for the second time of a (foreign) loan-word that has dropped out of currency; the phe-

nomenon of a word's being adopted separately or indepen-
dently in England and in America but with differing meanings,
e.g., "crevasse," "coulee."

double Dutch Unintelligible language; gibberish; "Greek."

Departures from the vocabulary, rules, and fetishes that we were
taught at school shake the foundations of our existence. A sort of
Double Dutch Elm Disease seems to be nibbling away at the roots
and branches of our language. —Philip Howard, *Weasel Words*

double duty See CANNIBALISM.

double-entendre [$d\overline{oo}''bl(ə)\cdot än\cdot tän' dr(ə)$] *n.* A provocative ambiguity in an expression, esp. a humorous or risqué connotation
in a word or phrase; double meaning. *British.* double-entente.

The editor was also often on the edge of panic about suspected *double
entendre,* and after thirty-one years I recall his concern about an Arno
drawing of one of his elderly gentlemen of the old school dancing with
a warmly clinging young lady and saying "Good God, woman, think
of the social structure!" Ross was really afraid that "social structure"
could be interpreted to mean a certain distressing sexual phenomenon
of human anatomy. —James Thurber, *The Years with Ross*

double negative The use of two negatives in a sentence where one
suffices, e.g., "It doesn't mean nothing"; reiterated denial that
is tantamount to an affirmative or positive statement.

In substandard speech, however, double negatives often reinforce a
strongly negative colour in an assertion. "I don't want nothing from
nobody" is a threefold declaration of independence, not a logical
seesaw. —G. W. Turner, *Stylistics*

doublespeak *n.* Deliberately unclear or obscure language to deceive, evade, impress, or in general make the questionable or
untrue seem true; double-talk; gobbledygook.

What I am writing this for is to call attention to a particularly egre-
gious example of doublespeak that the abortionists—"pro-choicers,"
that is—seem to have hit on in the current rhetorical war.
—Walker Percy, *The New York Times*

doublet *n.* Two words that are different forms of the same root
word but that often have different meanings or connotations,
e.g., "urban" and "urbane," "person" and "parson," "curt-
sey" and "courtesy," "frail" and "fragile"; phrase or idiom
with two terms, e.g., "fire and brimstone," "one and all."

double-talk *n.* Glib patter that mixes sense and nonsense, as used by certain entertainers; ambiguous language used to evade, confound, or deceive. See special entry THE LANGUAGE OF COMIC DOUBLE-TALK, p. 389. *V.* double-talk.

Perhaps because of its pomposity, the scholarly world often lends itself to hoaxes and flimflams. One case recently reported was that of three Southern California medical educators who hired a professional actor, dressed him up with a fictitious *curriculum vitae,* and presented him to lecture to groups of psychiatrists, psychologists, and social workers on the topic of "Mathematical Game Theory as Applied to Physical Education." The self-styled Dr. Myron Fox of Albert Einstein University lectured to the fifty-five educators, using academic jargon and double-talk, and making irrelevant, conflicting, and meaningless statements, both in his lectures and in the following question-and-answer periods. The comments of the audience? "Excellent presentation"; "Has warm manner"; "Lively examples"; "Extremely articulate." There was a single note of doubt: "Too intellectual." Not one of the audience saw through the phony, and all were convinced they had learned something.   —Mario Pei, *Weasel Words*

downright dunstable, plain dunstable *British* Very direct or plain-speaking; straightforward.

down style Individual or house writing style that minimizes capital letters; lower-case style (contrasted with up style).

dozens, (playing) the In the culture of American blacks, a contest of mutual insults concerning relatives, esp. the opponents' mothers, sometimes in rhymed couplets and often graphically sexual or scatological (the "dirty dozens"). See also SIGNIFYING.

His broad cultural approach to prizefighting is also illuminating. A discussion, for example, of the style of black boxers invokes jazz, "bad nigger" folk figures and a form of insult known as "the dozens."
—Diane McWhorter, *The New York Times*

drivel *n.* Stupidly silly or pointless talk; contemptible blather; pap. *Adj.* driveling, drivelling; *v.* drivel.

And your costume, though very becoming, is, in a sense, *traurnïy* (funerary). I'm spouting drivel.   —Vladimir Nabokov, *Ada*

drophead See special entry NEWSROOM HEADLINE JARGON, p. 386.

dropline See STEP HEAD under special entry NEWSROOM HEADLINE JARGON, p. 386.

drowned English See FRAMIS.

dryasdust See special entry BOOKISH APPELLATIONS, p. 406.

dual edition See special entry BOOK PUBLISHING TERMS, p. 361.

duckspeak *n.* George Orwell's term for speech so unconscious, thoughtless, and meaningless as to be a form of rote verbal noise; reflexive talk that is senseless, tautological, or otherwise asinine, however formal.

As he watched the eyeless face with the jaw moving rapidly up and down, Winston had a curious feeling that this was not a real human being but some kind of dummy. It was not the man's brain that was speaking; it was his larynx. The stuff that was coming out of him consisted of words, but it was not speech in the true sense; it was a noise uttered in unconsciousness, like the quacking of a duck.

—George Orwell, *1984*

durative See IMPERFECTIVE under special entry GRAMMAR ADJECTIVES, p. 399.

Dutch lead An "imagined" newspaper opening sentence or paragraph that is startling and in fact not true, as subsequently explained to the reader, and hence one used for dramatic effect, sometimes irresponsibly.

dysphemism *n.* Use of a disparaging or disagreeable term as a substitute for a standard, inoffensive one, e.g., "old lady" for "girlfriend"; gratuitous derogatory expression. *Adv.* dysphemistic.

For rival political systems, the entire rhetoric of the adversary becomes tinged with dysphemism, but special epithets are reserved for the routine taunts.

—Dwight Bolinger, in *The State of the Language*

E

earwig *v.* To pester with private persuasion, warnings, etc.; attempt to influence or to insinuate oneself through flattery.

echo See special entry WORD-GAME WORDS, p. 395.

echoic word, echo word A word expressive of the sound it stands for; onomatopoeic coinage, e.g., "kerplonk," "neigh," "ticktock," "tweet."

echolalia [*ek"ō·lā'lē·ə*] *n.* Habitual or pathological repetition of others' words or remarks, infantile imitation. *Adj.* echolalic.

> Most of us balk at her soporific rigmaroles, her echolaliac [*sic*] incantations, her half-witted-sounding catalogues of numbers; most of us read her less and less. —Edmund Wilson, *Axel's Castle*

echo phrase Porter Perrin's term for a phrase patterned on but different from a well-known expression, or an allusion in the form of a variant idiom of wordplay, e.g., "one man's humor is another man's poison." See also TWISTED PROVERB.

eclipsis *n.* Omission of a grammatical element necessary to the full meaning of a sentence. *Pl.* eclipses, eclipsises.

ecphonesis [*ek"fə·nē'sis*] *n.* Exclamation. *Pl.* ecphoneses.

> And there are the screeching italics and the inventive ecphonesis: " . . . But a red facade? A *color*? Well, I mean, my God—how very *bourgeois*!" —Christopher Lehmann-Haupt (quoting Tom Wolfe), *The New York Times*

edit *v.* To prepare or revise for presentation or publication, including correcting, rewording, adding, deleting, and styling; make correct, presentable, or readable; assemble or annotate a work, such as a scholarly collection; oversee a publishing enterprise. *Adj.* editorial; *adv.* editorially; *n.* editor.

> An editor's job is to shape the *expression* of an author's thoughts, not the thoughts themselves. The editor deletes jargon, redundancies, and irrelevancies—never ideas, unless the author consents. —Arthur Plotnik, *The Elements of Editing*

editio princeps See special entry SCHOLARLY (BIBLIOGRAPHIC) TERMS, p. 401.

editorial *n.* A newspaper or magazine column that voices the opinion of the editors or publisher, usually about an issue of current importance or interest; fervid or long-winded harangue. *Adj.* editorial; *adv.* editorially.

He knew he could probably write smarter editorials if he read *The Brothers Karamazov* and some of the other great works of all time, but there was the trouble: if he sat around reading the great works of all time, how would he ever get his editorials written?
—Richard Yates, *A Good School*

editorialize *n.* To express one's position or point of view; introduce opinion or bias into reporting of facts or information; admix comment with reportage; characterize or label. *N.* editorializer, editorialization.

Girls, Shmul editorialized in his little book, live a stone-age life in a blown-glass cave. —Grace Påley, *The Little Disturbances of Man*

editorial we "We" in place of "I" as a stylistic or journalistic device.

We, we, we—the smug editorial "we." My—it must be awfully cozy to be boringly married and use the editorial we. But is it conducive to art? —Erica Jong, *Fear of Flying*

Educanto *n.* The jargon of the teaching profession, characterized by highly abstract methodological terms having a sociological or psychological cachet, pedagogical and administrative generalities, and often barbarisms. Also EDUCATIONESE, PEDAGUESE.

Educationists—as distinct from teachers—are often addicted to a ponderous prose that James D. Koerner (in *The Miseducation of American Teachers*) calls "Educanto." In search for pseudoscientific status, teachers become "instructional personnel"; the classroom is "the teaching situation"; bright students are "fortunate deviates"; collecting information becomes "assemblizing imponderables"; and the teacher (or rather "director of experience") gets ahead by using ritual words such as "insightfulness" and progressing to formidable phrases like "the progressive familial subcultural mental retardation," "the normative, generalization reference cue," or "the extrinsic dualistic organization of coordinate administration." Mr. Koerner observes that such jargon "masks a lack of thought, and in fact makes thought of any important kind extraordinarily difficult."
—Robert Morsberger, *Commonsense Grammar and Style*

educationese *n.*   See EDUCANTO.

effective   See special entry GRAMMAR ADJECTIVES, p. 399.

effictio   See special entry RHETORIC TERMS, p. 403.

effiguration   See special entry RHETORIC TERMS, p. 403.

effusion *n.*   A pouring forth or overflowing; unrestrained or irrepressible expression; excessive emotionalism; gush. *Adj.* effusive; *adv.* effusively; *n.* effusiveness.

> Trace these to their cause, and how often will they be found to originate in the mischievous effusions of mercenary writers, who, secure in their closets, and for ignominious bread, concoct and circulate the venom that is to inflame the generous and the brave.
> —Washington Irving, *The Sketch Book*

eirenicon [*ī·ren'ə·kon*] *n.* *Chiefly British*   A statement to bring into harmony or synthesize conflicting doctrines; articulated compromise or reconciliation. Also IRENICON.

eisegesis *n.*   Reading one's own outlooks or ideas into an interpretation or a text. *Adj.* eisegetic, eisegetical.

either-or fallacy   See FALSE DILEMMA.

ejaculate *v.*   To utter abruptly and fervidly; cry out. *Adj.* ejaculatory, ejaculative; *n.* ejaculation.

> One inevitably thought of her in the act of love emitting florid *commedia dell' arte* ejaculations; one should not have thought of her in the act of love at all.   —Djuna Barnes, *Nightwood*

elegance *n.*   Gracefulness, harmony, and richness, as shown in a superior, fastidiously polished prose style; fluency and refinement; literary polish. *Adj.* elegant; *adv.* elegantly.

> He was an excellent essayist and knew it, but he couldn't make a living writing essays, and besides the form exposed his elegant prose to the often crude whimsies of editors.
> —Larry McMurtry, *The New York Times*

elegancy *n.*   Eric Partridge's term for a word or expression deemed by the semiliterate to be refined, delicate, or literary, including genteelisms, archaisms, literarisms, and euphemisms, e.g., "abode," "natal day," "powder room," "repast."

elegant variation   H. W. Fowler's term for strained avoidance of using the same word or expression twice in proximity, and

hence the resort to awkward or pretentious synonyms; gratuitous synonym.

The average contributor to this magazine is semi-literate; that is, he
is ornate to no purpose, full of senseless and elegant variations, and
can be relied on to use three sentences where a word would do.
— Wolcott Gibbs, in *Editors on Editing* ·

elegy *n.* A lamentational song or poem, esp. one for the dead
(and often in so-called elegiac couplets); any speech, musical
composition, or other expression of sorrow, regret, or contem-
plative yearning. *Adj.* elegiac, elegiacal; *adv.* elegiacally; *n.*
elegist, elegiast; *v.* elegize.

It is unsafe to trust the elegiac tone of this volume; he may also be
trying out his own funeral in advance, to see what a literary demise
could look like.   — V. S. Pritchett, *The Tale Bearers*

elenchus [*i·leng'kəs*] *n.* A refutation of an opponent's conclusion, esp. through a syllogistic proof of an alternative conclusion; logical disproof. *Pl.* elenchi; *adj.* elenctic, elenchtic,
elentical, elenchtical; *v.* elenchize.

Aall was hardly to be the victim of a juvenile Socratic elenchus.
— Edward Dahlberg, *The Confessions of Edward Dahlberg*

elephantine English *British* See GOBBLEDYGOOK.

elision *n.* The slurring over or omitting of a vowel or syllable in
pronunciation, as in dialectical speech; contraction; omission;
literary cutting or economy. *V.* elide.

"The journey from Lu to Magadha over the silk road took nearly one
year. . . . Much of the time, I was ill . . . I no longer remember, in
any detail, the exact route that we took. . . ." This sort of elision
is fairly frequent in the novel. . . .
— Paul Theroux, *The New York Times*

ellipsis *n.* Omission of an element within the sentence but of one
that is understood, without affecting overall meaning, as in
brief responses in conversational English; less than explicit
expression, often to avoid further involvement in conversation;
the punctuational use of three or four points of ellipsis (periods)
to represent omission or a trailing off of thought or expression.
Pl. ellipses; *adj.* elliptic, elliptical; *adv.* elliptically; *n.* elliptical-
ness.

Here was not just an excuse, but a demand, for every elliptical trick
in the bag.   — Clive James, *First Reactions*

elliptical illiteracy   William and Mary Morris's term for an awkwardly abbreviated sentence, truncated by omission of an understood word or phrase, e.g., "The dog wants out."

eloquence *n.*   Fluidly forceful, moving, or persuasive speech, or compelling verbal skills; fervid or powerful expressiveness; articulateness. *Adj.* eloquent; *adv.* eloquently.

But to return to eloquence; it is intuitive in its nature, and is "fed by an abundant spring." It flows when some dominant idea has mastery of the mind and orders the expression to the single purpose of that idea. Everything, every subordination and subtlety of style, is driven into one persuasive unity.

These three conditions are necessary to Eloquence—firstly, an adequate theme; then a sincere and impassioned mind; and lastly a power of sustainment or pertinacity.

—Herbert Read, *English Prose Style*

embolalia, embololalia *n.*   The use of virtually meaningless filler words, phrases, or stammerings (or so-called hesitation-forms) in speech, whether as unconscious utterings while arranging one's thoughts or as a vacuous, inexpressive mannerism, e.g., "you know," "well," "like," "I mean," "uh."

emendanda *n., pl.*   Errata. *Sing.* emendandum.

emendation *n.*   Scholarly change or correction of a text; an editorial or critical revision. *Adj.* emendatory; *v.* emend.

Icebreaking like that is what I do in my column, stimulating comment and emendation from peering peers (never co-equal) and backseat philologists.   —William Safire, *What's the Good Word?*

emunctae naris [*ā·mo͝ongk′tī″ när′is*] Of a wiped nose: of matured judgment; of nice discernment.

enallage [*en·al′ə·jē*] *n.*   The substituting of one grammatical form of a word for another, as by shifting its tense, mood, gender, number, or case, or (anthimeria) part of speech, e.g., using a singular verb where a plural verb would be expected or using a noun as a verb. Also FUNCTIONAL SHIFT.

en clair [*äN klâr*]   In plain, uncoded language, as in unclassified military communication.

I said it sounded bunkum, and rang off just as Mike Meakin, of wranglers, came through to say that all hell had broken out on the Czech air: half of it was coded, but the other half was *en clair*.
—John le Carré, *Tinker, Tailor, Soldier, Spy*

encomium *n.* A formal expression of high praise; fervent tribute. *Pl.* encomiums, encomia.

He had been tormented into speaking highly of royalty, flinging out encomiums with the force of small water made great by the pressure of a thumb.   —Djuna Barnes, *Nightwood*

end matter See BACK MATTER under special entry PARTS OF A BOOK, p. 363.

end paper, end leaf, end sheet See special entry PARTS OF A BOOK, p. 364.

English *v.* To render into English. *N.* Englishing, Englishment.

To be different, Alfred Jarry, in his play *Ubu Roi*, the first flatulency of the theatre of the absurd, opens with Ubu crying *Merdre*, which may be Englished as Shittle.   —Joseph Shipley, *In Praise of English*

en passant [*ä*N *pä·sän*] In passing; by the way; incidentally.

It may be mentioned *en passant* that more of these terms than is generally realized were of Germanic origin, having formed part of the ancestral Teutonic heritage of the Franks who incorporated them into their Salic laws and capitularies.   —Mario Pei, *The Story of English*

enthymeme [*en'thə·mēm''*] *n.* An argument (syllogism) or formulated conclusion in which a premise is understood but not stated, whether in reasoning, advertising, or humor , e.g., "He supports the nuclear freeze. He's warm to Communism." ("Nuclear freeze supporters are warm to Communism" is not stated); "I phoned my husband and told him a passionate woman awaited him at home. He asked where I was calling from." *Adj.* enthememmatic.

The higher modes of political lying make use of the same emthymeme, working it negatively as well as positively. By supporting Candidate A, the voter will indeed be aligning himself with Shirley MacLaine.   —Robert M. Adams, *Bad Mouth*

enunciate *v.* To state or propose in a definite or systematic way; propound or formulate; announce or proclaim; pronounce (words) distinctly; articulate. *Adj.* enunciable, enunciative; *adv.* enunciatively; *n.* enunciation, enunciator.

It always made the Major feel rather eerie to listen to them talking together in the quiet room. Their voices and enunciation were so precisely alike that they seemed to be softly echoing each other.
—Carson McCullers, *Reflections in a Golden Eye*

eo ipso [*ā″ō ip′sō*]   By it itself; by that fact alone.

What, then, about the first argument, that the rules should, in this particular instance, be waived? The argument is not *eo ipso* irresponsible.   —William F. Buckley, Jr., *The Governor Listeth*

epanaphora [*ep″ə·naf′ə·rə*] *n.*   See ANAPHORA.

epanorthosis   See special entry RHETORIC TERMS, p. 403.

epic *n.*   A long heroic poem; a voluminous or grand-scale novel having a majestic or heroic theme, or a nonfiction work recounting impressive historical events; something on a heroic scale or deserving of full or grandiloquent treatment. *Adj.* epic, epical; *adv.* epically.

The epic, I might put in here, is the form of all literary forms closest to the novel; it has the "boiler plate," the lists and catalogues, the circumstantiality, the concern with numbers and dimensions.
                    —Mary McCarthy, *On the Contrary*

epicrisis   See special entry RHETORIC TERMS, p. 403.

epideictic [*ep″i·dīk′tik*] *adj.*   For rhetorical or impressive effect; demonstrative or dramatic; deictic.

epigone [*ep′i·gōn″*] *n.*   A later aesthetic or philosophical disciple; devotee, esp. a second-rate imitator. *Pl.* epigones, epigoni; *adj.* epigonic, epigonous; n. epigonism.

In the early fifties emerged even younger Southern epigones, all born between 1914 and 1930, who were eager to do various kinds of academic-historical sweeping. . . .
                    —Richard Kostelanetz, *Literary Politics in America*

epigram *n.*   A wise, cleverly expressed saying, often with a memorably inverted or satiric twist; witty observation. *Adj.* epigrammatic, epigrammatical; *adv.* epigrammatically; *n.* epigrammatism.

The classic epigram is not a mosquito bite, which smarts awhile and goes away; it is a bee sting with the stinger left in, and it smarts forever.   —Willard Espy, *An Almanac of Words at Play*

epigraph *n.*   A signal quotation or precept (not necessarily stinging, like the epigram), such as a monument inscription or pertinent front-matter quote in a book; a saying indicating a theme. *Adj.* epigraphic, epigraphical; *adv.* epigraphically; *n.* epigraphy.

epilogue *n.* A summary speech or final scene in a play; concluding or additional section at the end of a literary work, often reporting an aftermath or jumping to a later period; concluding commentary.

Here is the epilogue; there always is one. In a world where love and sorrow float, there are many epilogues—and some of them go on and on. In a world where doom always muscles in, some of the epilogues are short. —John Irving, *The Hotel New Hampshire*

epiplexis See special entry RHETORIC TERMS, p. 403.

epistolary *adj.* Relating to or in the style of a personal letter, such as certain novels; composed in the form of correspondence between persons or characters. *N.* epistle.

Miss Strachey has tumbled all this with her own commentary and gossip into an admirable, almost epistolary family history, which is as quirky, episodic and frivolous as these things tend to be, but great fun to read. —Susan Bolotin, *The New York Times*

epitaph *n.* A memorial inscription on a gravestone or tomb; a saying, verse, or quotation serving to commemorate somebody deceased, esp. words that are personally appropriate; the final, summary truth about somebody or something, or a crucial act or statement that is an ironic harbinger or telling mistake. *Adj.* epitaphial, epitaphic.

Sir George Dyson, in his *The Progress of Music*, had written, long before, without intending it, a kind of epitaph for Orion, a prophetic appreciation of his son's involvement with the spacecraft. —Kenneth Brower, *The Starship and the Canoe*

epithet *n.* A characterizing word or phrase, whether a singular descriptive adjective or special appellation for a person or thing; personally disparaging expression or label; slur. *Adj.* epithetic, epithetical.

The British restrictions go back in part to a 1562 pronouncement of Commons that "no reviling or nipping words must be used." Today's guide prescribes rules of "good temper and moderation" for parliamentary debate and is an extension of Sir Thomas Erskine May's 1844 treatise on parliamentary usage. The following epithets are expressly forbidden: *lie, liar, villain, hypocrite, pharisee, criminal, slanderer, traitor, hooligan, blackguard, murderer, cad, dog, swine, stool pigeon, bastard, jackass, puppy* (or its extension, *cheeky young pup*), *ruffian, rat, guttersnipe, member returned by the refuse of a large*

constituency. Permitted, on the other hand, are *Parliamentary leper, purveyor of terminological inexactitude, goose,* and *halfwit.*
—Mario Pei, *The Story of the English Language*

epitome *n.* A concise presentation or brief summary; someone or something that is a consummate example or very essence of a type, class, or phenomenon; ultimate or ideal model. *V.* epitomize.

He wanted to indicate eager and devout recognition that should not at the same time imply firsthand knowledge of the work in question, in case Welch should demand an epitome of its argument.
—Kingsley Amis, *Lucky Jim*

epitrope   See special entry RHETORIC TERMS, p. 403.

eponym *n.* A person for whom something is named, or a personal name that is the source of or is identified with a word for a city, institution, movement, etc., e.g., "Pyrrhic victory"; namegiver; derived name. *Adj.* eponymous, eponymic; *n.* eponymy.

As a result of the play, Simon Pure, an aptronym, became an eponym, his name becoming proverbial for anything authentic, true, the real and genuine article, "the real McCoy," as we say more often today.
—Robert Hendrickson, *The Literary Life*

equivocate *v.* To use deliberately confusing language to mislead or deceive, or ambiguity through choice of words; make an evasive statement or double meaning. *Adj.* equivocal; *adv.* equivocally; *n.* equivocalness, equivocation, equivocator.

When I was chided by Balthazar for being equivocal I replied, without a moment's conscious thought: "Words being what they are, people being what they are, perhaps it would be better always to say the opposite of what one means?"   —Lawrence Durrell, *Clea*

equivoque *n.* An ambiguous statement or passage, often intentionally evasive or phrased to have two possible interpretations; double meaning; word play or pun.

ergoism *n.* Fussy adherence to logical protocols or forms.

eristic [*i·ris'tik*] *adj.* Involving controversy or provocative argumentation; spuriously or sophistically disputatious. *Adv.* eristically; *n.* eristic.

Later, the sophists exploited this duplicity for eristic purposes by first supporting one aspect of an ambiguity and then another by means of paradoxes.   —Noah Jacobs, *Naming-Day in Eden*

erotica *n.* Literature with an erotic, usually prurient theme or content, esp. heterosexual pornography; salacious writing.

The telephone bill was unpaid. The net of economic difficulties was closing in on me. Everyone around me irresponsible, unconscious of the shipwreck. I did thirty pages of erotica.
                                        —Anaïs Nin, *The Delta of Venus*

erotology *n.* The description of methods of lovemaking; the science of love.

errata *n.* Errors in written or published material, or notations of such mistakes along with corrections; corrigenda; a list of errors in a book, usually provided on an insert page. *Sing.* erratum.

As for the corrections and *errata*, I have made them in order that my words should be an absolute expression of my thoughts, and err neither through surplusage nor through being inadequate.
                                        —Oscar Wilde, *De Profundis*

Erziehungsroman [*er·tse′o͝ongs·ro·män″*] *n.* See BILDUNGSRO-MAN.

esemplastic [*es″em·plas′tik*] *adj.* Forming, by imagination, disparate parts into a whole; aesthetically unifying.

The prison walls of self had closed entirely around him; he was walled completely by the esymplastic [*sic*] power of his imagination—he had learned by now to project mechanically, before the world, an acceptable counterfeit of himself which would protect him from intrusion.
                                        —Thomas Wolfe, *Look Homeward, Angel*

esprit *n.* Lively intellect and cleverness; sprightly wit.

esprit de l'escalier [*e·spre də les·käl·ya*] Wishful thinking of a witty comment or retort that one should have made earlier; hindsight wit (said to derive from diplomats' reporting to their foreign offices as actual retorts the ripostes that occurred to them descending the host government's staircases). Also AFTER-WIT, LATTER-WIT, STAIRCASE WIT.

Yes, she had outflanked him, taken him unawares, and he had fired not one shot. *Esprit de l'escalier*—it was as he went upstairs that he saw how he might yet have snatched from her, if not the victory, the palm.   —Max Beerbohm, *Zuleika Dobson*

essay *n.* A short prose composition (from a few hundred to a few thousand words) treating a specific, limited subject analytically, evaluatively, or reflectively, either as a serious, dignified discourse (formal essay) or, more commonly, with a light or tentative personal flavor, a simple style, and often humor (informal essay); discrete critical commentary or exposition of a topic; brief treatise or article. *Adj.* essayistic; *n.* essayist.

What was formerly a ponderous history revives in the shape of a romance, an old legend changes into a modern play, and a sober philosophical treatise furnishes the body for a whole series of bouncing and sparkling essays.   —Washington Irving, *The Sketch Book*

état présent [*ā·tä prā·zä*N]   An exhaustive summary of up-to-date knowledge about a subject, as opposed to new information or original thought; compilation of others' thoughts and findings.

ethnicity *n.*   An ethnic euphemism or discreet generalization for a common but sensitive or questionable ethnic or racial term, e.g., "Native American" for "Indian."

ethnophaulism [*eth"nō·fôl'iz·əm*] *n.*   An ethnic slur.

etymological fallacy   The fallacy (a purist's pitfall) that the meaning of a word is necessarily determined by an earlier, historical, "original" sense, e.g., insistence that "decimate" must always denote destroying one out of ten people; linguistic reactionism.

etymology *n.*   The science of word history, specifically of the origin and development of a word from language to language or over time and of its changes in form and meaning; linguistic derivation; the origin or history of a word. *Adj.* etymological, etymologic; *adv.* etymologically; *v.* etymologize.

As Auden said, through etymology words become brief lyrics about themselves.
    —John Train, *Remarkable Words with Astonishing Origins*

etymon [*et'ə·mon"*] *n.*   The key, original element or form to the etymology of a word, such as a foreign word from which an English word derives; original meaning of a word. *Pl.* etyma, etymons.

eucharistia   See special entry RHETORIC TERMS, p. 403.

eulogy *n.*   A speech or written work extolling somebody or something, esp. a posthumous personal tribute; high praise or commendation. *Adj.* eulogistic; *adv.* eulogistically; *n.* eulogization, eulogist, eulogizer; *v.* eulogize.

Some of the eulogistic nicknames for American statesmen are familiar to every schoolboy, *e.g., the father of his country* for Washington,

Honest Abe for Lincoln, *Old Hickory* for Jackson, *the Little Giant* for Stephen A. Douglas, *the Great Commoner* for Clay and *the Commoner* for Bryan.　　—H. L. Mencken, *The American Language*

euonym [yōō′ ə·nim″] *n.*　A name that is suitable or appropriate. *Adj.* euonymous.

euphemism *n.*　Use of a milder or less direct word or phrase for one felt to be too starkly explicit, whether to avoid offending through bluntness or as a form of evasive double-talk, e.g., "passed away" for "died"; deliberately discreet wording; a tactfully or deliberately inexplicit expression. *Adj.* euphemistic; *adv.* euphemistically; *v.* euphemize.

At the same time that we have relaxed prohibitions of obscenities in the press and on the air and in the movies, we have clamped down on straightforward speech, and euphemisms teem; they do so with such a thunderous racket that it is next to impossible to tell what anybody is talking about.　　—Jean Stafford, *Saturday Review*

euphony *n.*　Harmony or agreeableness to the ear, as of a combination of sounds or syllables or a particular phrasing; trueness of sound; beauty of locution. *Adj.* euphonious, euphonous, euphonic; *adv.* euphoniously; *v.* euphonize.

My don had, I think, a natural gift for language, which it has been his business to cultivate; his taste appeared to me faultless. I was much struck by his insistence on the force of individual words. He liked the stronger word rather than the euphonious.
　　—W. Somerset Maugham, *The Summing Up*

euphuism [yōō′ fyōō·iz″əm] *n.*　Artificial, overly rhetorical prose, typically with self-consciously balanced sentences using antitheses, alliteration, and other stylistic devices; affectedly elegant writing (from two works, *Euphues, the Anatomy of Wit* and *Euphues and His England,* by John Lyly [1554?–1606]). *Adj.* euphuistic; *adv.* euphuistically; *n.* euphuist; *v.* euphuize.

The style veers between the densely sensuous and the irritatingly euphuistic, though the latter, I am afraid, predominates.
　　—D. M. Thomas, *The New York Times*

eusystolism [yōō·sis′tə·liz″əm] *n.*　The use of initials, instead of full words, in the interests of delicacy, e.g., "S.O.B." (son of a bitch).

ex animo [eks än′i·mō″]　From the soul: from the heart; sincerely.

ex cathedra [*eks″ kə·thē′drə*]   Pronounced from the seat of authority or by the right of one's office, as by a papal declaration; authoritatively judgmental, sometimes without explanation or justification; presumptuous. *Adv*. ex cathedra.

Both stamped Irving's "Hughes" samples as authentic, and both spoke forth with the certainty of the Holy Father making a pronouncement *ex cathedra*.

—James Phelan, *Scandals, Scamps and Scoundrels*

excerpt *n*.   A part of or selection from a book or other piece of writing; quoted passage. *N*. excerption; *v*. excerpt.

excerpta *n*.   Excerpts, bits of writing, or clippings.

exclusive *n*.   A news report, feature article, or interview acquired and published by only one newspaper or magazine; scoop.

ex concesso [*eks″ kon·kes′ō*]   Reasoning on the basis of an opponent's premise or admission of something. *Pl*. ex concessis.

excrescence *n*.   Abnormality; a markedly infelicitous use of language, such as a deplorable barbarism or redundancy. *Adj*. excrescent, excrescential; *adv*. excrescently; *n*. excrescency.

Inspired by the founding masters, Merleau-Ponty in philosophy and Gurvitch in sociology, a proliferating breed of literary contortionists has sprung up in France, who, by fusing a pot-pourri marxism with the worst excrescences of the Germano-American jargon, have broken the Boston supremacy and have made Paris into the most productive centre of mumbo-jumbo, often packaged under the labels of existentialism and structuralism.

—Stanislav Andreski, *Social Sciences as Sorcery*

excursus *n*.   A lengthy discussion, esp. an appendix offering further explication; incidental digression. *Pl*. excursuses, excursus; *adj*. excursive, excursory; *adv*. excursively.

In *The Magic Mountain,* there are famous passages on tuberculosis, recalling Boccaccio's description of the plague, and the famous chapter on time, a philosophical excursus like the chapter on whiteness in *Moby Dick* and the chapter on Freedom and Necessity in Tolstoy.

—Mary McCarthy, *On the Contrary*

execration *n*.   Contemptuous denunciation; express loathing; a curse; an object or target of curses. *Adj*. execrative, execratory, execrable; *adv*. execratively; *n*. execrableness, execrator; *v*. execrate.

Among terms of execration widely used by management are "unreasonable demands," "gouging practices," "demagogic leadership," "questionable political affiliations," all of which are attributed to the unions. . . . —Mario Pei, *Words in Sheep's Clothing*

exegesis *n.* Explanatory comment, esp. the critical analysis and interpretation of a text; expository scholarship. *Pl.* exegeses; *adj.* exegetic, exegetical; *adv.* exegetically; *n.* exegetics, exegete.

Finnegans Wake, despite the libraries of exegesis that have been erected, remains literally a closed book to the majority of serious readers of literature. —Anthony Burgess, *Joysprick*

exemplum *n.* A brief tale or anecdote offered to bolster an argument or suggest a moral, as in a medieval sermon; an example or illustration. *Pl.* exempla.

exergasia See special entry RHETORIC TERMS, p. 404.

exhort *v.* To call upon, urge, or caution through express advice or argument; appeal to earnestly. *Adj.* exhortative, exhortatory; *adv.* exhortatively; *n.* exhortation.

ex nihilo [*eks nē'ə·lō''*] Out of nothing; out of nowhere.

He was never a creator *ex nihilo;* he recomposed what he remembered, and he remembered most of what he had seen or had heard other people remember. —Richard Ellmann, *James Joyce*

exonym [*ek'sə·nim''*] *n.* A foreign-language synonym to a native or assimilated geographical name, e.g., German *Weichsel* or Russian *Visla* for the English word "Vistula."

exordium See special entry SCHOLARLY (BIBLIOGRAPHIC) TERMS, p. 401.

exotica *n.* Pornography that focuses on abnormal or deviant sexual activities, such as fetishism and sadomasochism.

ex parte [*eks pär'tē*] In part: from one side only or from but one point of view; partisan; on behalf of (in litigation).

expatiate *v.* To discourse at length or in detail; hold forth; enlarge upon or elaborate. *N.* expatiation.

When he showed no inclination to expatiate on this, Kolff asked no questions, but the comparison lodged in his mind, and not exactly in the way Von Braun intended. —James Michener, *Space*

expeditio See special entry RHETORIC TERMS, p. 404.

expletive *n.* A filler word, expression, or vocable that adds no
substantive meaning to a sentence but eases natural word order
or rhythm, serving as an anticipatory subject or object, or that
signals hesitation, e.g., "there" in "There is a problem"; an
exclamation, esp. a swearword. *Adj.* expletive, expletory.

Despite several thousand hours of discussion on the subject by writers and researchers and even senior editors, nobody had ever devised
a satisfactory explanation for why an educated man in his early sixties, a man sophisticated enough to preside over a national news-
magazine, should use the folksy expletive as his principal device for
communication.   —Calvin Trillin, *Floater*

explication de texte [*ek·splē·kä·syôn də tekst*] The close, systematic analysis of the parts of a written work as a method of
literary criticism, involving a detailing and synthesizing of the
work's expressive and thematic aspects and levels of meaning;
scrutinous interpretation. *Pl.* explications de texte.

We have examined the advertising of a technology in the spirit of that
great comparatist, Leo Spitzer, who wrote: "The present writer must
confess that it was by applying *explication de texte* to American advertising that he was given the first avenue (a 'philological' avenue)
leading toward the understanding of the unwritten text of the American way of life."   —Geoffrey Wagner, *On the Wisdom of Words*

exposé *n.* A factual report or public exposure of something dis-
creditable or criminal, esp. a revelatory article or book by an
investigative journalist.

The lunatic recovered miraculously two weeks after his capture, was
released, and sold to the *Banner* an exposé of the ill-treatment he had
suffered at the institution.   —Ayn Rand, *The Fountainhead*

exposition *n.* A stating or setting forth, as to clarify a purpose or
meaning; discourse that conveys information or explains,
rather than description, narrative, or argumentation; prose that
states or elucidates a case; statement of subject matter; in a
composition, the presentation of the subject or theme. *Adj.*
expositional, expository; *adv.* expositorily, expositively; *n.* ex-
positor.

Expository writing was rough, almost impossible going; he had never
been easy with the language of documents and directions on pack-
ages, and was not now with that of the natural and social sciences.
                                          —Thomas Berger, *Crazy in Berlin*

ex post facto From after the fact: by virtue of something done after a particular event; formulated later but retrospectively applicable or effective.

I'd see what the master minds thought now. Where were they anyway, and what profound conclusions were they drawing? What *ex post facto* lessons of history?　　　—Ralph Ellison, *Invisible Man*

ex post facto construction Theodore Bernstein's term for a sentence, unwittingly ludicrous, in which an adjective or result (or predication) is placed descriptively or "retroactively" early in the sentence (the subject), e.g., "Before the shot, the dead man grappled with his assailant," "The snow-covered ground was almost green before the blizzard struck."

expostulate *v.* To reason earnestly in order to demur, correct, or dissuade; remonstrate. *Adj.* expostulatory; *n.* expostulation.

As things are, we get ludicrous incongruities, like a highly placed academic I listened to at a conference in New York, who went on expostulating about some esoteric point of methodology but continued to use "suspect" for "suspicious"—declaring himself to be suspect of this and that—not just once or twice through a slip of the tongue but repeatedly throughout his lecture.
　　　　—Stanislav Andreski, *Social Sciences as Sorcery*

expound *v.* To state, put forth, or explain in a detailed way; articulate the nature or substance of.

expression *n.* The act or instance of setting forth or representing as a medium of communication or art; a rendering in words or putting into language; articulation; particular word or phrase; locution; manifestation; indication or instance. *Adj.* expressive; *adv.* expressively; *v.* express.

If poor Edward was dangerous because of the chastity of his expressions—and they say that that is always the hall-mark of a libertine—what about myself?　　　—Ford Madox Ford, *The Good Soldier*

expressionist, expressionistic *adj.* Describing nonnaturalistic writing that reflects the emotional or idiosyncratic outlook of the writer, usually through stylized description or dialogue, sensory distortion, or symbolism, and that often evokes an unreal or nightmarish atmosphere. *Adv.* expressionistically; *n.* expressionism.

Two things are essential to an expressionistic rhetoric; *sensibility* enough to be aware of one's individual reactions, and *emotion* enough

to enlarge this sensibility, to magnify and exploit it in the interest of
self-projection, self-expression, self-"creation."
　　　　　　　　　　　　—Herbert Read, *English Prose Style*

ex professo [*eks"prō·fes'ō*]　Expressly or avowedly.

expurgation *n.*　See BOWDLERIZATION.

ex silentio [*eks"si·len'tē·ō*]　From silence: basing an argument on
the lack or absence of evidence, data, firm proof, etc.

extemporaneous *adj.*　Carried out, composed, or uttered without
preparation; spoken after some preparation but without mem-
orization or use of written notes; offhand or improvised; adept
at speaking or performing without notice and preparation. *Adv.*
extemporaneously; *n.* extemporaneousness; *v.* extemporize.

Somebody else then, possibly Raynal, I don't remember, got up and
there were toasts, and then all of a sudden André Salmon who was
sitting next to my friend and solemnly discoursing of literature and
travels, leaped upon the by no means solid table and poured out an
extemporaneous eulogy and poem.
　　　　　　　—Gertrude Stein, *The Autobiography of Alice B. Toklas*

extempore [*ik·stem'pə·rē*] *adv.*　From the moment: without preparation; extemporaneously or ad lib; impromptu. *Adj.* extempore; *n.* extempore.

Francini, who also lectured at the evening university, advised him to
speak extempore, but Joyce, not wanting to risk mistakes, wrote
everything out.　　　　　　　—Richard Ellmann, *James Joyce*

extra　See INSTANT BOOK under special entry BOOK PUBLISHING
TERMS, p. 362.

extrapolate *v.*　To infer or conjecture not only on the basis of but
beyond the purview of given information, facts, evidence, or
experience; surmise or project. *Adj.* extrapolative, extrapola-
tory; *n.* extrapolation, extrapolator.

Meanwhile, H. H. Goddard, director of the research laboratory at the
Vineland Training School and Miss Kite's immediate superior, had
taken the genealogical charts that Miss Kite had painstakingly assembled, pondered them, extrapolated a bit, and published what became
a celebrated treatise on a family called Kallikak—a name that Goddard said he had invented to avoid doing harm to real people.
　　　　　　　　　　—John McPhee, *The Pine Barrens*

eyebrow See KICKER under special entry NEWSROOM HEADLINE JARGON, p. 386.

eye dialect The literary, or written, rendering of the uneducated or dialectal speech of a person or character, or a pseudo-phonetic "respelling" of words to indicate nonstandard pronunciation, e.g., "wanna" (want to), "feller" (fellow), "boid" (bird).

eyewash *n.* Discourse or explanation that is misleading, concealing something, or fulsomely flattering; bunk or hokum; florid nonsense.

If everyone is to have a radio or television set and is to be subliminally infused with the homogeneous palaver of the announcers and commentators and your friendly Chase Manhattan banker and the purveyors of mouthwash, eyewash, and hogwash, what is going to become of regional speech?   —Jean Stafford, *Saturday Review*

eye-word *n.* Mario Pei's term for a word that one seldom hears spoken (and hence is often mispronounced), e.g., "nonpareil," "recrudescence," "*pace*" (with all due respect to), "harrumph," and "cognoscenti."

F

fable *n.* A short didactic but often enchanting prose or verse tale having a moral, traditionally one with animals or objects of nature as characters; fanciful story; anecdotal popular story illustrating universal or typical human foibles; fictional concoction or falsehood. *Adj.* fabled, fabular; *n.* fabler, fabulist, fabulation; *v.* fable.

What one had instinctively suspected from the beginning is, unfortunately, true: the novel is a morality, a fable; Voltaire brought up to date and blown up big enough to fill a hoarding the size of Times Square. —T. J. Binyon, *Times Literary Supplément*

facetiae [*fə·sē′shē·ē*] *n., pl.* Humorous sayings or writings, esp. ribald witticisms, anecdotes, or tales.

façon de parler [*fä·sôɴ də pär·lä*] Way of speaking; manner of expression; natural or routine talk.

He certainly exposes the shams of casual, *façon de parler* anti-Semitism, such things as the changes of names, climbing, noting with glee that a certain Mr. Wood became a Lord Halifax (who was climbing then?). —V. S. Pritchett, *The New York Review of Books*

facsimile edition See special entry SCHOLARLY (BIBLIOGRAPHIC) TERMS, p. 401.

faction *n.* Reportage that is presented in a novelistic form, a mixture of fact and fiction; the so-called nonfiction novel.

This new style (will someone please coin a name for it, along the lines of "docudrama" and "faction"?) is a strange hybrid of heartfelt drama and apocalyptic farce.
—Annie Gottlieb, *The New York Times*

factitious *adj.* Produced through art or device rather than being natural, genuine, or spontaneous; artificial or conventionalized; contrived or forced. *Adv.* factitiously; *n.* factitiousness.

"Cold Heaven" is a chilly disappointment, a cheerless novel whose flat characters cannot sustain the weight of its factitiousness.
—Frances Taliaferro, *The New York Times*

factitive See special entry GRAMMAR ADJECTIVES, p. 399.

factoid *n.* A dubious or false assertion so repeated or publicized, as by the media, that it becomes accepted as fact. *Adj.* factoidal.

factualism *n.* Emphasis on the importance of facts, as in succinct, informative news writing or so-called hard news, as opposed to speculative or interpretive reporting. *Adj.* factualist, factualistic; *n.* factualist.

Factualism now uses such pitiful cover formulae as "Surveys show . . . " to introduce an undocumented point, which is then further simplified on the cover to sell copies. . . .
—David Cort, in *Language in America*

fadaise [*fa·dez'*] *n.* An obvious or silly remark.

fair comment The legal, journalistic right of comment, short of libel, allowing for an entertaining and even exaggerated style but requiring that a statement or story concerning a matter of public interest be fair and not malicious, and be clearly comment rather than allegations of fact. Also FAIR CRITICISM.

fair copy See special entry BOOK PUBLISHING TERMS, p. 361.

fair criticism See FAIR COMMENT.

fair use The legal principle allowing the brief excerpting without permission (for citation or criticism) of copyrighted material provided that its quoting or reprinting is done with accuracy and fairness, that appropriate credit is given, and that its use does not do a disservice to the material or infringe on expectable profits of the published original. See special entry FAIR USE, p. 368.

Mr. Zissu rejected both the fair use and free press arguments, labeling *The Nation*'s article as "vague stuff and a lot of hot air" rather than political speech protected by the First Amendment.
—David Margolick, *The New York Times*

fairy story *British* A fairy tale.

fairy tale A tale of magic or enchantment involving beings such as fairies, elves, dragons, witches, etc., esp. a fanciful story for children; highly improbable story or explanation; fabrication for the naïve. *Adj.* fairy-tale.

And there's Louise, wiping her eyes, talking about the beach at Nantucket, and her friend Tiffy—she's inseparable from this feminist, who thinks all the trouble in the world is the result of sexist fairy tales read to us when we were children.   —Ann Beattie, *Falling in Place*

fallacy *n.*   A statement or conclusion that is not valid according to logic's rules of inference or distribution; an illogical, erroneous argument, esp. one that is seemingly valid; specious reasoning; any false or misleading notion; error. *Adj.* fallacious; *adv.* fallaciously; *n.* fallaciousness.

A new fallacy in politics spreads faster in the United States than anywhere else on earth, and so does a new revelation of God, or a new shibboleth, or metaphor, or piece of slang.
                          —H. L. Mencken, *The American Language*

fallacy of accent   The fallacy of misleading or loaded emphasis (or deemphasis) in writing, as through large type or italics, positioning, taking out of context, etc.

It is said that Jeremy Bentham was so fearful of the fallacy of accent that he deliberately employed a reader with a perfectly monotonous voice.   —David Hacket Fischer, *Historians' Fallacies*

fallacy of accident   The fallacy of arguing from a general truth or rule to a special (accidental) case, or of assuming something accidental or particular to be essential, without taking into account circumstantial or background factors.

To take the general notion that the constitution reserved to the citizenry the right to have and bear arms and apply that to various specific instances is to commit the fallacy of accident.
                          —John B. Bennett, *Rational Thinking*

fallacy of composition   The fallacy of arguing from the distributive to the collective, or of making a collective, unitary assumption on the basis of what is known to be true only for the individuals or constituents that are members or parts of the unit.

She dropped to the floor and breathed deeply. "Also those fallacies. They made up as many fallacies as truths." She was calmer; we were still transfixed. "Fallacy of ambiguity, fallacy of equivocation," she droned. "Fallacy of composition, fallacy of division—I can't even remember all the fallacies."
                          —Lynn Sharon Schwartz, *Disturbances in the Field*

fallacy of division   The fallacy of applying the qualities of a unit or whole to the individuals or parts that make it up.

fallacy of the beard   The fallacy of arguing by grasping at a quantifiable aspect or stage of a situation, as by reasoning that "one more [day, purchase, attempt, etc.] won't matter''; attempt to fix or pinpoint something in an indeterminate context.

false cognate See FALSE FRIEND.

false comparative See ABSOLUTE WORD.

false dilemma A false statement or suggestion that there are only two possibilities, or that a situation is an either-or matter; dualistic oversimplification. Also BLACK-AND-WHITE FALLACY, EITHER-OR FALLACY.

false friend A foreign word (or phrase) similar to a familiar English word but of a different meaning and hence deceptive, e.g., *déception d'amour* (disappointment in love); verbal analogue that is semantically misleading (from the title of a French book, *Les faux amis,* on translation ''traps''). Also FALSE COGNATE.

false homonym See MONDEGREEN.

false illiteracy Eric Partridge's term for the pointless spelling of a standard word dialectally or phonetically, as in provincial dialogue, a ''false'' spelling since it suggests the same pronunciation that the standard, familiar word has, e.g., ''duz'' for ''does,'' ''wimmin'' for ''women.'' See also EYE DIALECT.

false lead In journalism, a misleading opening; topical red herring.

false singular An erroneous singular form or usage of a word that is properly always plural, e.g., a ''minute'' of a meeting.

false titles See COINED TITLES.

familiar *adj.* Natural and informal, as in casual, everyday discourse; colloquial; personal or intimate (contrasted with polite).

fanfaronade [*fan"far·ə·nād'*] *n.* Boastful or bullying speech or manner; braggadocio.

fanzine *n.* A specialty publication for fans or enthusiasts, such as a cheaply printed periodical for fantasy or celebrity devotees.

To appeal to the readers' interest does not mean to salute their every prejudice. No editor should make that mistake. Readers of even the

schlockiest fanzine or most rabid political journal are at least as interested in being challenged as being stroked.
—Arthur Plotnik, *The Elements of Editing*

farce *n.* Boisterous, swift-moving low comedy that develops out
of improbable and ludicrous situations, often complicated plot
ingredients and disclosures, and pronounced physical activity,
with characterization and dialogue minor elements, or a play or
other literary work in this category; absurd situational humor;
something ridiculously foolish, inadequate, or futile; a hollow
pretense or mockery; sham. *Adj.* farcical; *adv.* farcically; *n.*
farcicality, farcicalness.

Yet, he tells us that when he turned from the R and R of his first two
novels to the megalo-R and R of *The Sot-Weed Factor,* he moved
from "a merely comic mode to a variety of farce, which frees your
hands even more than comedy does."
—Gore Vidal, *Matters of Fact and Fiction*

farpotshket [*fär·poch'ket*] *adj. Yiddish* Bollixed up; crossed out
and erased and rewritten.

fascicle See special entry SCHOLARLY (BIBLIOGRAPHIC) TERMS,
p. 401.

FASGROLIA [*fas·grō'lē·ə*] *n.* The Fast Growing Language of
Initialisms and Acronyms (coined by *Time* magazine).

faux naïf [*fō nä·ēf*] *adj.* Falsely simple or naïve; feigning artlessness; stylistically disingenuous.

. . American style . . . has too great a fondness for the *faux naïf,* by
which I mean the use of a style such as might be spoken by a very
limited sort of mind. In the hands of a genius like Hemingway this
may be effective. . . When not used by a genius it is as flat as a
Rotarian speech.
—Raymond Chandler, *Raymond Chandler Speaking*

faux pas A social blunder or breach of etiquette; tactless or embarrassing remark. *Pl.* faux pas.

When anyone was witty about a contemporary event, she would look
perplexed and a little dismayed, as if someone had done something
that really should not have been done; therefore her attention had
been narrowed down to listening for *faux pas.*
—Djuna Barnes, *Nightwood*

feature *n.* A special story or article given prominence in a newspaper or magazine, often with a human-interest ingredient, as opposed to a straight news story; focused piece of background or personal journalism. *V.* feature.

The "feature" was the newspaper term for a story that fell outside the category of hard news. It included everything from "brights," chuckly little items, often from the police beat . . . There was this out-of-towner who checked into a hotel in San Francisco last night, bent upon suicide, and he threw himself out of his fifth-story window—and fell nine feet and sprained his ankle. What he didn't know was—the hotel was on a steep hill! . . . to "human interest stories," long and often hideously sentimental accounts of hitherto unknown souls beset by tragedy or unusual hobbies within the sheet's circulation area . . . In any case, feature stories gave a man a certain amount of room in which to write.   —Tom Wolfe, in *The New Journalism*

federalese *n.*   See GOBBLEDYGOOK.

Federal Prose   See GOBBLEDYGOOK.

felicity *n.*   A well-chosen and pleasing use of words; apt expression or stylistic grace. *Adj.* felicitous; *adv.* felicitously.

It is hard not to admire this kind of generosity, and it is likely that these warm, democratic convictions make possible the conversational felicities of her style—that sassy, breezy, gabby vernacular prose which makes you feel like you've been personally buttonholed by a wonderfully knowledgeable companion who won't let go of your lapel until she has persuaded you one way or another about a film.
        —Robert Brustein, *Critical Moments*

femme savant   See BLUESTOCKING.

Festschrift   See special entry SCHOLARLY (BIBLIOGRAPHIC) TERMS, p. 401.

fetish *n.*   H. W. Fowler's term for any current literary rule that is misapplied or unduly revered; a slavish, purist adherence to a "correct" practice, or aversion to a "violation," in usage or grammar.

A considerable number of readers of *The Times* are convinced beyond reason that the pronoun *none* is singular only. . . . The prudent if idle journalist, who wants to avoid having a lot of quibbling letters to answer, tries not to unadvisedly, lightly, or wantonly insult such popular fetishes—as well as the one against splitting infinitives.
        —Philip Howard, *Words Fail Me*

feuilleton [*foe·y(ə)·tôN*] *n.*   A section of a newspaper presenting light fiction, reviews, or other matter of popular entertainment; installment of a serialized novel; short, familiarly styled literary

composition or sketch, esp. a personal reminiscence. *N.* feuil-
letonism, feuilletonist.

I had always thought of the late S. J. Perelman as a fantasist. I'd
assumed that in one of his typical *New Yorker* sketches, or feuille-
tons, as he liked to call them, he would take a printed item that tickled
his sense of the absurd or satirical and simply start inventing around
it with his inimitably insane precision.
                         —Christopher Lehmann-Haupt, *The New York Times*

fiction *n.*   Imaginative but not necessarily nonfactual narrative
and dramatic prose literature, notably tales, stories, and novels; inventive or plot-structured prose writing; storytelling; a
mere imagining or illusion; untruth or concoction; a widely accepted falsehood; canard. *Adj.* fictional, fictionalistic; *adv.* fic-
tionally; *n.* fictionalization; *v.* fictionalize.

Going much further than Emily Brontë, Sterne or Proust, Gertrude
Stein has smashed up and pulverized her clock and scattered its fragments over the world like the limbs of Osiris, and she has done this
not from naughtiness but from a noble motive: she has hoped to
emancipate fiction from the tyranny of time and to express in it the
life by values only. She fails, because as soon as fiction is completely
delivered from time it cannot express anything at all, and in her later
writing we can see the slope down which she is slipping.
                         —E. M. Forster, *Aspects of the Novel*

fictionalization *n.*   The turning into or reworking as fiction, as of
a historical incident, biography, or news story, often to deal
more freely with events or to evade libel laws. *V.* fictionalize.

The own-worst-enemy, Jekyll-and-Hyde biography is a standard
amusement form, like the whodunit or the Western. Sometimes it is
frankly "fictionalized," and sometimes it just becomes fiction by the
interjection of a running commentary on the subject's gifts, thoughts,
and awful sufferings.   —A. J. Liebling, *The Press*

fictioneering *adj.*   The writing or marketing of fiction in quantity
that is of low or sensationalized quality. *N.* fictioneer.

fictive *adj.*   Of or characteristic of fiction; capable of imaginative
or literary creation; fictitious; imaginary. *Adv.* fictively.

It is this obsessional quality that makes one doubt the book's fictive-
ness; it is all seen from too close up, the anger verges on hatred, the
psychic pain is excruciating.
                         —Lore Dickstein, *The New York Times*

fiddle-faddle, fiddle *n.*   Foolishness, nonsense.

fifteeners See INCUNABULA.

figurative *adj.* Characterized by or using figures of speech, and hence having a meaning beyond the explicit or literal; rhetorical or metaphorical; imaginative or ornate in language; elaborately expressed. *Adv.* figuratively; *n.* figurativeness.

The metonymy *red tape* for the routine of bureaucracy, the synecdoche *mercury* for thermometer, the antithesis *Man proposes and God disposes*, the famous Dickens syllepsis (used preferably for humor only) *Miss Bolo went home in a flood of tears and a sedan chair . . .* , the allusion *He is the Croesus of the community*, the analogy *Chemical elements are to compounds as letters are to words*, and the editor's innuendo *Flames, James* written to an assistant named James, on the margin of a contribution which had been submitted with the request that it be printed entire or consigned to the flames—all are illustrative of the possibilities of figurative language in the cause of economy.   —John B. Opdyke, *Say What You Mean*

figure of speech Any of various expressive devices or imaginative modes of phrasing used in lieu of plain or literal speech for vivid depiction, graceful effect, emphasis or understatement, or comparison, such as antithesis, apostrophe, metaphor, and hyperbole; artful or picturesque locution; turn of phrase; trope.

His figures of speech contained all the distortions of dreams, creating a seemingly incomprehensible discourse, delivered with the authority of a political leader.   —Edward Rothstein, *The New York Times*

filler *n.* Written matter having no particular time reference that can be added to a newspaper or other publication as needed; additional and unimportant copy; brief newspaper item or squib; padding.

Our new idioms have a tendency to denote vagueness, and have the character increasingly of filler.
                      —Leon Botstein, in *The State of the Language*

fine writing Elegant, elaborately crafted prose writing; overly flowery writing that attempts to be "literary" but is strained and artificial; precious rhetoric; overwriting.

Finally, plain prose is almost requisite for handling violent or emotional scenes without eliciting dismay or nausea in the reader. We have long since tired of imitation fine writing, of bad fine writing, of the overwritten, gushing prose which we find not only in unskilled

literature but also in junk fiction—and we tire of it especially in the
wringingly emotional and violent scenes of which failed literature and
junk are made.   —Annie Dillard, *Living by Fiction*

fire-and-brimstone *adj.*   Impassioned and chastizing, esp. about
religious damnation; apocalyptic; unrestrainedly fervent about
a dire matter. *N.* fire and brimstone.

Then, having softened us up, he went into a glorious sermon, a fire-
and-brimstone sermon. Having proved that we, or perhaps only I,
were no damn good, he painted with cool certainty what was likely to
happen to us if we didn't make some basic reorganizations for which
he didn't hold out much hope.
                              —John Steinbeck, *Travels with Charley*

fish story   A far-fetched and unbelievable story; concocted explanation.

five W's   The journalist's traditional rule of thumb regarding
which six questions should be answered in the lead of a conventional news story: who, what, when, where, how, and why.
Also WHO, WHAT, WHEN, WHERE, HOW, AND WHY.

In modern journalism it is no longer felt that the five W's must be set
forth at once or completely. In the interest of clear and simple writing
it is now considered better to state the main point tersely, readably
and forcefully, letting the contributory facts follow in a natural development of the story. —Robert E. Garst and Theodore M. Bernstein,
                                          Headlines and Deadlines

flackery *n.*   Press-agentry; publicity or promotion. *N.* flack.

In education, as in the fast-food business, it's called "image enhance-
ment," and like all flackery, it's done with slogans and buzz words.
                              —Richard Mitchell, *The Graves of Academe*

flaneur   See special entry BOOKISH APPELLATIONS, p. 406.

flannel *n. British*   Smooth and insincere language; hypocritical
blarney or unctuous flattery.

flannelmouthed *adj.*   Oily-tongued; mellifluous; soft-soaping. *N.*
flannelmouth.

flap copy   See special entry BOOK PUBLISHING TERMS, p. 361.

flapdoodle *n.*   Foolish talk; nonsense.

He chewed my head off about the "threadsoul," "the causal body,"
"ablation," the Upanishads, Plotinus, Krishnamurti, "the Karmic

vestiture of the soul," "the nirvanic consciousness," all that flap-doodle which blows out of the East like a breath from the plague.
—Henry Miller, *Tropic of Cancer*

flash *n.* The language of the underworld; slick and showy cant.

flat head See DEADHEAD under special entry NEWSROOM HEAD-LINE JARGON, p. 386.

flatulent *adj.* Pretentiously windy and turgid; bombastic. *Adv.* flatulently; *n.* flatulence.

Fleet Street The journalistic profession in England; the London press; daily journalism.

flimflam *n.* Nonsense or twaddle; deception or trickery; pretentious mumbo-jumbo; humbug.

florilegium See special entry SCHOLARLY (BIBLIOGRAPHIC) TERMS, p. 401.

flubdub *n.* A dingbat. *British* Overblown or inept language; bombast.

fluency *n.* Ability to speak or write with smoothness; ready facility with language; effortless grace in expression; volubility. *Adj.* fluent; *adv.* fluently.

Ross couldn't have described perfection, because his limited vocabulary got tangled up in his fluency ("I don't want you to think I'm not incoherent," he once rattled off to somebody in "21"), but he recognized it when he saw it.   —James Thurber, *The Years with Ross*

fluff *n.* Thin and inconsequential matter or writing, as in a trite magazine article; innocuous or frivolous pap; a verbal blunder, as a bungling of a dramatic line. *V.* fluff.

I won't quote any of the better lines or situations: a Simon script is a one-time affair. Foreknowledge flattens fluff like this. The only real question is: Is the fluff fluffy? The answer here: Yes.
—Stanley Kauffmann, *The New Republic*

flummery *n.* Empty expression or literature; hollow compliments or flattering nonsense; humbug.

Jargons aim to define situations in flattering ways, and we are, as often as not, included in the flattery. But, as in the surgeon's case, the flattery seldom affects the surgery. It is, like his secretary's white uniform, part of the flummery that tries to justify exorbitant fees.
—Richard Lanham, *Style*

flyleaf   See special entry PARTS OF A BOOK, p. 364.

Foggy Bottom   The U.S. State Department and in particular its often turgid official language or jargon; diplomatic gobbledygook (from the so-named district associated with the State Department in Washington, D.C.).

> Thus, *Henry Kissinger White House Years* . . . provides the student of diplolingo with a feast of neologisms and a guide to current Foggy Bottom usage.   —William Safire, *On Language*

Fog Index   See special entry READABILITY: THE FOG INDEX, p. 407.

folderol, falderal *n.*   Foolishly elaborate talk or procedure; pseudoimportant nonsense.

> "They may be right of course," Quiz said, "though I hate to admit it.—Damned vultures. Death with dignity indeed! Folderol. Fiddle-dedee. The only reason they want to pull the plugs is to get at his fortune and power.—All those millions!"
> —Stanley Elkin, *The Living End*

folio   See special entry PARTS OF A BOOK, p. 364.

folk etymology   Popular modification of a borrowed, unfamiliar word out of a tendency to give the word a familiar form, or because of an erroneous notion of the original word's meaning, e.g., "eating humble pie" (originally "umble pie"), "Welsh rarebit" (for "Welsh rabbit"). Also POPULAR ETYMOLOGY; see also KLANG ASSOCIATION.

> Folk etymology is a notorious King Charles's head for amateurs. The ancient authorities from Homer to the Byzantine "grammarians" occasionally succumbed to the itch and offered explanations and derivations of the names of their characters; and jolly silly they often were, in the class of the etymology that was offered by sixteenth-century antiquarians for the origin of the name of the town of Windsor on the Thames: "Because the wind bloweth sore there."
> —Philip Howard, *Verbatim*

folk tale   A traditional, anonymous story that is part of a culture's oral heritage, often one involving remarkable characters and supernatural events and including fairy tales, tall stories, and husband-and-wife tales.

> Mars-Jones's pastiche of structural analysis of an urban folk tale (an adulterous husband has his hand superglued to his penis by the wife)

is both convincing *and* absurd, and as a result sharply judicious about the ease with which something can be made out of nothing.
—Thomas Sutcliffe, *Times Literary Supplement*

follow-up *n.* A subsequent newspaper story or installment on a subject, providing new or different information; sidebar. *Adj.* follow-up.

There were pictures of Morelli and a thirteen-year-old one of me in a pretty funny-looking hat, taken, I remembered, when I was working on the Wall Street explosion. Most of the follow-up stories on the murder of Julia Wolf were rather vague.
—Dashiell Hammett, *The Thin Man*

foot-in-mouth disease A tendency to make embarrassing gaffes when speaking, esp. by a public official; proneness to verbal blunders. See also DONTOPEDALOGY, MC KAY'S SYNDROME.

footnote *n.* A textual comment, explanation, or reference at the bottom of a page; a minor observation or additional remark or piece of information; afterthought. *V.* footnote. See special entry FOOTNOTE ABBREVIATIONS, p. 364.

The diary was now insatiable. It not only demanded its daily addition; it demanded footnotes, appendices, even illustrations.
—Louis Auchincloss, *Powers of Attorney*

foreignism *n.* A foreign word or expression; imitation of foreign usage.

forensic *adj.* Of or characteristic of a court, public forum, or debate; involving formal argumentation; rhetorical. *Adv.* forensically; *n.* forensic, forensics, forensicality.

He lifted his glass high. "To Lieutenant Barney Greenwald—a Cicero with two stripes—a Darrow with wings—the terror of judge advocates—the rescuer of the oppressed and the downtrodden—the forensic St. George who slew with his redoubtable tongue that most horrible of dragons—Old Yellowstain!"
—Herman Wouk, *The Caine Mutiny*

foreword See special entry PARTS OF A BOOK, p. 364.

formal fallacy An error in reasoning that constitutes a violation of any of logic's rules of inference or syllogism (contrasted with material fallacy and verbal fallacy). Also PARALOGISM.

formulaic *adj.* Having a fixed, prescribed, or conventional form or sequence, as a familiar prose technique or stereotypical response; established; rotely imitative or timeworn. *Adv.* formulaically; *n.* formula; *v.* formularize.

I was trying to get him to write his stories as well as he could and not trick them to conform to any formula, as he had explained that he did. —Ernest Hemingway, *A Moveable Feast*

formula writing Rote, hackneyed journalistic or fiction writing according to commercial formulas determining length of story or book, plot ingredients or sequence, and prose style, as in the case of much mystery, romance, and detective fiction.

Few stories in a newspaper are more addicted to formula writing than the obituary.
—Floyd K. Baskette and Jack Z. Sissors, *The Art of Editing*

fossil word A word no longer having a recognized, active meaning in itself but surviving solely as part of an expression or idiom.

Nonce is a curious fossil word, occurring only in the single phrase *for the nonce,* "for the occasion," "for the time being."
—James B. Greenough and George L. Kittredge,
Words and Their Ways in English Speech

foul copy See special entry BOOK PUBLISHING TERMS, p. 361.

found poem A passage or work of prose that unintentionally reads like poetry.

four-letter word A vulgar or taboo word, esp. one of the common four-letter scatological or sexual obscenities used in English; dirty word.

You see—oh well, let's have it out. Dolly has written a most obscene four-letter word which our Dr. Cutler tells me is low-Mexican for urinal with her lipstick on some health pamphlets which Miss Redcock, who is getting married in June, distributed among the girls, and we thought she should stay after hours—another half hour at least.
—Vladimir Nabokov, *Lolita*

fourth estate The journalistic profession (originally, a group exclusive of the nobility, the clergy, and the commons).

Fourth of July speech An ardent nationalistic speech appealing to patriotic emotions; flag-waving address.

"This country," he continued, more quietly, "has one tradition that is viable. It has been from the earliest times a haven of refuge from tyranny. The Puritans in New England, the Catholics in Maryland, the Irish peasants oppressed by the landlords, the victims of '48, Russian Jews fleeing military service, the refugees from Mussolini and Hitler.'' Harold Sidney coughed. ''What is this, Leo, a Fourth of July speech?'' he demanded with a self-conscious laugh.

—Mary McCarthy, *The Oasis*

fractured *adj.* Jumbled, barbarized, or not literate, but often colorfully expressive (and humorous) despite its oddity or malapropisms; idiomatically crude or disjointed. *V.* fracture.

''We expect then, who the little book for the care what we wrote him, and for her typographical correction, that may be worth the expectation of the studious persons, and especially of the Youth, as which we dedicate him particularly.'' With these words, José da Fonseca closed his introduction to the most famous and enduring of fractured English phrasebooks. —Michael Gorman, *Verbatim*

fragment *n.* An utterance lacking a subject, verb, or both, as distinguished from the elliptical but meaningful minor sentence; unfinished work nevertheless deemed worthy of publication. Also SENTENCE FRAGMENT.

The fragment is close to conversation. It is the laconic reply, the pointed afterthought, the quiet exclamation, the telling question.

—Sheridan Baker, *The Complete Stylist*

framis *n.* Comic double-talk blending actual words with made-up words, as performed by vaudevillians and later entertainers (often hired to pose as lecturers at conventions). Also DROWNED ENGLISH, SCRAMBLED WORDS. See special entry THE LANGUAGE OF COMIC DOUBLE-TALK, p. 389.

All I got from him was a lot of framis. Double-talk, a form of rapid, smoothly articulated, and well-modulated bafflegab with a normal syntax but with meaningless key words, has long been a popular specialty of comedians, and widely popularized in comic movies of the 1930's. The word (or rather the nonword) *framis* surfaced frequently in these comic routines; then, as Pinocchio turned into a real boy, *framis* turned into a real word by biting off its own comic nose and becoming a label for what it once was. ''The endomylogical concurrence of framis-analysis integration is parietal to the *sui generis* transcendence of the implicit'' (Fabrique du Jour, *Tergiversations*, trans. by John F. Nims). —John Ciardi, *A Browser's Dictionary*

frequentative See special entry GRAMMAR ADJECTIVES, p. 399.

Freudian slip   A speech error or inadvertent word that presumably reveals underlying concerns, motives, desires, or fears of the speaker; slip of the tongue that appears to be a telling disclosure or to have pointed reference to something else.

> A cultural artifact—whether suttee among the Balinese or baseball in America—is, in this view, analogous to a dream or Freudian slip.
> —Paul Robinson, *The New York Times*

frontispiece   See special entry PARTS OF A BOOK, p. 364.

frontlist   See special entry BOOK PUBLISHING TERMS, p. 361.

fudge *n.*   Foolish nonsense or humbug; a last-minute item, or patch of print, inserted in a newspaper edition.

fudge *v.*   To present or adjust a matter in a dishonest way, often expediently or clumsily; confuse the issue; fake or equivocate; hedge; insert for printing a last-minute news item.

> If Orwell occasionally fudged the truth about his Burmese days, the famous hanging, being down and out in either Paris or London, well, the fudging was in the service of a higher cause.
> —John Leonard, *The New York Times*

fudge factory *British*   The government bureaucracy as a purveyor of gobbledygook; any bureaucracy resorting to turgid jargon.

full stop *British*   The (punctuation mark) period.

> Bakorwa justice is based on beatings and the fear of beatings and shame, full stop. It's premodern.   —Norman Rush, *The New Yorker*

functional shift   See ENALLAGE.

furor loquendi   [*foŏr'ôr lô·kwen'dē*]   A passion to speak.

furor scribendi   [*foŏr'ôr skrē·ben'dē*]   A passion to write.

> If turnabout is fair play and a layman may diagnose his physician's complaint, the boys who wrote *The Horse and Buggy Doctor, Consultation Room*, and *Doctor, Here's Your Hat* are down with a thundering case of *furor scribendi*.
> —S. J. Perelman, "Boy Meets Girl Meets Foot"

furphy *n. Australian*   A false report or rumor (from a Furphy [manufacturer] sanitation cart in World War I Australia around which soldiers chatted).

fused metaphor   See special entry MIXED METAPHORS, p. 388.

fustian *n.*   Pompous or rustic bombast; overblown speech or writing; claptrap; padding. *Adj.* fustian.

Puns, fluffs, fumbled epigrams, wheezes of fustian, snorts of damning indignation, none of it escapes De Vries's notice, and from these faint swishes of nuance larger notions of style and paradox can be built.

—James Wolcott, *Harper's*

G

gabble *v.* To speak rapidly in an unintelligible way; chatter. *N.* gabble, gabbler.

The part of a language in use at any given time is hierarchically arranged in two great patterns, a vertical one rising to the pure and Olympian style of Santayana or Henry James, and sinking to the low and racy gabble of modern poets and used-car dealers.
—Guy Davenport, *The Geography of the Imagination*

gaffe *n.* A social blunder or verbal slip; blooper.

He is a trained pianist and musician who, fortunately, can write clear, coherent English, and thus there are none of the gaffes that so often happen when laymen try to write about music.
—Harold C. Schonberg, *The New York Times*

galimatias [*gal″ə·mā′shē·əs*] *n.* A confused or nonsensical mixture of words; confounding verbiage; gobbledygook.

Gallicism *n.* A French word or expression; an English phrase that is modeled on or is a loan-translation of a French idiom; witticism.

Meanwhile, *Le Figaro,* popular Parisian daily, conducted a weekly feature to determine which of the new Anglicisms were fit to find a place in French; was a word like *mixer,* the word for a culinary electrical device for combining foods, really necessary: Could not a Gallicism, or something approaching a Gallicism, be found?
—Charlton Laird, *Language in America*

gallionic [*gal″ē·on′ik*] *adj.* Showing carelessness or easygoing indifference.

Joyce detested the Gallionic, mildly ironical, adolescently cynical, leisurely gentlemanly, rather stodgy, certainly unexciting style adopted by so many novelists during the forty years beginning at 1900. —Eric Partridge and John W. Clarke,
British and American English Since 1900

gambler's fallacy An argument that because something has not occurred in the past, it is due or likely to occur.

gammon *n. British* Duplicitous nonsense; humbug.

garble *v.* To mix up, confuse, or scramble and misrepresent or distort the meaning of; make unintelligible; jumble. *N.* garble, garbler.

It is a mistake to think that the language of the bureaucrats is merely an ignorant, garbled jargon.
—Richard Mitchell, *Less Than Words Can Say*

garrulous *adj.* Irrepressibly talkative; given to chatter and rambling on; loquacious. *Adv.* garrulously; *n.* garrulity, garrulousness.

I had passed up lunch to retain my seat in the card game; so I was hungry. Moreover, it was evident that Graham was not going to wax garrulous on the subject of his scouting ability. I left him and sought the diner.
—Ring Lardner, "Harmony"

gasconade [*gas"kə·nād'*] *n.* Extravagantly boastful or vainglorious talk; blustering bravado. *V.* gasconade.

gatekeeper *n.* Journalist's slang for any organization or person that has the power to let newsworthy information through or to withhold it.

gaucherie *n.* Gracelessness or tactlessness, as in using language ignorantly or clumsily; socially inept act or expression; literary barbarism or gaffe.

When he repeatedly tried to attribute his political gaucheries to misquotation by the press, the reporters at first took it, then decided to gang up on him. Everything he said was taken down in shorthand and his quotations were printed verbatim in the papers.
—Theodore Bernstein, *The Careful Writer*

gazetteer *n.* A geographical dictionary; any book, as one on wines, treating a subject in terms of geographical distribution.

gee-whiz *adj.* Describing writing or reporting that attempts to arouse excitement or wonder regarding timely, local stories or unusual news items, as by emotional or melodramatic language; characterized by enthusiasm or wonder; showing or affecting ardent impressionability.

"I know, I know," Britt said impatiently, "but the headline doesn't have any dignity. The story doesn't either, for that matter—all this gee-whiz, boy's-magazine stuff. It's vulgar."
—Richard Yates, *A Good School*

gen [*jen*] *n. British* Information; dope (possibly from "general information")

"But you said you were writing it." "So I am. I give him all the gen, and he whips it into shape."   —S. J. Perelman, *The Last Laugh*

generality *n.* The quality or condition of being general, or commonly applicable or obtaining; broad, unspecific term or statement; vague abstraction; greater or main part or number; bulk.

It is possible to speak a language so commonized by generality or jargon or slang that one's own mind and life virtually disappear into it.
                        —Wendell Berry, *CoEvolution Quarterly*

generalization *n.* A broad, overall term, concept, or conclusion, such as a categorical noun, summary statement, or stereotypic idea; broad simplification; characterizing or describing in general terms. *V.* generalize.

They were both great talkers and good listeners, and each wore his best evening vehemence, ornamented with confident conclusions, large generalizations, and dark blue emphases.
                        —James Thurber, *The Years with Ross*

generic word A commercial-product word, formerly a brand name, no longer protected by trademark, e.g., "aspirin," "celluloid," "plexiglass"; nonproprietary term; word for a group or class.

genetic fallacy The fallacy that the nature or essence or validity of something is ascribable to its origin, or that something is invalid because of its origin or historical background, as in dismissing a book because its author was once in prison; assuming that something must have certain origins or that certain origins dictate certain outcomes. Also NOTHING-BUT FALLACY; see also REDUCTIVE FALLACY.

genitive See special entry GRAMMAR ADJECTIVES, p. 399.

genre *n.* A standard category or subject area of artistic composition, such as science fiction or the short story, having generally agreed-upon, traditional form and length and, in more specific categories, a characteristic method, style, and type of content; particular literary medium or class of book.

In "Have They Attacked Mary He Giggled—A Political Satire" (1917), she developed, however, still another genre, which at least partially left to language its common meanings—a sort of splintered stenographic commentary made up of scraps of conversation as they reverberate in the mind and awaken unspoken responses.

—Edmund Wilson, *Axel's Castle*

genteelism *n.* The affected use of refined or supposedly refined terms, typically by the less educated out of a notion of propriety; verbal overrefinement; finical euphemism; prudish word or expression.

Our modern timidity is not all kindness. It is indifference or fear, closely connected with the spread of genteelism—the use of "lady" for "woman" and "barn dressing" for "manure."

—Jacques Barzun, *Of Human Freedom*

Germanism *n.* A German word or expression; a compounding of several words into a single hyphenated (holophrastic) term, usually (but not always wisely) to label or to save space, e.g., "easy-to-read," "never-before-seen"; agglutination. Also TEUTONICISM.

ghost word A word created by an editor's or printer's error and hence existing by accident, e.g., in the 1944 Merriam-Webster *New International Dictionary of the English Language,* "dord," a misprint of "D or d" (for density); spurious term or erroneous reading. Also PHANTOM WORD, VOX NIHILI.

Many a ghost-word due to a seventeenth century misprint still gibbers at us from the more ambitious dictionaries of the eighteenth and nineteenth centuries. Sometimes, even—as in the case of *syllabus*—the ghost-word has acquired flesh and bones and become a respectable citizen of the world of words.

—Ernest Weekley, in *Dictionaries and That Dictionary*

ghostwriting, ghosting *n.* Writing for which another receives authorial credit or which is published under a pseudonym; speechwriting. *N.* ghostwriter (ghost); *v.* ghostwrite (ghost).

I went back to magazine writing, with a mental note that ghostwriting for big business executives—and dealing with high-powered agents like Paul Gitlin—was a line of work for which I possessed no talent whatever.   —James Phelan, *Scandals, Scamps and Scoundrels*

gibberish *n.* Unintelligible or meaningless language; nonsensical talk; impenetrably esoteric or barbarous jargon. *Adj.* gibbering; *v.* gibber.

An account executive, for example, might be entertaining an extremely important client in his own office, a little tête-à-tête of the

very first seriousness—perhaps with an emissary of one of the soap-
flake kings—when the door would burst open and in would fly the
president, scrambling across the room and under the desk, shrieking
pure gibberish, and then out he'd go again, scuttling crabwise over
the carpet, teeth and eyes blazing.

                                                    —Terry Southern, *The Magic Christian*

gibe *n.*   A mocking or teasing remark, usually in a light or trivial
vein; taunting aside; dig. *V.* gibe.

In proportion as Boston furnished the fundamentals for an ideally
cultivated life, it is not surprising that Boston should have received
her share of gibes and jests from many larger but less fortunate neighbors.   —John P. Marquand, *The Late George Apley*

gift book   See special entry BOOK PUBLISHING TERMS, p. 361.

glad handout   A public-service-styled advertisement gauged to in-
spire goodwill toward a product instead of baldly promoting its
sale.

glamour word   See BOSS WORD.

glib *adj.*   Speaking in an easy and fluent way, but often with superficiality; facilely clever or smug in expression. *Adv.* glibly;
n. glibness.

The farmer by the stove is brother to the men of the cities, and if you
listen you will find him talking as glibly and as senselessly as the best
city man of us all.   —Sherwood Anderson, *Winesburg, Ohio*

glittering generalities   See special entry PROPAGANDA DEVICES, p.
380.

gloss *n.*   An explanatory comment or translation of an expression
or passage, often provided between the lines of or in the margin
of a text; an extensive and continuous accompanying commentary; notes or glossary; a brief translation or explanation; a
misleading interpretation. *Adv.* glossingly; *n.* glosser; *v.* gloss.

If a university joke was handed on other than orally, it was in a musty
volume in Latin, or perhaps it was written as a gloss on some rare
manuscript.   —Robertson Davies, *One Half of Robertson Davies*

glossary *n.*   An accompanying special vocabulary defining or explaining difficult, unfamiliar, or foreign terms; a collection of
glosses. *Adj.* glossarial; *n.* glossarist.

The Glossary will be helpful for non-Scots (and even perhaps for Scots). Everybody knows that "houghmagandie" means fornication, but words like "biggonet" and "gamphrell" are more obscure.

—Gavin Ewart, *Times Literary Supplement*

glossolalia [*glos″ō·lā′lē·ə*] *n.* Individual nonsensical but patterned utterance, such as that of schizophrenics; ecstatic but unintelligible speechlike sounds, or the gift of tongues, as at certain revival meetings; curious babble.

Unlike the random sounds of gibberish, the utterances of glossolalia are structured and follow many of the rules of the speaker's own language, even though the speaker is not aware of it.

—Peter Farb, *Word Play*

glottogonic [*glot″ō·gon′ik*] *adj.* Of or concerning the origins of language.

glozing [*glō′zing*] *n. British* Flattery.

gnomic [*nōm′ik*] *adj.* Pointedly wise or expressive of human ways or universal truths; aphoristic, as a witty writer or his work; terse and quotable. *N.* gnome, gnomology.

"The flame of a candle gives Light, but it also Burns." Puzzled wrinkles appeared on Mr. Barbecue-Smith's forehead. "I don't exactly know what that means," he said. "It's very gnomic. One could apply it, of course, to the Higher Education—illuminating, but provoking the Lower Classes to discontent and revolution. Yes, I suppose that's what it is. But it's gnomic, it's gnomic."

—Aldous Huxley, *Crome Yellow*

gobbledygook *n.* Pretentiously stilted or periphrastic official writing, typically with many long words, passive constructions, euphemisms, and Latinate nouns; turgid bureaucratic jargon; unintelligible language. Also BAFFLEGAB, BARNACULAR, BUMBLERY, BUREAUCRAP, BUREAUCRATESE, CARCINOMENCLATURE, DOLICHOLOGIA, ELEPHANTINE ENGLISH, FEDERALESE, FEDERAL PROSE, GOVERNMENTALESE, GOVERNMENTESE, INVERTEBRATE ENGLISH, JARGANTUAN, JUNGLE ENGLISH, MUMBLESPEAK, MUSHMOUTH, POLLUTED ENGLISH, VERBOCRAP, WASHINGTON CHOCTAW, WHITEHALLESE. See also COMMERCIALESE, EDUCANTO, LEGALESE, OFFICIALESE, PENTAGONESE, PUDDER, SOCIOLOGESE.

Gobbledygook, meaning verbose, obscure, bureaucratic jargon, was coined by Maury Maverick, chairman of the Smaller War Plant Corporation, in a 1944 memo after attending a wordy committee meeting.

He later said the word just came to him but that perhaps he was thinking of the turkey gobblers back in his native Texas and of the "gobbledygobbling" sound they made while strutting so pompously, and that their gobbling ended in a "gook" sound. Gobbledygook was just a continuation of the New Deal's bureaucratic *officialese*, which delighted in such terms as *activation, clearance, coordinator, implementation, objective, to process* (this verb use dates back to 1884), and *roll-back*. By the early 1950s such talk or writing was also called *bafflegab* and by the early 60s *Pentagonese*.
—Stuart Flexner, *I Hear America Talking*

gobemouche   See special entry BOOKISH APPELLATIONS, p. 406.

Gonzo journalism   Free-wheelingly personal reportage, bizarrely idiosyncratic in viewpoint and prose style (and sometimes drug influenced), that is less than factual in its striving for colorful immediacy and liveliness (coined by Hunter Thompson).

good bad book   G. K. Chesterton's term for a modest work, in no wise a classic, that remains readable years later when more ambitious works are forgotten.

A type of book which we hardly seem to produce in these days, but which flowered with great richness in the late nineteenth and early twentieth centuries, is what Chesterton called the "good bad book": that is, the kind of book that has no literary pretensions but which remains readable when more serious productions have perished.
—George Orwell, "Good Bad Books"

good read   An enjoyably interesting and smoothly narrated book, esp. a work of popular fiction.

gospel *n.*   The teachings or apostolic accounts of Jesus Christ as a Christian message, or any of the first four New Testament books relating the life and precepts of Jesus (or a selection from them read at a service); message of a religion or a religious leader; a work, philosophy, or belief held to be unquestionably true; book or opinion revered as a reliable guide.

McMurphy was planning to sneak her out before the day crew came on but he didn't wake up. "Now what kind of crock are you giving us?" No crock. It's every word gospel. I was in on it.
—Ken Kesey, *One Flew Over the Cuckoo's Nest*

gossip *n.*   Curious talk or rumoring about the trivial, private, or titillating doings of others; repeated information or hearsay;

idle chatter; one who habitually talks about the immediate, rumored activities of others. *Adj.* gossipy; *n.* gossipry; *v.* gossip.

Carry on in the same vein, and he might just as well send her the local guide-book. What was required now was a splash of human interest. That gossipy stuff that girls like.
—P. G. Wodehouse, *The Luck of the Bodkins*

governmentalese, governmentese *n.* See GOBBLEDYGOOK.

gradatio See special entry RHETORIC TERMS, p. 404.

grammar *n.* The field of language concerning the functional classes (or parts of speech) of words, their accepted forms and inflections, and their relationships within sentences in conformity with established usage, as opposed to the study of word meaning (semantics); the formal structural rules of speech; a book on such linguistic rules; the practice of correct speech, as by an individual; any setting forth of a basic vocabulary or principles of a field of knowledge. *Adj.* grammatical; *adv.* grammatically; *n.* grammarian. See special entry GRAMMAR ADJECTIVES, p. 398

Most porn hacks cherish the hope of becoming real writers someday, so there comes a point when you start to fight back in obscure little ways. Since plot, characterization, imagery, allusion, tragedy, and comedy were all taboo, I took refuge in maniacally elegant grammar.
—Florence King, *When Sisterhood Was in Flower*

grammaticaster See special entry BOOKISH APPELLATIONS, p. 406.

grammaticism *n.* A principle, rule, or point of grammar.

grammatism *n.* Pedantry or hairsplitting about matters of grammar. *N.* grammatist.

grandiloquence *n.* Lofty, extravagantly styled language; grandiose speech. *Adj.* grandiloquent; *adv.* grandiloquently.

He also saw Joseph Hone at the London office of Maunsel & Co., and said grandiloquently, "I have crossed Europe to see you."
—Richard Ellmann, *James Joyce*

grandisonant [*gran·dis'ə·nənt*] *adj.* Stately sounding.

grangerize *v.* To fill out a printed book pictorially with illustrations, drawings, or the like taken from other sources; mutilate a book by cutting out its illustrations (from English clergyman

James Granger, whose book *Biographical History of England*
[1769] accommodated such inserted illustrations). *N.* granger-
ism.

graphospasm *n.* See WRITER'S CRAMP.

gratis dictum [*grat'is dik'təm*] An unsolicited or voluntary remark; mere assertion.

gravamen [*grə·vā'mən*] *n.* The formal basis or material point of
a grievance or charge against an accused party; specific criticism. *Pl.* gravamens, gravamina.

Grecism [*grē'siz"əm*] *n.* See HELLENISM.

Greek *n.* Incomprehensible language; indecipherably technical
or abstruse speech or writing.

And most pathetic was the melody of his long-forgotten Southern
vernacular, as he raved of swimming holes and coon hunts and water-
melon raids. It was as Greek to Ruth, but the Kid understood and felt
—felt as only one can feel who has been shut out for years from all
that civilization means.   —Jack London, "The White Silence"

griffonage [*grif"ə·näzh'*] *n.* Careless handwriting; illegible scribble.

grimgribber [*grim'gri"bər*] *n.* Technical jargon, esp. legalistic
gobbledygook.

grok *v.* To communicate warmly and sympathetically; understand through empathy (from a Martian power of perception in
Robert Heinlein's *Stranger in a Strange Land*).

Grub Street The world or situation of those struggling for a living
as hack writers (formerly a London street where impoverished
writers lived). *Adj.* grubstreet.

Grundriss [*groŏn'tris*] *n.* A careful, systematic "ground plan,"
outline, or overview of a field or subject, esp. a science. *Pl.*
Grundrisse.

guff *n.* Foolish and insistent nonsense; argumentative or trucu-
lent utterance; backtalk.

The opposite in Mailer is the hick who actually falls for all that guff
about screen queens, voodoo prize-fighters and wonder-boy Presidents.   —Clive James, *First Reactions*

gush *n.* Effusive and emotional language, esp. out of thoughtless enthusiasm; sentimental or rhapsodic drivel. *Adj.* gushy; *adv.* gushily; *v.* gush.

You should have seen the story! I couldn't possibly use it or the paper would have been a joke, but did they back me up? They did not. I finally had to run a half a stick about it, but I killed the gushy part, and so the Brombergs put their ad in again and I have to lick everybody's boots and kowtow to everybody that appears on the society page. —John O'Hara, *Appointment in Samarra*

gutter flyer A vicious, and not traceable, piece of political writing (that is always disavowed); opprobrious pamphlet.

gutter press *British* Journalism that panders to vulgar or depraved tastes.

H

hack *n.* A writer with commercial rather than literary standards, esp. one whose writing is facile, stale, or trite; unoriginal or mediocre writer of pulp fiction. *Adj.* hack.

I presume there exist readers who find titillating the display of mural words in those hopelessly banal and enormous novels which are typed out by the thumbs of tense mediocrities and called "powerful" and "stark" by the reviewing hack.　　—Vladimir Nabokov, *Lolita*

hackneyed *adj.* Predictable or commonplace from overuse; tritely stale or unoriginal; clichéd. *V.* hackney.

Here Le Bas, as usual, paused; probably from the conviction that the word "schooldays" had accumulated various associations in the minds of his listeners to which he was willing to seem to appeal. The use of hackneyed words had always been one of his preoccupations.
　　—Anthony Powell, *The Acceptance World*

hadeharia [*hā″dē·har′ē·ə*] *n.* Constant use of the word "hell."

hairsplitting *n.* Making too fine distinctions or criticisms; intellectual pettiness; cavilling. *Adj.* hairsplitting; *n.* hairsplitter; *v.* split hairs.

He became, I think, by far the most painstaking, meticulous, hairsplitting detail-criticizer the world of editing has known.
　　—James Thurber, *The Years with Ross*

half title　See special entry PARTS OF A BOOK, p. 364.

half-truth *n.* An assertion only partly true or that withholds certain facts, and hence a misrepresentation; statement of deceptive omission.

That's where the Devil keeps house, we like to say: down in the cities where merchants show their wares by uncertain light and pine sells for fruitwood, where sly politicians thread their lies through truths and half-truths till not even they themselves know which is which.
　　—John Gardner, *Freddy's Book*

hammer　See BARKER under special entry NEWSROOM HEADLINE JARGON, p. 385.

handle　See special entry BOOK PUBLISHING TERMS, p. 362.

handout *n.* A press release or official statement, issued by an organization or government, as opposed to a journalist's report or story; freely distributed circular.

A press handout is a story written by a political figure's press aide, or by himself, to be given to reporters at a press conference to save them the trouble of taking notes or asking questions. Good reporters profess to ignore "handouts" and dig for themselves; however, an informative handout can be helpful and timesaving. A *handout* is usually directly given by press agents to reporters; a *release* may either be handed out or mailed.
—William Safire, *The New Language of Politics*

hanger See DROPHEAD under special entry NEWSROOM HEADLINE JARGON, p. 386.

hanging comparative See AGENCY COMPARATIVE.

Hansard *n.* One of the official reports of British Parliamentary proceedings and debates (after Luke Hansard [1752–1828], first printer of the reports).

The *Washington Star* ran a long and heated correspondence in 1977 to try to establish whether *whoever* or *whomever* was right in the phrase: "To make that speech absolutely clear and lucid to *whomever* is listening." It read like Hansard of a parliament of owls: "Who-whom, who-whom." —Philip Howard, *Weasel Words*

hansardize *v. British* To point out or confront with one's previous, inconsistent remarks. *N.* hansardization.

hapax legomenon [*ha'paks li·gom'ə·non"*] Something said only once: a word or phrase occurring once in a document or in a literature; coinage or invented word never used again; chance verbal error that makes sense. *Pl.* hapax legomena.

We must, each of us for himself, decide what in it represents the best in usage—and what is merely a corruption that has become more or less widespread or is, indeed, a mere hapax legomenon. . . .
—John Simon, *Paradigms Lost*

haplograph [*hap'lə'·graf"*] *n.* An inadvertent omission of one of two similar letters, syllables, or words, e.g., "go in time" for "go in in time." *N.* haplography.

haplology [*ha·plol'ə·jē*] *n.* Contraction of a word by the elimination of one or two similar syllables, e.g., writing "interpretive" instead of "interpretative."

harangue *n.*   A long, vehement or impassioned speech; ranting lecture or tirade. *V.* harangue.

It would be senseless to try to list these failures, and besides that the purpose of this harangue is not to nail any one newspaper or magazine —but to point out the potentially massive effect of any story whose basic structure is endorsed and disseminated not only by *Time* and *Newsweek,* but by the hyper-prestigious *New York Times.*
—Hunter Thompson, *Hell's Angels*

hard-boiled *adj.*   Stoically direct and dispassionate, such as the laconic, realistic prose style of certain American detective-fiction writers; factual and unsentimental.

That's like the one they tell about another female writer. When this hard-boiled stuff first came in, she dropped the trick English accent and went in for scram and lam.
—Nathanael West, *Miss Lonelyhearts*

hard news   News of record, or the reporting of everyday, real-life events, as contrasted with feature writing, profiles, background material, etc.; spot news. See also AFGHANISTANISM, FACTUALISM, NEWSTHINK.

hard word   A word difficult to understand, explain, spell, or pronounce; long or technical word; *Pl.* blunt, unsoftened words; dire or discouraging news.

Donne was a mountebank who wrapped up his lack of meaning in hard words. The gulls were taken in; but the style would be out of fashion twelve months hence.   —Virginia Woolf, *Orlando*

harmless drudge   See special entry BOOKISH APPELLATIONS, p. 406.

hatchet job   A written attack on or derogation of somebody or something, or cutting down of an overblown reputation, as by a harsh review; one-sided castigating article or book; malicious detraction.

The irony of that charge is this: The reporter chosen by *Newsweek* editors to accuse *Times* editors of letting personal feelings affect editorial judgment was a young ex-employee of *The Times* who had stormed out of the newspaper in high dudgeon, with the editors' ready acquiescence; a hatchet job was inevitable.
—William Safire, *The New York Times*

haute vulgarisation [*ōt vül·gä·rē·zä·syô*N]   The popularization of complex or abstruse matters.

Thinking on the period of *haute vulgarisation* which preceded the French Revolution, one wonders whether such periods—a society making total inventory of its skills—are logical forerunners to political and social crisis.   —George Steiner, *Language and Silence*

haver *v. British*   To speak hesitantly or stall for time; dither; hem and haw; hedge.

Going down the stairs towards the Common Room, where coffee would now be available, he articulated these words behind closed lips: "You *ig*norant clod, you *stu*pid old sod, you *h*avering, *s*lavering . . ."   —Kingsley Amis, *Lucky Jim*

headlinese *n.*   The compressed, pidginized, space-saving jargon of poor newspaper and magazine headline writing, characterized by piled-up nouns, clipped words or abbreviations, commas instead of conjunctions, and sometimes a stark cluster of monosyllables.

The catatonic cacophony of headlines comprises three discordants: (1) the pitch of some copy editors that a headline has to "sound like a headline," as if it were written in some language other than English; (2) the theme of the progressives who think a headline is square unless, as Bernstein says in *Headlines and Deadlines,* it is "jazzed up"; and (3) the disgruntled wit of those who would compress an eight-note scale into four-letter words for the folks out there in Birdland. The result is a babel of babble like the croaking chorus from *The Frogs* of Aristophanes and Tin Pan Alley's, "Walla Walla Bing Bang."   —John Bremner, *Words on Words*

head-to-tail shift   See special entry WORD-GAME WORDS, p. 395.

hedge word   A word used protectively as a qualifier, esp. in journalism, in order to disclaim responsibility for certainty or truth, e.g., "reportedly," "conceivably."

Hellenism *n.*   A Greek word or expression. Also GRECISM.

hendiadys [*hen·dī'ə·dis*] *n.*   The "twinning" of one idea into two parts joined by a conjunction: specifically, using two words with an "and" (e.g., "nice and warm" instead of "nicely warm") or changing an infinitive construction (e.g., "try and catch me" instead of "try to catch me").

hermeneutic [*hûr"mə·n(y)ōo'tik*] *adj.*   Involving methodological scriptural or literary interpretation, as of a sacred text or scholarly paper, analytically interpretive. *Adv.* hermeneutically; *n.* hermeneutics, hermeneutic.

They took me aboard the aircraft and gave me a complete physical examination. I went along with it, as I had not had a checkup in two years. By now they had mastered my own language, but they still made simple mistakes like using "hermeneutics," when they meant "heuristic."   —Woody Allen, *Side Effects*

hesitation-form *n.*   An indeterminate word element or particle uttered as filler or pause in conversation or dialogue, usually as an expression of uncertainty, e.g., "uh," "mmm," "well." See also EMBOLALIA.

heteric spelling   See NOMIC SPELLING.

heterogenium   See special entry RHETORIC TERMS, p. 404.

heterography *n.*   Unorthodox, inconsistent, or incorrect spelling; the phenomenon of a single letter or letters representing different sounds in different words, and hence a source of difficulty in English spelling, e.g., "through," "bough," and "thought." *Adj.* heterographic, heterographical.

heterological *adj.*   Not self-descriptive, or not exemplifying its own meaning, e.g., the word "Italian" is not Italian, "capitalized" is not capitalized (contrasted with autological). *N.* heterolog.

heteronym *n.*   A word identical in spelling to another but different in pronunciation, meaning, and, strictly speaking, origin. e.g., "bass" (fish) and "bass" (musical instrument); a different term for the same thing, esp. a word that is a close, literal translation of a foreign word, e.g., "fish" and German *Fisch. Adj.* heteronymous; *adv.* heteronymously.

heterophemy [*het"ə·rə·fē'mē*] *n.*   The unconscious mistaken use of a word for one that it resembles in spelling or sound, e.g., "climatic" instead of "climactic"; an accidental twisting or reversing of syllables within a word, e.g., "nuculer" instead of "nuclear" (metathesis); the euphemistic use of a word with a pause or emphasis to indicate that another word is meant, e.g., "Mike and Sally are . . . *indisposed* . . . at the moment." *Adj.* heterophemistic; *v.* heterophemize.

heuristic [*hyŏŏ·ris'tik*] *adj.*   Serving the discovery of truth or furthering investigation, as in the case of a useful and stimulating (if not logical or conclusive) method, presentation, or argument, and esp. one used by a student to learn for himself. *Adv.* heuristically; *n.* heuristic.

My coarse distinctions between two kinds of fiction are useful heuristically, but they give a damaging impression of clear boundaries and a misleading impression of two armed camps.

—Annie Dillard, *Living by Fiction*

hiatus [*hī·ā'təs*[*n.* A break or missing element in written text; space in the sequence of a sentence or manuscript; pronunciation pause between successive like vowels, as in "cooperate." *Adj.* hiatus.

Hibernicism *n.* See IRISHISM.

hieroglyphics *n. pl.* Writing in the form of pictographic, symbolic script, or hieroglyphs (or hieroglyphics), rather than letters of an alphabet, such as the records of the ancient Egyptians; illegible handwriting; technical or cryptic writing difficult to decipher or understand. *Adj.* hieroglyphic.

As is the inevitable result of things unsaid, we find ourselves until today oppressed with a dangerous and reverberating silence; and the story is told, compulsively, in symbols and signs, in hieroglyphics; it is revealed in Negro speech and in that of the white majority and in their different frames of reference.

—James Baldwin, *Notes of a Native Son*

hierophant See special entry BOOKISH APPELLATIONS, p. 406.

highfalutin, hifalutin, highfaluten, highfaluting *adj.* Pompous in language; bombastic. *N.* highfalutin.

"Je ne comprends pas bien," I said in confusion, recalling all the highfalutin rigmarole which Americans believed—(little martyred Belgium protected by the allies from the inroads of the aggressor, etc.)—"why should the French put machine-guns behind you?"

—e. e. cummings, *The Enormous Room*

high-flown *adj.* Elevated or intellectually refined in language or tone; excessively lofty or inflated; bombastic.

But the style is admirable. I cannot imagine that English can be better written. Here are no flowery periods, fantastic turns of phrase or high-flown images. It is a civilized prose, natural, discreet and pointed.　　　　—W. Somerset Maugham, *The Summing Up*

highline See KICKER under special entry NEWSROOM HEADLINE JARGON, p. 386.

Hispanicism *n.* A Spanish word or expression used in English, e.g., "machismo," "olé."

historical present The present tense used to relate a past event or events, as to convey a sense of vivid immediacy or suspense.

Most of the people who eventually wrote about my style, however, tended to concentrate on certain mannerisms, the lavish use of dots, dashes, exclamation points, italics, and occasionally punctuation that never existed before : : : : : : : : : and of interjections, shouts, nonsense words, onomatopoeia, mimesis, pleonasms, the continual use of the historical present, and so on.
                                         —Tom Wolfe, in *The New Journalism*

hoarding *n. British* A billboard.

This was the lightless middle of the tunnel. Faith came down to a slogan, desperately re-worded to catch the eye, requiring to be pasted each time more strikingly on to hoardings and bases of monuments. . . .   —Elizabeth Bowen, *The Heat of the Day*

hobbyhorse *n.* A favorite topic, issue, or concern repeatedly harped on; pet personal cause or obsession.

Yet Miss Stafford, either blinded by her contumelious zeal or hanging on for dear life as her runaway hobby horse gallops into the sunset (possibly both), deplores the poverty-stricken imagery that is often the result of a combination of an impoverished imagination and a hyperactive gift of gab instead of ignoring it. . . .
                                         —Laurence Urdang, *Verbatim*

hobson-jobson *n.* The borrowing of a foreign word into English but in an adopted or altered form, e.g., the words "grouper" (from the Portuguese *garoupa*), "rosemary" (from the Latin *rōs,* dew, and *marīnus,* of the sea), and "hobson-jobson" (from Arabic *yā Ḥasan, yā Husayn!,* mourning cry for Mohammed's grandsons); Anglicized borrowing or corruption; popular altering of a borrowed word (formerly, Anglo-Indian vernacular).

hoc indictum volo [*hōk in·dik'təm wō'lō*] I wish this unsaid: I withdraw this statement.

hocus-pocus *n.* Bizarre or nonsensical words used as a formula in magic or conjuring; sleight-of-hand; trickery; mumbo jumbo.

It was when he was talking about everybody bowing and scraping and hocus-pocus and things like that, that Rufus began to realize that he was talking not just about Father Jackson but about all of them and that he hated all of them.   —James Agee, *A Death in the Family*

hogwash *n.* Ridiculously worthless writing, ideas, argument, etc.; obvious nonsense.

Music *is* a good thing; and after all that soul-butter and hogwash I never see it freshen up things so, and sound so honest and bully.
—Mark Twain, *The Adventures of Huckleberry Finn*

hoity-toity *n.* See RICOCHET WORD.

hokum *n.* A device or bit of fakery to create a desired response; impressive but hollow persuasion; overblown nonsense; bunk.

Time's West Coast legman lost no time in forwarding the terrible news to the Luce fortress, where it was immediately transformed into two columns of supercharged hokum for the National Affairs section: "Last week it [*The Wild One*] was back—and in real life!"
—Hunter Thompson, *Hell's Angels*

holograph See special entry SCHOLARLY (BIBLIOGRAPHIC) TERMS, p. 401.

holophrasis [*hə·lof'rə·sis*] *n.* The expression in one word or term of a whole idea, concept, or phrase, e.g., "More," "Thanks," "Ouch!" *Pl.* holophrases; *adj.* holophrastic; *n.* holophrase, holophrasm.

homily *n.* A religious or scriptural discourse delivered for edification; sermon; a pious, moralistic, or admonitory message, esp. one that is tedious. *Adj.* homiletic, homiletical; *adv.* homiletically; *n.* homilist; *v.* homilize.

"It takes brains *not* to make money," Colonel Cargill wrote in one of the homiletic memoranda he regularly prepared for circulation over General Peckem's signature. —Joseph Heller, *Catch-22*

hommage [*ôm·äzh*] *n.* An often subtle tribute in a work to an artist, writer, or composer, as by a special allusion or stylistic emulation.

Throughout Barthelme's work one notes various *hommages* to this writer or that (who lives at Montreux? and where will one hear the ultimate message *Trink?*); some are a bit too close.
—Gore Vidal, *Matters of Fact and Fiction*

homme moyen sensuel See special entry BOOKISH APPELLATIONS, p. 406.

homogenized we William Lambdin's term for the use in advertising of the word "we" to suggest general public involvement or appeal or "as a premise for selling products that benefit only a few."

homograph *n.*   A word identical in spelling to another but often having a different pronunciation, e.g., "row" (with oars) and "row" (a fight). *Adj.* homographic; *n.* homography.

homonym *n.*   A word having the same spelling and sound as another but a different origin and meaning, e.g., "bow" (bend over) and "bow" (of a ship); homograph or homophone; namesake. *Adj.* homonymic, homonymous; *n.* homonymy.

> In many of the punning expressions of Joyce, there is use of words not strictly homonymous.
> —Margaret Schlauch, *The Gift of Language*

homonym slip   The mistaken writing of one word for another that has the same (or almost the same) pronunciation, e.g., "too" instead of "two," "then" instead of "than." See also MONDE-GREEN, SONIC WRITING.

homophone *n.*   Words having the same pronunciation but not the same origin, spelling, or meaning, e.g., "peace" and "piece." *Adj.* homophonic, homophonous; *adv.* homophonically; *n.* homophony.

> The coat of arms of the Shakespeare family, which shows as its crest an eagle shaking a spear, is a kind of pun weakened by etymology, but when Joyce calls Shakespeare—very justly—"Shapesphere" he has gone a step further than homophony or homonymy. By changing two consonants he has interfered minimally with the shape of the name and enormously expanded its connotation.
> —Anthony Burgess, *Joysprick*

homo unius libri   See special entry BOOKISH APPELLATIONS, p. 406.

honorific *n.*   A term, epithet, or title conferring honor or respect, e.g., "sir," "honored guests." *Adj.* honorific, honorifical; *adv.* honorifically.

> But not all writers have been so simple and virtuous—what are we to make of those risen gentlemen, Shakespeare and Dickens, or those fabricators of the honorific "de," Voltaire and Balzac?
> —Lionel Trilling, *The Liberal Imagination*

hooey *n.*   Obvious falsehood or nonsense; baloney.

When riding the corner elevator, Becker always imagined the rhymes-with man dashing from wall to wall of the car on his chain, knocking his head against the padding now and then to jar out a rhyme, and chanting whatever rhymes he had produced that day: Ratatouille rhymes with lotta hooey.   —Calvin Trillin, *Floater*

hook *n.*   An initial narrative or plot device that captures the reader's interest, such as a tautly described crisis, provocative revelation, or arresting characterization; literary attention-grabber; advertising device to attract immediate attention. *V.* hook.

horribile dictu [*hô·rib'i·lē dik'tōo*]   Horrible to relate.

hospitable word   See special entry WORD-GAME WORDS, p. 395.

hot air   Empty or self-important talk; vainglorious rhetoric; verbiage.

The scholarly writer who is too lazy or too snobbish or too insecure to spell out what he means can produce sentence after sentence, paragraph on paragraph of hot air.
                    —Mary-Claire van Leunen, *A Handbook for Scholars*

hot-gospeller *British*   A rabid ideologue or puritan; violent preacher; ardent propagandist.

house ad   An advertisement appearing in a magazine or newspaper and publicizing the same, or one for another publication, product, etc. under the same ownership.

household word   A word, expression, name, or thing known far and wide; somebody or something ubiquitously familiar; byword.

After the movie version of *Trying to Grow* made Franny famous, and after the TV series of "The First Hotel New Hampshire" made Lilly Berry a household word, I suppose that Lilly wanted to "just write," as one is always hearing writers say.
                    —John Irving, *The Hotel New Hampshire*

house style   The copy or prose style adopted, traditionally or for consistency, by a publication, often one with its particulars and guidelines contained in a style book.

With a few celebrated exceptions the house style manages to be both turgid and lurid, a difficult combination to pull off.
                    —David Denby, *The New Republic*

howler *n.* A comically blatant verbal error; glaring gaffe or malapropism.

"Irezumi" is not an easy movie to respond to initially. It has its share of what are crudely called "howlers," especially in its subtitles.
—Vincent Canby, *The New York Times*

hucksterism *n.* Concerted, showmanlike selling, peddling, or hawking; petty merchandising; blatant advertising or promotion; use or abuse of words to sell, esp. of appealingly prestigious words and superlatives. *N.* huckstering, huckster; *v.* huckster.

hugger-mugger Newspaper jargon for a lead sentence that is crammed with details.

human-interest story An engaging, so-called people story in journalism, relating an unusual personal experience, esp. one that arouses sympathy or admiration.

By the time he was nineteen Bernstein was put on the reporting staff of the newspaper full-time as a summer replacement. At that time the *Star*'s editors featured a brightly written human-interest story across the top of the front page of the local news section every day.
—Leonard Downie, Jr., *The New Muckrakers*

humbug *n.* A pretense or pose intended to deceive, such as a hoax or false appeal; pretentious nonsense or sham; rubbish; fraud or poseur.

And looking back through my work, I see that it is invariably where I lacked a *political* purpose that I wrote lifeless books and was betrayed into purple passages, sentences without meaning, decorative adjectives and humbug generally. —George Orwell, "Why I Write"

Humpty-Dumpty *n. British* A person who makes words mean whatever he or she wants them to mean.

Humpty-Dumpty word A word used to mean whatever a speaker or writer wants it to mean.

But the negative sense is there, too—"belligerent," "arrogant"—which makes "feisty" confusing. The hottest word around turns out to be a Humpty-Dumpty word, a voguish befuddler, meaning what the speaker chooses it to mean. —William Safire, *On Language*

hwyl [*ho͞o'əl*] *n. Welsh* Fervid, emotional eloquence, esp. that associated with preaching and oratory. *Adj.* hwyl.

hybrid *n.* A word composed of elements from two different languages, e.g., "automobile," from Greek *autos* and Latin *mōbilis.* Also LOANBLEND.

hypallage [*hi·pal'ə·jē*] *n.* The reversal or fusing of two components of an expression for brevity or a telling effect, as by shifting an epithet to an unexpected position, e.g., "a careless cigarette," "hopeless efforts," "a curious fact," "a doubtful starter." *Adj.* hypallagic. Also TRANSFERRED EPITHET.

The Catholic Church has the beautiful hypallage (or transferred epithet) "invincible ignorance," referring to a state of paganism that is forgivable because the word of Christ was not available to it. . . .
—John Simon, *Paradigms Lost*

hype *n.* An instance of exaggerated, extravagant language used with marketing or publicity motives; inflated promotional or advertising statements or claims; sensationalizing; puffery. *V.* hype.

John Mosedale has put this history of Broadway, its journalists, pimps, gossip-mongers and publishers, its Runyonesque myths and Winchellian hype into rapid, slangy newspaper prose laden with clichés of the period. . . .
—Doris Grumbach, *The New York Times*

hyperbaton [*hī·pûr'bə·ton"*] *n.* A deliberate deviating from normal, idiomatic word order, or displacement of a particular word, e.g., "than whom none is fairer"; transposition. *Pl.* hyperbatons, hyperbata.

hyperbole *n.* Any mode of expression that is exaggerated for emphasis or rhetorical effect; extravagant figure of speech; overstatement (contrasted with meiosis). *Adj.* hyperbolic, hyperbolical; *adv.* hyperbolically; *v.* hyperbolize.

On these excursions Billy talked about his girlfriend, Marina. He described her as Botticellian, which I took to be the sort of hyperbole used by youthful romantics, but he showed me her photograph and I saw that he was only being accurate.
—Laurie Colwin, *The Lone Pilgrim*

hypercorrection *n.* A form, usage, or pronunciation in language that is strained (and usually erroneous) in an effort at correctness or avoiding a possible error, e.g., "Mary whom?", "between you and I''; self-conscious or stilted locution. *Adj.* hypercorrect.

Neoricans pick up the Black forms if they play with Black peers, as do, especially, those larger Puerto Rican boys who play basketball with the high school teams that are dominated by Black players. They also indulge in some of the same kind of hypercorrection: "Jack's Johnson's car."   —J. L. Dillard, *All-American English*

hyperdialectism *n.*   An attempt at rendering dialect or a special pronunciation that goes too far in its attempt at authenticity.

hyperurbanism *n.*   A dubious expression or pronunciation that results from an effort to emulate prestigious speech or avoid provincialism, or a questionable pronunciation by a speaker of one dialect attempting to imitate a more accepted dialect.

I am jarred only by such hyperurbanisms as "He is the one whom it is believed will be nominated."
—David B. Guralnik, quoted in Theodore Bernstein,
Do's, Don'ts, and Maybes

hypocoristic [*hĭ"pō·kə·ris'tik*] *adj.*   Relating to or characterized by a pet name or diminutive endearment as in baby talk; involving a doting epithet. *N.* hypocorism, hypocoristic. See also DIMINUTIVE.

hypocrisis   See special entry RHETORIC TERMS, p. 404.

hypophora [*hĭ·pof'ə·rə*] *n.*   A rhetorical posing of questions to oneself and answering them, or a reasoning aloud.

Julius Penrose is given to that kind of reasoning-with-oneself-aloud ("Let me hear no more complaining! The terms of payment? Not exorbitant, I think. What could be more generous?") which classical rhetoricians called *hypophora*.   —Richard Lanham, *Style*

hypostatize [*hĭ·pos'tə·tīz"*] *v.*   To treat a concept or name as being distinctly real, or symbolize or personify an abstraction; reify. *N.* hypostatization.

hypotaxis [*hĭ"pə·tak'sis*] *n.*   Sentence style that employs subordinate clauses; syntax with dependent, qualifying constructions (contrasted with parataxis). *Adj.* hypotactic; *adv.* hypotactically; *n.* hypotacticism.

All that can be said is that formulas are more typical of speech than of writing, just as hypotaxis, connectedness and a careful choice of individual words are more typical of writing than of speech.
—G. W. Turner, *Stylistics*

hypotyposis [*hī"pə·tī·pō'sis*] *n.*   Vivid pictorial description.

hysteron proteron [*his'tə·ron" prō'tə·ron"*]   The latter earlier: a figure of speech whereby the logical order or sequence of things is reversed, or the cart put before the horse, e.g., "Since you can't come over tonight, you're not invited"; the logical fallacy of presuming something at the outset that remains to be proved.

We can imagine academics at High Table roaring over that one, and explaining it to one another, and going into all the ramifications of the scholar's false logic, and quarrelling about whether it was a *hysteron proteron* or an *argumentum ad crumenam,* down through the generations.   —Robertson Davies, *One Half of Robertson Davies*

I

idée fixe [*ē·dā fĕks*]   A fixed, obsessive idea; unyielded notion, conviction, or focus; consuming preoccupation; hobbyhorse. See also KING CHARLES'S HEAD.

The Southern secessionists were certainly unbalanced in mind—fit for medical treatment, like other victims of hallucination—haunted by suspicion, by *idées fixes,* by violent morbid excitement; but this was not all.   —Henry Adams, *The Education of Henry Adams*

idée reçue [*ē·dā rə·sü*]   See RECEIVED IDEA.

idem per idem [*ī'dem" per ī'dem"*]   The same by the same: describing an allusion, illustration, or reference that adds nothing to the understanding of a matter.

idem sonans [*ī'dem" sō'nanz*]   Sounding the same: the principle in law that the misspelling of a word or name in a case, contract, etc., does not invalidate the document.

ideogram [*id'ē·ə·gram"*] *n.*   A symbol or drawing having a certain meaning, e.g., "$," as distinguished from a word or representation of a sound; graphic representation; logogram; logotype or trademark. Also IDEOGRAPH. *Adj.* ideogramic, ideogrammic, ideogrammatic.

. . . he might . . . have . . . found his period with the irreverent flappers or lapsed into the paternal delusions of the foreign diplomatic community enjoying with a smirk the Japanese discovery of besbol the humor of Adolph Menjou Lillian Gish speaking ideograms.
   —E. L. Doctorow, *Loon Lake*

idiolect [*id'ē·ə·lekt"*] *n.*   An individual's unique language, or that at a particular period of his or her life. *Adj.* idiolectal.

Thus, when Eric Sevareid, a widely respected pundit, solemnly pronounces particularly and regularly with penultimate secondary stress, he is certainly not using idiolectal pronunciations but rather ones that have been fairly widespread in Non-U speech for some time, though as yet unrecorded in dictionaries.
   —Thomas Pyles, *Selected Essays in English Usage*

idiologism [*id"ē·ol'ə·jiz" əm*] *n.*   A peculiarity or mannerism of individual speech, esp. a defective one.

idiom *n.* The particular language or usage of a group, community, or culture, or a current or prevailing dialect; tongue; a speech form or mode of expression peculiarly self-contained in its meaning, beyond its constituent words or literal elements, or one not literally translatable into another language; grammatically peculiar but common phrase familiar to the ear; special vocabulary; characteristic medium or manner of communication, or form of artistic expression. *Adj.* idiomatic, idiomatical; *adv.* idiomatically.

I stared through the Russian girl in her double-breasted gray suit, rattling off idiom after idiom in her own unknowable tongue—which Constantin said was the most difficult part because the Russians didn't have the same idioms as our idioms—and I wished with all my heart I could crawl into her and spend the rest of my life barking out one idiom after another. —Sylvia Plath, *The Bell Jar*

idiomatic *adj.* According with accepted usage and standard idiom, as opposed to awkward, unnatural, or artificial wording, and hence characteristic of the language; proper and familiar in phrasing; peculiar to a particular person or group. *N.* idiomaticness.

His style has always been hampered by an uncertainty about idiomatic English and a proclivity for German locutions, and, though his instinct for expressing himself has its own kind of sensitive precision, his language is always here a little cockeyed.
—Edmund Wilson, *Classics and Commercials*

idiosyncrasy *n.* A peculiar mode of expression characteristic of a writer; literary mannerism. *Adj.* idiosyncratic; *adv.* idiosyncratically.

An author has the right to cling to his idiosyncracies.
—William Bridgwater, in *Editors on Editing*

idioticon [*id″ē·ot′i·kon″*] *n.* A dialect dictionary.

idols of thought Francis Bacon's four types of fallacy to which humankind is subject, including: (1) idols of the tribe, or beliefs and dogmas arising from man's human nature, senses, and limited understanding; (2) idols of the cave, or individual frailties due to chance learning, partialities, and peculiarities; (3) idols of the marketplace, or the confusions and distortions wrought by language and human intercourse, or by the inconstancy of the meanings of words; and (4) idols of the theater, or human fallibility in the ever changing and false philosophical, theological, and logical systems of history, which are "so many stage plays."

The issue is subtler. It turns on the fact that the whole world of feeling (and therefore of expression) represented by sports and entertainment is accepted by many young people as the sole or main one worthy of emulation. That world, quite properly, has little to do with literacy. The Drs. DeBakey, keeping in mind the difficulties created for the English teacher by these idols of the tribe, put the case this way. . . .
—Clifton Fadiman and James Howard, *Empty Pages*

ifs, ands, or buts Protracted or involved comment, as out of hesitation, evasiveness, or self-justification; unwanted palaver.

ignoratio elenchi [*ig″nə·rä′tē·ō oi·leng′kē*] Ignorance of the refutation: the fallacy of arguing astray from the point at issue; stressing or "proving" what is irrelevant.

Or more specifically perhaps, Hugh, I was talking of nothing at all . . . Since supposing we settled anything—ah, *ignoratio elenchi,* Hugh, that's what. Or the fallacy of supposing a point proved or disproved by argument which proves or disproves something not at issue.   —Malcolm Lowry, *Under the Volcano*

ignotism [*ig′nə·tiz″əm*] *n.* A mistake due to ignorance.

Quite dead, on the other hand, is [the] old [word] "ignotism". . . . God rest his soul, we could have used him.
—Christopher Lehmann-Haupt, *The New York Times*

ignotum per ignotius [*ig·nō′təm per ig·nō′tē·əs*] The unknown (explained) by means of the more unknown: an annoyingly obscure explanation. See also OBSCURUM PER OBSCURIUS.

illeism [*il′ē·iz″əm*] *n.* Affected or excessive use of the third-person pronoun "he" (or "one"), esp. in reference to oneself. *N.* illeist. See also NOSISM, TUISM.

We're told that General Douglas MacArthur ranked high among practicing *illeists,* but even he, on the occasion of his most famous public pronouncement, was modest enough to use the first personal pronoun: "I shall return."
—William and Mary Morris, *Harper Dictionary of Contemporary Usage*

illiteracy *n.* Inability to read or write, or lack of aptitude or education in speech or language; an apparent but not heinous offense against literary idiom; word or expression not accepted even in colloquial usage; lapse.

He overcame the fact that he had absolutely no literary ability whatsoever by inventing a lingo which everyone mistook for a fresh and
unique style when it was really plain unadulterated illiteracy.
—Budd Schulberg, *What Makes Sammy Run?*

illiterate *adj.* Unable to read and write; devoid of learning or
familiarity with language and literature; ungrammatically written, filled with misspellings, etc.; unacceptable or uncouth as
expression. *Adv.* illiterately; *n.* illiterate, illiterateness.

They gave me *Out of Africa,* by Isak Dinesen. I thought it was going
to stink, but it didn't. It was a very good book. I'm quite illiterate,
but I read a lot. My favorite author is my brother D.B., and my next
favorite is Ring Lardner. —J. D. Salinger, *The Catcher in the Rye*

illocutionary *adj.* Pertaining to or describing an utterance that,
reflecting the speaker's emotions, conveys more or something
other than its literal meaning, such as a question implying dis-
satisfaction (as contrasted with locutionary and perlocutionary). *N.* illocution.

image advertising Advertising that builds product appeal around
a positive or prestigious image, as through associations with
success, vitality, or romance, rather than by describing the
product's specific qualities.

imagery *n.* Vivid descriptive words that evoke concrete mental
or pictorial images, often for emotional effect; colorful visual
representation; figurative writing or metaphor. *N.* image.

And he saw the town of Augusta first not in the drab hues of reality,
but as one who bursts a window into the faery pageant of the world,
as one who has lived in prison, and finds life and the earth in rosy
dawn, as one who has lived in all the fabulous imagery of books, and
finds in a journey only an extension and verification of it—so did he
see Augusta, with the fresh washed eyes of a child, with glory, with
enchantment. —Thomas Wolfe, *Look Homeward, Angel*

imitative *adv.* Designating a word formed to represent or evoke
a particular sound, as by mimicking a sound in nature; echoic;
onomatopoeic.

imperative See special entry GRAMMAR ADJECTIVES, p. 399.

imperfective See special entry GRAMMAR ADJECTIVES, p. 399.

imperscriptible *adj. British* Not supported or backed by written
authority; unrecorded.

impersonal one The pronoun "one" used in a general, formal manner.

implied metaphor An understood, derivative metaphor, or one developed from an explicit metaphor, e.g., "his cloven feet" (implying the devil). Also BURIED METAPHOR.

The implied metaphor is even more widely useful. It operates most often among the verbs, as in *snorted* and *tossed,* the horsy verbs suggesting "horse." Most ideas can suggest analogues of physical processes or natural history. Give your television system *tentacles* reaching into every home, and you have compared TV to an octopus, with all its lethal and wiry suggestions. You can have your school spirit fall below zero, and you have implied that your school spirit is like a temperature, registered on a thermometer in a sudden chill.
—Sheridan Baker, *The Complete Stylist*

imprecation *n.* An invoking of evil or a curse upon; an expression of ill will; malediction. *Adv.* imprecatory (chiefly British); *adv.* imprecatingly; *v.* imprecate.

And still from all the cross streets they were hurrying and rattling toward the converging point at full speed, and hurling themselves into the straggling mass, locking wheels and adding their drivers' imprecations to the clamor.   —O. Henry, "Mammon and the Archer"

impressionistic *adj.* Describing writing that, with selective detail, depicts a scene, situation, or character atmospherically for a general effect of vivid, subjective immediacy, by sensory impressions or associations rather than through objective description; evocatively and re-creatively subjective. *Adv.* impressionistically; *n.* impressionism.

Joyce and Woolf: he, shattering the English sentence into impressionistic pieces (as the pioneering Impressionists did on canvas before him) for every avant-garde novelist to come, attempting to tell nothing less than "the moral history of my country"; she, creating characters with intricate feelings. . . .
—Herbert Mitgang, *The New York Times*

imprimatur [im″pri·mä′tər] *n.* A license to publish, esp. that granted in the Roman Catholic Church by an authority or censor; official approval; prestigious endorsement.

Don't fuss about logic; that's the way it is. Idioms is idioms, and respect no imprimaturs. The English laugh at our "bums"; we laugh at their "I'll knock you up in the morning."
—William Safire, *What's the Good Word?*

imprint See special entry BOOK PUBLISHING TERMS, p. 362.

impropriety *n.* Misuse of a recognized or standard word; an erroneous usage; improper remark.

Indeed, it is rare these days to read or hear three sentences together without a gross impropriety of terms. When sense cannot be twisted, form is. One reads of self-indulge*ment,* of element*al* instruction, of a panel discuss*ant,* or a prim*al* dwelling place. . . .
—Jacques Barzun, *The House of Intellect*

inaniloquent [*in"a·nil'ə·kwənt*] *adj.* Talking foolishly; babbling. *N.* inaniloquence.

inarticulate *adj.* Uttered but not conforming to meaningful speech, and hence vocal but not verbal; incapable of speech; unable to express oneself understandably or coherently; inexpressive or not literate; unspoken. *Adv.* inarticulately; *n.* inarticulateness.

He sees that the majority of the letters are profoundly humble pleas for moral and spiritual advice, that they are inarticulate expressions of genuine suffering. —Nathanael West, *Miss Lonelyhearts*

incantation *n.* The recitation of words as ritualistic charms or magic spells; use of formulaic and often repetitive language, often without substance or content, for a beguiling effect or for political propaganda; sanctimonious slogan or shibboleth. *Adj.* incantational, incantatory; *v.* incant.

"For someone who's supposed to be so smart," Jean said softly, turning to me with a faint smile, "you don't use the old bean very much." This was a familiar phrase of Jean's, a favorite accusation against me, and always, like some final incantation at a religious rite, a signal that the dialogue was over, a reminder that Jean, as leader, was privy to secrets beyond my ken. —Frank Conroy, *Stop-Time*

inceptive, inchoative See INGRESSIVE under special entry GRAMMAR ADJECTIVES, p. 399.

incoherence *n.* Confusion in expression or meaning, or incongruence of sentence order; lack of sense; unintelligibility; inability to express oneself clearly. *Adj.* incoherent; *adv.* incoherently.

None of these books tells us anything really new about Ike, other perhaps than the fact that—his reputation for verbal incoherence notwithstanding—he was an excellent writer and a clear thinker.
—Ronald Steel, *The New York Review of Books*

incomparable *n.* See ABSOLUTE WORD.

incomparable absolute See ABSOLUTE WORD.

incunabula See special entry SCHOLARLY (BIBLIOGRAPHIC) TERMS, p. 401.

indicative See special entry GRAMMAR ADJECTIVES, p. 399.

indictment *n.* A charging with wrongdoing or criminal offense; express accusation; thoroughgoing negative critique. *Adj.* indictable; *adv.* indictably; *v.* indict.

Written in ink, in German, in a small, hopelessly sincere handwriting, were the words "Dear God, life is hell." Nothing led up to or away from it. Alone on the page, and in the sickly stillness of the room, the words appeared to have the stature of an uncontestable, even classic indictment. —J. D. Salinger, "For Esmé—With Love and Squalor"

indictum sit [*in·dik'təm sit*] Let it be unsaid.

indirect discourse Language that is not quoted exactly but related in terms of content or meaning in the grammatical framework of a longer sentence, most often in the past tense; reported utterance; paraphrase (contrasted with direct discourse).

indite *v.* To put into writing; compose; write. *N.* inditement, inditer.

in extenso At full length.

As it may be depended on to do, the *Times* covered matters *in extenso,* offering eight columns of Khrushchev quotes, full of a kind of anticlerical sanctimony and boasts about the rocket that he said had hit the plane.   —A. J. Liebling, *The Press*

infand [*in·fand'*] *adj.* Too odious to be mentioned; unutterable.

infelicity *n.* Inappropriate, unacceptable language; a misbegotten, ill-ringing expression; any awkward or clumsy wording. *Adj.* infelicitous; *adv.* infelicitously.

In such infelicities as "a man with one leg called Jones," a lacing of callousness adds its toll of spice.
                                        —Basil Cottle, *The Plight of English*

infix *n.* A sound element, letter, or syllable inserted into a word, rather than at the beginning or end, e.g., "a whole nother." *V.* infix; *n.* infixation, infixion. See also SANDWICH WORD, TMESIS.

inflection *n.* A change of form of a word to indicate gender, case, tense, person, mood, or voice; declensional or conjugational form of a word or an addition, such as a suffix, to fulfill a grammatical function; particular quality in or altering of word pitch, tone, or accent. *Adj.* inflected, inflectional, inflective; *adv.* inflectionally; *n.* inflectedness; *v.* inflect.

> The words are plain, but the sentences are subtly cadenced, and Joyce demonstrates his power to capture the inflections of speech.
> —Richard Ellmann, *James Joyce*

ingressive See special entry GRAMMAR ADJECTIVES, p. 399.

in invidiam [*in in·wid'ē·əm*] In ill-will or to excite prejudice.

initialese *n.* Language with many initialisms or acronyms, esp. that used by governmental agencies; bureaucratic shorthand; alphabet soup.

initialism *n.* An abbreviation for a person, organization, or institution made up of initial letters and not pronounced as a word, e.g., "F.B.I."

in-joke *n.* A subtle joke or allusion for initiates or a special audience.

> A scoffing Irish behaviorist, the sort in whom irony is so piled up on irony, jokes so encrusted on jokes, winks and nudges and in-jokes so convoluted, that anticlericism has become anti-anti-clerical, gone so far out that it has come back in as clericism and comes down on the side of Rome where he started. —Walker Percy, *Love in the Ruins*

inkhorn word A pedantic or recherché word, esp. a dubious borrowing or hybrid from classical Greek or Latin; erudite neologism. See also AUREATE LANGUAGE.

> Despite its well-known flaws—its prejudices . . . ; its pedantry . . . ; and its inclusion of outlandish inkhorn words (*ariolation, ataraxy, clancular, comminuible, cubiculary, deuteroscopy, digladiation, dignotion, incompossible*)—the publication of Johnson's Dictionary represented a turning point in the history of the English language.
> —Lincoln Barnett, *The Treasure of Our Tongue*

in malam partem [*in mäl'äm pär'tem*] In bad part: in a bad sense.

> Such fidelity, however, was taken *in malam partem* by the high Anglican authorities; they thought it insidious.
> —John Henry Cardinal Newman, *Apologia Pro Vita Sua*

in medias res [*in mā'dē·äs" rās'*]   In the middle of the thing, or directly into the course of a story or plot without any preliminaries.

innuendo *n.*   Indirect allusion, suggestion, or implication, esp. a derogatory intimation; subtle or oblique aspersion; insinuation. *Pl.* innuendos, innuendoes.

> Some critics are afraid of making "wrong" decisions. . . . Their writing reflects the tentativeness and often relies on weak innuendo, cleverly concealed qualifiers and evasive verb tenses, such as "presumably," "might have," "must have known," "surely," "perhaps," "indeed," "rather," "I presume" or "I gather" and of course, "I dare say."   —John English, *Criticizing the Critics*

inscription *n.*   The act of writing or printing on or marking (a surface); engraving; something set down as a formal or specific expression, such as a memorial quotation, personal dedication in a book, or epigraph; recorded group of words; entering of a name; enrollment. *Adj.* inscriptive, inscriptional; *adv.* inscriptively; *n.* inscriber; *v.* inscribe.

> My aunt, I remember, used sometimes to come into the shop in a state of aggressive sprightliness, a sort of connubial ragging expedition, and get much fun over the abbreviated Latinity of those gilt inscriptions.   —H. G. Wells, *Tono-Bungay*

instant book   See special entry BOOK PUBLISHING TERMS, p. 362.

intensive *n.*   An emphasizing word, such as an adjective or adverb, used to complement another word for forceful effect; modifier used to stress. *Adj.* intensive; *adv.* intensively.

> The American liking for intensives, especially marked during the pre–Civil War period, undoubtedly got a lift from the Irish newcomers.
>   —H. L. Mencken, *The American Language*

intensive *adj.*   See special entry GRAMMAR ADJECTIVES, p. 400.

intentional fallacy   The fallacy of judging or interpreting a literary work by what the reader takes (but often cannot know) to be the author's intention in writing it.

> Mr. Doctorow makes it quite clear that, as far as he is concerned, his theories about his books are no more qualified than anyone else's. He is, in the words of a mutual friend, a walking refutation of the intentional fallacy.   —Victor Navasky, *The New York Times*

inter alia [*in″tər ā′lyə*]   Among other things.

Communist China used to be celebrated by visiting writers in heroic vein, just as India was similarly romanticized by the West until Katherine Mayo wrote a disturbing account of its sexual practices from a woman's point of view. . . . Fox Butterfield's welcome book on China is not so specialized, although it does make the very Mayo-like point, inter alia, that the female orgasm seems elusive in that society.
—Dick Wilson, *Times Literary Supplement*

intercalation *n.*   An insertion or interposing, as of a word between other words in a sentence; interpolation; meaningless vocable or filler word, or an instance of embolalia. *Adj.* intercalary; *v.* intercalate.

An entire generation has grown up that distrusts language's ability to express a true picture of reality and that relies upon the empty intercalations of *like, you know, I mean.*
—Peter Farb, *Word Play*

interior monologue   The putting into words of an individual's or character's sequence of private thoughts and feelings, esp. in an extended passage in a novel. Also MONOLOGUE INTÉRIEUR.

Isabel comes to see this by way of an interior monologue—and as anyone knows who had [*sic*] tried it, it is terribly difficult to show a convincing change of heart in this form.
—Wilfrid Sheed, *The Good Word and Other Words*

interlinear   See special entry SCHOLARLY (BIBLIOGRAPHIC) TERMS, p. 401.

interlocutor *n.*   One who takes part in a conversation or dialogue; a partner or listener in a verbal interchange; in a minstrel act, the middle performer who engages in comic cross-talk with the so-called end men. *Adj.* interlocutory; *n.* interlocution.

"Maybe, Ace, I should tell him that I love him, I said." Amos forced out the words not looking anywhere, like a blind man who has lost the direction of where his interlocutor has placed himself.
—Malcolm Purdy, *Eustace Chisholm and the Works*

interpellation *n.*   A formal questioning or challenging regarding an action or policy; as of a government official; request for explanation. *N.* interpellant, interpellator; *v.* interpellate.

At Mr. Temple's interpellation, this smile faded from his face in a
flash, being replaced by a look of almost devotional intensity. . . .
                        —Anthony Powell, *A Question of Upbringing*

interpolation *n.* The inserting into a text of additional material,
or the adding of words, sometimes with a falsifying or corrupt-
ing effect; a writer's or scholar's interjection. *Adj.* interpola-
tive; *n.* interpolator; *v.* interpolate. See also SPATCHCOCK.

There's also a series of italicized interpolations putting us in touch
with the dream world of John Tremont's aged father, who has been
driven crazy by his wife's unrelenting carping and prudery.
                        —Benjamin DeMott, *The New York Times*

interpretive reporting Journalism in which judgments or a point
of view is generally implicit or which is emotionally colored;
reporting that not only provides information but indicates how
the reader is to feel about it (as contrasted with factualism).

Joseph Alsop and his brother Stewart, who until Korea pretty much
confined themselves to being experts and interpretive reporters, call
their syndicated column "Matter of Fact," even though it often contains a high percentage of opinion.   —A. J. Liebling, *The Press*

interrogative See special entry GRAMMAR ADJECTIVES, p. 400.

in toto In its entirety; totally.

How could an author—? But I'll depress *myself* in a minute. Anyway,
I insert the "masque" into these pages *in toto*.
                        —Gilbert Sorrentino, *Mulligan Stew*

introduction See special entry PARTS OF A BOOK, p. 364.

invective *n.* Vehemently abusive or denunciatory language; violent censure; vituperation. *Adj.* invective.

"Have you any special line?" asked the editor. "Yes," said the
bright lad, "I am rather good at invective." "Any special kind of
invective?" queried the man up top. "No," replied our hero, "just
general invective."   —P. G. Wodehouse, *Psmith Journalist*

inventory *n.* A listing or detailing of characteristics, elements,
objects, traits, etc.; descriptive itemizing or survey. *Adj.* inven-
torial; *n.* inventory.

The idea of food, after all, vibrates passionately in human lives, and
when it is elaborated to the lengths we find in Escoffier's book, it
bursts through all the strictures he attempts to lay upon it. Simply to

list and describe 114 recipes for sole unleashes the mind, and what is intended as a most precise kind of inventory becomes glittering caprice.
—Paul Schmidt, "As if a cookbook had anything to do with writing"

inversion *n.*   A reversal of normal word order, as for rhetorical effect, e.g., "Gone was all hope"; anastrophe. *Adj.* inverted; *adv.* invertedly; *v.* invert.

Inversion, of course, is not grammatically wrong; it becomes an irritant and the mark of a faulty style when it is overdone, or misplaces emphasis.
—Roy H. Copperud, *American Usage and Style: The Consensus*

invertebrate English *British*   See GOBBLEDYGOOK.

inverted commas *British*   Quotation marks.

This interpretation was backed by something more concrete I noticed about her: how everything she said, at least that evening, seemed to be in inverted commas, in some subtle way distinguished from some hypothetical sentence she might have more truthfully said.
—John Fowles, *Daniel Martin*

inverted pyramid   A conventional scheme for organizing a news story whereby major facts are given first and lesser details stated thereafter in descending order of importance (on the theory that many readers do not read beyond the first paragraph or two); rhetorically, catacosmesis. Also UPSIDE-DOWN PYRAMID.

"Hard news" stories like accidents and disaster will continue to be written in the traditional inverted pyramid pattern, even though that structure is dull, unimaginative and usually slowmoving.
—Floyd K. Baskette and Jack Z. Sissors, *The Art of Editing*

investigative journalism   Probing inquiry into uninvestigated, behind-the-scenes stories or backgrounds of stories, often an endeavor involving research, many interviews, and confidential sources.

We curiosity addicts were aptly described by Douglas Kennedy, editor of *True* magazine in its heyday, when it specialized in this genre. "An investigative reporter," he said, "is one who doesn't know when to quit." . . . True investigative reporting is brutally expensive, compared with the quick in-and-out of conventional deadline reporting.
—James Phelan, *Scandals, Scamps and Scoundrels*

invita Minerva [*in·wē'tä mi·ner'wä*] Minerva being unwilling: without any natural talent or inspiration.

invocation *n.* A calling on or entreating, as of a deity or the Muses, for guidance or support; earnest introductory prayer in a service of worship; a calling in, conjuring up, or bringing to bear, as to provide proof; adducing. *Adj.* invocative, invocatory, invocational; *v.* invoke.

> Her writing is sometimes awkward, and her psychologizing, even with the sudden invocation of slightly irrelevant quotations from Karl Abraham, is superficial.   —Richard Ellmann, *The New York Times*

ipse dixit He himself has said (it): an unsupported assertion, or a presumption bearing no evidence of its truth or validity; dogmatic statement. *N.* ipsedixitism. Also DIXIT; see also GRATIS DICTUM.

> Such a suggestion—that particular locutions be evaluated for their utility—is extremely rare in the history of discussion of language correctness, where either *ipse dixit* pronouncements or purely descriptive statements have held sway.
> —Edward Finegan, *Attitudes Toward English Usage*

ipsissima verba The very words.

> Furthermore, he has succeeded in freeing himself, after the first hundred pages or so, from the viscousness produced in *The Flowering* by his stirring into the stream of the story the *ipsissima verba* of his subjects.   —Edmund Wilson, *Classics and Commercials*

ipso facto By that very fact.

> I would not mean to imply that mystery novels written by women are *ipso facto* better than those written by men, or that women have a peculiar and gender-related talent for the genre.
> —Mary Cantwell, *The New York Times*

irenicon [*ī·ren'i·kon"*] *n.* See EIRENICON.

Irish bull A drolly paradoxical statement. See special entry IRISH BULLS, p. 392.

Irishism *n.* A word or expression peculiar to the Irish, e.g., the greeting "top o' the morning," initial use of "sure" to mean "surely." Also HIBERNICISM.

irmus See special entry RHETORIC TERMS, p. 404.

irony *n.* The use of words to suggest, through tone, understatement, or overstatement, the opposite of their literal meaning, often sardonically or cynically; mocking disingenuousness; the literary conveying of something opposite to what is ostensibly expressed or of naturalistic detachment; a sardonic expression or realization; in the theater, situational irony (dramatic irony); event casting a strange or sad light on what has occurred before. *Adj.* ironic, ironical; *adv.* ironically; *n.* ironist.

She was thinking about what she was going to do: She was going to talk about irony to students who, ironically, were too stupid to perceive irony. —Ann Beattie, *Falling in Place*

isogram See NONPATTERN WORD under special entry WORD-GAME WORDS, p. 396.

isomorph See special entry WORD-GAME WORDS, p. 395.

is splice Jacques Barzun's term for a presumptious or coy statement that glibly mismates ideas or things with use of the verb "is," as in certain advertisements or popular slogans, and often a fatuously cheap assertion, e.g., "General Motors is people."

Italianism, Italicism *n.* A word or expression from the Italian language, e.g., "ciao," "mamma mia," "salute."

italicize *v.* To call attention to or set apart by rendering in italic type; emphasize by underlining; accentuate. *Adj.* italic; *n.* italics.

Like a page where the commonest words are inexplicably thrown into italics, my mind is investing objects and sounds with a significance devoid of meaning. —Edmund White, *Forgetting Elena*

iterative See FREQUENTATIVE under special entry GRAMMAR ADJECTIVES, p. 399.

J

jabber *v.* To talk in an incessant, unintelligible way; babble. *N.* jabber.

And I heard—him—it—this voice—other voices—all of them were so little more than voices—and the memory of that time itself lingers around me, impalpable, like a dying vibration of one immense jabber, silly, atrocious, sordid, savage, or simply mean, without any kind of sense.　　　　　　　　　—Joseph Conrad, *Heart of Darkness*

jabberwocky *n.* Unintelligible speech or writing; artful or colorful nonsense; meaningless language, esp. provocatively motley and surreal blend words (coined by Lewis Carroll).

Jabberwocky is a fantastic extension of the pun, suitable for depicting the matter of dreams or hallucination, which frequently take an ambiguous or multiguous view of the material provided by waking experience.　　　　　　　　　—Anthony Burgess, *Joysprick*

Janeite *n. British* An admirer or devout reader of Jane Austen.

In the Glass Family, Salinger has created an object of almost Janeite interest for some, while others have found the increasingly elliptical and qualificatory manner of writing and the air of total knowledge-ability and of familial mutual appreciation distasteful.
　　—Arnold Goldman, *Penguin Companion to American Literature*

Janus word A word that can have either of two directly opposite meanings, e.g., "sanction," "cleave," "inflammable."

In English the subject has been noted, but not seriously studied, under the name of polarity, turncoat words, mirror words and oysterisms (referring to the hermaphrodite nature and erratic ways of the edible bivalve). . . . The Janus word is the paradox par excellence, the oxymoron compressed in one word, a one-word adynata.
　　　　　　　　　—Noah Jacobs, *Naming-Day in Eden*

jargantuan *n.* See GOBBLEDYGOOK.

jargon *n.* Unintelligible, incoherent, or nonsensical language; babble or gibberish; a hybrid of pidgin dialect, as used between two different peoples; a special terminology, formal or informal, favored by a particular profession, trade, group, or fellowship; homogenous lingo; any pretentiously obscure, indirect, sterilely abstract, or even illiterate language, esp. pseudo-official or pseudo-scholarly idiom; ponderous drivel or gobbledygook. *Adj.* jargonistic; *v.* jargonize.

Technical vocabulary pays its way honorably, while jargon elevates, inflates, obscures, magnifies, and sometimes even hallows. To cloak research in majesty one speaks of "realm of inquiry," and "conceptualizes" in order "to precipitate lines of reasoning."
　　　　　　　　—Robert K. Merton, quoted in Israel Shenker,
　　　　　　　　　　　　　　　　　Words and Their Masters

jargonaut *n.*　A person adept at speaking or writing in technical, scientific, or bureaucratic jargon.

American medical men, even more wanton jargonauts than their British counterparts, use *dichotomy* to mean fee-splitting by doctors.
　　　　　　　　　　　—Philip Howard, *Words Fail Me*

jawbone *v.*　To urge or admonish strongly, using the influence of one's office to win compliance with a certain policy; persuade with pressure or intimidation. See also BULLY PULPIT.

jawbreaker *n.*　A word difficult to pronounce. *Adj.* jawbreaking.

It is an irritable admiration, plagued by an inability to understand and not inconsistent with a readiness to mock the "jawbreakers" of scientists and the learned.　　　　　—G. W. Turner, *Stylistics*

je ne sais quoi [*zhoe nə sā kwä*]　I don't know what: an indescribable, elusive, or ineffable quality; rare and indefinable something. See also TERTIUM QUID.

S. J. Perelman, a wizard of the spontaneous effect, was asked by the *Paris Review* how many drafts he did of a story. "Thirty-seven," he said. "I once tried 33, but something was lacking, a certain—how shall I say?—*je ne sais quoi.*"
　　　　　　　　　—Anatole Broyard, *The New York Times*

jeremiad *n.*　A prolonged lament or complaint; a tale of woe or pessimism, often moralistic or denunciatory in tone; doleful tirade.

And they dominate the National Council of Teachers of English, which accounts, of course, for the fact that the Council's periodic jeremiads upon the sad state of English teaching place the blame on everything but the practice of teaching itself.
　　　　　　　　—Lincoln Barnett, *The Treasure of Our Tongue*

jeu de mots [*zhoe də mō*]　A play on words.

jeu d'esprit [*zhoe des·prē*]   A game of wit: a playful turn of phrase or literary vignette; clever squib or witticism; light and effervescent work.

The Torrents of Spring turned out to be a satirical *jeu d'esprit* with a serious critical core and a mean streak down the middle.
                                                                —Carlos Baker, *Hemingway*

jingle *n.*   Sound that is light, melodic, or tinkling because of its vowels and repetitions; an expression catchy to the ear; rhyme, echoing, or other similarity of sound that detracts from meaning, euphony, or seriousness in being a form of unwitting singsong. *Adj.* jingling; *adv.* jinglingly; *v.* jingle.

And the ponderous jingle of "deficiencies in the competencies" would nearly do for musical comedy.
                                                                —Sheridan Baker, *The Complete Stylist*

jive *n.*   Glibly deceptive language, often a slangy or colorful argot; insincere talk; cajolery; bumptious haranguing; mendacity; nonsense. *V.* jive.

What would they say? For the boys speak a jived-up transitional language full of country glamour, think transitional thoughts, though perhaps they dream the same old ancient dreams.
                                                                —Ralph Ellison, *Invisible Man*

joaning *n.*   See SIGNIFYING.

jocosity *n.*   High-toned jesting; a joking expression or observation, esp. a self-consciously learned or pompous comment; facetiously learned coinage. *Adj.* jocose; *adv.* jocosely.

This is as highly wrought as his lament for the National Letters, and I imagine that a few years later he would have shed such sophomoric jocosities as *Musca domestica* (for housefly) and *Homo neandertalensis* (for Neanderthal man).   —Alistair Cooke, in *On Mencken*

Joe Miller *British*   An often repeated joke.

John Garfield Still Dead story   A lame newspaper story that says nothing new but rather "milks" old news; perpetuated nonnews item.

Johnsonese *n.*   Language characteristic of Samuel Johnson, specifically pompous Latinate words, rhetorical balancing, and a general grandiloquence; haughty pontification.

Johnsonian *adj.* Typical of or resembling the thought, writing, or generally lofty, authoritative opinionizing of Samuel Johnson; showing good common sense and elevated diction, or derogatorily, pontifical and given to pompous, Latinate phraseology.

She had taught English at a girls' school and her sentences were Johnsonian in weight and balance.   —Elizabeth Bishop, *Vanity Fair*

Jonah word A word difficult for a stutterer to pronounce.

jottings *n.* Brief notes or personal memoranda; casual, spontaneous, or unpolished writing. *British* newspaper headlines.

And incidentally, if, as he claims, he really had to rewrite his prose 10 to 25 times in order to get it right, how come he writes so gracefully in these presumably spontaneous jottings?''
    —Christopher Lehmann-Haupt, *The New York Times*

journalese *n.* The gaudy, sensational writing style of some journalists, newspapers, tabloids, and "upbeat" magazines, characterized by breezy syntax, stock epithets and verbs, colloquialisms, clichés, "breathless" modifiers, occasional genteelisms and neologisms, glib or strident headlines and leads, and a general superficiality and carelessness of detail. Also NEWSPAPERESE.

He seems not to have left his library to talk to anyone himself. His writing lurches between academic inflation and tabloid journalese.
    —Tom Buckley, *The New York Times*

journalese attributives See special entry JOURNALISTIC ATTRIBUTION AND EVASION, p. 378.

journalism *n.* The gathering, writing, editing, and reporting of factual and current information of importance or interest to the public, including news and special or feature stories; the profession of newswriting or reporting on social and political events or phenomena; newspaper or magazine publishing or writing; reportage; the factual style characteristic of general or popular periodicals. *Adj.* journalistic; *adv.* journalistically; *n.* journalist.

As a piece of catching-the-moment, on-the-scene journalism, the profile has enough perceptive nuggets to make good reading; but its life should not have been prolonged beyond its occasion.
    —Eva Hoffmann, *The New York Times*

journal of record A reputable, reliable source of printed information; a respected and pertinent publication.

On June 26, the *Times,* as befitted a paper of record, printed the texts of the antithetical North and South communiques, in which each claimed to have been attacked.   —A. J. Liebling, *The Press*

jump head   See special entry NEWSROOM HEADLINE JARGON, p. 386.

jungle English *British*   See GOBBLEDYGOOK.

jus et norma loquendi [*yōos′et nôr′mə lô·kwen′dē*]   The law and rule of speaking: common usage.

juvenilia *n.*   A writer's youthful or early, and often immature, works; literature for young people.

Little doubt that my *juvenilia* was a hemorrhage of melancholia.
          —Edward Dahlberg, *The Confessions of Edward Dahlberg*

K

kangaroo word   See special entry WORD-GAME WORDS, p. 395.

Kauderwelsch [*kou'der·velsh''*]   Jargon; gibberish.

keeper *n.*   A news story kept in reserve until a more appropriate or newsworthy time, or for when it will have the greatest impact on public opinion.

kicker *n.*   An unexpected ending, startling comment, or the like; twist or punchline; unanticipated or hidden difficulty; a short line (in small type) over a headline to draw attention to or identify the subject or writer; characterizing or provocative tag.

For this audience Mr. Carpenter is careful to explain what *haiku* and *sestina* and *syllabic meter* mean and to provide little middle-brow kickers like "the French poet St-John Perse."
　　　　　　　　　　　　—Paul Fussell, *The New York Times*

kicker   See special entry NEWSROOM HEADLINE JARGON, p. 386.

King Charles's head   A favorite but irrelevant subject that repeatedly intrudes in or dominates the writing of one who cannot resist it; pet topic; hobbyhorse. See also IDÉE FIXE.

Upton Sinclair is his own King Charles' head. He cannot keep himself out of his writings, try though he may; or, by this time, try though he doesn't.　　　　—Dorothy Parker, *The Portable Dorothy Parker*

king's English   Standard English, or the educated dialect of England; English as it should be used or spoken; proper or accepted English.

The King's English means standard and correct usage. Don't mistake that for the President's English.
　　　　—John Chancellor and Walter R. Mears, *The News Business*

klang association   The phenomenon whereby a word's meaning to people is affected, and somewhat misconstrued, because of a familiar sound or word within that word, e.g., "greyhound" ("grey" is from the Norse word for dog), "niggardly"; word association, as in a psychology test. Also CLANG ASSOCIATION.

koan [kō'on''] *n.* A paradox or visionary riddle for meditation (and a teaching tool of Zen Buddhism), intended to make one transcend logic and reason to an intuition of enlightenment, e.g., "What is the sound of one hand clapping?"; instructive anecdote or story about the actions or words of an enlightened leader. *Pl.* koans, koan.

We were not ashamed of having had the abortion, but we were ashamed of having failed a test that we had not been aware we were taking until it was over. As with *koans,* the impossible Zen riddles we used to ask each other, there were no correct answers.
—David Black, *Like Father*

koine [koi·nā'] *n.* A dialect or idiom of one region that has become the standard language of a larger area or of different peoples; principal stock of a common tongue.

As one of the prominent groups on the frontier whose English had not undergone koine leveling, and as one that mixed notably with other minority groups, the Blacks were extremely important in the total situation.   —J. L. Dillard, *All-American English*

kudo [k(y)ōō'do] *n.* An award or expression of esteem; specific acknowledgment or praise; plaudit; compliment (back-formation from *kudos).*

kudos [k(y)ōō'dos''] *n.* Acclaim for or prestige from an act or accomplishment; esteem; praise.

"Yes. I heard reports of all he'd been doing organizing the gas works." "Oh yes," Julia said with a touch of her old dryness. "He's made a lot of kudos out of the strike."
—Evelyn Waugh, *Brideshead Revisited*

Künstlerroman [koŏnst'ler·rō·män''] *n.* A narrative or novel relating the struggles, maturing, and artistic development of an artist or writer, and hence a type of Bildungsroman. *Pl.* Künstlerromane, Künstlerromans.

L

label *n.*   An identifying designation; specific descriptive or classifying word or phrase, esp. one that oversimplifies or stereotypes; explicit characterization; epithet. *V.* label.

There is a curious preoccupation with *labeling* in Marxist polemics—a need to characterize the ideological position of an individual or a school of thought with an epithet.
>—S. I. Hayakawa, *Language in Thought and Action*

label head   See DEADHEAD.

label name   See APTRONYM.

laconic *adj.*   Terse or of few words; reserved or curtly dispassionate in expression. *Adv.* laconically; *n.* laconicism, laconism.

Hemingway used to present abrupt and laconic protagonists like Jake Barnes and Lady Brett, whose reluctance to verbalize was carefully contrasted with the explanatory loquacity of a jerk like Robert Cohn.
>—Robert M. Adams, in *The State of the Language*

lacuna *n.*   A space in a manuscript from which something is missing; an omission or oversight in the substance of something written; gap. *Pl.* lacunae, lacunas.

The Sherlockologists can't supply it, partly because most of them are nuts, but mainly because the deficiencies of Doyle's stories are what they thrive on: lacunae are what they are in business to fill, and they see Doyle's every awkwardness as a fruitful ambiguity, an irrevocable license for speculation.   —Clive James, *First Reactions*

ladies' club rhythm   Wolcott Gibbs's term for mannered suspensions or discontinuities in the styling of direct speech, or dialogue presented in sections or bits within a sentence.

I suffer myself very seriously from writers who divide quotes for some kind of ladies' club rhythm. " 'I am going,' he said, 'downtown' " is a horror, and unless a quote is pretty long I think it ought to stay on one side of the verb.
>—Wolcott Gibbs, in *Editors on Editing*

lallation [*la·lā'shən*] *n.*   Baby talk or infantile utterance; mispronunciation of the letter *l,* or using *l* for another sound or vice versa (lambdacism).

lalochezia [*la″lō·kē′zē·ə*] *n.*   Filthy talk to relieve tension. See also CATAROLYSIS.

lampoon *n.*   A boisterously polemical or scurrilous satire ridiculing someone or something; unrestrained, often highly entertaining caricature; spoof; caprice of university humor. *N.* lampoonery, lampooner, lampoonist; *v.* lampoon.

Their present differences could become so polemical that Sheldon might think it worthwhile lampooning Shernmaker in his column.
                                        —Anthony Powell, *Books Do Furnish a Room*

lamprophony [*lam·prof′ə·nē*] *n.*   Shining, ringing oratory.

language *n.*   Audible human speech or vocal articulation; the body of words mutually understood by a social group, community, or people, or an established tongue, whether oral, written, or both; any codified means of communication or expression of information, ideas, or feelings; manner or terminology in verbal expression; the particular vocabulary or idiom of a field, profession, or person.

Some of Andrew's friends say that although he is ordinarily a polite and gracious man he does not like people watching him as he works, and when people do watch him he swears lightly at first, letting the words patter around just under his breath, and then, after a time, he gets the words up there on his breath at a high mutter, and, with a little more time, a little more watching, the language rises and eventually breaks into a thoroughgoing crescendo that drives all the women back up the road, stilting along like scared blue herons.
                                        —John McPhee, *The Crofter and the Laird*

languaging up   Stephen Potter's term for confounding and one-upping others in conversation by using actual or sham foreign words.

To "language up" an opponent is, according to Symes' *Dictionary of Lifemanship and Gameswords,* "to confuse, irritate and depress by the use of foreign words, fictitious or otherwise, either singly or in groups."

The standard and still the best method is the gradual. If the subject is the relative methods of various orchestral conductors, for instance, say something early on about the *"tentade"* of Boult. Three minutes later contrast the *"fuldenbiener"* of Kubelik, and the firm *"austag, austag"* of his beat "which Brahms would have delighted in."

A general uneasiness should now be developing and the Lifeman may well feel he has done enough. But for Advanced Languaging I recommend the Macintosh Finisher, invented by H. Macintosh, the tea planter. During one of the lengthening pauses, he will quote one of seventeen genuine *Ballades* in Medieval French which he has learnt by heart. "Of course, you know this," he begins . . .

"Ah, vieille septance du mélange" and so on, with reverberating accents on the silent "e." After two of these, half his audience will be completely silent for fifteen minutes and the rest may actually have gone. —Stephen Potter, *Lifemanship*

langue *n.* The structurally homogeneous quality inherent in a language, above all its complete grammatical system used by an entire group or community (contrasted with parole).

A famous linguist (Bally) defined style as the force *parole* exerts on *langue.* —Richard Lanham, *Style*

lapse *n.* A minor error, such as an inadvertent or careless mistake in grammar or diction; slip of the tongue; solecism.

lapsus calami [*läp′səs käl′ə·mē*] A slip of the pen. Also LAPSUS PENNAE.

lapsus comicus [*läp′səs kō′mi·kəs*] Willard Espy's term for an amusingly truistic or tautological statement, "a simple verbal confusion" rather than a malapropism or mixed metaphor, e.g., "He looks so much older than he did when he was younger," and " 'I haven't been to South Bend,' she remarked, 'since the last time I was there.' "

lapsus linguae [*läp′səs ling′gwī″*] A slip of the tongue; lapsus loquendi. Also LUBRICUM LINGUAE.

Poetry . . . that depends so much on settings, on objects, touches, at times, animism . . . , delights as much in spoonerisms as in Freudian *lapsus linguae* or James's "torment of taste."
—Robert Mazzocco, *New York Review of Books*

lapsus pennae [*läp′səs pen′ī″*] See LAPSUS CALAMI.

Latinate *adj.* Describing a word having its origin in or being modeled after a Latin word; Latin-like in diction, such as a learned, classical prose style.

And for all of Johnson's fame as a pedantic old grouch rumbling out latinate words, it is he and not a modern dictionary who can be counted on to blurt out a simple, blunt definition.
—Guy Davenport, *The Geography of the Imagination*

Latinism *n.* A Latin expression used in English; a Latinate word or expression in English, esp. an abstract or technical term; an expression imitative of Latin.

He mixes the scientistic latinisms of the old sociology ("participation framework," "referent-response") with the weird ungrammatical coinages of the new ("say-foring," "commentary-like," "self-talk").
—Geoffrey Nunberg, *The New York Times*

latter-wit *n.* See ESPRIT DE L'ESCALIER.

laundry list Any long itemization of facts, reasons, places, etc.; descriptive inventory.

In his first speech as President on this subject, he is free to point the way, leaving the laundry list of achievements and assessments to the "state of the world" address eight months hence.
—William Safire, *The New York Times*

lead *n.* The opening sentence or paragraph of a news story, often capsulizing the essential facts; introductory summary; the most important news story of the day; part of a news story (second lead, third lead, etc.).

Don't you see? Look. Make it something like this: "James Parker Killed In England." Then your lead ought to be: "James H. Parker, class of '39, was killed after steering his crippled fighter plane away from the English village of Whaddyacallit last month," period.
—Richard Yates, *A Good School*

leader *n. British* A newspaper editorial, esp. the principal one. Also LEADING ARTICLE.

You were not impressed by the information that such and such a paper was being edited and brought out at Lisbon or Innsbruck if you chanced to see the principal leader-writer or the art editor lunching as usual at their accustomed restaurants.
—Saki, "The Yarkand Manner"

leaderette *n. British* A short editorial paragraph following the main one.

leading article See LEADER.

leading question A question so framed as to lead to or suggest the desired answer; phrasing, in interrogation, that is a form of prompting, e.g., "Why does a paste deodorant make such perfect sense?"

Leading questions elicited that he was one of that pitiable class of men for whom the gods have provided everything but a career.
—Frederick William Rolfe (Frederick Baron Corvo), *Hadrian the Seventh*

lection See special entry SCHOLARLY (BIBLIOGRAPHIC) TERMS, p. 401.

legalese *n.* The elaborate, serpentine jargon of law, characterized by special nomenclature, long procedural sentences with qualifying clauses, self-referring phrases, archaic locutions, frequent repetition and redundancy, and a generally flat proclamatory or cautionary tone.

The New York State Attorney General was puzzled by this sentence: "The liability of the bank is expressly limited to the exercise of ordinary diligence and care to prevent the opening of the within-mentioned safe deposit box during the within-mentioned term, or any extension or renewal thereof, by any person other than the lessee or his duly authorized representative and failure to exercise such diligence or care shall not be inferable from any alleged loss, absence or disappearance of any of its contents, nor shall the bank be liable for permitting a co-lessee or an attorney in fact of the lessee to have access to and remove the contents of said safe deposit box after the lessee's death or disability and before the bank has written knowledge of such death or disability."
—Richard Haitch, letter to *The New York Times*

legalism *n.* A formal principle or term from law, esp. an expression that appears meaningless in or remote to real life.

"What must be attacked, uprooted and destroyed," the academician explained, "is, generally, the tendency to place legalisms above the interests of society, and, individually, the tendency of the law above the understood goals of justice." —Martin Cruz Smith, *Gorky Park*

legend *n.* An unverified but valued or repeated story, often with a historical basis, handed down over generations and part of a people's culture; the realm of such traditional, apocryphal stories; the historical myths of a nation or culture; something or someone with the force of unforgettable myth or romance; inscription or motto; wording; brief accompanying description, key, or caption with an illustration or map. *Adj.* legendary; *adv.* legendarily; *n.* legendry.

There was a contagion in the very air that blew from that haunted region; it breathed forth an atmosphere of dreams and fancies infecting all the land. Several of the Sleepy Hollow people were present at Van Tassel's, and, as usual, were doling out their wild and wonderful legends. —Washington Irving, "The Legend of Sleepy Hollow"

legend See CUTLINE under special entry NEWSROOM HEADLINE JARGON, p. 386.

legenda *n. pl.* Stories or biographical accounts intended to be morally instructive or religiously edifying, such as those recounting the lives of saints.

leitmotif, leitmotiv *n.* A specific recurring theme or expression in a literary or musical work, in association with a particular idea, person, circumstance, or emotion; a signal repeated note, effect, or term, such as a Homeric epithet. Also MOTIF.

By tomorrow he would be into the D.T.'s, preaching on the evils of prostitution—a favorite subject—and waving the meat cleaver. The leitmotif of these performances was "gonna cut off your balls and serve 'em for breakfast."
—Christopher Buckley, *Steaming to Bamboola*

leptologia [*lep″tə·lō′jē·ə*] *n.* Subtle speech or quibbling.

lethologica [*leth″ə·loj′i·kə*] *n.* Inability to remember the right word; tip-of-the-tongue-ness.

lethonomia [*leth″ə·nō′mē·ə*] *n.* A propensity for forgetting names.

letter change See special entry WORD-GAME WORDS, p. 395.

letter deletion See special entry WORD-GAME WORDS, p. 396.

letter insertion See special entry WORD-GAME WORDS, p. 396.

letter rebus See special entry WORD-GAME WORDS, p. 396.

letters *n.* The realm or profession of literature or of language and literary learning; belles-lettres; bookish culture.

But Petrescu, his loyalty to American letters affronted beyond endurance, insisted that they leave after the first act.
—John Updike, *Bech: A Book*

lexeme *n.* Any speech form or element that is, in itself, a meaningful unit in a language; basic item of vocabulary. *Adj.* lexemic.

lexicography *n.* The writing of dictionaries, or the compiling and defining of words. *Adj.* lexicographic, lexicographical; *adv.* lexicographically; *n.* lexicographer.

Few words have more than one literal and serviceable meaning, however many metaphorical, derivative, related, or even unrelated, meanings lexicographers may think it worth while to gather from all sorts and conditions of men, with which to bloat their absurd and misleading dictionaries. —Ambrose Bierce, *Write It Right*

lexicology *n.* The science of word derivation, meaning, and application. *Adj.* lexicologic, lexicological; *n.* lexicologist.

lexicomane See special entry BOOKISH APPELLATIONS, p. 406.

lexicon *n.* An alphabetical list or book of defined words; word-book; glossary or dictionary; the vocabulary of a particular language, class, group, or individual; word-hoard; complete record or domain, as of a particular field. *Pl.* lexicons, lexica; *v.* lexiconize.

Among several reasons why the Women's Liberation Movement (an interesting metaphor in itself) runs into resistance is that both men and women have internalized a rich lexicon of metaphors, about the subjects of sex, love, and domesticity.
—Neil Postman, *Crazy Talk, Stupid Talk*

lexiphanicism, lexiphantism [*lek"si·fan'ə·siz"əm*] *n.* Bombastic, over-Latinized writing; pretentious vocabulary or grandiose phraseology. *Adj.* lexiphanic; *n.* lexiphanes.

lexis *n.* The vocabulary of a language, person, field, topic, etc.; pertinent idiom.

Pragmatic politicians live in a world whose lexis is as slippery as its motives are hypocritical. —Philip Howard, *Words Fail Me*

libel n. The publishing of something manifestly untrue or detrimental to another's reputation; defamation in print, as opposed to slander, which is oral. *Adj.* libelous, libellous; *adv.* libelously, libellously; *v.* libel. See special entry LIBEL, p. 366.

"It's not them sue you for libel," Solly mused, "it's you sue them for saying your book's libellous. That's if they put it in writing."
—Muriel Spark, *Loitering with Intent*

ligature *n.* A written or printed character that conjoins (with no space between) two or more letters, sometimes with a superscribed connecting stroke or bar, e.g., "æ."

limehouse *n. British* Abuse of one's political opponents (from a July 30, 1909, speech by Lloyd George at Limehouse, London).

limn *v.* To convey or portray in words, esp. in a depictive or pictorial way; describe.

line *n.* A horizontal row of type or written characters; a sentence, standard horizontal segment of verse, or single utterance by a character in a play; a personal letter or note; the rationale or direction of development, as of a story or argument; an approach to explain, flatter, or win over, esp. one that is obvious and tiresome; expressed opinion or viewpoint.

"Jack," he said, "you know what the *Chronicle* line is in this election."   —Robert Penn Warren, *All the King's Men*

line See special entry BOOK PUBLISHING TERMS, p. 362.

line editing Close perusal and correcting of a manuscript, line by line, not only for grammar, spelling, and style but also for content and organization. *N.* line editor; *v.* line edit.

The compleat line editor can spot a faulty classical allusion in an article on the Nauruan phosphate industry as well as a transposed subscript in $Ca_3(PO_4)_2$, a dangling participle in the lead sentence, and a libelous crack about a plant manager.
—Arthur Plotnik, *The Elements of Editing*

lingo *n.* Language regarded as special or unfamiliar, such as foreign speech, a trade idiom, or "thick" slang; special vocabulary; jargon.

. . . Some invented slang, not all, becomes current among the people it is invented for. If you are sensitive to this sort of thing, I believe you could often, not always, distinguish between the colored-up lingo that writers produce, and the hard simplicity of the terms that originate in the circle where they are actually used.
—Raymond Chandler, *Raymond Chandler Speaking*

lingua franca Frankish language: a hybrid language that serves as a common mode of discourse between groups or peoples speaking different languages, esp. as a commercial or trade jargon; a useful makeshift lingo (formerly a language used in Mediterranean commerce).

The thought came to Holliwell that he had spent much of his life depending on a few local people, speaking some lingua franca, hovering insect-like about the edge of some complex ancient society which he could never hope to really penetrate.
—Robert Stone, *A Flag for Sunrise*

linguistic *adj.* Of or relatmg to a language or to linguistics; involving speech or expression; verbal. *Adv.* linguistically.

This tape, you might be interested in knowing, was submitted to prompt psychiatric, neurological, and linguistic examination. With the aid of our latest-model computers, our teams have analyzed Gardiner's vocabulary, syntax, accent, gestures, facial and other characteristics. —Jerzy Kosinski, *Being There*

linguistic chauvinism Militant partiality and protectiveness regarding one's language, particularly out of nationalistic feelings and resistance to adopting foreign words; elitism or snobbery about established speech.

The Midwest has always been the chief center of linguistic chauvinism. . . . —H. L. Mencken, *The American Language*

linguistics *n.* The science of language, esp. of the elements, modifications, and structural and relativistic aspects of units of speech; study of a particular language.

But they lead me on to the English of advertising, a study which I know has been called the small change of linguistics; here is a jargon that lies all around us. —Basil Cottle, *The Plight of English*

linkade See special entry WORD-GAME WORDS, p. 396.

lipogram See special entry WORD-GAME WORDS, p. 396.

lip service Avowal of intention, agreement, or regret in word only; perfunctory or pro forma interest or concern.

And yet, in the late 1970s and early 1980s, a high academic official who paid lip service to the humanistic verities while passing out paychecks to a pack of joyous literary barbarians was not necessarily a hypocrite. —Bryan Griffin, *Harper's*

lirripoop See special entry BOOKISH APPELLATIONS, p. 406.

litany *n.* A prayer rite with congregational responses to the supplicational phrases of the leader or pastor; any familiar recitation or accounting, often repetitious or monotonous; itemization or recapitulation.

Polly led the way down a long corridor past the assertiveness-training class, from which bloodcurdling screams of "This steak is tough!" and "I demand to see the manager!" poured forth like a perpetual litany from a demented abbey.
—Florence King, *When Sisterhood Was in Flower*

lit crit The profession or idiom of literary criticism.

She must be among the most scholarly characters in fiction; talking in great swabs of lit crit, even in bed, she announces theories on everything *but* Hamlet's grandson being Shakespeare's grandfather.
—Michael Malone, *The New York Times*

literacy *n.* The state or quality of being able to read and write; intelligence and expressiveness; education and articulateness; familiarity with literature.

She did not read herself, though at the time of her marriage she had been able to read a little. She did not practice it much then and during the last forty years she had lost even that habit, preferring now to be face to face with the living breath of event, fiction or news either, and being able to comment and moralise upon it. So she saw no need for literacy in women.   —William Faulkner, *The Hamlet*

literal *adj.* According to the evident, primary meaning of a word or words rather than figurative, symbolic, or metaphorical; plain or explicit; exact or verbatim, rather than paraphrased or interpreted; concerned chiefly with facts; prosaic; involving letters or written characters. *Adv.* literally; *n.* literalness, literality; *v.* literalize.

The general tone of novels is so literal that when the fantastic is introduced it produces a special effect: some readers are thrilled, others choked off: it demands an additional adjustment because of the oddness of its method or subject matter—like a sideshow in an exhibition where you have to pay sixpence as well as the original entrance fee.   —E. M. Forster, *Aspects of the Novel*

literal *n.* A spelling or printing error; typo.

literalism *n.* Adherence to the exact word or explicit sense, or to the stated meaning, often unwisely or narrow-mindedly; precise and unidealized representation; following the letter; a literal expression. *Adj.* literalistic; *adv.* literalistically; *n.* literalist.

The new translators dislike metaphor, and are much happier with the literalisms which release us from too much bondage to the metaphor.
                                    —Margaret A. Doody, in *The State of the Language*

literarism *n.* A cultured or high-brow word favored by the literary, e.g., "sempiternal," "prescient," "rebarbative."

literary *adj.* Pertaining to the craft of writing or to works of literature; involving or concerned with books or the professions of publishing or journalism; characterized by serious, polished expression, esp. in writing, rather than by informal use of language; engaged in or familiar with literature; earnest about writing; well-read; bookish. *Adv.* literarily; *n.* literariness.

Why hadn't he written it? Partly because he found he could only write in one language, the dialect of Pater, Proust, and Henry James, the style that is common to mandarin academic circles given over to clique life and introspection. This dead literary English, with its long sentences, elaborate similes and clever epithets effectually blocked any approach to a new vernacular.

—Cyril Connolly, *The Rock Pool*

literaryism *n.* Affectedly literary style or expression or an instance of it; overrefinement in writing.

literate *adj.* Able to read and write; properly articulate; educated; appreciative of literature; involving or concerning respectable literature; well crafted or readable; worthily written; polished. *Adv.* literately; *n.* literateness.

He has always been a literate and sweetly humorous writer for children and he does conjure up some amusing and quite lyrical moments but they are left to sparkle from a rather routine travelogue.

—Karla Kuskin, *The New York Times*

literati [*lit″ə·rä′tē*] *n. pl.* The literate or bookishly educated; men of letters or scholars. *Sing.* literato, literatus.

Another ancient monopoly, the monopoly of the literati, was being dissolved and its powers were being dispersed into the whole people.

—Daniel Boorstin, *The Americans*

literation *n.* The representing of sounds or of words by written letters; rendering in characters.

literature *n.* The work or works of authors, including prose and verse and esp. writings of relative excellence and lasting or universal appeal; artistically worthy writing; letters or belles-lettres; the body of writings in a particular field or on a particular subject; historical or available documents; printed matter.

As talk, no doubt, it was charming, and certainly the writer is a good fellow to meet over a bottle of beer. But literature is stern; it is no use being charming, virtuous, or even learned and brilliant into the bargain, unless, she seems to reiterate, you fulfil her first condition— to know how to write.   —Virginia Woolf, *The Common Reader*

Literaturwissenschaft See special entry SCHOLARLY (BIBLIO-GRAPHIC) TERMS, p. 401.

litotes [*līt′ə·tēz″*] *n.* Understatement, irony, or innuendo by use of a negative or inverted phrasing, e.g., "Not bad," "I'm not exactly displeased"; affirming something by negating its con-

trary; oblique emphasis. *Pl.* litotes. See also MEIOSIS, PARA-
DIASTOLE.

Henry James used the litotes continually, and successors of James to
such an extent that one sometimes wonders what meaning is thereby
being passed, if any.
                                    —Geoffrey Wagner, *On the Wisdom of Words*

littérateur *n.* One whose calling or career is literature; man of
letters; professional writer or critic.

I could count back the years on one hand to the time when I was
teaching the young genius and littérateur not to say ain't.
                                    —Budd Schulberg, *What Makes Sammy Run?*

loa *n.* An introductory address or prologue intended to win sympathy or support; flattering speech to an audience.

loaded attribution See special entry JOURNALISTIC ATTRIBUTION
AND EVASION, p. 379.

loaded question A yes-or-no question that, containing a tacit assumption, may trap or incriminate the person responding. See
also QUESTION-BEGGING.

loaded verb A verb that subtly editorializes rather than reports,
framing what may be questionable as fact and harboring a value
judgment or prejudice, e.g., "Jones pointed out that Smith was
a racist" (rather than "Jones said that Smith was a racist") or
(often) the verbs "emphasize," "admit," "stress," and
"note"; verbs that palliate value judgments.

loaded word An emotional word charged with implication or association, either favorably or unfavorably, e.g., "racist," "un-
American," "appeasement"; prejudiced or pregnant term.

Loaded language, like loaded firearms, can be hidden where least
suspected, and the laws against concealed weapons do not apply.
                                    —Dwight Bolinger, *Language—The Loaded Weapon*

loanblend *n.* See HYBRID.

loan-translation *n.* See CALQUE.

loan-word *n.* See BORROWING.

localism *n.* A word, expression, or pronunciation peculiar to a
particular locality, such as a dialectical idiom. *Adj.* localistic.

Pervading these and other facets of the country is that extraordinary
language, which dots his text with such expressions as "in the ease

of the world," "while the life was in her," "giving him the hard word." The text tingles with these localisms.

—Richard Ellmann, *The New York Review of Books*

locus classicus [*lō'kəs klas'i·kəs*]   A place of the highest class: illustrative, model passage from a literary work or classic that is commonly cited for its style, usage, etc.; authoritative source. *Pl.* loci classici.

... the chronology of "The Good Soldier" is hopelessly muddled, and not only to a lazy reader. This novel, a masterpiece of the storyteller's art, a *locus classicus* for discussion of the unreliable narrator, is full of contradictions.   —Margaret Drabble, *The New York Times*

locus communis [*lō'kəs ko·mōō'nis*]   A public place: commonplace passage that is often quoted; cliché expression; (usually plural) a general, all-purpose argument. *Pl.* loci communis.

locution *n.*   A particular word, phrase, or expression, esp. one considered critically from the standpoint of aptness, unusualness, or style; wording or phraseology; mode of speech.

In the staff editorial conferences he was fond of uttering such locutions as "Wolfe used to say to me . . ." Or, "As Tom wrote to me so eloquently just before his death . . ."

—William Styron, *Sophie's Choice*

locutionary *adj.*   Pertaining to or describing an utterance that is manifestly meaningful, such as "The train is here on time" (contrasted with illocutionary and perlocutionary).

loganamnosis [*log"ən·am·nō'sis*] *n.*   A mania to recall forgotten words.

logic-chopping *n.*   See CHOPLOGIC.

logion [*lō'jē·on"*] *n.*   A traditional saying or religious teacher's maxim, esp. a saying of Jesus unrecorded in the Gospels (or one of the so-called agrapha) or one of certain sayings of Mohammed. *Pl.* logia.

logodaedaly [*log"ə·dēd'ə·lē*] *n.*   Verbal legerdemain, esp. in the imaginative or capricious coining of new words; word skill.

He mimed and mocked me. His allusions were definitely highbrow. He was well read. He knew French. He was versed in logodaedaly and logomancy.   —Vladimir Nabokov, *Lolita*

logogogue   See special entry BOOKISH APPELLATIONS, p. 406.

logogram *n.*   A symbol, figure, or letter used to represent a word, e.g., the symbol "#" for "number" or the ampersand (&). Also LOGOGRAPH. *Adj.* logogrammatic; *adv.* logogrammatically.

logogriph *n.*   A word puzzle in which a single word must be discovered from combinations of synonyms, other words, or verses; anagram. *Adj.* logogriphic.

Per contra, she suggested to Van that verbal circuses, "performing words," "poodle-doodles," and so forth, might be redeemable by the quality of the brain work required for the creation of a great logogriph or inspired pun and should not preclude the help of a dictionary, gruff or complacent.   —Vladimir Nabokov, *Ada*

logology *n.*   The science of words, esp. the field of orthographic and homophonic word games. *Adj.* logological. See special entry WORD-GAME WORDS, p. 394.

Here "logology," with its gift for fanning out families of semi-cognate words like a deck of cards, for shuttling between high and low levels of speech, for seeing the personal in the abstract and vice versa, not only delights the spectator but illuminates the text.
—Robert M. Adams, *Times Literary Supplement*

logomachy [*lō·gom'ə·kē*] *n.*   A dispute over words; semantic contention getting away from issues or reality; duel with opprobrious words; word game. *Adj.* logomachic, logomachical; *n.* logomachist; *v.* logomachize.

Conducted with "shattering candour" (as one has said who is in spirit a member of this Club, though not yet, alas, inducted), the meetings may sometimes resolve themselves into a ribaldry, sometimes into a truthful pursuit of Beauty, sometimes into a mere logomachy.
—Christopher Morley, "Creed of the Three Hours for Lunch Club"

logomisia [*lō"gō·mis'ē·ə*] *n.*   Disgust for particular words.

logophag   See special entry BOOKISH APPELLATIONS, p. 406.

logophile   See special entry BOOKISH APPELLATIONS, p. 406.

logophobia *n.*   Fear of words.

Exaggerated anxieties about language's ability to express reality result in the pathology or "logophobia". . . . Logophobia has found popular expression in recent decades in the movement known as General Semantics.   —Peter Farb, *Word Play*

logorrhea *n.* Protracted or uncontrollable talk; compulsive garrulousness. *Adj.* logorrheic.

What Young doubtless meant was that Cosell had logorrhea, and what he intended to write—in euphemistic reference to the inelegant but functional phrase "diarrhea of the mouth"—was "an articulate diarrhetoric." —Roy Blount, Jr., *More*

logrolling *n.* The exchanging of favors, such as the writing of reciprocally flattering reviews; conniving literary cronyism or back scratching. *V.* logroll.

Sherwood would be able to whoop it up for me in a half-dozen periodicals which had come to consider his word as artistic law. Flushed with these visions of logrolling, I sat down opposite Sherwood in our favorite restaurant. . . . —Ben Hecht, *The New York Times*

longueur [*lông·gûr'*] *n.* A long and tedious section of a book, play, etc.; boring prose passage.

But how about the dreadful bogs and obstacles that one has to get over in Scott? the interpolated essays in Hugo? the leaking tap of Thackeray's reflections on life, in which the story is always trickling away? Is there anything in first-rate modern fiction quite so gratuitous as these *longueurs*? —Edmund Wilson, *Classics and Commercials*

loose sentence A sentence that contains a complete thought before its end, that is, one with a main clause followed by subordinate elements (contrasted with periodic sentence).

loquacity, loquaciousness *n.* Extreme talkativeness; garrulousness. *Adj.* loquacious; *adv.* loquaciously.

Yet he had learned that there was something about Barry, despite his outrageous conceit and his blatant toadying, despite his never-ending loquacity and his abominable jokes, that made the other clerks put up with him, at times even like him.
—Louis Auchincloss, *Powers of Attorney*

lost positives Whimsically coined or archaic words of which only the negative or an inflected (prefixed) form is in common usage, e.g., "ept" (from "inept").

Lost positives are words like "couth," "sheveled," and "kempt," which some people think formerly existed as positives of "uncouth," "disheveled," and "unkempt." They are simply common words stripped of their usual prefixes. . . .

One of our column readers suggested "ane" (inane), "descript" (nondescript), "gruntled" (disgruntled), and "digent" (indigent). It

was the late James Thurber who first devised "gruntled." Asked to comment on fellow staff members on the Paris *Herald Tribune* during the halcyon days following World War I, Thurber called them "the most gruntled group I ever knew."
> —William and Mary Morris, *Harper Dictionary of Contemporary Usage*

lubricum linguae [*lōo'bri·kəm ling'gwī"*]   See LAPSUS LINGUAE.

lucidity, lucidness *n.*   Clarity of thought, meaning, or expression; aptness or directness of style; express understandableness. *Adj.* lucid; *adv.* lucidly.

The test of lucidity is whether the statement can be read as meaning anything other than what it intends.
> —Evelyn Waugh, *A Little Order*

lucubration *n.*   Nocturnal or assiduous study or writing, esp. that showing toil rather than inspiration; studious meditation; an overly abstruse or artificial piece of scholarship; pedantic discourse. *Adv.* lucubratory. See also OLET LUCERNAM.

lucus a non lucendo [*lōo'kəs ä nōn" lōo·ken'dō*]   "Grove" (must be) from "not shining" [since a grove admits no light]: an absurd word derivation; illogical explanation or non sequitur.

lugging *n.*   See SIGNIFYING.

lurry *n.*   Something repeated by rote; jumble of sounds.

lyricism *n.*   Songfulness, or the quality or state of being richly or sonorously expressive, as in brilliantly descriptive prose; appealing, evocative language; poetic style; enthusiastic, inspired, or ardent outpouring of feeling. *Adj.* lyrical; *adv.* lyrically.

The melting passage slows the reader down and even trips him up with its coy allusion to earmuffs, its repetitions and pauses, and its peculiar mixture of lyricism and banality.
> —Christopher Lehmann-Haupt, *The New York Times*

M

macrology *n.* Excessive or repetitious wording; redundancy.

Madison Avenue The New York City street identified with the American advertising industry; hence, values, methods, or language characteristic for its advertising or promotional purport; glib and slick hucksterism; glamorized language.

His own regular contributions as Critic represent a unique journalistic achievement and provide a piece of one-man social history, neither objective nor unbiased, but piquant, and, as they say along Madison Avenue, personalized. —Malcom Muggeridge, *Things Past*

magniloquence *n.* Grandly high-flown, lofty speech; pompous language. *Adj.* magniloquent; *adv.* magniloquently.

As late as 1935 Herbert Horwill called it [donate] a word which in England is eschewed by good writers as a pretentious and magniloquent vulgarism. —Albert Marckwardt, *American English*

magnum opus A great work of art or literature, esp. a writer's culminating and greatest achievement; masterpiece. *Pl.* magna opera, magnum opuses.

It was the magnum opus of a fat spoiled rich boy who could write like an angel about landscape and like an adolescent about people. —Norman Mailer, *Cannibals and Christians*

maieutic [*mā·yōo′tik*] *adj.* Pertaining to or involving the Socratic method or instructive, guided dialectic.

majuscule *n. Chiefly British* A capital, or upper-case, letter.

makebate See special entry BOOKISH APPELLATIONS, p. 406.

mala fide [*mal′ə fī′dē*] In bad faith: falsely, deceitfully, or insincerely.

malapropism A glaring, usually humorous use of a wrong (similar) word. *Adj.* malaproptistic. See special entry MIXED METAPHORS, p. 388.

malarkey *n.* Glib talk intended to cover up or impress; nonsense.

malediction *n.*   An invoking of evil or harm upon somebody or something; pronounced curse; evil talk or slander. *Adj.* maledictive, maledictory.

He caught up the empty pewter mug at his right and threw it at the clumsy lad with a malediction.
                                          —Willa Cather, *Death Comes for the Archbishop*

malonym   See special entry MIXED METAPHORS, p. 388.

mamaloshen, mame loshn [*mä"mə·lô'shən*] *n. Yiddish*   Mother's language: straight talk or down-to-earth language.

. . . some Jewish writers express a yearning for Jewishness . . . from Philip Roth's vulgarly Americanized Yiddish clichés . . . to Saul Bellow's lyrical quotations from the "mamaloshen."
                                          —Kathryn Hellerstein, in *The State of the Language*

managed news   Information provided and distributed by the government (or other official body) in its own interest; "orchestrated" official releases.

managed text   See special entry BOOK PUBLISHING TERMS, p. 362.

man-bites-dog story   A newspaper story having a curious human-interest, often humorous flavor, such as one profiling a person with a hobby that would seem to be a role reversal.

The defendant was what the N-boys like to call a Scion (of a wealthy family of former oleomargarine manufacturers, in this instance), which, in the same idiom, qualified him as a Socialite. Scions are seldom accused of procuring, which gave the case a bit of the man-bites-dog-aspect that the schools of journalism talk about.
                                          —A. J. Liebling, *The Press*

mandarin English *Chiefly British*   Extremely formal, sophisticated, or elegant verbal style.

In general, the short-sentence boys cannot lengthen the line to stillness, and the mandarins can't jab worth their hats.
                                          —Wilfrid Sheed, *The Good Word and Other Words*

manifesto *n.*   A public declaration of advocated opinion, intent, viewpoint, etc., esp. a political exhortation or proclamation of aesthetic principles; avowal; credo. *Pl.* manifestos, manifestoes.

How often he had seen her, as they sat together in the evening lamplight, with a pad of it propped on her knee as she drafted a letter to

her Congressman, or a flaming manifesto for one or another of the
ecological causes into which she threw herself, and sometimes him.
—Peter De Vries, *Madder Music*

mannerism *n.* An author's marked or habitual peculiarity of
style; characteristically individual locution or stylistic idiosyncrasy; artificiality. *Adj.* mannered, manneristic.

Much of what struck foreign observers as bizarre in American description was a new linguistic confusion of present and future, fact
and hope. This became a mannerism, or even a mode of American
speech. Statements which foreigners took for lies or braggadocio,
American speakers intended to be vaguely clairvoyant.
—Daniel Boorstin, *The Americans*

mantra *n.* A Vedic hymn or text intoned in prayer; a particular
word or incantation used as a ritual chant in Buddhist meditation; any personal word or formula used mystically.

"You can get high on a mantra," he says. "But I'm holy on acid."
—Joan Didion, *Slouching Towards Bethlehem*

Märchen [*mâr'khin*] *n. German* A folk tale or fairy tale. *Pl.*
Märchen.

marginalia *n.* Comments or notes in the margins; matters of less
importance or of mere detail.

Though Mr. McLuhan's reading of *King Lear* is absurdly unconvincing, he has fascinating marginalia on Rabelais, Cervantes, Pope, and
Joyce. —George Steiner, *Language and Silence*

marrowsky [*mə·rou'skē*] *n.* See SPOONERISM.

marsupial See KANGAROO WORD under special entry WORD-
GAME WORDS, p. 395.

mass-market paperback See special entry BOOK PUBLISHING
TERMS, p. 362.

mataeology [*mat"ē·ol'ə·jē*] *n.* Useless or pointless discourse;
worthless conversation.

matching parts Wilson Follett's term (from Le Baron Russell
Briggs) for the principle of proper balance and parallel phrasing
in a sentence; consistency of structure as it lends itself to a
smooth train of thought; rhetorical keenness.

material fallacy An error in reasoning arising from the question
of the subject matter of an argument (contrasted with formal
fallacy and verbal fallacy). Also REAL FALLACY.

matronym, matronymic *n.* A name derived from that of one's mother or a maternal ancestor, usually by addition of a suffix or prefix. *Adj.* matronymic, matronymical; *adv.* matronymically. Also METRONYMIC.

maunder *v.* To talk uncertainly or idly in a disconnected, desultory way; chatter aimlessly; whine or grumble. *Adj.* maundering; *adv.* maunderingly; *n.* maunderer.

The title story of the book allows two drunken couples to maunder in an all-too-familiar vein about love.
—Anatole Broyard, *The New York Times*

mauvaise plaisanterie [*mō·vez' plä·zäN"·t(ə)rē'*] An inappropriate or badly timed joke.

maxim *n.* A summary universal truth, fundamental principle, or rule of conduct; proverbial or sententious saying.

I guess I was seven when I first heard the maxim that only people with a small vocabulary use "dirty" words. I am forty-seven and have just received a communication from a reader delivering that maxim as though he had invented it.
—William F. Buckley, Jr., *Execution Eve*

McKay's Syndrome Russell Baker's term for a witless admission of empty rhetoric or hypocrisy in political speechmaking, a form of foot-in-mouth disease.

Ronald Reagan's early campaign founderings disclose a severe case of McKay's Syndrome, a deadly political affliction named for Douglas McKay, an Oregon car dealer who ran for the Senate some years ago.
  McKay's case became terminal during a rousing campaign rally in which he delivered the customary speech stuffed with the customary banalities, evasions and bromides, to the customary applause from the party claque. Not content to quit while he was behind, McKay then laid aside his prepared text, looked over the audience and said, "Now I'd like to say a few words of my own."
—Russell Baker, *The New York Times*

mealymouthed *adj.* Unwilling to be candid about facts or one's opinions; not plainspoken; evasive or coyly euphemistic to the point of insincerity. *Adj.* mealymouthedly; *n.* mealymouthedness.

And in 1949 Hemingway writes—but does he mail?—an exuberant diatribe to Cardinal Spellman accusing him of "mealy mouthed arrogance," nastiness toward Eleanor Roosevelt, strike-breaking "against Catholic workers" and telling lies "about the Spanish Republic."   —Irving Howe, *The New York Times*

medela See special entry RHETORIC TERMS, p. 404.

megillah [*mə·gil′ə*] *n.* *Yiddish* A tediously long or overly involved recital, story, or explanation; rigmarole; folderol.

MEGO *n.* My Eyes Glaze Over: a political or official speech that is sleep-inducing; rhetorical soporific.

meiosis [*mī·ō′sis*] *n.* Rhetorical understatement, or representing something as less or more minor than it actually is as a form of ironic emphasis (contrasted with hyperbole). See also LITOTES, PARADIASTOLE.

What was a rhetorical device in the Classical schools of oratory— *meiosis* or under-emphasis—and came into facetious use in Victorian times (e.g., "Pedestrianism in November is a matter of not a little unpleasantness") is now second nature to most Englishmen, and has lost its original ironic purpose. It now means modesty. . . . Conversationally this style can be charming, but in prose it makes for irrelevancy, material omission, faulty connexion, logical weakness, and, eventually, boredom.
        —Robert Graves and Alan Hodge, *The Reader over Your Shoulder*

melioration *n.* An elevation or bettering: in language, a hitherto or otherwise derogatory word's acquiring a favorable meaning; positive rather than negative connotation (contrasted with pejoration). *Adj.* meliorative; *v.* meliorate. Also AMELIORATION.

Thus when I arrived in America *compromise* was a meliorative term in Britain, pejorative in America. This tells you quite a bit about the social history of the countries concerned.
        —Geoffrey Wagner, *On the Wisdom of Words*

mellifluous *adj.* Richly sweet and smooth in speech or tone; resonant and flowing; honeyed. *Adv.* mellifluously; *n.* mellifluousness.

The best American essay on him, in my opinion, was by Edmund Wilson, dry and to the point. There was no mellifluous English nonsense about the "inimitable" and "incomparable."
        —V. S. Pritchett, *The Tale Bearers*

melliloquence *n.* Euphonious speech; sweet talk.

memoir *n.* A historical memorandum or record, or an individual's narrative, recollections, or observations illuminating a pe-

riod or subject; contemporary personal chronicle. *Pl.* an autobiographical account, esp. by an eminent person; memorial biography; report of something notable; record of investigations
or the recorded proceedings of a learned society or the like. *N.*
memoirist.

She had bought *Le Temps* and the *Saturday Evening Post* for her
mother, and as she drank her citronade she opened the letter at the
memoirs of a Russian princess, finding the dim conversations of the
nineties realer and nearer than the headlines of the French paper.
                                     —F. Scott Fitzgerald, *Tender Is the Night*

memorandum *n.*   A brief note or reminder or a record kept for
future reference; a particular interoffice notice or staff communication; directive; informal diplomatic summary or outline, as
of a decision or policy; official statement or observation for the
record. *Pl.* memorandums, memoranda.

The authors evidently failed to understand that a memorandum for
the President was only a writer's device to sell books, not a framework that had to be taken literally. . . . Instead of capturing the emotion and suspense of politics at the center, the authors have indeed
produced an overlong memorandum.
                                     —Edward Cowan, *The New York Times*

mempsis   See special entry RHETORIC TERMS, p. 404.

mendaciloquence [*men″də·sil′ə·kwəns*] *n.*   Lying as a fine art;
adroit prevarication. *Adj.* mendaciloquent.

merged quotation   Jacques Barzun's term for a quotation incorporated within a sentence of the main text or exposition, e.g.,
"She knew that 'the real deals are made behind closed doors,'
as more than one lobbyist had told her."

merism [*mer′iž″əm*] *n.*   A pairing of contrasting terms to express
a totality, and thus a form of synecdoche, e.g., "now and
then," "black and white." Also PAIRED OPPOSITES.

metabasis   See special entry RHETORIC TERMS, p. 404.

metachronism *n.*   See ANACHRONISM.

metagraphy *n.*   See TRANSLITERATION.

metalanguage *n.*   A language or idiom used to discuss or describe
another language (or object language), such as the text of a

linguistics book; speech about speech (contrasted with object language).

Long saturated by the prolixity of ads that told of the advantages of product use and promised satisfaction with results, the consumer allows himself to be more open to commercials that work simply on the level of an invocation. Henceforth he becomes the reader of a metalanguage that does not "act the things," as Barthes declares, but rather "acts their names." —Robert E. Ziegler, *Verbatim*

metalinguistics *n.* The study of language in terms of its interrelationship with other behavioral phenomena of culture or society. *Adj.* metalinguistic; *adv.* metalinguistically.

metallege See special entry WORD-GAME WORDS, p. 396.

metanalysis *n.* See AFFIX-CLIPPING.

metaphor *n.* The figure of speech denoting implied comparison: an imaginative or analogous term used in place of a given word or concept, or an expressive and comparable figurative term; word or image that is suggestively equivalent and ornamental but not synonymous; application of a comparable, figurative word or words. *Adj.* metaphoric; metaphorical; *adv.* metaphorically.

The Speaker of the House is not a goddamned metaphor; I have never been a metaphor and, God willing, I never shall be.
—Thomas P. ("Tip") O'Neill, quoted in *The New Republic*

metaphrase, metaphrasis *n.* A translation, esp. a word-for-word translation, as contrasted with a paraphrase. *V.* metaphrase.

metastasis See special entry RHETORIC TERMS, p. 404.

metathesis [*mi·tath'ə·sis*] *n.* Transposition of letters, syllables, or sounds within a word, either as a historical, permanent change in the language or as an individual speech lapse, e.g., Old English "brid" to modern "bird" or "nuclear" being pronounced "nuculer." *Pl.* metatheses; *adj.* metathetic, metathetical; *adv.* metathetically; *v.* metathesize.

metonymy *n.* The figurative or symbolic use of the name of one thing for that of another with which it is associated, or of an attribute for the whole, e.g., "brass" for military officers. *Adj.* metonymic, metonymical; *adv.* metonymically; *n.* metonym.

A full set would also have included the brazen Perelman pun ("My choler wilted" for "My anger subsided") . . . the Perelman micro-metonymy ("Hanna listened to the veins throbbing in my temple" for "I was speechless with anger at Hanna"), and the Perelman extrapolation of cliché into metaphor ("The whole aviary in my head burst into song" for "I was bird-brained").

—Tom Wolfe, *The New York Times*

metric prose   H. W. Fowler's term for prose that is unwittingly poetical in its rhythm, often the result of inflated, pretentious writing.

metronymic *n.*   See MATRONYM.

micrology *n.*   Excessive attention to or discussion of details or minor differences; nitpicking. *Adj.* micrological, micrologic.

mid-Atlantic *adj.*   Of, characterized by, or using English that is a mix of British and American idiom or pronunciation, esp. in the field of news reporting, entertainment, and the theater.

Homeless, permanently mid-Atlantic—and in spite of the way he clung to his Englishness in accent and idiom, the kind of parenthesis he always let you see round his Americanism, and his queer old patriotism—what I thought of sometimes as his Visit-Britain self, chatting with picturesque old gaffers in an oak-beamed country pub and quaffing your tankard of ale. . . .

—John Fowles, *Daniel Martin*

mimesis *n.*   Imitation or representation, as of nature or of speech, behavior, etc., of an individual or people; cultural expression. *Adj.* mimetic; *adv.* mimetically.

Benjamin's essays . . . belong to our theme . . . and the essay on Paris, instigated by Baudelaire's *Tableaux de Paris,* whose shape is a mimesis of the city, district following district with sudden avenues or winding alleys between them.

—George Steiner, *Language and Silence*

minced oath   Richard Spears's term for a euphemized profanity, e.g., "Cripes!" (instead of "Christ!").

mincing word   An affectedly dainty or coy word for a sexual term, swearword, etc.; puritanical euphemism; genteelism; elegancy.

Despite greater frankness and more frequent use of "gutter obscenities" in print, film, and theater, Mincing Words are still popular. Most people still prefer "birthday suit" or "stark naked" to "bare." "Nude" is a tepid compromise.   —Arthur Herzog, *The B.S. Factor*

mingle-mangle *n.* A hodgepodge; speech that is a confused jumble of words from different languages. Also SORIASMUS.

minor sentence A sentence that lacks words or complete predication but that makes sense, e.g., "Absolutely not," "And then?" and "In a manner of speaking."

minuscule *n. Chiefly British* A small, or lower-case, letter.

minutiae [*mi·n(y)ōo'shē·ē"*] *n. pl.* Minor or trivial details. *Sing.* minutia.

But its relentless detail and technical concentration are exhausting for the undisciplined armchair historian who might prefer the flavorful bacon of opinion to the dry minutiae of Rumanian pig exports in discussions of inter-war foreign policy and diplomacy.
—Neal Johnston, *The New York Times*

mirabile dictu [*mi·rä'bə·lä dik'tōo*] Wonderful to relate.

miscellanea *n.* A collection of sundry things or writings.

mischsprache [*mish'shprä"khə*] *n.* A language that is a mixture of two or more established languages. *Pl.* mischsprachen.

miscorrection *n.* A new error made in the course of correcting an old one. *V.* miscorrect. Also SCHLIMMBESSERUNG.

miserabile dictu [*miz'ə·rä'bi·lē dik'tōo*] Sad to relate.

misnomer *n.* Misnaming; a misapplied or wrong term, esp. in the case of a title or appellation; incorrect word or name.

Was I gifted or were these facts known to all travelers and wouldn't giftedness be a misnomer for a faculty that could not be exploited?
—John Cheever, *Bullet Park*

misology [*mi·sol'ə·jē*] *n.* Hatred of logical discussion or reason.

There is an appropriately ugly name for this prejudice: misology, or logic-hating. Its continuing existence among academic historians explains their failure to refine a logic of historical thought.
—David Hackett Fischer, *Historians' Fallacies*

misprint *n.* A typographic error; misspelling in print. *V.* misprint.

Lowell's book of literary essays, *My Study Windows,* was one of those read for the Dictionary, and James had found amongst the slips of quotations from it a strange word—*alliterates.* So he wrote to Lowell to ask its meaning, at the same time expressing warm appreciation of his writing and enclosing a copy of the annual report on the progress of the Dictionary. Lowell replied, saying that the unknown word was certainly a misprint for *illiterates*.

—K. M. Elisabeth Murray, *Caught in the Web of Words*

misquotation *n.*   Inaccurate quotation or an instance of it. *V.* misquote.

He paused, about to expose the heart of the matter, the root of the distaste, the fracture of the rules that bothered him more than the alleged misquotations, more than the intimation that he was no longer the Ringo Kid.   —Joan Didion, *Slouching Towards Bethlehem*

misreading *n.*   An inaccurate or careless reading; misunderstanding or misinterpretation. *V.* misread. See also GHOST WORD.

Mr. Givens's sentences sound as if he has misread both Leonard Michaels and Joan Didion.

—Anatole Broyard, *The New York Times*

misspeak *v.*   To mispronounce; express wrongly; speak in error or inadvisedly.

"Fired them?" I asked. "No, I misspoke myself. I mean he gave them their space to resign in."   —Herbert Gold, *Newsweek*

misspelling *n.*   An incorrect spelling. *V.* misspell.

I suspect that the popularity of all dialect stuff derives in part from flattery of the reader—giving him a pleasant sensation of superiority which he gets from working out the intricacies of misspelling, and the satisfaction of detecting boorishness or illiteracy in someone else.

—E. B. White, *Essays of E. B. White*

mistaken metaphor   See special entry MIXED METAPHORS, p. 389.

misstatement *n.*   A wrong or false statement. *V.* misstate.

All this, of course, was a tissue of lies. *The Autobiography of Alice B. Toklas* was so full of misstatements that many of her former associates felt that the book called for public contradiction.

—Carlos Baker, *Hemingway*

misword *n. Chiefly British*   An unkind word. *V.* to word incorrectly.

mixaprop   See special entry MIXED METAPHORS, p. 389.

mixed metaphor   A use of incongruous or clashing metaphors. See special entry MIXED METAPHORS, p. 388.

But that was nothing. Ray Kerrison flew into a berserk frenzy of mixed metaphors that left Media Person gasping for breath.

In the space of a few sentences, Kerrison had the contest *pick up*

steam, though it was too early *to get* a handle on all the candidates who were *jousting* and beginning to *sling the mud,* while at the same time trying to *blow Mayor Koch out of City Hall.* Nothing to do there but drag the man away with butterfly nets.
　　　　　—Lewis Grossberger ("Media Person"), *7 Days*

mnemonic [*nē·mon'ik*] *n.*　A verbal formula to assist memory, such as a special acronym, rhyme, or other form of verbal key or shorthand, e.g., Every Grizzly Bear Digs Figs (EGBDF) for the lines of the treble clef in music. *Adj.* mnemonic, mnemonical; *adv.* mnemonically.

I used to have a mnemonic to help me remember the difference between "invidious" and "insidious," as well as "stalagmite" and "stalactite," but I kept forgetting how to spell mnemonic.
　　　　　—William Safire, *On Language*

Möbius Mot [*moe'bē·əs mō'*]　Donald Westlake's term for a sentence in which a manner of expression or metaphor is an unwitting literal-sense echo of another word within the sentence, or an unconscious (and often distracting rather than funny) double meaning, e.g., "You can really get fleeced buying a sheepskin coat," "Banning the pill is inconceivable," "You could scour the city looking for a pot like that."

What I've come across is a sentence that, all unsuspected by the person speaking it, turns back on itself with a useless and irrelevant self-reference. It's a sentence with a short-circuit in it—a Möbius Mot.　　　　　—Donald Westlake, *The New York Times*

mock-heroic *adj.*　Satirizing a heroic or elevated theme or style, as through a humorously aggrandized treatment of the trivial; stylishly burlesquing. *Adv.* mock-heroically; *n.* mock-heroic.

This conversation takes place in Welch's car, and the continuation illustrates how Amis exploits stylistic incongruity for comic purposes in a very traditional way (it goes back to Fielding and mock-heroic).
　　　　　—David Lodge, *Language of Fiction*

mock ruralism　Leon Stolz's term for a self-consciously folksy, often illiterate, expression.

Following is some advice from Leon Stolz of the Chicago *Tribune* in *English I* (June 1968): "If you hold your quota to one mock ruralism a century, your readers will not feel deprived." Expressions such as "seeing as how" or "allowed as how" are supposed to give a folksy touch. They don't. They merely make the writer sound stupid.
　　　　　—Floyd K. Baskette and Jack Z. Sissors, *The Art of Editing*

modernism *n.* A modern word or expression; recent or contemporary coinage. *Adj.* modern; *v.* modernize. See also ARCHAISM.

mogigraphia *n.* See WRITER'S CRAMP.

mome See special entry BOOKISH APPELLATIONS, p. 406.

mondegreen [*mon'də·grēn"*] *n.* Sylvia Wright's term for an instance of mistaken interpretation of heard speech because of homophony or sound-alike words (from Wright's childhood interpretation of a line in a Scottish ballad as "They hae slain the Earl Amurray, And Lady Mondegreen," when the actual final words were "And laid him on the green.") Also FALSE HOMONYM. See also HOMONYM SLIP, SONIC WRITING.

When far from an office, I dictate my copy over the telephone to a machine in the recording room of *The Times;* a human transcriber of uncanny accuracy then takes my shouted transmission from Nanjing or wherever and types it into the computer that sets type. Mondegreens can be expected, but occasionally human error is creative enough to produce neologisms.   —William Safire, *On Language*

monepic [*mo·nep'ik*] *adj.* Consisting of one word, or of one-word sentences.

monoglot [*mon'ə·glot"*] *n.* A person knowing only one language (contrasted with polyglot); text written in one tongue. *Adj.* monoglot.

Yet one wonders whence the recruits to such a calling will come when it is so ill rewarded, when the study of foreign languages is hampered by the abolition of the native grammar, and when more and more of our university students can barely rank as monoglots.
        —Jacques Barzun, *The House of Intellect*

monograph *n.* A scholarly paper or book on a particular subject; special essay or treatise on a single thing or topic. *Adj.* monographic, monographical; *adv.* monographically.

I have, as you know, devoted some attention to this, and written a little monograph on the ashes of 140 different varieties of pipe, cigar, and cigarette tobacco.
        —Arthur Conan Doyle, "The Boscombe Valley Mystery"

monologophobia *n.* See SYNONYMOMANIA.

monologue *n.* A long speech by one person or, in writing, an extended discourse by an author, character, etc., sometimes self-indulgent or tedious. *Adj.* monologic, monological; *v.* monologize, monologuize.

> Sidney's prose is an uninterrupted monologue, with sudden flashes of felicity and splendid phrases, which lends itself to lamentations and moralities, to long accumulations and catalogues, but is never quick, never colloquial, unable to grasp a thought closely and firmly, or to adapt itself flexibly and exactly to the chops and changes of the mind.
> —Virginia Woolf, *The Common Reader*

monologue intérieur See INTERIOR MONOLOGUE.

monosyllables *n. pl.* One-syllable words; rudimentary or limited vocabulary; subliterate language; terse response. *Adj.* monosyllabic; *adv.* monosyllabically; *n.* monosyllabicity.

> Why had I thought I could learn anything about the land? For the last hundreds of miles I had avoided people. Even at necessary stops for gasoline I had answered in monosyllables and retained no picture.
> —John Steinbeck, *Travels with Charley*

moonshine *n.* Fatuous, illusory talk or notions; airy nonsense. *Adj.* moonshining.

morkrumbo *n.* Conventional, perfunctory journalistic writing, esp. typified by identification or "bogus titling" of people discussed with piled-up modifiers; routinely factual news copy; the making up by bureaucrats of impressive-sounding job titles, such as "animal welfare officer" for the post of exterminator.

> Certainly we should avoid what Wallace Carroll, former editor of *The Winston-Salem Journal and Sentinel,* called "Morkrumbo," the language of the Morkrum printer, which chattered, "Former North Carolina State University's head basketball coach Everett Case today declared. . . ." —William Safire, *The New York Times*

morology *n.* Deliberate nonsense or foolishness for effect.

morpheme *n.* Any of the smallest units of meaning or form within a language, or a verbal element that cannot be further reduced and still retain meaning, e.g., the word "woman," the prefix "un-," and the inflection "-ize." *Adj.* morphemic; *adv.* morphemically.

mot *n.* A clever comment or witticism; bon mot.

> The characteristic handling of wit in the circle was not merely that a *mot* would be remembered, but that it would also be recalled with the

name of the person who originally said it (which is not a bad way to
start feuds).   —William Barrett, *The Truants*

motif *n.* See LEITMOTIF.

mot juste [*mō zhüst*] The perfect, fitting word or phrase; precisely apt expression. *Pl.* mots justes.

It was a straight answer and Ezra had never given me any other kind
verbally, but I felt very bad because here was the man I liked and
trusted the most as a critic then, the man who believed in the *mot
juste*—the one and only correct word to use—the man who had
taught me to distrust adjectives as I would later learn to distrust
certain people in certain situations; and I wanted his opinion on a
man who almost never used the *mot juste* and yet had made his people
come alive at times, as almost no one else did.
                                      —Ernest Hemingway, *A Moveable Feast*

mot propre [*mō prôp·r(ə)*] The correct or necessary word. *Pl.*
mots propres.

motto *n.* A characterizing, usually idealizing word, phrase, or
sentence adopted to be appropriate to or representative of
something, such as a Latin inscription or rallying cry. *Pl.* mot-
toes, mottos; *adj.* mottoed.

History develops, Art stands still, is a crude motto, indeed it is almost
a slogan, and though forced to adopt it we must not do so without
admitting it vulgarily. It contains only a partial truth.
                                      —E. M. Forster, *Aspects of the Novel*

mouthpiece *n.* Somebody or something that speaks for a person
or a point of view, such as a press agent or propagandistic
newspaper; spokesperson or voice.

The newspaper press is organized so as to be a more perfect expression of public opinion than it possibly could be in your day, when
private capital controlled and managed it primarily as a money-mak-
ing business, and secondarily only as a mouthpiece for the people.
                                      —Edward Bellamy, *Looking Backward*

Mrs. Grundy A straitlaced, prudish person, or in matters of language one whose views are strict and conventional; censorious
purist (from a character in Thomas Morton's play *Speed the
Plough* [1798]). *Pl.* Mrs. Grundys.

In this first era of national life, when American speech was acquiring
its new vitality, many American academic students of language and
American literary writers were trying to keep the language "pure."

These Mrs. Grundys, the self-appointed censors of linguistic morality, never worked harder.   —Daniel Boorstin, *The Americans*

mucker pose   The pose of being ignorant or uncultivated, sometimes proudly, sometimes insincerely; assuming a guileless,
humble idiom.

... There is a good deal of this, for example, in Mark Twain ...
some clearly with tongue in cheek. The extreme of such an attitude
has at times been called the "mucker pose," one which certain politicians . . . have at times found it profitable to adopt.
                          —Albert Marckwardt, *American English*

muckraking *n.*   The searching out or exposure, as by a writer or
newspaper, of wrongdoing committed by prominent individuals
or institutions, esp. of political corruption or scandal; sensational revelatory journalism. *Adj.* muckraking; *n.* muckrake,
muckraker; *v.* muckrake.

Having failed in her basement, I thought to have her here, in the loft
of the parish hall, where a leaky old skylight made vivid the woody
forms of miniature crèches and lifesize mangers, wise kings' crowns
and shepherds' crooks, Victorian altar furniture and great padded
Bibles no longer thumped by the virile muckraking parsons of the first
Roosevelt's reign, plywood palm trees and temples of gilded card-
board.   —John Updike, *A Month of Sundays*

mudslinging *n.*   The use of malicious accusations or epithets to
slur an opponent, esp. in politics. *N.* mudslinger.

The words hit the headlines of the evening papers, and people began
to shrug and say that the case was simply a mud-slinging competition
between two angry women.
                          —Louis Auchincloss, *Powers of Attorney*

multum in parvo   Much in little: containing or suggesting much in
few words; holophrastic.

multisyllable *n.*   See POLYSYLLABLE.

mumblespeak *n.*   See GOBBLEDYGOOK.

mumbo jumbo   An idol, fetish, or figure of dread; cryptic gibberish used in a ritual, such as voodoo incantation; self-impor-
tantly obscure or complicated terminology or folderol; meaningless or purposeless language.

Mr. Appleman decorates this framework with considerable Norse and
Persian legendry, astrological mumbo jumbo, runic inscriptions,

clumsily expository dialogue that strains to pass as snappy patter and a proliferation of bad baseball metaphors.
— Rachel Billington, *The New York Times*

mumchance [*mum'chans"*] *adj. British* Tongue-tied or stupidly silent. *Adv.* mumchance.

But ahead of me now, a gathering. They stand mum-chance, carelessly, effortlessly, blinking their eyes.
— J. P. Donleavy, *Meet My Maker the Mad Molecule*

mumjummer See special entry BOOKISH APPELLATIONS, p. 406.

Mummerset *n. British* Any invented countrified or provincial accent used by British actors (from "mummer," or actor).

Some slang, for example tilly-valley (a sixteenth century exclamation of impatience: nonsense! fiddle-sticks!, is preserved as in amber in historical dictionaries and the Mummerset of period theatricals and the Gadzookery of historical novels.
— Philip Howard, *Weasel Words*

mumpsimus [*mump'si·məs*] *n.* An erroneous word or spelling that through long usage, has become absorbed into the language; an incorrect manuscript reading blindly adhered to by some scholars; stubborn adherence to a mistaken verbal form in the face of correction; person determined to perpetuate a wrong usage or word (from mispronunciation of "sumpsimus" in Latin mass by a priest refusing to be corrected) (contrasted with sumpsimus)

mush *n.* Cloyingly sentimental talk or writing, esp. about love; maudlin drivel. *Adj.* mushy.

mushmouth *n.* See GOBBLEDYGOOK.

must *n.* Newspaper jargon for matter that somebody in authority has ordered printed or published; an admonition that copy must not be changed in any way. Also MUSTY.

muster *n.* A news story considered important enough to sacrifice other stories to make space for it.

musty *n.* See MUST.

mutatis mutandis [*m(y)ōo·tä'tis m(y)ōo·tän'dis*] The (necessary) changes having been made, or the respective differences having been considered or allowed for: used as a qualifier in regard to alterations or corrections.

It was, he said, the same in Weymouth, mutatis mutandis. Mutatis and mutandis are bosom companions of those with classical educations; so long as British sports writers use them, we will know that Britain's literary tradition abides.

—Edwin Newman, *Strictly Speaking*

mycterism [*mik′tə·riz″əm*] *n.* Derision or sarcasm that is somewhat veiled; subtle or partly concealed gibe.

mystagogue See special entry BOOKISH APPELLATIONS, p. 406.

myth *n.* An enduring story of unknown origin but certain cultural significance or overtones, typically concerning deities, superhumans, and a drama of creation, transformation, victory, etc.; the realm of such stories; invented, imagined, or unreal story; fallacious belief or notion. *Adj.* mythic, mythical; *adv.* mythically; *n.* mythology; *v.* mythicize, mythify.

How humiliating it would be now if one were, say, an earnest left-philistine like Harvey Swados or Herbert Gold to grant that the mythic "we" of the declining fifties was constituted by a no-talent novelist called Jack Kerouac and his friends.

—Leslie Fiedler, *The Collected Essays of Leslie Fiedler*

N

name-calling   See special entry PROPAGANDA DEVICES, p. 380.

name-dropping *n.*   Vain mention of well-known or prestigious people to impress others. *N.* name-dropper; *v.* name-drop.

> Famous television names—from Rona Barrett to Marvin Hamlisch—are worked slavishly into what seems like every line of his script, for the sole purpose of idle name-dropping.
> —Frank Rich, *The New York Times*

narration *n.*   The telling or sequential detailing of a story, whether real or fictional, as by an author or through a character; factual or imaginative recounting; running commentary, as for a documentary film. *Adj.* narrational; *n.* narrator; *v.* narrate.

> Avant-garde methods of narration did not interest him either.
> —Richard Ellmann, *James Joyce*

narrative *n.*   Discourse in the form of a telling or describing of sequential events, or the expressive continuity of a story; related account; recitation; story-telling. *Adj.* narrative; *adv.* narratively.

> All right, we come next to the stage in your narrative where your folks have moved to a cotton plantation in Dixie.
> —S. J. Perelman, *The Last Laugh*

natter *v. Chiefly British*   To chatter.

naturalistic *adj.*   Describing writing presented as dispassionate or scientific observation of life, and implying immutable natural laws of cause and effect and human instinct and denying the supernatural; starkly realistic, with a nonidealized, often pessimistic or coarse depiction of human existence. *Adv.* naturalistically; *n.* naturalism, naturalist.

> In doing this, he manages to create a convincing world, delineating in quick strokes of naturalism what life is like amid the burned-out lots and after-hours joints of the South Bronx.
> —Michiko Kakutani, *The New York Times*

naturalized word   See BORROWING.

nay-saying *n.* A denying, refusal, or protest; negative or adverse response; rejection; reflexive pessimism or defeatism. *Adj.* naysaying; *n.* nay-sayer; *v.* naysay.

Among those who abhor the trend toward thumbs-up-thumbs-down criticism is Stanley Kauffmann, who wrote . . . "For many American decades, approximately since the heyday of Mencken, the chief hallmark of critics on 'journals of opinion' and quarterlies, has been naysaying." —John English, *Criticizing the Critics*

needled lead A newspaper lead that purposely overstates or exaggerates the truth of its story and hence is misleading.

In his effort to get the maximum punch in his lead, the overzealous reporter may "needle" the opening. That is, he lets the lead overreach the story.
—Floyd K. Baskette and Jack Z. Sissors, *The Art of Editing*

needless quotation marks See special entry JOURNALISTIC AND EVASION ATTRIBUTION, p. 379.

Negroism *n.* A word, phrase, or manner of expression distinctive or thought to be distinctive of Negro speechways.

By the nineteenth century, at any rate, Southern observers regarded expressions like *to sorta palaver on,* "to go on talking," as typical Negroisms. —J. L. Dillard, *All-American English*

neologism *n.* A newly coined word or phrase, or a novel expression in increasing usage (as contrasted with a nonce word); a new meaning for an old word. *Adj.* neological, neologistic; *n.* neology, neologist, neologian; *v.* neologize.

He landed in lexicography footnotes first, with an appendix to his M.A. thesis—listing neologisms committed by English romantic poets. —Israel Shenker, *Harmless Drudges*

nervus probandi [*ner'vəs prō·ban'dī"*] The strong point of the proving: crux of the argument; central issue or piece of evidence.

New Journalism Journalism that employs the techniques of fiction, generally reportage that is unconventional and distinctively personal, is written in a lively, idiosyncratic style, and that often involves sources or characters that are composites or probing interviews that may be partly fabricated. Also PARAJOURNALISM.

This article was by no means like a short story, despite the use of scenes and dialogue. I wasn't thinking about that at all. It is hard to

say what it was like. It was a garage sale, that piece . . . vignettes,
odds and ends of scholarship, bits of memoir, short bursts of sociology, apostrophes, epithets, moans, cackles, anything that came into
my head, much of it thrown together in a rough and awkward way.
That was its virtue. It showed me the possibility of there being something "new" in journalism.   —Tom Wolfe, *The New Journalism*

newsbreak *n.*   A newsworthy event or sudden development in
news; brief news item; quotation used as a filler in a column,
often one that is humorous because of an error in writing.

news hole   Space reserved for news in a newspaper, as opposed
to that for advertising.

newspaperese *n.*   See JOURNALESE.

Newspeak *n.*   From George Orwell's *1984,* simplistic state propagandistic language to subvert thought and manipulate public
opinion, and that changes in meaning to accommodate shifts in
the government's policies, esp. through use of labels; deceptive, false, or ambiguous communication as a strategy; empty
vogue idiom.
    . . . Christopher Reed declared that psychobabble is "the Newspeak
of our age—puerile pap, specious speech, yet a dangerously pretentious nonsense talk which one day could engulf us all."
                —David Lodge, in *The State of the Language*

news point sentence   In journalism, a sentence that summarizes
the whole story.

news release   See PRESS RELEASE.

Newsthink *n.*   Arthur Herzog's term for the vested interest of the
news media in creating news and for the means sometimes used
to that end, including exaggeration, misquotation, and "tag-
ging, trending, and countertrending"; the journalistic imperative.

newsworthy *adj.*   Worthy of journalistic coverage; important or
interesting enough for public readership. *N.* newsworthiness.

nickname *n.*   A descriptive name used in addition to or instead of
the actual name of a person, place, or thing; shortened or familiar form of a proper name. *V.* nickname.
    But of all the team nicknames in American sports, one defied theft. It
was also the best, and it belonged to the minor league hockey team
known as the Macon Whoopees.
                —Dave Anderson, *The New York Times*

nihil ad rem [*ni'hil ad rem'*] Nothing to the matter: not pertinent; irrelevant.

nihil obstat [*ni'hil ob'stat"*] Nothing stands in the way: in Roman Catholicism, certification by an examining censor that a book contains nothing contrary to church doctrine in faith and morals; seal of approval.

Raskin, Bernstein, and Adams, my sources say, had the full support of the *Times*'s managing editor, Turner Catledge, but what I find almost unbelievable is that Raskin's story had the *nihil obstat* of his publishers. I doff my bowler. —A. J. Liebling, *The Press*

nodus [*nō'dəs*] *n.* A crucial or difficult point. *Pl.* nodi. See also QUIDDITY.

nom de guerre [*nom də gâr*] A pen name or alias; pseudonym.

Harry Argonaut wasn't his real name. It was his nom de plume or, more accurately, his nom de guerre.

—Irwin Shaw, "Small Saturday"

nom de plume [*nom də plōōm*] See PEN NAME.

nomenclature *n.* A system of names for designating the things or member elements of a particular science, field, or discipline; categorical labeling; terminology; list or set of names. *Adj.* nomenclative, nomenclatorial, nomenclatural; *adv.* nomenclatorially, nomenclaturally.

Nailles claimed not to be a superstitious man but he did believe in the mysterious power of nomenclature. He believed, for example, that people named John and Mary never divorced.

—John Cheever, *Bullet Park*

nomic spelling [*nom'ik*] Conventional spelling, as distinguished from phonetic spelling. Also HETERIC SPELLING.

nominative See special entry GRAMMAR ADJECTIVES, p. 400.

nonbook *n.* A book of scant literary or lasting merit, such as a hastily compiled biography for fans of a frivolous humor book published to exploit a current popular fascination or trend.

Mr. Fadiman offers his opinion on the difference betwen real books, which assume a certain seriousness, and non-books, such as Jane Fonda's exercise lessons, in which "the little they have to say could be contained in a pamphlet."

—John J. O'Connor, *The New York Times*

nonce word A word devised for one occasion or publication and usually short-lived, as contrasted with a neologism; makeshift or convenient term, such as one invented by a novelist for a special usage or meaning.

non est disputandum [*nōn est dis″ p(y)ōō·tän′dəm*] It is not to be disputed.

nonfiction *n.* Prose other than novels and short stories such as books about science or nature, biography, hobbies, and history; bookstore stock exclusive of fiction, drama, and poetry.

She extolled the uses of reading nonfiction, which could teach such practical things as "how to make love" or "how to be a hooker," and which sounded rather like a curriculum based on the collected works of Gail Sheehy.   —John Simon, *Paradigms Lost*

nonliterate *adj.* Having no written language or written form; not orthographic.

nonpattern word See special entry WORD-GAME WORDS, p. 396.

non possumus [*non pos′ ə·məs*] A statement of inability to do something. *Pl.* non possumes.

nonrestrictive *adj.* Denoting a modifying or descriptive clause, phrase, or term that is not essential to the sentence's fundamental meaning and that hence is usually set off by commas; subordinate or extrinsic to the main thought; not dependent on a referent; parenthetical.

"There's also a grammar error," it went on. "You can't say, 'by a rising tide of mediocrity that threatens our very future.' What they have constructed is a sentence with a nonrestrictive clause. You can't start a nonrestrictive clause with 'that.' You have to start it with a 'which.' If they weren't such mediocre grammarians they would have written 'a rising tide of mediocrity which threatens our very future.' "
—Russell Baker, *The New York Times*

nonsense *n.* Language that makes no sense or that is empty or incomprehensible in its ideas; incoherence or absurdity; worthless or false communication; humbug; something trifling or irritating. *Adj.* nonsensical; *adv.* nonsensically; *n.* nonsensicality, nonsensicalness.

There is a kind of nonsense that isn't really nonsense, it's just phrased that way: "Matched stereo speakers which are unmatched."
—Arthur Herzog, *The B.S. Factor*

nonsense word A meaningless word; word having no orthodox or definite derivation but sometimes a memorable or catchy quality and a suggestion of sense; bizarre coinage.

When sending important coded messages it was the custom in the United States Navy to preface crucial details with nonsense words and to close with others.   —James Michener, *Space*

nonsentence *n.* An expression that is not a complete sentence; fragment or minor sentence.

Mr. Kleinfield also tries to describe everybody, often in staccato nonsentences ("Glasses. Short brown hair, plastered down. A blue striped suit, white shirt, red and blue tie."), and this he shouldn't do.
     —Martin Mayer, *The New York Times*

non sequitur [*non sek′wi·tŏŏr″*] A sentence posing a false connection between its clauses or elements—logically, an inference that does not follow from the premise—often because of the writer's desire to compress information; a statement that does not follow logically; an irrelevancy or false conclusion; nonplussing, unanswerable statement.

A single page is impressive, two are "stimulating," five raise serious doubts, ten confirm them, and long before the hardy reader has staggered to page 359 the accumulation of contradictions, nonsequiturs . . . and chronic rhetorical vagueness has numbed him to the insights. . . .   —Dwight Macdonald, *McLuhan Hot & Cool*

non serviam [*nōn ser′vē·äm*] I will not serve: an assertion or refusal to accept or submit; statement of demurral or defiance; objection, protest, or renunciation.

Buckle responds to this with an admirable *non serviam* hurled at the collective ignorance of the unwashed. . . .   —John Simon, *Esquire*

nonsexist English English that is free of or consciously avoids presumption of gender in its point of view or its generalizations, and esp. of male gender, notably by use of generic ("human") words and female pronouns.

Non-U *adj.* Non-upper class: characteristic of the speech and manners of English people not belonging to the educated upper class; using or involving unlearned, unprestigious, or common speech.

"Gallus" is another of these widespread words, splendidly and aggressively Non-U, but as rightfully and naturally part of the English language as fish and chips is part of the English diet.
—John Moore, *You English Words*

nonword *n.* A dubious or infelicitous neologism; questionable coinage.

I wonder whether his argument isn't so much against Romanticism as it is against godlessness. And I wish he wouldn't use nonwords such as "cloudification."   —John Leonard, *The New York Times*

Normanism *n.* A Norman word of expression, or an English word derived from Norman French, e.g., "noble," as contrasted with an Anglo-Saxonism.

nosism [*nō′siz″əm*] *n.* Use of "we" in speaking of oneself; conceit or self-exaltation by a group. *N.* nosist. See also ILLEISM, TUISM.

The love of our own is an elementary form of narcissism or nosism, and forms the most powerful ingredient in the love of family and country. . . .   —Noah Jacobs, *Naming-Day in Eden*

notabilia *n.* Things worth noting.

notandum *n.* A thing to be noted. *Pl.* notanda, notandums.

nothing-but fallacy See GENETIC FALLACY.

nothosonomia [*nō″thō·sə·nō′mē·ə*] *n.* Calling someone a bastard.

notice *n.* A written or printed announcement; a formal notification, statement of intent, or warning; published informative or critical review or mention of a play, book, etc., esp. an advance report for the public.

I am distressed, because my first novel, *Proud Emetic*, has been coolly received by the critics. Its one favorable notice, in the *Times*, was vitiated by the last sentence, which called the book "a miasma of asinine clichés unrivalled in Western letters."
—Woody Allen, *Side Effects*

not un- formation George Orwell's term for the mannered use of a double negative or "not un-" expression rather than a straightforward declarative statement; litotes.

One can cure oneself of the *not un-* formation by memorizing this sentence: *A not unblack dog was chasing a not unsmall rabbit across a not ungreen field.*
—George Orwell, "Politics and the English Language"

noun-banging *n.* The excessive clustering of nouns, or the stringing together of nouns attributively before a noun subject or object, esp. of abstract words in bureaucratic jargon, e.g., "missile guidance center personnel office equipment maintenance" (apparently coined by Arnold Lazarus, Andrew MacLeish, and H. Wendell Smith in *Modern English*, 1971). Also NOUN PLAGUE, NOUNSPEAK.

noun plague See NOUN-BANGING.

nouns of assemblage See VENEREAL NOUN.

nounspeak See NOUN-BANGING.

nouveau roman See ANTI-NOVEL.

novel *n.* A work of prose fiction, usually an extended narrative but often idiosyncratic in structure, that tells a story or uses incident and setting to dramatize human experience and individual character, whether through imagination, re-creation of real-life existence, intricate or rich plot, the author's particular vision or persona, or all of these; the genre of this type of prose writing. *Adj.* novelistic; *adv.* novelistically; *v.* novelize.

At this late date—partly due to the New Journalism itself—it's hard to explain what an American dream the ideas of writing a novel was in the 1940s, the 1950s, and right into the early 1960s. The Novel was no mere literary form. It was a psychological phenomenon. It was a cortical fever. It belonged in the glossary to *A General Introduction to Psychoanalysis*, somewhere between Narcissism and Obsessional Neuroses. —Tom Wolfe, *The New Journalism*

novelese *n.* H. W. Fowler's term for stock, long deflated phrases used by young writers because they remember such expressions as having stirred them emotionally with their earlier reading of novels; trite fictional writing.

novelette *n. British* A work of light, popular fiction, esp. a sentimental romance novel; novella.

. . . in English the word for short novel is novelette, which quickly became pejorative, meaning a rather cheap love story and giving rise

to the damning adjective "novelettish" before passing out of use altogether. Nobody talks of novelettes any more.
— Mary McCarthy, *New York Review of Books*

novelization *n.*   The transforming of a story, play, event, or work of nonfiction into a novel, or an example thereof. *V.* novelize.

As Washington reporters, both Mr. Wise and Mr. Szulc wrote about government secrecy, espionage, international terrorism and the Central Intelligence Agency. "A lot of that material lends itself beautifully to novelization," said Mr. Wise.
— Barbara Gamarekian, *The New York Times*

novella *n.*   A prose narrative that is relatively brief and has a compressed plot (often focused on a single event or conflict) and circumscribed setting, esp. a tale with an illustrative or satiric intent or a moral; long short story or a short novel. *Pl.* novellas, novelle. See also CONTE.

His latest book, *Breakfast at Tiffany's,* is a collection of a short novel or, if you wish, a long short story (I promised my mother I would never use that wretched word "novella") and several stories.
— Dorothy Parker, *The Portable Dorothy Parker*

nuance *n.*   A slight or subtle distinction or expressive variation; shade or nicety of meaning; overtone; connotation.

To be sure, a less idiosyncratic writer would have softened his interpretation, introduced more nuances, perhaps shown more compassion.   — Peter L. Berger, *The New York Times*

nudis verbis [*nōō'dis ver'bis*]   In naked word.

O

oath *n.*   A solemn avowal, with God or somebody venerated as a witness, that one is speaking the truth, will carry out something intended, etc.; sworn declaration that what one says or will say is true; the actual form of words of a statement of attestation or promise; swearword, esp. one profaning God.

Then Don Severo began to bang the crude wooden table, and each phrase of his discourse, emphasized with disgraceful oaths, was underlined by thwacks of his whip on the table, the other pieces of furniture, and the door. . . .
—B. Traven, *The Rebellion of the Hanged*

obelize *v.*   To note (with a ÷ or × mark) as being doubtful or spurious. *N.* obelism. Also ATHETIZE.

It is out of exasperation with Nabokov's verbal excesses that Wilson, in attacking his former friend's translation of *Eugene Onegin* in his notorious polemic against that work in the *New York Review of Books* (July 15, 1965), wrote about "my departures from the 'literal,' which have been obelized by Mr. Nabokov (I hope he has to look up that word). . . ." I doubt, though, whether Nabokov had to, but *you* might want to do so.   —John Simon, *Paradigms Lost*

obfuscation *n.*   Making obscure, difficult, or complex, often deliberately and pretentiously; unclear technical language; bewilderingly turgid or high-flown pedantry or jargon. *Adj.* obfuscatory; *n.* obfuscator; *v.* obfuscate.

The present authors are not in these respects typical sociologists for they have a style of obfuscation wholly their own.
—P. B. Medawar, *New York Review of Books*

obiter dictum [ō' bi·tər dik'təm]   An opinion expressed incidentally by a judge and thus not legally binding; incidental observation or remark; author's aside. *Pl.* obiter dicta.

Both profess belief in the deep wisdom of the uncorrupted common people, although Maistre's mordant *obiter dicta* about the hopeless barbarism, venality and ignorance of the Russians cannot have been to Tolstoy's taste, if indeed he ever read them.
—Isaiah Berlin, *The Hedgehog and the Fox*

obiter scriptum [ō′ bi·tər skrip′təm]   Something written by happenstance or off-handedly; an incidental composition. *Pl.* obiter scripta.

objective correlative   T. S. Eliot's term for a situation or chain of events that will unfailingly evoke a particular or proportionate emotional response because of its sensory effect on a viewer or reader, and hence a formula for artists; a factual or structural circumstance having an inescapable, dramatic subjective effect.

With Hemingway, on the other hand, the objective correlatives are not so much inserted and adapted as observed and encompassed.
                                                        —Carlos Baker, *Hemingway*

object language   A language that addresses or refers only to specific things apart from itself and thus is not self-referring, that is, does not discuss its own vocabulary, grammar, etc.; the language described by a metalanguage (contrasted with metalanguage).

object-speak *n.*   William Lambdin's term for impersonal jargon whereby objects or abstractions seemingly communicate or otherwise act like people, as through indirect or collective phrasings, e.g., "Our government has the right to lie if it wants to," "A Message from the Desk Of."

objurgation *n.*   An earnest denunciation, rebuke, or scolding; harsh criticism. *Adj.* objurgatory, objurgative; *adv.* objurgatorily; *n.* objurgator; *v.* objurgate.

Macdonald . . . had even agreed to edit my work-in-progress. The chapters I sent him came back marked up like freshman themes. His challenges, objurgations, rebukes—and occasional praise—defaced every page.   —James Atlas, *The Atlantic*

obloquy *n.*   The state of bad repute borne by one being harshly criticized; abusive condemnation, esp. personal defamation. *Adj.* obloquial, obloquious.

Typically he takes no credit whatever for the nine months of jail and fifteen years of obloquy that followed; the unfriendly witnesses thought they would win, he explains simply.
                        —Wilfrid Sheed, *The Good Word and Other Words*

obnubilation [ob·n(y)ōō″bə·lā′shən] *n.*   Beclouding or obscuring; obfuscation. *V.* obnubilate.

By dint of referring to . . . "the interpersonal resentment factor" for both an old grudge and the trivial friction of daily life, we have taught people the art of—let us be pedantic too—*reifying and obnubilating.* . . . —Jacques Barzun, *The House of Intellect*

obscenity *n.* Offensiveness to taste, modesty, or morals; abhorrent language; an unsavory or lewd thing, expression, fact, act, etc. *Adj.* obscene; *adv.* obscenely.

Now he was prosperous, thanks mostly to his powers of persuading his lawyers and printers to let him publish increasingly obscene American authors. —John Updike, *Bech: A Book*

obscurantism *n.* Hindering the spread of knowledge, or obscuring information or truth from the public; deliberate abstruseness, as in pedantic, jargonistic writing; obfuscation. *Adj.* obscurant, obscurantic, obscurantist.

Such sesquipedality is grandoise and obscurantist unless it is put to comic use; even then, however, it works only if you can sneak in an explanation and so keep your readers or listeners.
—John Simon, *Paradigms Lost*

obscurum per obscurius [əb·skyo͞or'əm per əb·skyo͞or'ē·əs] (Explaining) the obscure by means of the more obscure. See also IGNOTUM PER IGNOTIUS.

Conferring is an act, but an unintelligible one; conferring power, acquiring it, using it, is not at all like eating or drinking or thinking or walking. We remain in the dark: *obscurum per obscurius.*
—Isaiah Berlin, *The Hedgehog and the Fox*

Occam's razor, Ockham's razor The principle of economy formulated by William of Occam, holding that theories, terms, concepts, etc., ought not be unnecessarily multiplied and that the simpler explanation is preferable to the more complex.

And such is the Occam's Razor that Professor Fussell wields to surprise and provoke us in his multileveled examination of British travel literature. . . . —Christopher Lehmann-Haupt, *The New York Times*

odium aestheticum [ō'dē·əm es·thet'i·kəm] The bitterness of aesthetical controversy.

odium scholasticum [ō'dē·əm skə·las'ti·kəm] Acrimony between scholars or pedants; academic quibbling.

odium theologicum [ō'dē·əm thē"ə·loj'i·kəm] Bitter hatred between rival theologians.

The kind of language Lenin employed, with its metaphors of the jungle and the farmyard and its brutal refusal to make the smallest effort of human understanding, recalls the *odium theologicum* which poisoned Christian disputes about the Trinity in the sixth and seventh centuries, or the Eucharist in the sixteenth.

—Paul Johnson, *Modern Times*

oeuvre [*oe'vr*(ə)] *n.* The complete body of work of an artist, composer, or writer; lifetime artistic accomplishment; single artistic work.

He was driven to create an oeuvre by a terrible urgency that pushed like an unseasonable tide into the coves of his imagination to flush out material that should have had more time to develop.

—Hilary Masters, *Last Stands*

officese *n.* See COMMERCIALESE.

officialese *n.* Official or bureaucratic jargon; gobbledygook.

Theirs, however, is often the worst officialese, by a two-fold technique: first, their spokesmen take on polysyllables as Laocoon and his boys took on the serpents, reluctantly and to their own throttling. . . .   —Basil Cottle, *The Plight of English*

off-the-cuff *adj.* Spoken extemporaneously or casually; ad-lib.

As one remedy, the Reagan high command decided to assign a top-level political adviser to curb the former California Governor's penchant for off-the-cuff remarks on the stump and to help screen his speeches for comments that might stir controversy.

—Hedrick Smith, *The New York Times*

off the record *adj.* Said or answered in confidence and not for publication; discreetly personal rather than official.

olet lucernam [*ō'let lōō·ker'näm*] It smells of the lamp: describing something written that is belabored or overwrought. See also LUCUBRATION.

omniana [*om"nē·an'ə*] *n. pl.* Varied bits of information; miscellaneous facts.

omnibus word See COVERING WORD.

omnilegent [*om·nil'ə·jənt*] *adj.* Reading or having read everything; having encyclopedic curiosity and knowledge.

omphalopsychites [*om"fə·lō·sī'kīts"*] *n.* H. L. Mencken's term for literary Anglophiles who wish American English to emulate or ape British English.

on-dit [*ōn·dē*] *n.* An unsubstantiated report, rumor or piece of gossip.

one-liner *n.* A brief joke or witticism, esp. a wry line of dialogue or patter.

The face Mr. Galbraith chooses to wear, as in his previous works, is that of the wry, detached observer, who can be depended upon to come up with a precise, deflating one-liner that will combine wit with seriousness—and who knows just how apt his comments are.
—James Fallows, *The New York Times*

one-note *adj.* Belaboring one point, aspect, etc.; single-mindedly narrow.

Instead we get Broadway plays that imitate the real junk of prime time—namely, those situation comedies that are tied to one principal set, three or four major one-note characters, and toilet and jiggle jokes. —Frank Rich, *The New York Times*

onomastic [*on"ə·mas'tik*] *adj.* Pertaining to a proper name or names. *N.* onomastics, onomatology.

The Amerindians gave names to all prominent aspects of the continents they filled, in most instances many names, in what may have been the most extensive onomastic orgy of all time.
—Charlton Laird, *Language in America*

onomatomaniac See special entry BOOKISH APPELLATIONS, p. 406.

onomatopoeia [*on"ə·mat"ə·pē'ə*] *n.* The forming of or use of a word that imitates in sound what it denotes; use of imitative or echoic words; echoic word. *Adj.* onomatopoeic, onomatopoeical, onomatopoetic, onomatopoeian; *adv.* onomatopoeically, onomatopoetically; *n.* onomatope, onomatopy.

onus probandi [*ō"nəs prō·ban'dī"*] The burden of proof.

open letter A published statement, often a summary exhortation or protest, in form addressed to a specific party but in effect a plea or advertisement to the public; proclamatory position paper.

. . . he and several other prominent Soviet sympathizers . . . had the ill luck to sign an uncritical open letter of all-out support for the USSR —Philip Nobile, *Intellectual Skywriting*

open punctuation   A style of minimal punctuation in sentences, free of commas where possible (contrasted with close punctuation).

opprobrium *n.*   Disgrace, shame, or ignominy; stigma or bad odor; disdainful reproach or scorn; animadversion. *Adj.* opprobrious; *adv.* opprobriously.

The thrill of seeing her, and knowing she knew, and knowing nobody else knew what they had so freely, and dirtily, and delightfully indulged in, less than six hours ago, turned out to be too much for our green lover despite his trying to trivialize it with the moral corrective of an opprobrious adverb.   —Vladimir Nabokov, *Ada*

opuscule [*ō·pus'kyōol*] *n.*   A minor composition of work. Also opusculum.

oracle *n.*   A shrine where deities were consulted for prophecies or revelations; a priest or other interpreter of supernal pronouncements or prophecies; any person thought to be a source or medium of divine communication, or one revered for his profound knowledge, foresightful wisdom, or authoritative counsel; a divinely inspired utterance, esp. an enigmatic or ambiguously allegorical statement; a wise or purportedly wise opinion. *Adj.* oracular, oraculous; *adv.* oracularly; *n.* oracularity, oracularness.

Presumably he prefers the anonymous "it"; and likes to see an expression like "I think that . . ." replaced by "it is hypothesized . . .", which (apart from expurgating the dirty word "to think") ministers to the bureaucratic underling's predilection for submissive anonymity combined with oracular authority.
                    —Stanislav Andreski, *Social Sciences as Sorcery*

oracy *n.*   The ability to use and understand language that is oral; fluency in vocal speech; talk.

Our is a time that trusts talk; the "talk show" is a symbol of that trust. Now, a culture stressing "oracy," as against literacy, is not in itself dangerous. Risk ensues when oracy gains so much authority that a television interviewer whose mental powers are obviously not limitless can earn, or receive, $1 million a year. Risk ensues when in a modern society an oral culture is not checked or balanced by a culture of the responsible written word.
                    —Clifton Fadiman and James Howard, *Empty Pages*

oral *adj.* Expressed by or involving the mouth or vocalized speech; uttered or spoken rather than written; communicated from person to person. *Adv.* orally.

But by this time the poor Consul had already lost almost all capacity for telling the truth and his life had become a quixotic oral fiction.
—Malcolm Lowry, *Under the Volcano*

oration *n.* A formal and usually ceremonial public address; grandiloquent discourse; a carefully presented speech in a debating competition.

Volumes of past orations and addresses, however apposite or impressive at the time, soon hang like flags on a windless day.
—Malcolm Muggeridge, *Things Past*

oratio obliqua [*ô·rä′tē·ō ə·blē′kwə*] Indirect speech: reported speech, or relating by another that is modified and indirect; indirect discourse.

oratio recta [*ô·rä′tē·ō rek′tə*] Straight speech: actual or direct speech; verbatim discourse.

oratory *n.* The art of public speaking; rhetorical skill; eloquence; formal or stylized speech. *Adj.* oratorical; *adv.* oratorically; *n.* orator; *v.* orate.

Oratory pleased them, whatever its subject; sermons, educational lectures, political programmes, panegyrics of the dead or living, appeals for charity—all had the same soporific effect.
—Evelyn Waugh, *Scoop*

ore rotundo [*ō·re rō·tōon′dō*] With a round mouth: eloquently; with considered emphasis.

orismology [*ôr″iz·mol′ə·jē*] *n.* The science of defining or explaining technical terms. *Adj.* orismologic, orismological.

orismus See special entry RHETORIC TERMS, p. 404.

ornament *n.* A literary embellishment or nicety, such as a metaphor or foreign expression. *Adj.* ornamental.

A phrase, a situation suggests a whole train of striking or amusing ideas that fly off at a tangent, so to speak, from the round world on which the creator is at work; what an opportunity for saying something witty or profound! True, the ornament will be in the nature of a florid excrescence on the total work; but never mind.
—Aldous Huxley, *Collected Essays*

orotund *adj.* Forceful and resonant in sound or tone; sonorously grandiloquent; overblown or bombastic. *N.* orotundity.

> But he had learned his rôle of dignity now, and though he observed, "Dandy day, Shorty!" he was quick to follow it up unhesitatingly with an orotund "I trust that you have been able to enjoy the beauty of the vernal foliage in the country this week."
> —Sinclair Lewis, *Elmer Gantry*

orthography *n.* The writing of words with proper or accepted letters or symbols; the written or printed representation of speech sounds; the study or field of spelling or characters in a language; specific mode or system of spelling; correct spelling. *Adj.* orthographic, orthographical; *adv.* orthographically.

> In these records we find numerous misused words, neologisms, and phonetic spellings remarkable even in that relatively freewheeling orthographic age, spellings like *kow ceeper* and *piticler, pharme* and *elc, engiane* and *injun*.   —Mary Dohan, *Our Own Words*

orthology *n.* The correct use of words.

Orwellian *adj.* Comparable to the impersonal totalitarian society depicted in George Orwell's *1984*, esp. with respect to manipulative governmental name-calling or double-talk (Newspeak).

> In one weekend's reading in the professional literature this year, we encountered the word *purist* twenty-eight times. It is a catch-all curse, designed to bring anyone who questions the ideology of the new grammar or new English to his knees. It is used in the most Orwellian manner possible.   —Arn Tibbetts and Charlene Tibbetts,
> *What's Happening to American English?*

O.S.S. An obligatory sex scene; expected erotic passage in a conventional novel. See also PORNOPATCH.

otiose [*ō'shē·ōs"*] *adj.* Useless, ineffective, or weak; lame or flat in expressiveness; verbose. *Adj.* otiosely; *n.* otiosity, otioseness.

> The argument that we need "overly" for the negative statement "not overly" is otiose; we have "overmuch," "excessively," "very," and several others to choose from.   —John Simon, *Paradigms Lost*

overblown *adj.* Exaggerated or puffed up in style or self-importance; excessive; inflated or pretentious.

The sections of the book are called "Genesis," "Exodus," "The Promised Land" and "Kings," and the prose is often comparably overblown. —Janet Maslin, *The New York Times*

overline See special entry NEWSROOM HEADLINE JARGON, p. 386.

oversimplification *n.* Simplification that is so excessive or reductive that it distorts; too broad or facile analysis. *V.* oversimplify.

Mailer's novels, at least for me, personify the dilemma of novelists who are deeply concerned with history but dangerously oversimplify it; if they seem consumed by their interest in sex it is because they are always seeking some solution for "the times." —Alfred Kazin, in *Writing in America*

overstatement *n.* Statement in terms too strong or emphatic; excessive treatment; magnification or exaggeration. *V.* overstate.

Evelyn Waugh . . . wrote to Nancy Milford that "American polite vocabulary is very different from ours . . . [it] is pulverized between two stones, refinement and overstatement." —Israel Shenker, *Words and Their Masters*

over-the-roof head See SKYLINE HEAD under special entry NEWSROOM HEADLINE JARGON, p. 386.

over the transom See special entry BOOK PUBLISHING TERMS, p. 362.

over-title See SKYLINE HEAD under special entry NEWSROOM HEADLINE JARGON, p. 386.

overtone *n.* Implicit or secondary meaning; suggestion or intimation; vague implication; nuance.

One of my purposes was to listen, to hear speech, accent, speech rhythms, overtones and emphasis. For speech is so much more than words and sentences. —John Steinbeck, *Travels with Charley*

overwrite *v.* To write in an excessively elaborated, wordy, or strained way, as in overly detailed newswriting or flowery, pseudo-poetic prose; compose in earnest but belabored language.

William O'Rourke is enormously articulate. . . . So it is a mystery why Mr. O'Rourke has used his gifts to create a novel so constricted in its vision and so relentlessly overwritten. —David Quammen, *The New York Times*

oxymoron [*ok″si·môr′on″*] *n.* A pairing of incongruous or contradictory terms for a startling expressive effect, e.g. "an acute dullness." *Pl.* oxymora; *adj.* oxymoronic. Also ANTISYZYGY.

When it was first announced, John Ashbery's new book had a title— *Paradoxes and Oxymorons*—that called up Donne's *Paradoxes and Problems*. . . . Ashbery's witty variation placed propositional impossibility (paradox) next to figurative impossibility (oxymoron) to tell us that he was about to propose contradictions of life in the contradictions of rhetoric. An oxymoron . . . is . . . the show-off among figures of speech.   —Helen Vendler, *New York Review of Books*

P

pabulum *n.* Mindlessly unnourishing, oversimplified, obvious, or worthless ideas or writing; shallow drivel; pap.

At that rate he'd be able to talk for eleven and a half minutes as his notes now stood. Some sort of pabulum for a further forty-eight and a half minutes was evidently required, with perhaps another minute off for being introduced to the audience, another minute for water-drinking, coughing, and page-turning, and nothing for applause or curtain calls. —Kingsley Amis, *Lucky Jim*

pace [*pā′sē*] *prep.* With all due respect to: despite the claims of; notwithstanding.

My own feeling (*pace* Balthazar) is that Justine became slowly aware of something hidden in the character of this solitary endearing long-suffering man; namely a jealousy all the more terrible and indeed dangerous for never allowing itself any outlet.
—Lawrence Durrell, *Balthazar*

package See special entry BOOK PUBLISHING TERMS, p. 362.

padding *n.* Deliberate and contrived wordiness, esp. turgid explication or secondary information added for length or to divert from the weakness of one's case or lack of proper research; verbosity; filler; deadwood. *V.* pad.

Really, there is a lot of crude oil in "The Devil's Alternative," Frederick Forsyth's new novel, and more plot than any typewriter deserves, and so much padding that I am, in my cell, brain-mushy from banging my head against pointless digressions.
—John Leonard, *The New York Times*

paean [*pē′ən*] *n.* A joyous hymn or song, as of praise, victory, or thanksgiving; fervent laudation or tribute; rhapsody.

From "Legal Tender" (a juiced-up rocker about the pleasures of counterfeiting) to "Butter Bean" (a paean to vegetable love), the album's first side is sweeter than Nehi Grape, more fun than daytime TV. —D. D. Guttenplan, *Vanity Fair*

page-turner *n.* An enthralling book, esp. a work of popular formula fiction, such as a rags-to-riches novel or a thriller.

"The Englishman's Daughter," a suspense novel by Peter Evans, is not a "page-turner." No good novel ever is. If a book is worth anything at all, it makes you reluctant to turn the pages. It holds you, encourages you to hang around and relish a scene or mull over an idea.　　　　　—Anatole Broyard, *The New York Times*

paired opposites　See MERISM.

pair isogram　See special entry WORD-GAME WORDS, p. 396.

pairs and snares　See CATCHFOOLS.

palaver *n.*　A usually protracted negotiation or conference; talk, esp. idle, lengthy, or beguiling conversation; cajolery. *Adj.* palaverous; *n.* palaverer; *v.* palaver.

I'm reading it over, line by line, standing by the stones. It sounds nutty to me, all this palaver about life and death and things happening so fast. Nothing is happening that I can see, except the usual calamities on the front page.　　　　　—Henry Miller, *Tropic of Cancer*

palilogy, palillogy *n.*　Repetition of a word for emphasis, esp. immediate repetition.

palindrome　See special entry WORD-GAME WORDS, p. 396.

palinode *n.*　A poem or song counterbalancing or retracting what is expressed in an earlier poem; a written retraction. *Adj.* palinodial; *n.* palinodist.

Then, crazedly reversing himself: "You don't owe me nothin'. Leave me alone!" And then, in a truly abject palinode: "Don't leave me alone! Don't leave me! *Stay!*"　　　　　—John Simon, *Vanity Fair*

palter *v.*　To talk insincerely, evasively, or equivocally; prevaricate; act in a trifling or capricious way; bargain or haggle. *N.* palterer.

pamphlet *n.*　A small, thin, usually cheaply bound publication having a paper cover, esp. one dealing with a special subject or current issue; controversial or doctrinaire treatise, esp. a political argument; tract. *Adj.* pamphletary; *v.* pamphletize.

For all the studies it cites, "The Cinderella Complex" is not a social science document. It is a political pamphlet, designed to shift the burden of responsibility for women's low status from systematic discrimination in the labor market to women themselves.　　　　　—Carol Tavris, *The New York Times*

pamphleteer *n.* A writer of pamphlets, esp. a zealous ideologue. *V.* pamphleteer.

The writing falls somewhere between huckster copy (paeans to the favored product, diatribes against all other brands and their venal or deluded purchasers) and ideological pamphleteering: denouncings, exhortations, code words, excommunications, programs, threats.
—Renata Adler, *New York Review of Books*

pan *n.* An emphatically negative or derogatory appraisal; unequivocally bad review (contrasted with rave). *V.* pan.

He had never been a good critic, because among other things, he could not pan a friend.
—Wilfrid Sheed, *The Good Word and Other Words*

panegyric *n.* A formal or elaborate tribute in writing or speech, usually extolling a person or a work; encomium. *Adj.* panegyrical, panegyric; *adv.* panegyrically; *v.* panegyrize.

The Marcuse obituary, characteristically, is less a panegyric than a critique. —Elinor Langer, *The New York Times*

pangram See special entry WORD-GAME WORDS, p. 396.

pap *n.* Insipid, simplistic ideas, argument, or substance, esp. obvious sentimental or moralistic talk or writing; reading matter that is infantile or obvious; valueless escapist entertainment.

paperback original See special entry BOOK PUBLISHING TERMS, p. 362.

parable *n.* An illustrative moral or religious story, usually brief and with generalized, simple characters and universal human application; telling or cautionary account.

I have never read a story better than *Endurance,* Alfred Lansing's account of the Shackleton expedition to Antarctica; but no one considers it literature. If Mailer had written it, might we not read the same text as a parable of something or other?
—Annie Dillard, *Living by Fiction*

paradiastole [*par"ə·dī·as'tə·lē*] *n.* The use of a softened or more positive word or phrasing for something suggesting stronger terms, whether euphemistically or ironically, e.g., describing an extremely drunk person as "unsure of footing" or a person's uncontrolled rage as "spirited behavior"; gentle circumlocution or understatement. See also MEIOSIS.

paradigm *n.*   An exemplary pattern or model; a list for reference of the various inflectional forms of a word; declension or conjugation. *Pl.* paradigms, paradigmata; *adj.* paradigmatic, paradigmatical; *adv.* paradigmatically.

This last satirical flourish, aimed at the whole mystique of corporation capitalism, is embodied in the fantastic adventures of Milo Minderbinder, the company mess officer, and a paradigm of good natured Jonsonian cupidity.   —Robert Brustein, in *The Critic as Artist*

paradigma   See special entry RHETORIC TERMS, p. 404.

paradigmatic *adj.*   By grammatical example or form; inflectional; determining the meaning of a word apart from a prose context, that is, in terms of its individual forms (declensions or conjugations) or how it differs from other individual words (contrasted with syntagmatic).

paradox *n.*   An evidently self-contradictory statement that nonetheless may be true, valid, or expressive in its own way; logical absurdity; any situation, action, or person that is inexplicably inconsistent or unresolved; behavioral riddle. *Adj.* paradoxical, paradoxal, paradoxial, paradoxic; *adv.* paradoxically; *n.* paradoxicality, paradoxicalness, paradoxology.

I knew, for one, that the brother-killer had put on the Shaper's idea of the hero like a merry mask, had seen it torn away, and was now reduced to what he was: a thinking animal stripped naked of former illusions, stubbornly living on, ashamed and meaningless, because killing himself would be, like his life, unheroic. It was a paradox nothing could resolve but a murderous snicker.
                                              —John Gardner, *Grendel*

paragoge [*par'ə·gō"jē*]   See CURTAILMENT under special entry WORD-GAME WORDS, p. 395.

paragram *n.*   A pun made by changing a letter in a word or name, esp. its initial letter, a "himpoverished her," "an XXX-ploitation movie."

parajournalism *n.*   See NEW JOURNALISM.

paraleipsis [*par"ə·līp'sis*] *n.*   See PRETERMISSION.

paralinguistic *adj.*   Relating to communicational factors that complement language, such as tone of voice, gestures, facial expressions, and speech tempo; kinesic. *N.* paralinguistics.

Such ostentatious taboo is usually accomplished by well-known paralinguistic features—qualifiers such as smirking, the arched eyebrow,
a slyness of manner.   —Allen Walker Read, *Verbatim*

paralipomena [*par″ə·li·pom′ə·nə*] *n., pl.* Secondary or incidental things not included in a work but added elsewhere or as a
supplement.

parallelism *n.* Structural correspondence of word and clause elements within a sentence for harmoniously equivalent or contrasting phrasing and rhythm; orderly, complementary syntax;
consistency in sentence arrangement.

paralogism [*pə·ral′ə·jiz″əm*] *n.* See FORMAL FALLACY.

paraphrase *n.* Rewording or recapitulating to express the same
meaning; a restatement in different words, as to clarify the
meaning of or to discuss when exact quotation is not possible;
a free or loose rendering of a line, passage, or text. *Adj.* para-
phrastic, paraphrastical; *adv.* paraphrastically; *n.* paraphrasis,
paraphraser; *v.* paraphrase.

As the American essayist Christian Boves said, paraphrasing Swift:
"There are few wild beasts more to be dreaded than a communicative
man having nothing to communicate."   —Bryan Griffin, *Harper's*

parasynesis [*păr″ə·sin′ə·sis*] *n.* The corruption of a word or
words owing to a misunderstanding of their elements, as ex-
emplified by folk etymology, e.g., "chaise lounge" instead of
"chaise longue." *Adj.* parasynetic.

parataxis *n.* Sentence style without connectives, and thus syntax
that is a series of simple clauses without conjunctions; coordinate rather than subordinate syntax (contrasted with hypotaxis). *Adj.* paratactic, paratactical; *adv.* paratactically; *n.*
parataxicism.

A related risk is run today by an American school of "deadpan"
writers who betray no sense of shock as they record the shocking
details of our own times, usually in a paratactic syntax which declines
to present or arrange the raw details of the narrative.
                                          —G. W. Turner, *Stylistics*

parciloquy [*pär·sil′ə·kwē*] *n.* Moderation in words; speaking little. Also BREVILOQUY, PAUCILOQUY.

parergon [*pa·rûr′gon″*] *n.* A subordinate or secondary piece of
writing, such as something done at one's leisure; a literary by-
work. *Pl.* parerga; see also OBITER SCRIPTUM.

Mr. Casaubon had adopted an immediate intention. there was to be a new *parergon,* a small monograph on some lately traced indications concerning the Egyptian mysteries whereby certain assertions of Warburton's could be corrected.   —George Eliot, *Middlemarch*

par exellence *adj.* Preeminently: to a supreme degree; beyond compare.

The title story, for example, is about a girl who lives with an old Eskimo man, a storyteller *par excellence.*
—N. Scott Momaday, *The New York Times*

parlance *n.* Manner of speaking; characteristic usage; idiom or vernacular; conversation; formal debate.

He also preferred the disciplinary anarchy of the river to the competitiveness of the cricket field, so he became, in Eton parlance, a "wet-bob" rather than a "dry-bob." He was strong but not skilled, both in rowing and swimming.   —Bernard Crick, *George Orwell*

parody *n.* The art of imitative ridicule; literary imitation of a work or author's writing that apes or exaggerates the particular traits of its model with ridicule or humor; stylistic satire. *Adj.* parodic, parodical, parodistic; *n.* parodist; *v.* parody.

That Miss Alther's second novel is not successful is partly because her first was: the parody, it seems, was published before its target.
—Mary Cantwell, *The New York Times*

paroemiology [pə·rē″mē·ol′ə·jē] *n.* The subject or coining of proverbs.

parole *n.* An individual's particular use of language (contrasted with langue); idiolect; word of honor or explicit promise; military password or watchword.

The other usage is that of "right" as a ubiquitous tag. . . . It is fundamentally expressive of doubt and fear, of so to speak hopeless *parole* in search of lost *langue.*   —John Fowles, *The Ebony Tower*

parolist [pə·rōl′ist] *n.* A person who uses affected words.

paronomasia [par″ə·nō·mā′zhə] *n.* Punning; a pun.

In short, he was Eveless, or to use the quaint paronomasia of a modern critic, "Adam missed his missus."
—Noah Jacobs, *Naming-Day in Eden*

paronym *n.* A word having the same derivation or root as another; similar word in a foreign language, or a cognate to a foreign word. *Adj.* paronymic, paronymous.

parrhesia [*pa·rē'zhə*] *n.* Boldness or frankness of speech; liberal expression.

parrot *v.* To repeat or imitate without necessarily understanding or without reflection; reiterate rotely or mechanically; slavishly adopt, as another's ideas or opinions. *N.* parrot.

Most of our plays, for all the light they throw on American life, might have been written by a Visagoth in the Year 1, while the others merely parrot the liberal prejudices of the audience or hide their meaning (if it is disturbing or controversial) under a mountain of allegory. —Robert Brustein, in *Writers in America*

parse *v.* To divide a sentence into its syntactic parts so as to understand their functional relationship; analyze grammatically. *Adj.* parsable; *adv.* parsably.

Few characters in British society novels of the day speak more formally, more elegantly, more parsably than Cooper's noble savages. . . . —Thomas Pyles, *Words and Ways of American English*

Parthian shot A critical or antagonistic comment made while departing or (as it were) retreating; valedictory reproof (after tactic of Parthian archers, who released their arrows while feigning retreat). Also PARTING SHOT.

particle *n.* An uninflected word or speech element having only an abstractly specifying, connective, or qualifying function in a sentence and including definite and indefinite articles, most conjunctions and prepositions, and certain verbs and adverbs; prefix or suffix.

To speak of an adverb as being an intransitive particle is heresy in terms of our Latinized grammar books—but it is a very sensible way to describe how the English language works. —Jim Quinn, *American Tongue and Cheek*

parting shot See PARTHIAN SHOT.

parti pris [*pär·tē prē*] Side taken: a preconceived opinion; partiality or prejudice. *Pl.* partis pris; *adj.* partis pris.

The sexual *parti pris* that governs the evocation of the archaic in this fiction is anything but obscure. —Hilton Kramer, *The New York Times*

partitive See special entry GRAMMAR ADJECTIVES, p. 400.

part of speech   In grammar, one of the traditional classes used to designate words according to role or form and function within a sentence, in English including noun, pronoun, verb, adjective, adverb, conjunction, preposition, and interjection (and, to some grammarians, article).

pasquinade [*pas"kwə·nād'*] *n.*   An abusive or coarsely satirical anonymous comment inscribed or posted in a public place; scurrilous graffito; lampoon; satire. *N.* pasquil; pasquinader; *v.* pasquinade.

All that has appeared so far is Cyril Connolly's *From Oscar to Stalin* (represented under the title *Where Engles Fears to Tread*), a brilliant pasquinade of 1937 which, incidentally, provides a leper's squint into Cyril's own life as an undergraduate.
—Evelyn Waugh, *A Little Learning*

passim *adv.*   Here and there; throughout: applied to a word, phrase, or reference that recurs frequently in a book.

Yet *passim* there is the sense of frustration that, having escaped the middle-class world of childhood, he should find that this was indeed still his material.
—Wilfrid Sheed, *The Good Word and Other Words*

password *n.*   A secret word of entry or access; watchword; entree.

The Adult world seems to be some kind of secret society that has its own passwords, handclasps, and countersigns.
—Jean Shepherd, *In God We Trust, All Others Pay Cash*

pastiche *n.*   A literary work that draws on styles, formats, etc., of other sources and thus is eclectic and derivative, and often whimsical or irreverent (but not with humor as a primary intent); book or story made up of borrowings from other writers; hodgepodge; stylistic imitation of a writer or work; parody. *N.* pasticheur.

His novels were pastiches of the work of the best people of his time, a feat not to be disparaged, and in addition he possessed a gift for softening and debasing what he borrowed, so that many readers were charmed by the ease with which they could follow him.
—F. Scott Fitzgerald, *Tender Is the Night*

patavinity [*pat"ə·vin'ə·tē*] *n.*   Use of local or regional words; provincial diction or dialect.

pathetic fallacy   The ascribing of human traits and feelings to inanimate objects or nature, or the use of anthropomorphic images or metaphors. Also ANTHROPOPATHISM.

John Ruskin coined the name and a later writer, James Thurber, created our favorite example of the *pathetic fallacy* in a cartoon caption for *The New Yorker:* "It's a naive domestic Burgundy without any breeding, but I think you'll be amused at its presumption."
—William and Mary Morris,
Harper Dictionary of Contemporary Usage

pathopoeia [*path″ə·pē′ə*] *n.*   The arousing of passions through rhetoric; literary passage or scene written to arouse passionate feeling.

patois *n.*   A regional, usually subliterate parlance that differs from the standard form of the language; crude dialect, jargon of a group.

They danced gratefully, formally, to some song carried on in what must be the local patois, while no one paid any attention as long as they were together, and the children poured the family nickels steadily into the slot machines, walloping the handles down with regular crashes and troubling nobody with winning.
—Eudora Welty, "No Place for You, My Love"

patronym, patronymic *n.*   A name derived from that of one's father or a paternal ancestor, usually by addition of a suffix or prefix; surname. *Adj.* patronymic, patronymical; *adv.* patronymically.

In the Middle Ages Lindum Colum was the name of a town and a shire, and, corrupted to Lincoln, thus could be the name of anybody from those areas. It became the patronymic of a poor settler in Illinois, the name of a great president of the United States, and hence the name of all sorts of places throughout the western part of the country.   —Charlton Laird, *The Miracle of Language*

patter *n.*   Any glib or rapid-fire talk or routine monologue, such as that of a comic performer or auctioneer; specialized vernacular or argot; frivolous talk or chatter. *V.* patter.

The cheaper the crook, the gaudier the patter.
—Dashiell Hammett, *The Maltese Falcon*

patterned form   A word or idiom modeled on or inspired by another word, e.g., "viewership" (from "readership"), "single-entendre" (from "double-entendre"), "Gray Panther" (from "Black Panther"); imitative coinage. See also ABSTRACTED FORM, BOOSTED COINAGE.

pauciloquy *n.* See PARCILOQUY.

paucis verbis In few words.

pedaguese *n.* See EDUCANTO.

pedantic humor See POLYSYLLABIC HUMOR.

pedanticism, pedantism *n.* An unduly fine or niggling point, concern, or expression.

> . . . Laurence Urdang disagrees: " 'Data' used as a plural strikes me as a pedanticism." —William Safire, *On Language*

pedantry *n.* Finical adherence to bookish learning, details, or rules, esp. to display one's learning or to affect rigorous erudition; overconcern with formal, precise, and minor matters; narrow-mindedness; snobbish schoolmarmishness. *Adj.* pedantic; *adv.* pedantically; *n.* pedant.

> There are characters, such as Mrs. Gamp and Mrs. Malaprop, who add splendour to language by their very misuse of it; and not all the careful pedantry in the world has given it as much glory as one bewildered sentence of poor word-intoxicated Pistol when he said of the dying Falstaff "His heart is fracted and corroborate."
> —John Moore, *You English Words*

peg *n.* The central event, ingredient, or axis of a news story on which the journalist builds his or her written treatment; the reference in a news or feature story to its main source of justification; assumption or premise behind a speech or literary work.

> I was not the only reporter who talked regularly with Angleton, but I think I stuck with it longer than most, even though he rarely "leaked" any information that could serve as the peg upon which to hang a news story. —David C. Martin, *Wilderness of Mirrors*

pejoration *n.* The erosion or dilution of a word's integral meaning, hence semantic depreciation; development of a "worse" or less favorable meaning by a word, or the downgrading of a word by adding to it a particular suffix, etc., e.g., "poetaster" from "poet" (contrasted with melioration). *V.* pejorate.

Stevens avoids the possible vulgarity of a too particular word so that we may feel the pure impact of pejoration without the punch of a pejorative. ("It is the word *ratface* that hurts.")
—John Leonard, *The New York Times*

pejorative *n.* A derogatory word or phrase; disparaging expression. *Adj.* pejorative; *adv.* pejoratively.

While he avoids any pejorative reference to participants, he gives a fair picture of the vast real-estate caper accomplished under Robert Moses's juggernaut.
—Lincoln Kirstein, *The New York Review of Books*

penalty book See special entry BOOK PUBLISHING TERMS, p. 362.

Penguinize *v. British* To publish in paperback.

pen name A name used by an author other than his or her own. Also NOM DE PLUME, PSEUDONYM.

We drank coffee and shared the egg cookie. Esther put down her cup. "I can't believe that I'm sitting with you at this table. I read all your articles under all your pen names. You tell so much about yourself I have the feeling I've known you for years. Still, you are a riddle to me."
—Isaac Bashevis Singer, "The Cafeteria"

penny-a-line *adj. British* Cheap and inferior (writing or journalism). *N.* penny-a-liner (hack writer).

They did not demean themselves by showing much gratitude for the extraordinary generosity of the man who had been dismissed by his father as "a greengrocer" and a contemptible "penny-a-liner."
—V. S. Pritchett, *The Tale Bearers*

pensée [*pän·sā*] *n.* A thought, observation, or reflection expressed with lucid, literary cogency.

We are not talking here about the kind of notebook that is patently for public consumption, a structural conceit for binding together a series of graceful *pensées;* we are talking about something private, about bits of the mind's string too short to use, an indiscriminate and erractic assemblage with meaning only for its maker.
—Joan Didion, *Slouching Towards Bethlehem*

penster See special entry BOOKISH APPELLATIONS, p. 406.

Pentagonese *n.* The jargon of the U.S. military-industrial establishment, a bureaucratic and strategic gobbledygook characterized by technocratic words, military acronyms, and abstract euphemisms for the realities of weaponry, warfare, and death.

As *Newsweek* noted in 1967, nuclear weapons "unleashed a fallout of acronyms, neologisms, euphemisms and technical jargon," and the development of antiballistic missiles "has produced a second generation of Strangelovisms." Among the additions to Pentagonese: *megadeaths,* for millions of deaths; *credible deterrent,* a defense that needn't be effective as long as the enemy thinks it is; *preferential defense,* protecting some areas but not others; *rippled attack,* sending missiles in salvos to trick an enemy into using defensive missiles on the first few waves, leaving no defense for later waves.
—William Safire, *The New Language of Politics*

per contra [*pûr kon′trə*]   On the contrary; in contrast.

Per contra, the omission of panties was ignored by Ida Larivière, a bosomy woman of great and repulsive beauty (in nothing but corset and gartered stockings at the moment) who was not above making secret concessions to the heat of the dog-days herself; but in tender Ada's case the practice had deprecable effects.
—Vladimir Nabokov, *Ada*

periodic sentence   A sentence structured so that the sense or complete thought is suspended until the end, with intermediate phrases or clauses preceding the main, closing verb or object (contrasted with loose sentence).

I only had this one criticism to offer: As I sat back in the dim part of the room watching you stand on the stage beside the secretary with your papers, I could not avoid thinking of all the other lives which I had heard read out from that platform in sonorous, periodic sentences.   —John P. Marquand, *The Late George Apley*

period piece   An artistic or literary work distinctively depicting or evoking a particular historical era.

Dorothy Parker's original introduction to *Men, Women and Dogs* is itself a period piece, as enviable and unreachable as a face in a train window.   —Wilfrid Sheed, *The Good Word and Other Words*

period style   A prose style adopted to evoke or reflect a past era, as a formal, somewhat archaic style in a historical novel.

A "period" style can be cultivated with the expectation that the reader will recognize it only if the style is a recent one, as in Thackeray's *Henry Esmond* or John Fowles's *The French Lieutenant's Woman.*   —G. W. Turner, *Stylistics*

periphrasis [*pə·rif′rə·sis*] *n.*   The use of more words or of roundabout phrasing rather than straightforward language; circumlocution. *Adj.* periphrastic; *adv.* periphrastically; *n.* periphrase; *v.* periphrase.

Thus a war becomes "a war situation," two rival mobs are not fighting but "in a conflict situation," a firm losing money has "moved into a loss situation," partly due perhaps to having been "involved" (a related periphrastic word) "in strike situations."

—J. Enoch Powell, in *The State of the Language*

perissology *n.* Verbal superfluity; pleonasm or tautology.

Both quotation marks and adjectives may be omitted and the word itself repeated in its intensified or pregnant sense: What's what, Business is Business, Keep politics out of politics, There teachers and teachers, Coffee 10¢ but coffee, and the quaint perissology eggs is eggs (a corruption of the logical formula X = X).

—Noah Jacobs, *Naming-Day in Eden*

perlocutionary *adj.* Pertaining to or describing an utterance having a specific effect on another's feelings, thoughts, or behavior, including statements that sympathize, ridicule, persuade, frighten, etc. (contrasted with illocutionary and locutionary).

permissive *adj.* Tolerant or lenient; having a liberal, uncensorious attitude toward language usage and writing. *Adv.* permissively; *n.* permissiveness.

Dictionary buffs will find your work permissive, descriptive or prescriptive. Which shall it be?

—Israel Shenker, *Harmless Drudges*

peroration *n.* Climactic summary; a formal, forceful conclusion to a speech or argument; recapitulation; formal or rhetorical speech. *Adj.* perorational; *v.* perorate.

He went into the peroration. The year 2000 was coming. A great period of celebration and joy at being alive in America was ahead. "I see a day," he began to say, as Martin Luther King had once said, "I have a dream." —Norman Mailer, *Miami and the Siege of Chicago*

perpilocutionist See special entry BOOKISH APPELLATIONS, p. 406.

per se [*pûr sā'*] By or in itself; being so or such; intrinsically.

Colette's understanding of the male sex amounted to an amazing identification with man per se, to which was added her own uterine comprehension of women, more objective than feminine.

—Janet Flanner, *Janet Flanner's World*

persiflage [*pûr′sə·fläzh″*] *n*.   Banter that is a mixture of seriousness and flippancy, generally good-natured but often becoming
sardonic; light or frivolous raillery.

His hatred for sham literary posturing was profound, and in conversation he had a capacity for rough and bear-like persiflage that reminded at least one reader of Goldsmith's remark about Dr. Samuel
Johnson: "When his pistol misses fire, he knocks you down with the
butt end of it."   —Carlos Baker, *Hemingway*

persona *n*.   The conscious or self-conscious "mask" assumed by
a person: in literature, esp. narrative fiction, the distinctive
speaker or second-self adopted by an author or implicit in his
or her voice or narrator, which may be a story device. *Pl*.
personae.

His admirers might say that the persona created is self-confident,
resourceful and witty; his critics might say that it is arrogant, self-
indulgent, reckless and contradictory.
                            —Marcia Chambers, *The New York Times*

personalia *n*.   Personal details or anecdotes, such as reminiscences; biographical items.

personification *n*.   Giving human form or personal attributes to
something inanimate or abstract, as by using a divinity or allegorical character to represent a virtue; a rhetorical or imaginary
figure or representation having human qualities; incarnation or
embodiment. *Adj*. personificative; *v*. personify. Also PROSOPO-
POEIA.

By habitually talking of the nation as though it were a person with
thoughts, feelings and a will of its own, the rulers of a country legitimate their own powers. Personification leads easily to deification; and
where the nation is deified, its government . . . claims to give orders
by divine right and demands the unquestioning obedience due to a
god.   —Aldous Huxley, *Collected Essays*

petitio principii   See QUESTION-BEGGING.

pet name   An affectionate nickname, often a diminutive form of
another word.

When I say Garry I mean Sir Gareth. Garry was my private pet name
for him; it suggests that I had a deep affection for him, and that was
the case.
                —Mark Twain, *A Connecticut Yankee in King Arthur's Court*

pettifoggery *n.* Cunning fussiness over trivialities; foolish, obfuscating pettiness or chicanery; niggling or quibbling. *Adj.* pettifogging; *n.* pettifogger; *v.* pettifog.

What do we care for what (most of) the critics say? They (we know only too well) are not criticizing *us,* but, unconsciously, themselves. They skew their dreams into their comment, and blame us for not writing what they once wanted to. You we can trust, for you have looked at life largely and without pettifogging qualms.

—Christopher Morley, "The Perfect Reader"

phantom word See GHOST WORD.

phatic *adj.* Denoting speech or noises as a means of sharing feelings or establishing sociability rather than for the communication of ideas of information. *Adv.* phatically.

You would think, from the unexamined god-term Clarity has become, that students of prose had never heard of nonreferential language—emotional, phatic, symbolic, purely social.

—Richard Lanham, *Style*

philippic *n.* A denunciatory discourse or declamation; a bitter, acrimonious speech (from Demosthenes's orations against Philip of Macedonia in the fourth century *B.C.*).

But after a fairly spirited philippic comes Philip's dispiriting cop-out: "I'm afraid that, in spite of the efforts of the [Edwin] Newmans and [E. B.] Whites, all these little horrors are embedded in the language, along with 'like' for 'as,' and 'you know.' "

—John Simon, *Paradigms Lost*

philippize *v.* To speak or write under bribery or corrupt influence (from Greek word meaning "to be on Philip's side").

philodox See special entry BOOKISH APPELLATIONS, p. 407.

philology *n.* The study of language, its use in written records and literature, and its historical development, or of the role of speech in culture; historical or comparative linguistics; formerly, love of learning and letters; classical literary scholarship. *Adj.* philological, philologic; *adv.* philologically; *n.* philologist; *v.* philologize.

There was an ashtray on the table and Smiley set to work trying to read the writing round the edge. After much manipulation of the glass he came up with what the lapsed philologist in him described as the asterisk (or putative) form of the letters "A-C-H-T," but whether as a word in their own right—meaning "eight" or "attention," as well as certain other more remote concepts—for as four letters from a larger word, he could not tell.   —John le Carré, *Smiley's People*

philosophaster   See special entry BOOKISH APPELLATIONS, p. 407.

philophronesis   See special entry RHETORIC TERMS, p. 404.

phonaesthesia [*fŏn″əs·thē′zhə*] *n.*   The phenomenon of certain sounds' or word elements' seeming not only to be imitative or onomatopoeic but to have an innate meaning or flavor, e.g., "st" signifying fixity (as in stone, stolid, stiff), "sl" signifying a gliding down (as in slither, slobber, slide, slope), and "gl" suggesting a shining quality (as in glow, gleam, glimmer).

phoneme *n.*   A basic, distinctive unit of speech constituting one of the characteristic utterances in a language, and that, while represented by one symbol, may include several somewhat different sounds that are heard by native speakers as being the same sound. *Adj.* phonemic; *adv.* phonemically; *n.* phonemics.

This unit may be theoretically useful, but no one has ever learned to speak or write by the study of phonemes. As all babies soon find out, the raw material is words, strung into phrases and short sentences or quasi-sentences.
          —Clifton Fadiman and James Howard, *Empty Pages*

phonetic *adj.*   Of or pertaining to the transcription of sounds or symbols representing pronunciation, as in the so-called phonetic alphabet; denoting speech sounds or specific sound of utterance rather than conventional verbal meaning, as in literally reproduced dialect. *Adv.* phonetically; *n.* phonetics; *v.* phoneticize.

This original life in a word (as in the word "talent") burns low as it is: sensible spelling might extinguish it altogether. Suppose any sentence you like: suppose a man says, "Republics generally encourage holidays." It looks like the top line of a copy-book. Now, it is perfectly true that if you wrote that sentence exactly as it is pronounced, even by highly educated people, the sentence would run: "Ripubliks jenrally inkurrij jollidies." It looks ugly: but I have not the smallest objection to ugliness. My objection is that these four words have each a history and hidden treasures in them: that this history and hidden treasure (which we tend to forget too much as it is) phonetic spelling tends to make us forget altogether.
          —G. K. Chesterton, in *The Man Who Was Chesterton*

phoneticism *n.* A word spelled to emphasize its sound or pronunciation, as opposed to its conventional spelling, e.g., "fer sherr" (for sure).

When I first came to America I was confronted with the public use—brazen in neon—of phoneticisms like TONITE . . . DEE-LUX. This appalled me. —Geoffrey Wagner, *On the Wisdom of Words*

phonology *n.* The science or study of speech sounds and their changes, including the fields of phonetics and phonemics; system or principles of speech sounds in a language. *Adj.* phonological, phonologic; *adv.* phonologically; *v.* phonologize.

Joyce's fondness for puns, and his generally elaborate exploitation of the phonological level of language, probably make *Ulysses* a more formidable task for the translator than the *Odyssey*.
—David Lodge, *Language of Fiction*

phrase *n.* A group of words, lacking a subject and predicate, constituting a syntactic unit or segment of meaning, such as a prepositional or adverbial expression; wording; brief expression; locution. *Adj.* phrasal; *adv.* phrasally; *v.* phrase.

"Messy stuff," was the delicate phrase bestowed by one of our greatest dailies on his poetry.
—Rebecca West, *Rebecca West: A Celebration*

phrasemaker *n.* One who coins eloquent, memorable, or pithy phrases. *N.* phrase-making.

That soldier had in him the very soul of literature; he was one of the great phrase-makers of modern thought, like Victor Hugo or Disraeli. —G. K. Chesterton, in *The Man Who Was Chesterton*

phrasemonger *n.* One prone to quoting the words of others, and hence who traffics in clichés, platitudes, and secondhand expressions.

She asked him why did he not write out his thoughts. For what, he asked her, with careful scorn. To compete with phrasemongers, incapable of thinking consecutively for sixty seconds?
—James Joyce, *Dubliners*

phraseology *n.* Choice and manner of wording or phrasing; diction; terminology. *Adj.* phraseological; *adv.* phraseologically.

There were piles of silver all over the counter, and her sister had looked up at her sadly and she had said: "Here's somebody who thinks I'm to blame for the phraseology of the phone company's dunning letters, and that I deserve some shit."
—Ann Beattie, *Falling in Place*

pi, pie *n.* A jumbling of printing type; chaos. *Adj.* pi; *adv.* pi; *v.* pi, pie.

piano word See special entry WORD-GAME WORDS, p. 396.

picaresque *adj.* Of or characterized by realistically detailed, often humorous adventures of resourceful rogues or vagabonds; describing or resembling a tale having colorful and earthy episodes. *N.* picaresque (someone or something picaresque).

He was an adventurous, extremely magnetic, and generous man. (After having spent so many years laboriously begrudging him those picaresque adjectives, I feel it's a matter of life and death to get them in here.)   —J. D. Salinger, "De Daumier-Smith's Blue Period"

Pickwickian sense, in a In an odd or droll way; to be understood only in a special, facetious, or whimsical sense; not literally.

An open mind, says Chesterton, is like an open mouth, swallowing all that comes its way. But Chestertonian truth must be taken in a Pickwickian sense.   —Ellery Sedgwick, in *Editors on Editing*

pidgin *n.* A mixed, bastardized language combining elements of dissimilar languages in a simplified grammatical form that allows groups to communicate or conduct trade; any odd, broken form of speech or awkward idiom. *N.* pidginization; *v.* pidginize.

By the time he had left, they had learned each other's names and a few words in the respective languages—afraid, happy, sleep, love . . . the beginnings of a new tongue, a pidgin which they were perhaps the only two speakers of in the world.

     —Thomas Pynchon, *Gravity's Rainbow*

pidgin English A simplified, commercial form of English as used in the South Pacific and the Orient, showing either Melanesian or Chinese influences; any idiom of English-based jargon; crude or corrupted English.

The weak face now stepped forward, and asked me gently: "Hugh er a merry can?"—so I carried on a brilliant conversation in pidgin-English about my relatives and America until interrupted. . . .

     —e. e. cummings, *The Enormous Room*

piffle *n. Chiefly British* Trite, futile, or inept discourse or ideas; vacuous nonsense. *Adj.* piffling; *v.* piffle.

Indeed the suggestion that his soul might have inhabited even briefly the body of such a beast seemed to make him very angry; for he declared that Crowley's story was "ostrobogulous piffle" from beginning to end. —John Moore, *You English Words*

pig iron Newsroom jargon for serious or dull news copy.

pi-jaw [*pī'jô"*] *British* Sermonizing or pious cant; tedious moral or religious lecture.

"He read the young gentleman something of a lecture. What the young gentleman described as 'pi-jaws.' And I happen to know that hard feelings existed as a consequence on the latter's side. So much so, indeed, that I received the impression that he had been planning something in the nature of a reprisal."
—P. G. Wodehouse, *Thank You, Jeeves*

pillow talk Conversation between people in bed together, esp. intimate or amorous confidences; romantic or seductive talk. See also CURTAIN LECTURE.

The main story of "Sauce for the Goose" concerns the love affair between Daisy Dobbin, the troubled feminist, and Dirk Dolfin, a cocoa tycoon whose notion of pillow talk is to discuss what theological implications the 1618 Synod of Dort held for the policies of the Dutch Reformed Church. —Peter Andrews, *The New York Times*

pilpul [*pil'pōol"*] *n.* Subtle rabbinical disputation or dialectic; penetrating inquiry or scholarship; hairsplitting analysis or argumentation (from the Hebrew word meaning to spice or to dispute violently). *Adj.* pilpulistic; *n.* pilpulist.

This was almost like the pilpul my father had told me about, except that it really wasn't pilpul, they were twisting the texts out of shape, they seemed more interested in b'kiut, in straightforward knowledge and simple explanations of the Talmudic passages and commentaries they were discussing. —Chaim Potok, *The Chosen*

pink *v.* *Chiefly British* To comment so as to wound or ridicule, esp. with the wit of understatement, irony, or double meaning; mordantly tease or tweak.

In general, the English pink more deftly than Americans. Benjamin Disraeli remarked that a traveler, learning that Lord John Russell was leader of the House of Commons, "may well begin to comprehend how the Egyptians worshipped an insect." Disraeli used his rival, William Gladstone, to illustrate the difference between a misfortune and a calamity: "If Gladstone fell into the Thames, it would be a misfortune. But if someone dragged him out again, it would be a calamity" —Willard Espy, *An Almanac of Words at Play*

piracy *n.*   The excerpting from or reproduction of copyrighted or patented work without the permission of the owner, but sometimes legally, as in the case of a book reproduced in a country not subscribing to international copyright laws; literary appropriation or theft. *Adj.* piratical; *n.* pirate; *v.* pirate. See also PLAGIARISM.

There was other incontrovertible evidence of Irving's piracy. In one spot, Noah had told me a political story, and I'd fleshed it out with some background information of my own. Irving had the story, reworded, but he had used the same background context that I had supplied.   —James Phelan, *Scandals, Scamps and Scoundrels*

pitch *n.*   An earnest, pressuring talk to sell or persuade; glib sales presentation; spiel.

There are so many now who actually believe that what we do is really important. This happens not only to salesmen, who repeat their various sales pitches aloud so often they acquire the logic and authority of a mumbo-jumbo creed, but to the shrewd, capable executives in top management who have access to all data and ought to know better.   —Joseph Heller, *Something Happened*

plagiarism *n.*   The use without knowledge of the ideas or words or both of another writer, thereby passing them off as one's own, or an example of this; unethical paraphrasing or copying; literary theft. *Adj.* plagiaristic; *n.* plagiarist; *v.* plagiarize.

Whenever the enemy drew close, he would invariably instruct the men not to shoot "till you see the whites of their eyes!" Having made the line famous at Bunker Hill, he tended to plagiarize himself, to the amusement of everyone except those officers who thought the firing ought to begin long *before* the whites became apparent to some of our myopic riflemen.   —Gore Vidal, *Burr*

plain English   Simple, direct, and understandable English; honest and forthright language, as opposed to circumlocution, cant, or jargon; candid expression; truth.

Her heart was really so bad that she would have succumbed to anything like an impassioned embrace. That is the plain English of it, and I suppose plain English is best.
          —Ford Madox Ford, *The Good Soldier*

plain folks   See special entry PROPAGANDA DEVICES, p. 380.

plain style   A straightforward and simple prose style that eschews rhetorical artificialities, sonorously oratorical cadences, and florid diction, as contrasted with more ornate, Ciceronian styles that also have their origins in sixteenth-century England.

Orwell did, indeed, teach himself "the plain style" for which he is deservedly celebrated, and he taught himself in the only way a writer can—by doing it over until you get it right. When he began to write, an acquaintance recalls, "he was like a cow with a musket."

—John Leonard, *The New York Times*

plain talk Candid discussion; down-to-earth language; hard words.

planiloquence [plə·nil'ə·kwəns] *n.* Plain-speaking.

plant *n.* A story given to a single, favored reporter or publication by a source, such as a politician, for his or her own benefit or purposes; covertly self-serving publicity item. *V.* plant.

platform rhetoric Oratorical language, or hollow, perfunctory grandiloquence typical of politicians; campaign oratory; speechifying.

platitude *n.* A flat and obvious observation or comment, esp. when uttered or written with an air of wisdom; dull truism; trite profundity. *Adj.* platitudinal, platitudinarian, platitudinous; *adv.* platitudinously; *v.* platitudinize.

The editing tends to be too jazzy, Hughes is occasionally bug-eared cute (as when he turns up in goggles and motorcycle gear), and some of the commentary lapses into survey-course platitude.

—James Wolcott, *Village Voice*

play *n.* A dramatic work or theatrical piece; the determination of how a news story is to be presented in terms of space and importance in a publication (or other medium), for example, whether it is to be a front-page story or buried in back pages. *V.* play.

"A reporter cannot promise anonymity from the editor," said A. M. Rosenthal, executive editor of *The New York Times*. "It is important to trust a reporter, but it is not only a question of trust, it is a question of judging the story and knowing how to play it."

—Jonathan Friendly, *The New York Times*

pleonasm *n.* The use of more words than necessary, or repetition in a sentence or expression that could be forgone without changing the meaning; wordiness, usually ill-advised but sometimes deliberate for emphasis; redundancy. *Adj.* pleonastic; *adv.* pleonastically.

At most a certain tendency to pleonasm, not unpleasant if a trifle pompous, can be detected: "he shrinks *in some measure* from a *public* appearance in the House" is really absurd, since a member . . . either does or does not appear in the house, and if he does is bound to do so publicly.   —J. Enoch Powell, in *The State of Language*

ploce [*plō′sē*] *n.*   Repeating a word but giving it a new significance for emphatic, rhetorical effect, e.g., "more Irish than the Irish." See also POLYPTOTON.

plug *n.*   A favorable mention of something to promote it, often brief but usually obvious in intent; gratuitous endorsement. *V.* plug.

On your car, plug the horn, the lock on the gas tank, the paint job, the speed and the low gas consumption. That's all. Leave out about the brakes, the knee-action, and all that. They never heard of it, and you're just wasting your time. Better let me write those plugs, and you let your announcers translate them.
                                                            —James M. Cain, *Serenade*

plurisyllable *n.*   A word of more than one syllable.

poetic *adj.*   Of or relating to poets or poetry; written in verse; having the characteristics of poetry, such as lyricism, romanticism, or elevated, evocatively crafted language; artful in imagery or metaphor; figurative; artificial or precious in language or style. *Adv.* poetically; *n.* poeticality, poeticalness; *v.* poeticize.

The secret of biography is to let your imagination flourish in key with your subject's. In this way you will achieve a poetic truth that is the jewel for which facts are merely the setting. Be poetic, dear boy, be poetic, and take your text from d'Aurevilley—*La verité m'ennuie.*
                                                            —Tom Stoppard, *Lord Malquist & Mr Moon*

poeticism *n.*   An archaic expression or touch of fine writing, esp. an expression or scrap of verse that appears rarefied or ornamental in a modern prose context.

poetic license   A poet's or writer's departure from proper, conventional form, rules, diction, etc., to achieve a desired effect or purpose; artistic prerogative.

poetic prose   See POLYPHONIC PROSE.

pointer phrase   Speechwriter's term for a verbal cue or "underlining" signaling an essential point in a speech; a locution calling attention to what is to follow.

polemic *n.* A concerted attack on or refutation of a doctrine, policy, etc.; an earnest counterargument; contesting opinion; *pl.* the art of disputation or the protocol of controversy, notably of theological refutation. *Adj.* polemic, polemical; *adv.* polemically; *n.* polemicist; *v.* polemicize.

His new book, "The French Ideology," is a shrill polemical exposé of France's home-grown tradition of fascism before, during and after Vichy. . . .   —Roger Shattuck, *The New York Times*

polite *adj.* Describing language that is culturally refined, as the English of belles-lettres; elegant; socially correct (contrasted with familiar).

Politeness, however, can be separated from formality within language, since it is possible to have language which is both polite and informal, as in "I say, Jim, you wouldn't have such a thing as a spanner handy, would you?", and conversely one can use very formal language to be cheeky, as every schoolboy knows.

—G. W. Turner, *Stylistics*

polluted English See GOBBLEDYGOOK.

polyglot *adj.* Fluent in several languages; multilingual; involving or expressed in several languages; involving a medley of languages. *Adv.* polyglottally; *n.* polyglot, polyglottism.

"Only our people know how to enjoy themselves with civilized freedom," they write. "We are generous, warmhearted, hospitable, sensitive," they go on, and they mean it to be read not only by themselves but by the polyglot barbarians of the upper plateau who obstinately go on regarding Veracruz as merely a pestilential jumping-off place into the sea.   —Katherine Anne Porter, *Ship of Fools*

polygraphy *n.* Notable literary productivity and versatility; prolific and varied writing. *Adj.* polygraphic; *n.* polygraph.

Barzun is the historian as polyhistor, one of those rare scholars who give polygraphy a good name.   —John Simon, *Paradigms Lost*

polyonymous *adj.* Having many names. *N.* polyonymy.

polyphonic prose Prose having the attributes of verse, combining meter, alliteration, recurrent imagery, etc., and associated chiefly with Amy Lowell; quasi-poetic writing. Also POETIC PROSE.

The purpose of Joyce is the achievement of the efforts of polyphonic music in verbal writing. . . . Joyce substitutes for melodies polysemantic verbal patterns realized by means of distortions.

—Margaret Schlauch, *The Gift of Language*

polyptoton *n.* Repetition of a word but in a different case or inflection, for rhetorical effect, as by following a verb with its adverbial form, e.g., "Tell your lie but do it tellingly." See also PLOCE.

polysemy *n.* Multiplicity or diversity of meaning in one word. *Adj.* polysemous; *n.* polysemant (word with more than one meaning).

The "messiness" of language, its fundamental difference from the ordered, closed, systematization of mathematics or formal logic, the polysemy of individual words, are neither a defect nor a surface feature which can be cleared by the analysis of deep structures.
—George Steiner, *After Babel*

polysyllabic humor H. W. and F. G. Fowler's term for the use of long words or droll pedanticisms in a facetious way; sesquipedalian jocosity. Also PEDANTIC HUMOR.

It is a popular misapprehension that Winston Churchill eluded the convention with "terminological inexactitude." This famous example of polysyllabic humour has been generally misunderstood as a nice substitute for "lie," but the context makes it clear that this was not what was intended.   —Philip Howard, *Words Fail Me*

polysyllable *n.* A word having more than three syllables; a long, obscure, or pretentious word. *Adj.* polysyllabic, polysyllabical; *adv.* polysyllabically; *n.* polysyllabism. Also MULTISYLLABLE; see also PLURISYLLABLE.

Probably I was deep in thought imagining myself orchestrating rhythmic, polysyllabic replies to Green's thrusts without tripping over a single vowel or consonant.
—Joseph Heller, *Something Happened*

polysyndeton *n.* The use of many conjunctions, esp. the repetition of "and" with a series of phrases or clauses. *Adj.* polysyndetic; *adv.* polysyndetically.

poncif [*pôn·sēf*] *n.* A hackneyed notion or expression offered with an air of authority or originality; a banality.

pons asinorum Asses' bridge: a crucial and critical test of understanding; a problem of matter difficult for beginners or people of limited wit.

One began at last to see that a great many impressions were needed to make a very little education, but how many could be crowded into

one day without making any education at all, became the *pons asinorum* of tourist mathematics.
—Henry Adams, *The Education of Henry Adams*

pontificate *v.* To pronounce or comment with haughty, oracular authority or dogmatism; posture officiously or pompously. *Adj.* pontifical; *adv.*pontifically; *n.* pontification, pontificator.

The bureaucrat struts his power by pontificating—and pontificating is virtually a synonym for polysyllabic language.
—Louis B. Lundborg, in *The State of the Language*

pony *n.* See CRIB.

poppycock *n.* Absurd, senseless talk; nonsense.

"Captain, they're both naval officers—"
"Oh, don't give me that poppycock." Queeg took a pair of steel balls from the bowl on his desk. —Herman Wouk, *The Caine Mutiny*

popular etymology See FOLK ETYMOLOGY.

popularization *n.* A work or version of a work intended to be understandable and enjoyable to the lay person, such as a simplified book on a scientific subject. *N.* popularizer; *v.* popularize.

popularized technicality H. W. Fowler's term for a faddish or pretentious word borrowed from the professions or the sciences, often resulting in amateurish warping of its original meaning through thoughtless misapplication or needless use when simpler words exist, e.g., "entropy," "osmosis," "parameter," "alibi." See also SLIPSHOD EXTENSION.

Listen to television and you find that the spoken word ranges from the sophisticated lingo of the advertiser to the modish patter of the master of ceremonies. In between, the common man who is interviewed delivers as many popularized technicalities as the news analyst or other expert delivers vogue phrases and conciliatory slang.
—Jacques Barzun, *Simple & Direct*

pork *n.* Newspaper jargon for matter that is repeated in a subsequent edition, or that is taken from one day's final edition for use in the next day's early edition. See also TIME COPY.

pornography *n.* Printed matter that is sexually arousing in its intent, esp. writing or photographs that are explicitly titillating; erotica. The production or publishing of prurient material. *Adj.* pornographic; *adv.* pornographically; *n.* pornographer.

"It's true," Vanya now, "look at the forms of capitalist expression. Pornographies: pornographies of love, erotic love. Christian love, boy-and-his-dog, pornographies of sunsets, pornographies of killing, and pornographies of deduction—*ahh,* that sigh when we guess the murderer—all these novels, these films and song they lull us with, they're approaches, more comfortable and less so, to that Absolute Comfort."   —Thomas Pynchon, *Gravity's Rainbow*

pornopatch *n.*   A gratuitous passage of explicit sex inserted in a novel by an author or editor to give the book more selling appeal. See also o.s.s.

portmanteau word   See BLEND WORD.

poshlost [*pôsh'ləst*] *n.*   Vladimir Nabokov's term, borrowed from Russian, for any of various instances of vulgar, shallow, or hackneyed writing or opinion; trash.

The failure to make such distinctions has landed many Western observers of Russia in a swamp of *poshlost,* an untranslatable word whose meanings Vladimir Nabokov summarized as "corny trash, vulgar clichés, Philistinism in all its phases, imitations of imitations, bogus profundities."   —Susan Jacoby, *The New York Times*

position paper   A detailed summary statement articulating a philosphical or political opinion on an issue or recommending a course of action; a policy statement.

But Howe may reasonably be characterized as the "iron man," the Lou Gehrig of the Old Left, who is always there when you need him with a clutch position paper on the cold war, Vietnam, Eugene McCarthy, confrontation, or sexual politics.
                                    —Philip Nobile, *Intellectual Skywriting*

post-hoc-ergo-propter-hoc fallacy   After this, therefore because of this: the error of presuming that an occurrence or situation has to have arisen because of something previous; false attributing of cause on the basis of sequence.

Sports figures are inclined to *post hoc* reasoning. A pitcher will shift his quid to change his luck. A batter will enter the batter's box from only one angle of approach.   —John B. Bennett, *Rational Thinking*

postscript *n.*   A note or comment after the close or signature of a letter; supplementary remark or tag; final thought or afterthought; ensuing development.

Let us ignore, for the moment, those novels of oppression written by Negroes, which add only a raging, near-paranoic postscript to this statement and actually reinforce, as I hope to make clear later, the principles which activate the oppression they decry.

—James Baldwin, *Notes of a Native Son*

potboiler *n.* A book of little literary worth written chiefly for money; hack commercial novel.

Conan Doyle, it seems, worked conscientiously to document his historical romances, which he considered his serious work, but he regarded Holmes and Watson as the paper dolls of rather ridiculous and undignified potboilers, and he paid so little attention to what he wrote about them that the stories are full of inconsistencies. . . .

—Edmund Wilson, *Classics and Commercials*

potshot *n.* A random, easy, or cheap criticism; a sniping comment.

It was the *Hollywood Megaphone*. I began to read the lead editorial in the corner. The editor was taking pot shots at the Writers' Guild again. —Budd Schulberg, *What Makes Sammy Run?*

potted *adj. British* Abridged or simplified, e.g., "potted" Shakespeare.

pourparler [*poŏr″pär·lä′*] *n.* An informal conference or conversation prior to an official occasion, such as the signing of a treaty; parley.

praecisio See special entry RHETORIC TERMS, p. 404.

pragmatographia *n.* Vivid description of an action or event.

prate *v.* To talk foolishly or with annoying insistence; jabber; expound or harp on. *Adv.* pratingly.

prattle *n.* Empty or innocuous talk; silly chatter; infantile, repetitive noises. *Adv.* prattlingly; *n.* prattler; *v.* prattle.

Mars-Jones couches his tale in the weighty language of history, its pomposity infected with amiable prattle to match the disease's disorienting course. —Deborah Rae Cohen, *Village Voice*

precept *n.* An instructive rule of conduct or guiding principle for the individual; moral rule of thumb. *Adj.* preceptive; *adv.* preceptively.

Whether for reasons of indifference, incapacity, or indolence, they all ignore Dr. Johnson's crucial precept: "What is written without effort is in general read without pleasure."

—Lincoln Barnett *The Treasure of Our Tongue*

précieuse See special entry BOOKISH APPELLATIONS, p. 407.

preciosity *n.* Extremely fastidious but overrefined and rapturous language, typically having affected diction, elaborate and strained sentence construction, or a general narcissism or self-consciousness. *Adj.* precious; *adv.* preciously.

It is simply too full of self-conscious literary devices—passages that whimsically break into the urgent present tense . . . precious sentences such as "How could you compare flesh with stone?" "She'd gentled down in the middle of it" and "But water magics everything". . . .   —Christopher Lehmann-Haupt, *The New York Times*

précis *n.* A careful, point-by-point summary; concise capsule version; recapitulation.

A *précis* of any chapter might cause us to wonder whether the book has any appeal whatsoever: a toy bear and a toy pig follow their own tracks around a tree until they are told by a small boy that this is pointless, and all retire for lunch.
                                   —Frederick C. Crews, *The Pooh Perplex*

precisian, precisionist *n.* One who is scrupulously strict about standards; purist; stickler or hairsplitter. *N.* precisianism.

One poem was accidentally printed in two different issues in 1925; a building located by the *New Yorker* at Sixth Avenue and 55th Street was actually at Sixth Avenue and 54th Street; the name of George Eliot was spelled with two *l*'s, and Carolyn Wells was called Caroline, two mistakes that were pointed out by that old precisionist, F.P.A., whose hawk eye was ever alert for inaccuracies.
                                   —James Thurber, *The Years with Ross*

preface See special entry PARTS OF A BOOK, p. 364.

prescriptive *adj.* Showing concern for the rigorous adherence to precise, established rules and forms and authoritative guidelines, esp. with regard to language; strictly conservative or orthodox in matters of grammar. *Adv.* prescriptively; *n.* prescriptiveness.

The second contribution demonstrates that Bernstein's humanity had limits—he invented in his role of liberal prescriptive grammarian, a straw man who represented everything old-fashioned and nitpicking about illiberal prescriptive grammar.
                                   —Jim Quinn, *American Tongue and Cheek*

press release A prepared representative statement, to announce, inform, or promote, given to the media concerning an organization, product, etc., such as a bulletin distributed by a governmental agency, a corporation, or a public relations firm; publicity handout. Also NEWS RELEASE, RELEASE.

There is nothing more humbling than to sit down at a desk stacked with handouts—our word for press releases—or speech texts, and be forced to sort out all the verbiage and turn it into a story to meet a deadline. But there are few things more satisfying than the experience of wading through it all and finding a lead which gives coherence and structure to the whole uncoordinated mess of information.
—John Chancellor and Walter R. Mears, *The News Business*

prête-nom [*pret·nôn*] *n.* One who lends his or her name; a front.

preterition *n.* See PRETERMISSION.

pretermission *n.* Letting pass without mention or with scant mention; disregarding. Also PARALEIPSIS, PRETERITION.

prevarication *n.* Deviation, evasion, or perversion of truth or fact; misleading or equivocal discourse; waffling; lying. *Adj.* prevaricative, prevaricatory; *n.* prevaricator; *v.* prevaricate.

primary source A firsthand, direct source of information or research, such as the words of the person who is the subject, official government records, or the memoirs of others (with allowance made for bias); document examined that has not been emended by a third party (contrasted with secondary source).

privative See special entry GRAMMAR ADJECTIVES, p. 400.

procès-verbal [*prō·sā·ver·bäl*] *n.* An official record of a diplomatic negotiation, legal presentation or inquiry, or similar formal proceeding; transcript; minutes. *Pl.* procès-verbaux.

It seemed to me, since what I regarded as the high point—the *procès-verbal*—had been passed and since the hotel-keeper was once again in possession of his sheet, that we might reasonably expect to be released from police custody in a matter of hours.
—James Baldwin, *Notes of a Native Son*

proem *n.* A preliminary or introductory discourse or comment; preface.

profanity *n.* Irreverence toward the sacred; secularrsm; word or expression showing disrespect for what is venerable, esp. a derisive expletive; irreverent vulgarism; abusive language;

swearing; curse word. *Adj.* profane, profanatory; *adv.* profanely; *n.* profanation, profaneness, profaner; *v.* profane.

She waited with sympathy and amusement, and with habituated dread of his fury and of the profanity she was sure would ensue, spoken or unspoken.   —James Agee, *A Death in the Family*

profile *n.* A brief and usually thoughtful and vividly personal sketch of an individual. *V.* profile.

During the late twenties and very early thirties *The New Yorker* frequently ran a type of profile of rich and successful men that was only superficially distinguishable from the Success Stories in the late *American Magazine.* (The difference was that the *New Yorker* writer might attribute to the protagonist some supposedly charming foible like wearing crimson ties although he had attended Princeton.) The hallmark of this kind of profile was a sentence on the order of "Although Jeremy P. Goldrush is as rich as rich, you would think from his plain old two-hundred dollar suits that he was more than an ordinary weekend polo player."   —A. J. Liebling, *The Press*

prolegomenon See special entry SCHOLARLY (BIBLIOGRAPHIC) TERMS, p. 401.

prolepsis *n.* The representing of something expected or in the future as if it were already present or accomplished; the anticipation and answering of an opposing argument or objection, thereby neutralizing or disposing of it; a summary, as of a story, preliminary to its being related in detail; the use of an adjective in an anticipatory way, presuming a result or situation that is not yet an existing consequence. *Adj.* proleptic, proleptical; *adv.* proleptically.

The field's name was the Old Batch—batch from bake, some ancient farm's own annual bread was always grown there. The sky's proleptic name was California; the imperial static blue of August.
                              —John Fowles, *Daniel Martin*

prolixity *n.* Speech or writing that is wordy or lengthy, sometimes tediously; a tendency to long-windedness; verbosity. *Adj.* prolix; *adv.* prolixly.

Mann writes in a manner inimitable by anyone else; the density and prolixity of his novels would be intolerable in a writer who did not also possess his extraordinary sweep and complexity of mind.
                              —Robertson Davies, *One Half of Robertson Davies*

prolocutor *n.* One who speaks or interprets for another; spokesperson; mouthpiece.

prologue *n.* A prefatory discourse; introductory part of a dramatic or other work; preliminary section, usually foreshadowing what follows; initial scene, event, passage, etc.; preface or introduction.

Romantic, talkative women made him impatient. He sought out those who didn't require what he called "a prologue and an epilogue."
—Isaac Bashevis Singer, "Dr. Beeber"

prolusion *n.* A prefatory discussion or discourse; prologue.

proneur See special entry BOOKISH APPELLATIONS, p. 407.

pronouncement *n.* A formal declaration or decision; official statement; authoritative opinion, judgment, or conclusion. *V.* pronounce.

She made no effort to speak but stood rigidly as if waiting for some dread pronouncement, like a convicted prisoner at the bar about to receive sentence.   —S. S. Van Dine, *The Bishop Murder Case*

pronunciamento [*prō·nun"sē·ə·men'tō*] *n.* An edict proclaiming a coup d'état; autocratic or dogmatic pronouncement; decree; ukase.

proofreading *n.* The reading of text to detect typographical errors, usu. of galleys or proofs before publication; perusing copy for mistakes. *N.* proofreader; *v.* proofread.

Little crudities of a mechanical sort were observable here and there, but there were not enough of them to amount to anything, and it was good enough Arkansas proofreading, anyhow, and better than was needed in Arthur's day and realm.
—Mark Twain, *A Connecticut Yankee in King Arthur's Court*

propaedeutic [*prō"pi·d(y)ōo'tik*] *adj.* Providing preparatory or introductory instruction; an introductory course of study. *N.* paedeutic, propaedeutics.

A teacher must be propaedeutic before turning heuristic; a student must learn precise, unambiguous expression before he can start contemplating the relativity of the universe and all its components.
—John Simon, *Paradigms Lost*

propaganda *n.* Information, doctrine, ideas, or rumors spread to promote or discredit a cause, institution, or person, esp. systematic political persuasion; self-serving or proselytizing material. *Adj.* propagandist, propagandistic; *adv.* propagandistically; *n.* propagandism, propagandist; *v.* propagandize. See special entry PROPAGANDA DEVICES, p. 380.

> Each end of the political spectrum has, I suppose, its own favorite style of propaganda. The Right tends to prefer gross, straightforward sentimentality. The Left, a sort of surface intellectualizing.
> —Neil Postman, *Crazy Talk, Stupid Talk*

propound *v.*   To offer for consideration or acceptance, as a theory; set forth; propose.

proprietates verborum [*prō·prē"ə·tä'tes wer·bôr'əm*]   The proper meanings of words; orthodox usage.

prosaic *adj.*   Characteristic of prose rather than of poetry; factual or expository; unimaginative or unexceptional; pedestrian; dull. *Adv.* prosaically; *n.* prosaism, prosaicism, prosaicness, prosaist.

> Enid's cigars somehow enhanced a naturally aristocratic bearing, besides emphasizing her independence. " 'The Love Song of J. Alfred Prufock' is full of those prosaic lines, like, let's see, it's so long since I've read it. 'I have measured out my life with coffee spoons.' "
> —Peter De Vries, *Madder Music*

prosateur *n.*   A prose writer.

prose *n.*   The ordinary, idiomatic mode of human expression, spoken or written, as opposed to the metrical, figurative mode of poetry; writing that is narrative, expository, or conversational; literature besides poetry, including drama not in verse, fiction, and nonfiction; writing; craftsmanship and style; language. *Adj.* prose; *n.* prose; *v.* prose.

> He talked his prose, Agee prose. It was hardly a twentieth century style; it had Elizabethan colors. Yet it had extraordinarily knowledgeable content. It rolled just as it reads; but he made it sound natural—something just there in the air like any other part of the world. How he did this no one knows.
> —Walker Evans, *Let Us Now Praise Famous Men*

prose poem   A form of poetry with a prose format, which may display richness of imagery and all the familiar devices of verse except end-stopped lines.

> By armature here I mean the factual frame as designed for that book; and by its dislocation I *don't* mean the kind of fantastic coincidence

or improbability which we find, for instance, in Dickens. Dickens' plots are perfectly to his purpose. He is a romantic prose poet dealing in melodrama.   —Joyce Cary, *Art and Reality*

prosographia [*pros"ə·graf'ē·ə*] *n.* Vivid description of a person or character.

prosonomasia [*pros"ə·nō·mā'zhə*] *n.* A humorous variant of a person's name, or a punning nickname, e.g., "Fred A-Stairs"; use of similar sounds in a pithy expression, e.g., "Don't lose it, use it."

prosopopoeia [*prə·sō"pə·pē'ə*] *n.* See PERSONIFICATION.

prosy *adj.* Conventional or unremarkable in style; commonplace; dull. *Adv.* prosily; *n.* prosiness.

Mr. Cortázar, who is internationally famous for his novel, "Hopscotch," and for his short stories, makes even Lawrence Durrell sound prosy.   —Anatole Broyard, *The New York Times*

pro tanto [*prō tan'tō*] For so much: to some extent; good enough as far as it goes; for what it's worth.

Now we must enter two caveats: "making explicit" is not the same as describing or stating (at least philosophers' preferred senses of these words) what I am doing. If "making explicit" conveys this then pro tanto it is a bad term.
                    —J. L. Austin, *How to Do Things with Words*

provection See AFFIX-CLIPPING.

proverb *n.* A quotation from the Book of Proverbs; a well-known, venerable popular saying, esp. one rooted in philosophical or religious wisdom; instructive, often metaphorical maxim. *Adj.* proverbial; *adv.* proverbially.

The aphorism is a personal observation inflated into a universal truth, a private posing as a general. A proverb is anonymous human history compressed to the size of a seed.   —Stefan Kanfer, *Time*

provincialism *n.* A provincial or local peculiarity of speech or idiom; a word or idiom characteristic of a local dialect; unpolished or parochially narrow ways. *Adv.* provincial; *adv.* provincially.

The exclusiveness, whether real or imagined, drives him to an extreme form of defiant provincialism, so that he flaunts his vulgarity and his special form of American speech self-consciously
                    —Margaret Schlauch *The Gift of Language*

proviso *n.*   A clause, article, or addendum making a specific stipulation in a document; restricting or qualifying note; condition. *Pl.* provisos, provisoes. *Adj.* provisory.

Unfortunately neither of the possible editors suggested by James, namely the Rev. A. L. Mayhew and Henry Bradley, were free at that time and in October 1884 both parties at length accepted an agreement, based on Hucks Gibbs' earlier proposals, but with the proviso that if the Editor failed to produce 700 pages a year, he would be prepared to accept the division of the work between himself and a co-editor.   —K. M. Elisabeth Murray, *Caught in the Web of Words*

prunes and prisms   Affected, prim, priggish language.

This book will make you realize that contemporary users of liquid protein and diet pills aren't the only masochists, that women once buckled themselves into 18-inch corsets, painted their faces with arsenic and went around with words like "prunes" and "prisms" on their lips because those words gave their mouths the proper, pursed appearance.   —Michiko Kakutani, *The New York Times*

pseudandry [*sōo'dan"drē*] *n.*   The use of a masculine pen name by a female writer (contrasted with pseudogyny).

pseudepigrapha   See special entry SCHOLARLY (BIBLIOGRAPHIC) TERMS, p. 402.

pseudepigraphy [*sōo"di·pig'rə·fē*] *n.*   The false attribution of an article, novel, etc., to a certain writer; spurious authorship. *Adj.* pseudepigraphic, pseudepigraphal, pseudepigraphical; pseudepigraphous; *n.* pseudepigraph.

pseudodox *n.*   A false opinion or doctrine. *Adj.* pseudodox; *n.* pseudodoxy.

pseudograph *n.*   A false piece of writing or spurious document; forgery; pseudepigraph.

pseudogyny [*sōo·doj'ə·nē*] *n.*   The use of a feminine pen name by a male writer (contrasted with pseudandry).

pseudological *adj.*   Falsified in a romantic way; wildly exaggerated or untrue. *N.* pseudology.

pseudologue   See special entry BOOKISH APPELLATIONS, p. 407.

pseudomenos   See special entry RHETORIC TERMS, p. 404.

pseudonym *n*   See PEN NAME

pseudo-paragraphs *n.* Jacques Barzun's term for a sequence of brief paragraphs of nonsentences or single words, often a structural evasion or straining for effect by an undisciplined writer.

pseudostatement *n.* A statement that is unverifiable, such as a poetic assertion; sentence that is grammatically unobjectionable but that makes no literal or logical sense, such as one mixing metaphors or a message in code words.

psilology [*sī·lol'ə·jē*] *n.* Empty talk.

psilosophy [*sī·los'ə·fē*] *n.* Shallow philosophy.

psittacism [*sit'·ə·siz"əm*] *n.* Parrotlike speech without thought as to meaning; boring, mindlessly repetitive language.

> The other usage is that of "right" as a ubiquitous tag to all manner of statements that do not require it. I know it is also so commonplace among the young that it may be dangerous to see more in it than a mere psittacism—a mindless parroting.
> —John Fowles, *The Ebony Tower*

psychobabble *n.* R. D. Rosen's term for the colloquial, self-involved, and ostensibly candid jargon of devotees of various psychological and human-potential disciplines and therapies, typified by simplistic and self-reassuring catch-phrases, glib barbarisms, and a general repetitious confessional content; familiar self-improvement patter.

> Psychobabble, as a style of speech . . . is more than anything else a feature of contemporary decorum, a form of politesse, a signal to others that one is ready to talk turkey, to engage in *real dialogue*. Unfortunately, in the rush for revelation, real dialogue often turns out to be real monologue. —R. D. Rosen, *Psychobabble*

Public School Standard See RECEIVED STANDARD.

publish or perish A slogan denoting the departmental peer pressure in academia to publish scholarly writings, often at the expense of teaching responsibilities.

> "But Halberstadt's problem with 'publish or perish' is not my problem ," said Mr. Gitlin, who is also executor of the estates of Sinclair Lewis and Christopher Morley.
> —Edwin McDowell, *The New York Times*

pudder *n. British* Gobbledygook.

"At this moment in time . . ." still rules the sound-waves as a pompous piece of pudder that fills a little time while the speaker works out what sonorous banality he or she is going to emit next."

—Philip Howard, *Words Fail Me*

puff *n.* A publicity release that is self-serving in its praise of a person, organization, etc., and hence of little news value; a praising mention or notice; blurb or plug. *V.* puff.

puffery *n.* Exaggerated praise, esp. extravagant publicity or endorsement for promotional purposes; laudatory testimonial or crowing commendation; fluffery.

Indeed, only if he is the beneficiary of literary-political puffery can a serious novelist survive a best-seller, because one function of critical allies is to protect a respectable reputation against the likely charge of "selling out."—Richard Kostelanetz, *Literary Politics in America*

puff piece A newspaper or magazine article that praises or promotes its subject and is thus fatuous or obvious from the standpoint of objective or meaningful journalism.

pulp *n.* A magazine printed on cheap, unglossy paper, as opposed to a so-called slick magazine; cheap, commercial book, esp. a formulized melodramatic or sensational novel, such as a Western or romance. *Adj.* pulp, pulpy.

Girodias himself would probably regard *Naked Lunch* as his crowning discernment. I don't see it. The book strikes me a strident bore, illiterate and self-satisfied right to its heart of pulp.

—George Steiner, *Language and Silence*

pun *n.* A suggestive, humorous play on word meaning, either by virtue of two or more senses of one word or by the similar sound or form of different words; pointed, usually humorous double meaning. *Adv.* punningly; *n.* punster; *v.* pun.

"He's thinking of going into advertising, but he's hesitating. He says he feels it would be crossing the Young and Rubicam."

A sweet voice came from the kitchen. "Would you like some tea, Daddy?"

"Yes, my darjeeling, daughter." He turned back. "She sounds so sad these days. You'd think a girl pretty enough to be a model would be happy."

"It's modeling that's done it. It's turning her into a mannaquin-depressive."

The sweet voice rose in anger. "It isn't. It's these hot, cross puns. Will you two never stop?"

They did.

So will I, in spite of having a reserve that includes Pilat project, buying cigars from the Good Humidor man, détente saving time, Gdansk, ballerina, Gdansk as advice to a Polish girl unable to make it with the Bolshoi, a worried Dutch conductor with the Concernedgebrow, a Middle Eastern psychiatrist known as the shrink of Araby, and a Japanese robot functioning shakily because of a recent frontal robotomy. —Edwin Newman, *Strictly Speaking*

punch line The climactic and telling line of a joke, story, or speech, usually a humorous surprise; ultimate or crucial point of something told; clincher.

Hutchins had stood here for ten minutes hearing the distant sound of Gerhardt's voice in the rhythm of a comedian's, setting up punch lines, and at the expected intervals he'd heard all their laughter rise and break and fall away. —Richard Yates, *A Good School*

punctatim [*pungk·tā'tim*] Point for point.

punctilious *adj.* Showing or characterized by rigorous concern about fine points or details of correctness or social convention; scrupulously precise. *Adj.* punctiliously; *n.* punctiliousness.

No one expects (or even wants) students to be as punctilious as Dominic Boubours, the French grammarian who in 1702 remarked on his deathbed, "I am about to—or I am going to—die; either expression is correct." —Donna Cross, *Word Abuse*

punctuation *n.* The act or system of using recognized marks or symbols in written matter to set apart, stress, or otherwise clarify elements of sentence relationship and meaning. *Adj.* punctuational, punctuative; *n.* punctuator; *v.* punctuate.

The best rule I can give for literary punctuation is the old or perhaps legendary practice of typesetters: "Set type as long as you can hold your breath without getting blue in the face, then put in a comma; when you yawn put in a semicolon; and when you want to sneeze, that's time for a paragraph."
—Robert Hendrickson, *The Literary Life and Other Curiosities*

pundigrion [*pun·dig'rē·ən"*] *n.* A play on words; a pun.

punnigram *n.* A punning epigram.

purism *n.* Strictness or fastidiousness about language; concern with or insistence on the niceties of correctness or orthodox usage. *Adj.* purist, puristic; *adv.* puristically; *n.* purist.

. . . Would you convey my compliments to the purist who reads your
proofs and tell him or her that I write in a sort of broken-down patois
which is something like the way a Swiss waiter talks, and that when
I split an infinitive, God damn it, I split it so it will stay split. . . .
                    —Raymond Chandler, *Raymond Chandler Speaking*

purple prose, purple passage, purple patch   Elaborately styled or
   floridly ornate prose; esp. a particular passage; overwrought,
   overly poetic writing.

The Well of Loneliness is overblown, rhetorical, composed like a 19th
century novel that wells with self-conscious regularity into purple
passages pronouncing on Art, Passion, and The Meaning of Life.
                              —Vivian Gornick, *Village Voice*

purr-word *n.*   S. I Hayakawa's term for a subjective expression
   that is a signal of great favor or approval and hence is a "pre-
   symbolic form of nuzzling"; word or expression that soothes
   or lulls (contrasted with snarl-word).

Now it may seem picky to notice such a mousy nothing of a word,
but in the last six or seven months I've been keeping track of all the
times "nice" has appeared in the cultural pages of the *Times*—ever
since a fellow writer tipped me off that "nice" was the paper's favorite purr word.   —James Wolcott, *Village Voice*

put-down *n.*   An action or comment that belittles, deflates, or ridicules; pointed, snubbing retort. *V.* put down.

But Ms. Murphy had proven as difficult and inscrutable as Kate and
his daughter Joan, both of whom had become so hypersensitive to
"anti-feminist put-downs" in the last year that they oinked at him, in
concert, just about every time he opened his mouth.
                              —Cyra McFadden, *The Serial*

pysma   See special entry RHETORIC TERMS, p. 404.

Q

Q.E.D. (quod erat demonstrandum) Which was to be demonstrated: used to indicate that something has just been shown or proved.

By making this call—which reduces both characters to still more tears—Vito miraculously learns to "stop hating himself." He then decides, Q.E.D., that the time has come to quit his ad-agency job and settle down with Theda to collaborate on hit plays.
—Frank Rich, *The New York Times*

qua *prep.* In the capacity or role of, or by virtue of being; in its very nature as.

Then it's back to pretentious abstraction spinning "qua" this and "modulo" that. Quite a performance.
—Carlin Romano, *Village Voice*

quadriliteralism *n.* Use of four-letter (taboo) words.

Worse, not only have the porn racketeers predictably cashed in on the increased freedom to exploit the titillatory and surviving shock value of quadriliteralism: so have purveyors to superficially more serious and scholarly readers.
—Randolph Quick, in *The State of the Language*

qualifier *n.* A word, phrase, or sentence, esp. an adjective or adverb, that limits, restricts, or makes conditional the meaning of a statement; stipulating term or expression; modifier. *N.* qualification; *v.* qualify.

What they amount to, basically, is the art of printing a story without taking legal responsibility for it. The word "alleged" is a key to this art. Other keys are "so-and-so said" (or "claimed"), "it was reported" and "according to." In fourteen short newspaper paragraphs, the *Times* story contained nine of these qualifiers.
—Hunter Thompson, *Hell's Angels*

quality paperback See TRADE PAPERBACK under special entry BOOK PUBLISHING TERMS, p. 363.

query See special entry BOOK PUBLISHING TERMS, p. 362.

question-begging *n.* Reasoning or arguing with prejudicial, loaded words that beg or presume the conclusion at issue, or phrasing whereby something unproved is assumed to be true; persuasion that is speciously self-proving, tautological, or circular. *Adj.* question-begging. Also BEGGED QUESTION, CIRCULAR REASONING, PETITIO PRINCIPII. See also LOADED QUESTION.

Indeed, a good exercise in verbal sincerity is to give a group the task of writing one of President Johnson's speeches, on a given subject, before he delivers it. The language will be bound to be bafflingly question-begging and soporifically vague, so that an intelligent student can sometimes provide whole paragraphs in advance.
—Geoffrey Wagner, *On the Wisdom of Words*

quibberdick See special entry BOOKISH APPELLATIONS, p. 407.

quibble *n.* A minor or petty criticism or reservation; cavil; an evasion or irrelevancy. *Adj.* quibbling; *adv.* quibblingly; *n.* quibbler; *v.* quibble.

Reports came in at the rate of two or even three a month, and the standard, according to the customers, continued excellent, but Control's name was seldom mentioned and he was never invited to comment. Occasionally the evaluators produced quibbles.
—John le Carré, *Tinker, Tailor, Soldier, Spy*

quickie See INSTANT BOOK under special entry BOOK PUBLISHING TERMS, p. 362.

quiddity *n.* The quality that makes something what it is; essence or crux; subtle distinction or point. *Adj.* quidditative.

Nothing is quite that simple: I know it. But when circumstances grow unbearably complex, it is natural that we should grope about for a very simple credo. And so, after all, we tell ourselves, man's real quiddity is that he is a human being, not that he is a Zionist, a Communist, a Socialist, a Jew, a Pole, or, for that matter, a Nazi.
—John Hersey, *The Wall*

quid multa? [*kwid mōōl'tə*] Why so many (words): why be so long-winded?

quidnunc See special entry BOOKISH APPELLATIONS, p. 407.

Quinalpus *n.* A dragged-in authority to clinch an argument.

Quine sentence Douglas Hofstadter's term for a type of self-referential (autological) sentence in which a phrase or clause is preceded by itself in the form of a quotation, e.g., " 'Is a sentence fragment' is a sentence fragment," " 'Yields falsehood when preceded by its quotation' yields falsehood when preceded by its quotation" *(after philosopher Willard Van Orman Quine).*

quip *n.* A light, often wry or sarcastic offhand remark; passing jest or jibe. *Adj.* quippish; *n.* quipster; *v.* quip.

The shirtless one, the sockless one, the one dispensing shots and pills like a gumball machine, with a song in his heart and a quip on his lip?
—Chris Chase, *The New York Times*

quoad hoc [*kwō' äd" hōk'*] So far as this point is concerned; to this extent.

quodlibet [*kwod'li·bet"*] *n.* A fine or subtle point for scholastic argument or formal debate; knotty or debatable matter; fine point. *Adj.* quodlibetic, quodlibetical; *adv.* quodlibetically. See also PILPUL.

" 'Ecology' gets defined in about an inch of type; 'pollution' gets about two inches, and yet a few pages later the editors devote more than half a page to the 'popinjay.' The editors have it all wrong. The world is not going to be polluted by the popinjay. But enough of the quodlibets." —Charles R. Larson, *Academia Nuts*

quodlibetarian [*kwod·lib"ə·târ'ē·ən*] *n.* One who fancies quodlibets or impractical, trivial questions, esp. a smugly disputatious person; arguer of fine points; quibbler.

quotable *adj.* Lending itself to being quoted or excerpted; useful, memorable, or effective as a quotation; fit for repeating or publication. *Adv.* quotably; *n.* quotability, quotableness.

Ring Jr. cannot explain his family, it would shatter their code, but he describes them splendidly in a prose like his own light-comedy writing, not so much quotable as steady and pleasing. . . .
—Wilfrid Sheed, *The Good Word and Other Words*

quotation, quote *n.* The repeating of utterance or writing; something spoken or written that repeats or reproduces, usually with acknowledgment of the source; statement or passage offered for evidence, illustration, etc.; citation; reported saying or line; reference to another person or book as an authority; blurb. *V.* quote.

So his speeches were cut to that measure. It was a weird mixture of facts and figures on one hand (his tax program) and of fine sentiments on the other hand (a faint echo, somewhat dulled by time, of the quotations copied out in the ragged, boyish hand in the big ledger).

—Robert Penn Warren, *All the King's Men*

Quote Fact Arthur Herzog's term for a mere assertation or opinion that, simply because it is heard or read as a quotation, is regarded as factual or authentic.

Many people appear to believe that because something is quoted it is necessarily true. A Quote Fact is not itself a fact but someone's opinion which becomes a fact or datum by virtue of having been quoted. If I say X, it is no more than Opinion X. If I quote Y on X, it may still be Opinion X but, because I have quoted it, it takes on the authority of Fact X.   —Arthur Herzog, *The B.S. Factor*

quotemanship, quotesmanship *n.* Shrewdness or fluency in using quotes from others, often to sound authoritative without doing proper research or to affect erudition.

quotha [*kwō'thə*] *interj.* Said he: used as an ironic or contemptuous comment after a quoted passage or for self-assertion.

quoth proverb See WELLERISM.

R

raconteur [*rak″on·tûr′*] *n.* An adept or engaging storyteller. *N.* raconteuse (female).

> I listened attentively: the Club Bore, that first hour, strikes one as a great raconteur.   —Paul Theroux, *The Consul's File*

rant *n.* Intemperately vehement or extravagant speech or language; loud or violent harangue; bombastic declamation. *Adv.* rantingly; *n.* ranter; *v.* rant.

rap *v.* To hold forth or converse, esp. informally and frankly in a personal or mutual idiom; chat.

> The qualities are: exaggerated language (unusual words, High Talk); mimicry; proverbial statement and aphoristic phrasing; punning and plays on words; spontaneity and improvisation; image-making and metaphor; braggadocio; indirection (circumlocution, suggestiveness); and tonal semantics. A black rap can have one, all, or any combination of these. Rappers must be skillful in reading the vibrations of their audience and situation, for the precise wording depends on what is said to whom under what conditions.
>   —Geneva Smitherman, *Talkin and Testifyin*

ratiocination *n.* Methodical or intellectual step-by-step reasoning, as to deduce something or to devise or decipher a logical scheme; specific inquiry or train of thought. *Adj.* ratiocinative; *n.* ratiocinator; *v.* ratiocinate.

> In "Sheiks and Adders," his usual hero, Sir John Appleby, the retired head of the London police, is given to what might be called arch ratiocination. He goes to a local fête at Drool Court, for example, merely out of a curiosity to know why Cherry Chitfield's father "was being so intransigent over the detail of a particular piece of miming or charade."   —Anatole Broyard, *The New York Times*

rave *n.* An unreservedly favorable critical review, as of a book or dramatic production; an extravagant, utterly admiring personal judgment (contrasted with pan). *V.* rave.

re *prep.* In the matter of; with regard to; concerning.

readable *adj.* Legible; easy to read; reasonably coherent or literate; interesting or compelling in content. *Adv.* readably; *n.*

readableness, readability. See special entry READABILITY: THE FOG INDEX, p. 407.

Doubtless I'm being more than a sliver harsh. Irving can be devilishly readable—just as your attention begins to flag, he sends in a troupe of midgets, pulls back incestuous sheets, tosses off a daring piece of slapstick.   —James Wolcott, *Esquire*

reading line   See Special entry BOOK PUBLISHING TERMS, p. 362.

read out   See DROPHEAD under special entry NEWSROOM HEAD-LINE JARGON, p. 386.

real fallacy   See MATERIAL FALLACY.

realistic *adj.*   Describing writing that is rendered in a factual, de-tailed way as to be faithful to actuality or real life, rather than being idealized, romanticized, or impressionist; unsentimental; re-creating with telling detail and objectivity; vivid and believ-able; graphic. *Adv.* realistically; *n.* realism, realist.

In his earlier days he was praised or blamed for his realism; according to the idiosyncrasy of his critics he was extolled for his truth or cen-sured for his coarseness.   —W. Somerset Maugham, *Cakes and Ale*

rebus   See special entry WORD-GAME WORDS, p. 396.

received idea   An obvious, conventional "truth" that is an igno-rant cliché or a trite, parroted opinion; rote, reflexive platitude; stale, secondhand notion. Also IDÉE REÇUE; see also BEN TRO-VATO.

You can observe the shift in each generation of undergraduates. At first they say "I think," and follow it with a mish-mash of received ideas. But in a few weeks they've learned the ropes, and then you hear "Hegel thinks" and "Freud thinks" and "Aristotle thinks."
                              —Mary-Claire van Leunen, *A Handbook for Scholars*

Received Pronunciation *British*   The elite British public school ac-cent, or the pronunciation of Received Standard English. Also R.P.

Those who speak RP are set apart from other educated people by the fact that when they talk, one cannot tell where they come from.
                                            —Norman Schur, *English English*

Received Standard (English) *British*   The most prestigious dialect (southeastern) of British English, being that used by public school and Oxford and Cambridge graduates, most Conservative members of Parliament, etc.; upper-class or Oxbridge English. Also PUBLIC SCHOOL STANDARD.

In George Bernard Shaw's play *Pygmalion* and its musical version, *My Fair Lady*, Received Standard is the speech taught by Professor Henry Higgins to the cockney flower girl Eliza Doolittle. Until recently this speech form, especially its accent, was almost essential to social success. This rigidly snobbish attitude has now softened somewhat. Forms of modified Standard are heard almost everywhere, and a certain amount of regionalism and even lower classism has its own cachet, rather like the wave of ethnic pride that has been sweeping America. —*Success With Words*

recension *n.* The scholarly production of a revised text, esp. of that of an early or ancient writer, by critically reviewing and appraising various sources or variant manuscripts to be incorporated in it; revised text. *V.* recense.

The pattern of entities as distinct as *Rashomon, The Ring and the Book,* and *The Alexandria Quartet* involves relating the same story several times over from several different, and mutually destructive, points of view, one potential conclusion being that nobody possesses more than a fraction of the truth, and that the next recension of the story may cast doubt even on that.
—Robert M. Adams, in *The State of the Language*

recherché [*rə·sher"shā'*] *adj.* Sought after: rare or prized; exquisite; too studiously or obscurely fine or erudite; precious or highfalutin.

This is of course a very simple example of the stylistic misuse of language, and I think that certain writers are under a compulsion to write in recherché phrases as a compensation for a lack of some kind of natural animal emotion.
—Raymond Chandler, *Raymond Chandler Speaking*

récit [*rā·sē*] *n.* A tale or brief novel, esp. one that tells a simple story with literary care and structural economy.

For example, "Coup de Grâce," written four years later, is among the purest examples extant of the classically unified récit, all understated lucidity, ease, and tragic force.
—Stephen Koch, *The New York Times*

recitation *n.* A repeating from memory, as of prepared answers or a passage, esp. a spoken presentation before other people; pupil's speech learned by heart; litany or enumeration; rote or parroted message or discourse. *V.* recite.

During that last recitation of his ("I am totally corrupt, you torture
me too much, I cannot stand your purity," etc.) we had both been
quite drunk.   —Francine du Plessix Gray, *Lovers and Tyrants*

recto   See special entry PARTS OF A BOOK, p. 364.

recursive *adj.*   Involving self-containing or nested objects, art
forms, or other structured phenomena, such as a doll within a
doll, a story within a story, or a parenthetical comment within
a parenthetical comment. *Adv.* recursively; *n.* recursion.

red herring   A deceptive or irrelevant issue introduced as an evasion; a topic that is a deliberate diversion; smokescreen; fiction
writer's plot device to mislead the reader, as in a mystery
novel.

This book, they cry, ranks well beside the *Confessions* of Rousseau;
and I, diverted, as is every layman, by any plump red herring, mutter,
"Oh, Rousseau, my eye," and am preoccupied with that.
          —Dorothy Parker, *The Portable Dorothy Parker*

reductio ad absurdum   Disproof of an assertion or argument by
reasoning the ultimate absurdity of its logical, inevitable conclusion. Also REDUCTIO AD IMPOSSIBILE.

A sufferer from the Simplex Complex can be identified by his predilection for finding simple answers to complex questions, which causes
him to commit the fallacy of exclusive linearity (uncritical attempts
to bring everything under one principle or category), the *reductio ad
absurdum,* and other grievous errors.
          —Arthur Herzog, *The B.S. Factor*

reductio ad impossibile   See REDUCTIO AD ABSURDUM.

reductive fallacy   Jacques Barzun's term for the fallacy of reducing or equating something to one thing or aspect, for example,
the attributing of the American Revolution to a question of
overtaxation; forming a conclusion that is too simplistic or exclusive.

redundancy *n.*   Needless repetition or rephrasing, e.g., "regain
their strength back"; wordiness that only reiterates; unnecessary, expendable word or expression. *Adj.* redundant; *adv.* re-
dundantly.

To be inundated is to be overwhelmed by a wave, and to be redundant
is to be overflowing, unnecessarily wordy, tautologous, overabun-
dant, excessive, or using too many synonyms in a single definition.
          —William Safire, *On Language*

reduplicative See FREQUENTATIVE under special entry GRAMMAR ADJECTIVES, p. 399.

reduplicative word See RICOCHET WORD.

reefer *n.* In a newspaper, a brief front-page notice referring the reader to a story on an inside page.

reflexive See special entry GRAMMAR ADJECTIVES, p. 400.

regionalism *n.* A word or expression characteristic of a particular region; localism; provincialism; literary emphasis of a particular locale, dialect, etc. *Adj.* regionalistic.

register *n.* The level or variety of language used in a given instance considered in terms of social appropriateness or etiquette, or relative formality or informality in choice of words.

rehash *n.* A mere rewriting or reworking of old material; repetition or paraphrase that adds nothing. *V.* rehash.

As for the play, which Grace was sure to love, it turned out to be a rehash of "Cradle Snatchers" and "Sex," retaining the worst features of each.　　　—Ring Lardner, "Old Folks' Christmas"

reification *n.* Investing an idea or word with a reality of its own, or using it as if it were something concrete or absolute, as when a name acquires the cachet of a certificate; regarding of an abstraction as a material thing (as opposed to a metaphor, which compares two concrete things); hypostatization. *V.* reify.

I wonder, truly, if "love" (old whore of a word, we'll let you in this once, fumigated by quotation marks) is not a reifying rather than dereifying process, and "sex object" not the summit of homage.
　　　—John Updike, *A Month of Sundays*

rejoinder *n.* A verbal response, esp. a counteranswer to another's reply. *V.* rejoin.

The party were too intimate for reserve, and they soon fell on Adam's hobby with derision which stung him to pungent rejoinder: "The American man is a failure! You are all failures!" he said.
　　　—Henry Adams, *The Education of Henry Adams*

relative See special entry GRAMMAR ADJECTIVES, p. 400.

release *n.* See PRESS RELEASE.

release copy News copy prepared in advance, such as the text of an important political speech or the obituary of a person whose death is imminent.

remainder   See special entry BOOK PUBLISHING TERMS, p. 362.

remonstrate *v.*   To state in reasoned opposition, as to counter or protest an expressed statement or opinion; plead against; show disapproval; object. *Adj.* remonstrant, remonstrative; *adv.* remonstrantly, remonstratingly; *n.* remonstrant, remonstration.

remplissage [*räm·plē·säzh*] *n.*   Filling or padding in (music or) literature.

repartee *n.*   Witty and sprightly conversation that becomes an interchange of pointed observations and retorts, often with teasing wordplay; heady, lighthearted verbal fencing; verbal quickness; clever rejoinder.

> Her words bore the full gravity of life's tragedy and no repartee of his could cheapen them.   —Patrick McGinley, *Bogmail*

repetend *n.*   A repeated word, phrase, or part of a word; recurrent sound; refrain.

reportage [*rep″ər·täzh′*] *n.*   The reporting of news; factual, topical writing that comes from direct observation or documentable events or situations; news writing; news story.

> Under Brown's aegis, book-reviewing approached levels typical of travel reportage, where most subjects are indiscriminately praised in columns adjacent to *paid* advertisements. . . .
> —Richard Kostelanetz, *Literary Politics in America*

reportorial *adj.*   Involving or characteristic of a reporter or reportage, and hence of factual news gathering or a journalistic account. *Adv.* reportorially.

> Indeed, Mr. Klein is so aggressively reportorial, so intent on keeping things moving, that he often resorts to labels instead of images. . . .
> —Jack Sullivan, *The New York Times*

reprint   See speical entry BOOK PUBLISHING TERMS, p. 363.

restrictive *adj.*   Denoting a clause, phrase, or term that limits or qualifies what it modifies and, being indispensable to full meaning, is usually not set off by commas, e.g., "that was correct" in "I sought the word that was correct"; not extraneous or parenthetical; integral and limiting. *Adv.* restrictively; *n.* restrictiveness.

résumé *n.* A summary or brief recapitulation; digest; outline of one's professional career experience.

It fell face downwards, and on the back he saw a neat little *résumé* in Miss Pembroke's handwriting, intended for such as him. "Allegory. Man = modern civilization (in bad sense). Girl = getting in touch with Nature." —E. M. Forster, *The Longest Journey*

retort *v.* To reply in a prompt, pointed way to a criticism or accusatory question; answer or counter. *N.* retort.

He was giving birth to groups of words that lived inside of him as things, a jumble of the retorts he had meant to make when insulted and the private curses against fate that experience had taught him to swallow. —Nathanael West, *Miss Lonelyhearts*

retraction *n.* The withdrawing or recanting of a statement, charge, etc.; admission or correction of error in something said or published; acknowledgment of misinformation. *N.* retractor; *v.* retract.

retronym *n.* Frank Mankiewicz's term for an adjective-noun pairing that arises because newer senses of the noun, or new products, have made its meaning less clear, requiring the somewhat redundant modifier to restore its original or earlier sense, e.g., "hardcover book" (because of the advent of softcover books), "stage play" (because of the advent of the television play), "natural turf" (after the advent of "artificial turf").

reversal See special entry WORD-GAME WORDS, p. 397.

reverse kicker See BARKER under special entry NEWSROOM HEADLINE JARGON, p. 385.

review *n.* A descriptive critical discussion in a periodical, esp. a literary report-cum-appraisal by an arts writer for a newspaper or magazine; critique; notice; journal or periodical of critical or intellectual content. *V.* review.

I think we must get it firmly fixed in our minds that the very occasions on which we should most like to write a slashing review are precisely those on which we had much better hold our tongues. The very desire is a danger signal. —C. S. Lewis, *Studies in Words*

Reviewer's Basic Stephen Potter's term for tactically useful words, phrases, and pretenses that may be exploited by the crafty book reviewer, whether for attacking another's writing, bestowing "safe" faint praise, or logrolling.

J. Betjeman, in a series of conversations with me, has reminded me
that in Reviewer's Basic, which he has studied for so many years,
any attack on the author under review is essentially friendly. J. Betjeman has kindly turned aside from his second volume on *Periodship*
to summarise for us his findings. They are as follows:

Friendly attacks should begin with faint praise, but be careful not
to use adjectives or phrases of which the publisher can make use in
advertisements. Safe faint praise adjectives are *catholic*—i.e. too
wide in treatment to be anything but superficial; *well-produced*—i.e.
badly written. Alternatively—"The illustrations, of course, are excellent." *Painstaking*—i.e. dull.

Useful words for friendly attacks are *awareness, interesting,
tasteful, observant.*

Effective methods of attack are:

(i) To quote from a book no one else has read but you.

(ii) To imply that you are in some college or institution where the
subject under review is daily discussed, so, of course, you know
better but think this author quite good for one who has not had your
opportunities of acquiring more knowledge.

(iii) To begin "Serious students will perhaps be puzzled . . ."

(iv) To say "In case there should be a Second Edition . . ." Then
note as many trivial misprints as you can find.

It may well be that the author you are reviewing is someone who
may be useful to you in the future. In that event write one signed and
favourable review, and attack the book anonymously in another review in *The Times Literary Supplement* or the *Listener*. These papers
specialise in unsigned friendly attacks and so do most antiquarian
journals.

—Stephen Potter, *The Theory and Practice of Gamesmanship*

rewrite *n.*   A revised or reworded piece of writing, usually with
substantial changes; recomposed or restructured draft; revision. *V.* rewrite.

He wrote and re-wrote his reports of tedious port authority meetings,
dehydrating them of superfluities till they, unlike the real meetings,
crackled with crispness.   —Gail Godwin, *Glass People*

rhematic [*rē·mat'ik*] *adj.*   pertaining to word formation; based on
or derived from a verb.

rhetoric *n.*   The art of effective writing or speaking through attention to coherence, style, balance, and other aspects of prose
composition; the art and science of oratory, esp. with regard to
persuasive devices formulated by critics since ancient times;
elegant and persuasive discourse; a particular idiom or style of

expression; language that is hollow and inflated, esp. in political speechmaking; orotund verbiage; empty or hypocritical talk. *Adj.* rhetorical; *adv.* rhetorically; *n.* rhetoricalness, rhetorician. See special entry RHETORIC TERMS, p. 402.

He rode awhile in silence, then spoke again. "That was mere rhetoric, I'm sure you noticed. 'Walk on foot to China.' I live on rhetoric, like a spider on its threads. Perhaps I imagined I could outride the edge of my rhetoric. More rhetoric, you'll notice."
—John Gardner, *Freddy's Book*

rhetorical question   A statement or understatement posed, for effect, in the form of a question, and hence a comment or a bid for agreement rather than a sincere question; question whose answer is obvious.

"Well," he said, "do you think you destroyed me?" The question was rhetorical. Neither of us was prepared to admit the answer.
—David Black, *Like Father*

rhopalic   See special entry WORD-GAME WORDS, p. 397.

rhubarb   *n. British*   A vocal dispute or argument; murmurous or muttered general conversation (a word repeated by actors to simulate this in crowd scenes). See also WALLA-WALLA.

rhyparography   [*rī″pə·rog′rə·fē*] *n.*   Filthy writing: the literary depiction (originally, painting) of unworthy or sordid subjects. *Adj.* rhyparographic.

ribaldry   *n.*   Indecently earthy or course sexual mockery or humor in behavior or language; lewd vulgarity. *Adj.* ribald; *adv.* ribaldly.

The attitudes of philistinism and vulgar ribaldry which showed signs of becoming unconscious mannerisms in *That Uncertain Feeling,* are here pushed to the extreme of conscious self-parody.
—David Lodge, *Language of Fiction*

ribbon   See BANNER.

ricochet word   A word that is a combination of elements of similar form or sound, that is, of tautophony, e.g., "harum-scarum." Also HOITY-TOITY, REDUPLICATIVE WORD.

riddle   *n.*   A challenging question or elliptically enigmatic statement whose answer or explanation requires a certain ingenuity, often because it is framed with paradox or figures of speech; conundrum; perplexing problem, situation, person, etc. *N.* riddler; *v.* riddle.

rigmarole *n.* Rambling or confused language; incoherent verbiage or nonsense; endless yarn; complicated or ritualized procedure. *Adj.* rigmarole, rigmarolish.

Why had Judith told him all that rigmarole, ending with the story of the preposterous harnessing of Spot? Probably just because she had felt that way, and with no ulterior motive whatever.
—Michael Innes, *Appleby's End*

riposte *n.* A sharp, countering reply; retort. *V.* riposte.

Theirs is an exercise in journalism in depth—the riposte of written journalism to the visual television variety, or, in McLuhan terms, the Message struggling to exist outside the Medium.
—Malcolm Muggeridge, *Things Past*

rocket head See special entry NEWSROOM HEADLINE JARGON, p. 386.

rodomontade [*rod"ə·mon·tād'*] *n.* Bragging speech or writing; boastful idiom; braggadocio. *Adj.* rodomontade; *v.* rodomontade.

I leave it, then, (4) that Mr. Macdonald is not willing, under intense public scrutiny, to break the law particularly, preferring to tweak the law by rodomontade. . . .
—William F. Buckley, Jr., *The Governor Listeth*

roman à clef A novel with a key: a novel whose characters, despite fictitious names, represent actual people in life, as in a disguised portrayal of a historical incident or a celebrity's life. *Pl.* romans à clef.

Even with a roman à clef, which *Ulysses* largely is, no key quite fits. Art lavishes on one man another's hair, or voice, or bearing, with shocking disrespect for individual identity.
—Richard Ellmann, *James Joyce*

roman à thèse [*rō·män ä tez*] See THESIS NOVEL.

roman-fleuve [*rō·män·flœv*] *n.* A long, fictional chronicle usually published as a series of interrelated novels and depicting, through several generations, the lives of many characters or of a family or portraying a milieu of society. *Pl.* romans-fleuves. Also SAGA NOVEL.

Like Nick Jenkins, the amiable narrator of his *roman-fleuve,* "A Dance to the Music of Time," Mr. Powell tends to be self-effacing and reserved when it comes to talking about himself.
—Michiko Kakutani, *The New York Times*

romantic *adj.* Describing writing that serves imaginative, visionary, heroic, or sentimental storytelling that is colorful and idealized, such as that in tales of adventure or love, rather than factual literature; involving narrative relating to great events or strong human emotions; fanciful and humanistic; descriptive; ardent; individualistic. *Adv.* romantically; *n.* romanticism, romantic, romanticist; *v.* romanticize.

roorback *n.* A defamatory falsehood in politics; bogus slanderous story or canard printed as truth by a newspaper or periodical (from name of imaginary traveler whose "account" was meant to reflect badly on James K. Polk in 1844).

Nor is the journalist's credulity confined to such canards and roorbacks from far places. He is often victimized just as easily at home, despite his lofty belief that he is superior to the wiles of press agents. The plain fact is that most of the stuff he prints now emanates from press agents, and that his machinery for scrutinizing it is lamentably defective. —H. L. Mencken, *Gang of Pecksniffs*

rot *n. British* Nonsense.

There had been a lot of such rot let loose in print and talk just about that time, and the excellent woman, living right in the rush of all that humbug, got carried off her feet.
—Joseph Conrad, *Heart of Darkness*

R.P. See RECEIVED PRONUNCIATION.

rubbish *n.* Unredeemably worthless writing, content, or ideas.

From one of the little white tables between the cots Theresa picked up an opened book incautiously left there the night before, read below her gray mustache with the still inward smile of her great-boned face, its title—*The Common Law*, by Robert W. Chambers—and gripping a pencil in her broad earthstained hand, scrawled briefly in jagged male letters: "Rubbish, Elizabeth—but see for yourself."
—Thomas Wolfe, *Look Homeward, Angel*

rubric *n.* A title or heading in a manuscript or book that is underlined of a different color, etc., so as to stand out; name, title, or category under which something falls or is subsumed; designation or classification; aegis. *Adj.* rubric, rubrical; *adv.* rubrically.

The stories were to be found in collections under one rubric or another but could take place in any of a variety of Central European areas at any given time under diverse political registrations. . . .
—Thomas Berger, *Crazy in Berlin*

rule-out *n.*   Newspaper term for a non-news story published on a slow, uneventful day to fill space.

So named because one of the sure-fire signals of such a story is the phrase, "The (name of official) absolutely *ruled out* today any chance of (whatever it was the official never intended to do in the first place)."   —Joel Homer, *Jargon*

running joke   A recurring joke or humorous allusion.

This is what is known as a running joke. The only thing is, I don't know who it's on.   —Walter Kerr, *The New York Times*

run-on sentence   A sentence lacking an appropriate punctuation stop (semicolon, period, or colon) between its clauses, and hence a faulty running together of two clauses. See also COMMA SPLICE.

The rarity of capital letters and the run-on sentences in Molly's monologue are of course related to Joyce's theory of her mind (and of the female mind in general) as a flow, in contrast to the series of short jumps made by Bloom, and of somewhat longer ones by Stephen.
                                              —Richard Ellmann, *James Joyce*

runover *n.*   Text set in type that runs in excess of the anticipated or allotted space for it in a publication; the jump, or part of an article or story continued on another page or pages. Also BREAKOVER.

If you read all the way off the first page and deep into the runover of the story, you found out that the woman and her daughter had long before been moved out of the hotel room they had been occupying and had since then been receiving only $162.20 a month from the department.   —A. J. Liebling, *The Press*

Russianism *n.*   A Russian word adopted into English.

Soon another sort of Russianism came; Russia became one of the leading world powers, expansive both politically and industrially, so that borrowings included words like *soviet, commissar, troika, nyet, MIG,* and *cosmonaut,* although many such loans were reborrowings of Western words from Greek, Latin, French, or German.
                                              —Charlton Laird, *The Word*

sacred cow   A person, idea, or thing regarded as being unassailable, as for reasons of established veneration or special sensitivity; a sacrosanct matter; in journalism, a story that must be printed or aired because it is important to the publisher or top editors, who favor or fear the person or thing involved.

saga *n.*   A historical (predominantly) prose narrative relating the experiences and exploits of lofty personages, both actual and legendary, esp. one of the medieval Scandinavian accounts of such adventures; tale or history of marvelous events; roman-fleuve; event, adventure, or chronicle suggesting or considered worthy of such narrative treatment.

saga novel   See ROMAN-FLEUVE.

salacious *adj.*   Erotically provocative or arousing, or clearly sexual in content; obscene; lecherous. *Adv.* salaciously; *n.* salaciousness, salacity.

Oh yes, oh yes, ostensibly pronouncing on the contemporary American novel or Teddy Boys or Canadian politics, he was really writing for an audience of one, spinning love letters in the sober pages of the *Statesman* with hidden salacious messages, just for her.
—Mordecai Richler, *Joshua Then and Now*

sales talk   A persuasive speech in order to sell a product or service; presentation or argument intended to convince somebody of something; pitch.

He wrinkled his nose fastidiously, in self-mockery. "A few words to say informally in a little after-dinner speech—you know, nothing blatant, no vulgar sales talk—only a few well-chosen thoughts on the responsibility of realtors to society, on the importance of selecting architects who are competent, respected and well established. You know, a few bright little slogans that will stick to the mind."
—Ayn Rand, *The Fountainhead*

sally *n.*   A surprising, deft remark or witticism; audacious or imaginative passage.

samizdat [*sä'mēz·dät"*] *n.* The circulation or smuggling of self-published dissident Russian writing proscribed in the Soviet Union; underground press network.

For years, the most interesting writing to come out of the Soviet Union has been samizdat—literally, self-published—those unorthodox works, banned by the state, that are circulated hand to hand, sometimes finding a sizable readership and a reputation for their authors.   —Walter Goodman, *The New York Times*

sandwich word Harold Wentworth's term for a word of at least two syllables into the middle of which (by tmesis) another word has then been inserted, usually for humorous or sarcastic effect, e.g., "absogoddamnlutely." See also INFIX.

sans phrases [*sän fräz*] Without (roundabout) phrases: direct and to the point; without beating around the bush.

sarcasm *n.* Language that is deprecating, wearily cynical, or caustic about somebody or something, or wit in the form of wry suspicion or pessimism; derisive, sneering humor; sour gibe or taunt. *Adj.* sarcastic; *adv.* sarcastically.

Like too many *Voice* pieces, the article consisted of a mass of circumstantial evidence driven forward by moral outrage and sarcasm.
                                        —David Denby, *The New Republic*

sardonicism *n.* Archly disdainful skepticism or oblique derision, or an expression thereof; acidulous mockery or cynicism; sarcasm. *Adj.* sardonic, sardonical; *adv.* sardonically.

The saving grace of "Dreamland" is the sardonic and witty Orville, whose deadpan humor provides much needed relief from Reno's uncouth banality and Jennifer's upper-crust whining.
                                —Philippe Van Rjndt, *The New York Times*

satire *n.* The use of humor with ridicule to expose vice, folly, pretension, or the like; pointed literary mockery, irony, or wit; the branch of literature characterized by an intent to ridicule; a literary work that is bitingly or amusingly derisive. *Adj.* satiric, satirical; *adv.* satirically; *n.* satirist; *v.* satirize.

In fact, the form Mr. Trow, a 38-year-old New Yorker writer of short stories and dry satires of WASPish and corporate follies, has invented for this essay is so original and idiosyncratic that on entering it one experiences a kind of reading vertigo.
                                        —Eva Hoffman, *The New York Times*

satis verborum [*sä'tis wer·bôr'əm*] Enough of words; enough said about this.

savoire-dire [*sav"wär·dēr'*] *n.* Ability to express oneself persuasively; verbal adeptness; articulateness.

Where but in England could there be a Captain the Lord Louis Mountbatten, a royalty with *savoir-dire* sufficient to pose his candidature (candidacy) as he did in World War II, for the post of Anglo-American interpreter? —Israel Shenker, *Words and Their Masters*

saw *n.* An old, often repeated popular saying or piece of folk wisdom.

The cool practicality of this advice, its smug recourse to millennia of peasant saws and aristocratic maxims, to all that civilized wisdom America had sought to flee and find an alternative to, angered him. —John Updike, *Bech: A Book*

saying *n.* A familiar, conventional thought or observation expressed in particular words, such as a saw, proverb, or epigram.

He did not have the gift of being able to throw out a sentence or a metaphor which suddenly illuminates some dark corner of life—his role implied that he should be full of "sayings" and specific insights, yet he never was. —Lionel Trilling, *The Liberal Imagination*

scandal sheet A newspaper or magazine accenting alleged scandal and often factitious celebrity gossip; lurid tabloid.

I folded the paper and wedged it between the slats of the park bench. It was what my mother called a scandal sheet, full of the local murders and suicides and beatings and robbings, and just about every page had a half-naked lady on it with her breasts surging over the edge of her dress and her legs arranged so you could see to her stocking tops. —Sylvia Plath, *The Bell Jar*

scanmag (from *scandalum magnatum*) *n.* Scandal about great ones: malicious words about people of renown or high station; scandalous gossip.

scanning speech A deliberative or hesitant manner of speech with pauses between words or syllables; syllable-by-syllable utterance.

scarehead See special entry NEWSROOM HEADLINE JARGON, p. 386.

scatology *n.* The study of or preoccupation with feces; interest in or treatment of excretory functions, as in literature with ribald or taboo content; obscenity having an excremental or toilet theme. *Adj.* scatologic, scatological; *n.* scatologer, scatologist.

For all his obsession with the sordid and scatological, his abusive tirades against his own characters, his penchant for scenes of sudden death, he really wants to be liked.
—James Atlas, *The New York Times*

scesis onamaton See special entry RHETORIC TERMS, p. 404.

Schimpflexikon [*shimpf'lek"si·kōn"*] *n.* Abuse dictionary; dictionary or anthology of invective, such as one published by H. L. Mencken recording abuse directed at himself.

Schlimmbesserung [*shlim'bes"se·roŏng"*] *n.* See   MISCORRECTION.

schlock *n.* Inferior or vulgar merchandise, art, or literature, such as a sentimental or sensational formula novel; trite or lurid trash.

scholasm *n.* A pedantic or academic expression; inkhorn term.

scholium See special entry SCHOLARLY (BIBLIOGRAPHIC) TERMS, p. 402.

schoolgirl style Immature and extravagantly gushy or sentimental writing, characterized by trite diction (counterwords), too many adjectives and adverbs, and emphatic punctuation (underlinings, exclamation points, dashes); confessional adolescent writing.

schoolmarmish *adj.* Fussily pedantic; priggish and punctilious about language or learning. *N.* schoolmarm.

. . . Flaubert himself became something of a pedant. In the Dictionary he grows schoolmarmish over common expressions that are justifiable and useful, such as that which marks the contrast between warmed air in a sheltered spot and the open air which is cooler.
—Jacques Barzun, Introduction to Gustave Flaubert,
The Dictionary of Accepted Ideas

Schwank [*shvängk*] *n.* A comic folk tale or anecdote (from German word for comical tale).

schwärmerei [*shvâr'me·rī"*] *n.* Excessive enthusiasm or sentiment; treacle (from the German word for ardent enthusiasm).

scientism *n.* The assumptions, methods, and viewpoints characteristic of the natural sciences, but more recently as misapplied, with simplifications and distortions, to the social sciences and humanities as well; scientific and pseudoscientific language, generally to impart a solemn tone and air of authority to writing, and hence a cause of turgid abstraction and jargon. *Adj.* scientistic; *adv.* scientistically.

Scientism is the fixation that the research methods of the natural sciences are the only valid means of acquiring knowledge in any academic discipline. Scientism is the science of making a science out of something that isn't a science, such as communicology.
—John Bremner, *Words on Words*

sciolism [*sī'ə·liz"əm*] *n.* Superficial knowledge or pretended scholarship; shallowness. *Adj.* sciolistic, sciolous; *adv.* sciolistically; *n.* sciolist.

His style was geological, so to speak, consisting of various strata deposited at various periods. The surface stratum, representing the Kainozoic Time, consisted of the platitudinous bombast characteristic of the common or oratorical demagogue. Below that, corresponding to the Mesozoic Time, came the ridiculous obsequious slang of the bagman of commerce. Below that again, corresponding to the Paleozoic Time, appeared the gelded English which muscleless feckless unfit-for-handicraft little sciolists acquire in school-board spawning beds.   —Frederick William Rolfe (Frederick Baron Corvo), *Hadrian the Seventh*

scissors-and-paste *adj.* See CUT-AND-PASTE.

scoop *n.* A news story or item obtained by a single reporter or publication, and hence an advantage or success against competitors in the news media; journalistic coup; information, esp. essential facts or confidential data. *V.* scoop.

Scotticism *n.* A Scottish word, expression, or pronunciation used in English, e.g., "bonnie," "wee." *V.* Scotticize.

He had been teased in Scotland for his immense learning and bookish ways: in London, he must have seemed a very odd character to his fellow clerks in the bank, with his Scotticisms and his rather prim views on religion and morals.
—K. M. Elisabeth Murray, *Caught in the Web of Words*

scrambled words See FRAMIS.

screamer See special entry NEWSROOM HEADLINE JARGON, p. 386.

screaming gin and ignorance *British* Bad newspaper writing.

screed *n.* A lengthy speech or discourse; protracted harangue; diatribe.

A tirade is in itself a perfectly respectable literary form; there are many splendid modern examples, ranging from the grand harangue of Shaw's mouthpiece, Don Juan, in "Man and Superman," to the screeds of Nathanael West's surrogate, Shrike, in "Miss Lonely-hearts." —Harold Bloom, *The New York Times*

scribblative *adj.* Describing hasty and verbose writing.

scribble *v.* To make meaningless marks on; write down hastily and carelessly or thoughtlessly, sometimes illegibly; compose casually or with no particular literary intent; dash off. *N.* scribble, scribbler.

Thus, Lévi-Strauss puts the conventional sign for "to minus one power" where the word "opposition" or "contrast" is appropriate. For instance: since many cosmologies treat fire and water as opposites, he writes "fire $=$ water$^{(-1)}$"—a strange and meaningless scribble which is neither an equation nor a sentence.
—Stanislav Andreski, *Social Sciences as Sorcery*

scripturient *adj.* Having a great urge to write or be an author.

sculler See special entry BOOKISH APPELLATIONS, p. 407.

scurrilous *adj.* Using or characterized by grossly abusive language, such as that of a gutter flyer, or vulgarly jocular; foul-mouthed. *Adj.* scurrilously; *n.* scurrility, scurrilousness.

One of the scurrilous cheap-shooters, aghast and nonplussed at the French Smith counterattack, whimpered in print that a man in the position of attorney general "must start acting immediately like Caesar's wife." —William Safire, *What's the Good Word?*

secondary source A derivative or indirect source of information in research, such as comment by a historian, an encyclopedia article, or a critical essay (contrasted with primary source).

They are all educated women, though—in that age group which learned its courtesies from its own mothers; its loves from Paolo and Francesca, Bronte, Joyce, and even O'Hara; and all the solid enthusiasms in its cast of mind from what we used to emphasize were not anthologies, textbooks, or other secondary works, but from originals, the works themselves. —Renata Adler, *Speedboat*

second coming type See special entry NEWSROOM HEADLINE JARGON, p. 386.

sedulous ape See special entry BOOKISH APPELLATIONS, p. 407.

Sekundenstil [*ze·koŏn'den·shtēl"*] *n.* A literary style based on exact, minute observation of detail, but especially the phonographic reproduction of spoken words as a style of naturalistic writing.

The "consistent" naturalism of his early work moved towards an interior "Sekundenstil," until, finally, flights of the imagination and eruptions of the unconscious more or less displace any empirical *donnée*. —Anthony Phelan, *Times Literary Supplement*

self-referential *adj.* Denoting a sentence, statement, novel, etc., that refers to itself, such as certain paradoxical statements and works of experimental or avant-garde fiction. *Adj.* self-referring. See also AUTOLOGICAL.

Does this quintessentially self-referential experiment, which could be described as a meditation on the possibilities of the novel form, still warrant the term "novel"?
—Francine du Plessix Gray, *The New York Times*

selling idea A headline phrase or slogan used as the central theme of an advertisement or advertising campaign.

semantic, semantical *adj.* Pertaining to meaning in language or in philosophy; involving choice of words; terminological. *Adv.* semantically; *v.* semanticize.

semantics *n.* The science of verbal meaning, including the historical development and changes in the significations of words or linguistic forms, meliorative and pejorative influences, cultural and psychological associations, and factors of linguistic context; the denotations, connotations, and ambiguities of words; the use or manipulation of connotation; the issue of the choice and interpretation of words; terminology. *N.* semanticist.

Semantics is not now the lively concern that it was a few years ago, but the mythology of what we may call political semantics has become established in our intellectual life, the belief that we are betrayed by words, that words push us around against our will.
—Lionel Trilling, *The Liberal Imagination*

semiliterate *adj.*   Showing barely adequate or limited literacy; inferior in use of or familiarity with language; poorly read. *N.* semiliteracy.

> Semiliterates don't read Flaubert and intellectuals don't as a rule read the current fat slab of goosed history masquerading as an historical novel.   —Raymond Chandler, *Raymond Chandler Speaking*

sentence fragment   See FRAGMENT.

sententiae [*sen·ten'chē·ē"*] *n. pl.*   Brief and memorable sayings; aphorisms. *Sing.* sententia.

sententious *adj.*   Pithy and epigrammatic, as a passage with sentences that seem discrete and provocative in themselves; showing or given to self-important moralizing; high-sounding and opinionated. *Adv.* sententiously; *n.* sententiousness.

> Far from sharing Guillam's bewilderment, he seemed curiously confident—even complacent—to the extent of allowing himself a sententious aphorism from Steed-Asprey on the arts of double-cross; something about not looking for perfection, but for advantage, which again had Guillam thinking about Camilla.
> —John le Carré, *Tinker, Tailor, Soldier, Spy*

septic verbs   A. P. Herbert's term for pseudo-scientific or pseudo-official verbs ill-born from nouns, such as "eventuate," "finalize," "spectate"; bureaucratic or pedantic verb barbarisms meant to sound authoritative.

seriatim [*sir"ē·ā'təm*]   In series; point by point.

sermocination [*sûr·mos"ə·nā'shən*] *n.*   Answering one's own question.

sermo vulgus   Popular speech or idiom; vernacular.

> Rather curiously, the *sermo vulgus* was for long as diligently neglected by the professional writers of the country as by the philologians.   —H. L. Mencken, *The American Language*

service feature   A newspaper or magazine article catering to personal or consumer interests of the readership, such as one providing information on health or available products (sometimes those of its advertising clients); feature summarizing or explaining a complex news matter.

sesquipedalian *n.*   A very long word. *Pl.* sesquipedalia; *adj.* sesquipedalian; *n.* sesquipedalianism, sesquipedality.

It would actually be effrontery on my part to call medical and scientific English a jargon, once it is out of the quagmire of formulas and sesquipedalian words; this language is not trying to look pretty, but has a duty to be exact, clear, and in a highly conventional style.

—Basil Cottle, *The Plight of English*

sesquipedality *n.*   Use of long words; sesquipedalian style.

The hate letters I receive at *New York* magazine just for my alleged sesquipedality are legion.   —John Simon, *Paradigms Lost*

set piece   A composition or writing segment that is conventional and formal in its presentation, sometimes self-conscious or meant to impress; scene having a prescribed structure; part of a larger work that is self-contained or sui generis.

It is a style admirably suited to the flaming set-piece, the rapid vignette, the picaresque excursion. But it is not so well suited to a sustained and complex action, or a lengthy flow of experience, or a tragic plot, or what George Moore, in discussing the nature of fiction, called the "rhythmic sequence of events."

—Irving Howe, in *The Critic as Artist*

shaggy-dog story   A long and improbable, if not absurd, fablelike yarn or conundrum that promises a surprise ending but instead winds down to a deflatingly trite, quasi-humorous conclusion; long joke with an irrelevant punch line; belabored groaner.

He laughed all through the exposition, not nervously as people will who are afraid of missing the point, but heartily, relishing every moment of it for its own sake and only slightly less than he did the payoff, which he greeted with a final roar of delight. The fact that it was a shaggy dog story fortified Tattersall's damaged faith in his capacity for special humor.

—Peter De Vries, *The Cat's Pajamas*

shelf life   See special entry BOOK PUBLISHING TERMS, p. 363.

Sherman statement, Sherman   A politician's final, irrevocable announcement that he or she will not be a candidate, though not always lived up to (from General William T. Sherman's refusal to be a presidential nominee, or to serve if elected, in a wire to the Republican National Convention in 1884).

. . . Mr. Ford is showing that he, too, knows all the lines and bits of business. . . . To a group of Congressmen about such statements as the one in Nashville: "That's not a Sherman."

—Tom Wicker, *The New York Times*

shibboleth *n.* A criterion, watchword, or pet phrase, or a self-identifying slogan; term of acceptance or conformity; sacred cow; peculiarity of speech distinctive to a particular group of people.

Overhearing a conversation between two practitioners of such jargon gives one the impression that neither understands the other any more than he understands himself, which is just as well, since neither is saying anything anyway; most such "conversations" are mere attempts by some ninnyhammer to impress his counterpart that he is familiar with the trendy shibboleths of the current scene.
                                                    —Laurence Urdang, *Verbatim*

shirttail *n.* A brief, related, or late-breaking news item appended to the end of an article.

shmooz, shmoos, shmooze *v. Yiddish* To have a heart-to-heart chat; hobnob; gossip.

And as a master social mountaineer, he was the doctor who had time to nosh with them, schmooze with them, counsel their adored children, . . . who had the time to sit up all night with them if the situation required.   —Shana Alexander, *Very Much a Lady*

shocker *n. British* A sordidly sensational story or book; piece of cheap pulp fiction; thriller (novel).

shoptalk, shop *n.* An informal occupational vocabulary, esp. slang terms and abbreviations in lieu of more formal technical language; colloquial professional jargon; conversation about one's job or field of interest.

On my desk, at the moment, I have the letters that Ring wrote to us; here is a letter one thousand words long, here is one of two thousand words—theatrical gossip, literary shop talk, flashes of wit but not much wit, for he was feeling thin and saving the best of that for his work, anecdotes of his activities.
                                    —F. Scott Fitzgerald, in *The Critic as Artist*

short *n.* A brief or filler item in a newspaper.

shorthand *n.* A symbolic or phonetic system for writing rapidly; any handy, abbreviated manner of expression; expedient language. *Adj.* shorthand.

By connoting entire legends, historical events, literary plots, and other concepts in single words or phrases, allusions form a kind of shorthand.   —Clifton Fadiman, *Britannica Book of English Usage*

short story A piece of fiction of limited scope but self-contained or unified in its focus on a single, salient theme and effect.

> In Toronto, before we had ever come to Paris, I had been told Katharine Mansfield was a good short-story writer, even a great short-story writer, but trying to read her after Chekov was like hearing the carefully artificial tales of a young old-maid compared to those of an articulate and knowing physician who was a good and simple writer.
> —Ernest Hemingway, *A Moveable Feast*

shriek See SCREAMER.

shtick *n.* A worked-up, contrived form of talent or self-presentation to entertain or win attention; an idiosyncratic routine or particular forte; mannerism.

> Rebuttal is inappropriate. For what we have here is no argument but a *shtick,* as we used to say in vaudeville, an antic, a bit, a thing.
> —Donald Kaplan, in *Language in America*

shucking and jiving Posturing in speech and gesture to give a false impression or deceptive information, either to protect oneself or deal with authority; misleading or distracting fast-talk; verbal bluffing and dissembling.

sic *adv.* Thus, or as it appears in the sentence: used after a questionable word or spelling in quoted matter to indicate that it has been left intact and uncorrected. V. sic.

> But he twice misspells "plagiarize" as *plagerize,* which the editors duly note with a *sic*. —John Simon, *Paradigms Lost*

sic passim Thus throughout, or found in various other places in the book, as in the case of a particular expression or spelling.

sidebar *n.* A brief sidelight news story accompanying a major story to provide additional information; follow-up.

> "What the hell do we keep you in London for if you can't produce a simple sidebar?" an editor would say. "Your last expense account looks like the national debt. You're always taking a diplomat to lunch on us. You ought to be able to get ahold of some of them now and find out what they think about Stalin."
> —John Chancellor and Walter R. Mears, *The News Business*

signed *adj. British* Having a byline.

significatio See special entry RHETORIC TERMS, p. 404.

signifying *n.*   In the culture of American blacks, a verbal game of exchanged insults, whether in the form of imaginative circumlocutions or one-upping one-liners; taunting, opprobrious repartee; duel of put-downs. Also CAPPING, CRACKING, JOANING, LUGGING, SOUNDING, WOOFING. See also DOZENS, (PLAYING) THE.

> Another unique characteristic of signification is that it can be both light and heavy. Sounding, capping, joaning, and lugging are generally lightweight, that is, for verbal posturing. Signifying, on the other hand, can also be heavy, that is, a way of teaching or driving home a cognitive message but—and this is important—without preaching or lecturing. An example of lightweight siggin or cappin is provided in the playful name-calling rituals, such as: "You so ugly look like you been hit by a ugly stick," and "Yo natural look like this broad on the wall" (pointing to a picture of Medusa).
> —Geneva Smitherman, *Talkin and Testifyin*

signpost line   An authorial statement in the text that serves to tell the reader what has already been said, what is to come, etc., such as a statement of purpose, transition, or summary; notational sentence; pregnant allusion or portentous line.

> The dialogue is full of signpost lines ("There are some things in the past you don't like to think about") and salty Texas talk that pales beside that of such shows as "A Texas Trilogy," "Lone Star" and "The Best Little Whorehouse in Texas."
> —Frank Rich, *The New York Times*

signpost writing   John Bremner's term for exposition cluttered with references such as "above-mentioned," "aforesaid," "discussed below," etc.; self-consciously procedural scholarly prose.

sillabub, syllabub [*sil'ə·bub*] *n.*   Floridly inane language that is frothy and unsubstantial; vapid discourse.

sillograph   See special entry BOOKISH APPELLATIONS, p. 407.

silly season   A slack, stagnant period for news, when newspapers resort to trivialities to fill space, esp. the month of August; journalistic dog days.

silver fork diction, silver fork school   The preciously genteel prose in novels (notably those of Edward Bulwer-Lytton) about aristocratic characters, the social graces, etiquette, etc., and in some cases by authors unfamiliar with such a milieu

Much else in Disraeli's mode of life was equally perilous. Writing novels—and such novels: romans à clef caricaturing people who were important to his career, "silver fork" novels romanticizing (and ridiculing) high society, a historical novel fantasizing and eulogizing the Hebrew "race"—that was hardly a prescription for political success.
—Gertrude Himmelfarb, *The New Republic*

simile *n.* An expressive or evocative comparison of two essentially unlike things, usually after the word "like" or "as"; figurative likening.

His turbulent and undisciplined rhetoric had acquired, by the regular convention of its usage, something of the movement and directness of classical epithet: his similes were preposterous, created really in a spirit of vulgar mirth, and the great comic intelligence that was in the family—down to the youngest—was shaken daily by it.
—Thomas Wolfe, *Look Homeward, Angel*

simplistic *adj.* Presented or interpreted with a false simplicity, ignoring complexities; oversimplified. *Adv.* simplistically; *n.* simplism.

And change is life. The slang of the poor, the new technical terms and jargon of the professionals, the cant of journalism, the simplistic language notions of pop grammarians—all keep language from going stale.
—Jim Quinn, *American Tongue and Cheek*

singsong *adj.* Characterized by verselike monotony of sound, rhythm, or both, esp. with rhyme or a mechanical rising and falling of pitch. *N.* singsong; *v.* singsong.

Only the ears busy to catch the speech are not alone; the ears are caught tight, linked tight by the tendrils of phrased words, the turn of a joke, the singsong fade of a story, the gruff fall of a sentence.
—John Dos Passos, *The Big Money*

sit venia verbis [*sit wen'ē·ə wer'bēs*] Pardon my words.

sizzle seller A product that is successfully advertised and marketed by image, or attractive or prestigious associations, rather than by worth or substance.

skeletonize *v.* To render writing in an abbreviated or outline form; reduce to essentials or a framework; shorten, for monetary reasons, news copy to be cabled to another office, usually by eliminating articles and other expendable words. *N.* skeletonization

skimble-skamble *adj.* Confusingly rambling or disconnected; senseless. *N.* skimble-skamble.

> "You don't know what you're doing! Stop making this sentence, and begin instead to make Moholy-Nagy cocktails, for those are what we really need, on the frontiers of bad behavior!" and then he falls to the floor, and a trap door opens under him, and he falls through that, into a damp pit where a blue narwhal waits, its horn poised (but maybe the weight of the messenger, falling from such a height, will break off the horn)—thus, considering everything carefully, in the sweet light of the ceremonial axes, in the run-mad skimble-skamble of information sickness, we must make a decision as to whether we should proceed, or go back. . . .   —Donald Barthelme, *City Life*

skyline head   See special entry NEWSROOM HEADLINE JARGON, p. 386.

slander *n.*   Malicious charges, misrepresentation, or falsehood (but when written treated as an instance of libel) that is injurious to the reputation of another; spoken defamation. *Adj.* slanderous; *adv.* slanderously; *v.* slander.

> But Pinsky's outraged lawyers put in an immediate appeal, on the grounds that Mr. Justice Boyer had misdirected the jury with a blatant and inexcusable racial slander.
>   —Mordecai Richler, *Joshua Then and Now*

slang *n.*   Informal, highly metaphorical idiom or language that arises out of newly coined words and phrases and, with a generally appealing liveliness in its easy, elliptical irreverence or humor, is typified by clipped words, vivid epithets, and playful exaggeration or terse immediacy; colorfully expressive nonstandard speech; lingo or jargon that sets a group apart; cant. *Adj.* slangy, slangish; *adv.* slangily; *n.* slanginess; *v.* slang.

> Standard English, by Webster's own definition, excludes slang; yet slang—at any rate, transatlantic slang—is well represented. *Hep, beatnik, hipster, square, in the groove,* are all there. . . .
>   —Christopher Small, *Dictionaries and That Dictionary*

slanging match *British*   A heated or prolonged exchange of insults, esp. between supposedly dignified parties; abusive quarrel.

slanguage *n.*   Slangy speech or writing.

> The English seldom differentiate between American slang and Americanisms in respectable use; both they label as the American slanguage.   —H. L. Mencken, *The American Language*

slant *n.* A presenting or construing in a one-sided way, as through loaded wording, intrusive phrases, or omission, overemphasis, or deemphasis; dishonest or prejudiced reporting; particular point of view behind a report, news story, etc., that caters to a specific audience or reflects the opinion of the writer or his publication; appeal to a certain readership. *Adj.* slanted; *v.* slant.

He had noticed the cautious "slanting" of news stories, the half-hints, the vague allusions, the peculiar adjectives peculiarly placed, the stressing of certain themes, the insertion of political conclusions where none was needed. If a story concerned a dispute between employer and employee, the employer was made to appear guilty, simply through wording, no matter what the facts presented.
—Ayn Rand, *The Fountainhead*

slate *v. British* To criticize severely; berate; pan.

sleight-of-mouth *n.* Cleverly equivocal or deceiving use of words; suspicious verbal adroitness.

slice-of-life *adj.* Showing or characterized by an unselectively naturalistic rendering of day-to-day life, as in a short story portraying starkly working-class existence; depicting actual experience.

slick *adj.* Describing or characteristic of high-circulation magazines printed on glossy, coated paper, as contrasted with cheaper (but not necessarily inferior) pulp publications. *N.* slick.

Incidentally, for the slicks you do need certain rudimentary entertainment skills—a comic use of the first person, a bag of shiny phrases. For the rest, simple waltz steps will do.
—Wilfrid Sheed, "The Politics of Reviewing"

slip of the tongue An error in speech or writing, usually trivial but sometimes telling or belying; verbal lapse.

Words, phrases, skipped through my mind; I saw the blue haze again. What had I meant by saying that I had become "more human"? Was it a phrase that I had picked up from some preceding speaker, or a slip of the tongue? —Ralph Ellison, *Invisible Man*

slipshod extension H. W. Fowler's term for the ignorant bending of word meaning by the careless or uninformed, typically because the misused word has to them a better ring than a similar, more common term, e.g., the current broader meanings of "di-

lemma" and "protagonist"; semantic degeneration. See also
POPULARIZED TECHNICALITY.

The recent slipshod extension to describe any sort of graded organization, as in the upper *echelons* of management, is otiose (there are simpler words to do the job), and weakens the vocabulary by destroying the special meaning of echelon.

—Philip Howard, *Words Fail Me*

slipslop *n.* See MALAPROPISM.

slogan *n.*   A statement or expression adopted to bespeak a position, attitude, or goal or to characterize or represent; rallying cry; brief promotional phrase or motto used for attention-getting advertising. *Adj.* sloganistic; *adv.* sloganistically; *v.* sloganize.

He has come here to-night to help you with your moral and spiritual problems, to provide you with a slogan, a cause, an absolute value and a *raison d'être*.   —Nathanael West, *Miss Lonelyhearts*

sloganeer *v.*   To coin or use slogans to influence or persuade, as in political campaigning or advertising.

Sloganeering consists largely of ritualistic utterances that are intended to communicate solidarity. . . . The first thing, then, that needs to be stressed is that sloganeering, by definition, is a repudiation of individual thought, another example of what Huxley calls "herd poisoning."   —Neil Postman, *Crazy Talk, Stupid Talk*

slur *n.*   A disparaging remark or insinuation; insult, aspersion, or sleight; derogation or stigma; a sliding over without due consideration or attention; in utterance, a blurring or omitting of sounds, thereby running syllables or words together. *V.* slur. See also CHARIENTISM.

This slurring of words into a refined cadence until they cease to be words at all is due partly to the Englishman's disinclination to move his lips. Evidently the lips and teeth are held stationary for the most part, open just wide enough to let in air for breathing (many Englishmen must breathe through their mouths, otherwise they would not breathe at all) with an occasional sharp pursing of the lips on a syllable which does *not* call for pursing the lips.
—Robert Benchley, "The King's English: Not Murder but Suicide"

slurvian *n.*   John Davenport's facetious name for American speech characterized by carelessly slurred pronunciations, e.g., "c'mon," "whaddja do"; a speaker of slurvian. *Adj.* slurvian; *n.* slurvianism.

Unfortunately for the fun, however, these slurred forms happen to be the accepted, standard pronunciations. Though they may not be for long. The emphatic righteousness of the anti-slurvians is having an immense effect among the half-educated and the insecure.

—Bergen Evans, *Comfortable Words*

slush *n.*   Cheaply sentimental or obvious writing; maudlin drivel.

I never would have believed him capable of the revolting slush which now proceeded from his lips at the rate of about two hundred and fifty words to the minute. When I tell you that the observation "There, there, little girl!" was the only one I can bring myself to quote, you will be able to gather something of the ordeal to which I was subjected. And, to make matters worse, on an empty stomach, mind you.

—P. G. Wodehouse, *Thank You, Jeeves*

slush pile   See special entry BOOK PUBLISHING TERMS, p. 363.

small talk   Casual talk of no consequence, often out of social protocol; idle, trivial conversation. *V.* small-talk.

Once Yossarian had driven him back from the nose, Aarfy was free to cower on the floor where Yossarian longed to cower, but he stood bolt upright instead with his stumpy arms resting comfortably on the backs of the pilot's and co-pilot's seats, pipe in hand, making affable small talk to McWatt and whoever happened to be co-pilot and pointing out amusing trivia in the sky to the two men, who were too busy to be interested.   —Joseph Heller, *Catch-22*

smear word   A word that besmirches or slanders somebody or something, esp. a malicious political epithet, e.g., calling a political candidate an "agent for big business" or an "anti-Semite."

He is stigmatized as a "liberal" (a smear word nowadays in this particular context), as "permissive," as one who "has no standards," all because he conceives it to be his primary function to record, study, and, if he is lucky, to make some significant comment on the facts of linguistic change.

—Thomas Pyles, *Selected Essays on English Usage*

smoking-room story   A racy or indecent story; smutty anecdote or joke.

smut *n.*   Plainly indecent and unredeemed obscenity, such as a graphic and vulgar pornographic work; degraded art or literature. *Adj.* smutty; *adv.* smuttily; *n.* smuttiness.

Look around, for heaven sakes; actual pornography clipped from those smut books and pinned on the walls—she was planning, inci-

dentally, to see to it that the Main Building made an investigation of the *dirt* that had been brought into this hospital.
—Ken Kesey, *One Flew Over the Cuckoo's Nest*

snarl-word *n.* S. I. Hayakawa's term for a subjective expression that, a verbal equivalent of a snarl, growl, or angry gesture, is a form of emphatic judgment rather than a report or statement and is used to express disapproval or, often, to determine whether others also disapprove; emotionally laden derogatory word or expression (contrasted with a purr-word).

Racist has become a snarl word, roughly synonymous with the sound *ugh!*   —Neil Postman, *Crazy Talk, Stupid Talk*

sneer word A word used with irony or contempt to cast aspersion on a person or thing, or an adjective used to express dissociation from a particular term or concept, e.g., "self-styled"; derisive epithet or qualifier.

snow job A wordy presentation, intended to be persuasive, that is insincere, hollow, or cunningly complimentary, such as a fulsome explanation or padded term paper; glib bluffing or fakery; flattery or self-excuse.

soapbox *adj.* A street orator's platform, hence pertaining to or describing personal speechmaking, esp. self-important political oratory or public haranguing. *N.* soapbox; *v.* soapbox.

His style is that of the soapbox orator who has to make his points and be quick about it because the police will be by at any moment asking him to move along.   —Donal Henahan, *The New York Times*

sobriquet *n.* A fanciful or humorous designation or appellation; nickname.

Lady Emmeline not only refrained from denouncing the speech of Americans; she actually praised their habit, then in full tide, of giving grandiloquent sobriquets to their cities.
—H. L. Mencken, *The American Language*

sob sister A journalist or columnist who presents mawkish human-interest stories or letters and offers personal advice; sentimentalist or do-gooder.

The twins brought the one-liner into what had once been strictly sob-sister territory. The cutting edge of urban Jewish humor and the puncture-the-pompous quip are what make "Dear Abby" so readable.
—Caryl Rivers, *The New York Times*

sob story, sob stuff A sentimental or sad account intended to arouse sympathy.

sociologese *n.* Turgid jargon in the field of sociology, characterized by pseudo-scientific terminology, human and social-institution generalities, and a general abstractness.

The following passage appeared in a journal for sociologists and social psychologists: "The purpose of this article is to demonstrate that media influence is a function of the receptiveness of message recipients to communications in general. It is also to show that this receptiveness is a scalable predispositioning attitude which is directly and positively correlated with the number of types of media to which message recipients are exposed, the impact these media have, and the overt behavior induced by media exposure and contact." Which, being interpreted, means: "I intend to show that newspapers and television and other 'mass media' are influential if people pay attention to them, and that the more people are bombarded with any given message, the more they will respond to it." A truism about human behavior is all that lurks behind the verbiage.
— Robert Altick, *A Preface to Critical Reading*

sockdolager [*sok·dol′ə·jər*] *n.* A decisive answer or argument (or blow) that settles an issue.

Socratic irony The pretense of innocence or ignorance in discourse in order to expose the weakness or falsity of an opposing viewpoint; adroitly disingenuous reasoning or questioning.

Suddenly he was the "good soldier Schweik," politely stupid, obsequiously confused, maddeningly witty, a master of Socratic irony.
— John Hersey, *The Wall*

Socratic method Directed discussion or philosophical inquiry by means of progressive questions, posed by the teacher, that lead to a logical conclusion or concession. See also MAIEUTIC.

Wu was not a very good novelist, but he was a smart man. He knew that I was homesick and depressed and he tried, in his way, to help me. Sometimes, in the manner of Confucius, he gave me advice, but more often his approach was gently Socratic.
— Larry McMurtry, *All My Friends Are Going to Be Strangers*

soft soap Language that attempts to sweeten or varnish; cajolery or flattery; smooth talk. *V.* soft-soap.

Dave bawled him out and accused him of stalling. Kane stalled just the same. Then Dave soft-soaped him, told him how he'd burn up the

league and how we were all depending on him to put us in the race
and keep us there. But he might as well have been talking to a
mounted policeman.   —Ring Lardner, "Hurry Kane"

soi-disant [*swä'dē·zän'*] *adj.*   Self-styled, or presumptuously so-
called; supposed or pretended.

It is a pity Jonathan Miller did not include in his team . . . a novelist
or playwright. We might have learned more from them than from
some of the *soi-disant* experts whom he did include.
                              —Stuart Sutherland, *Times Literary Supplement*

solecism *n.*   Any violation of grammatical rule, syntax, or proper
idiom in usage, such as a malapropism, dangler, or mixed metaphor; misused word; impropriety or illiteracy. *Adj.* solecistic,
solecistical; *adv.* solecistically; *n.* solecist; *v.* solecize.

After an honorable fellow in righteous wrath has told a blackguard
what he is, to wit, a murderer, a blasphemer, and a rapist, what more
is there to say than that he is an utterer of solecisms?
                              —Charlton Laird, *The Miracle of Language*

soliloquy *n.*   A dramatic or literary monologue, usually medita-
tive or philosophical and uttered in the context of solitude;
discourse with oneself. *Adv.* soliloquizingly; *n.* soliloquist; *v.*
soliloquize.

Lonigan kept nodding his head in thought, and soliloquizing that he
didn't know what to say, because she was right, and yet a lot of this
education was nothing but booklearning, nothing but bunk. He had
some new thoughts, and these fed further soliloquizing.
                              —James T. Farrell, *Young Lonigan*

solipsism *n.*   The philosophy or conviction that the self can know
only its own states or experiential changes, or that the self is
all that exists; extreme absorption with oneself, esp. that of an
artist; egoism. *Adj.* solipsistic; *adv.* solipsistically; *n.* solipsist.

Joyce and Woolf bade their characters think on the page to deepen
the characters, not to flatten the world solipsistically.
                              —Annie Dillard, *Living by Fiction*

somniloquence *n.*   Talking in one's sleep.

sonic writing   John Bremner's term for unwittingly misspelled
words prompted by their similarity in sound to the correct
words, e.g., "under weigh," "polls apart"; malapropistic homophony. See also HOMONYM SLIP, MONDEGREEN.

sonorous *adj.* Full, deep, or rich in sound; resonant; impressively and euphoniously high-sounding; compellingly worded or styled. *Adv.* sonorously; *n.* sonority, sonorousness.

His sonorous periods, his mystic vocabulary, his bold flights into the rarefied air of the abstract, were thrilling to a fancy unhampered by the need of definitions.

—Edith Wharton, "The Angel at the Grave"

sooterkin [*soot'ər·kin*] *n. British*   An abortive scheme or enterprise; imperfect or supplementary literary composition.

sophism *n.*   Clever or intellectually impressive but specious disputation; deceptive point or argument.

sophistry *n.*   Subtly or cleverly persuasive but fallacious reasoning. *Adj.* sophistic, sophistical; *adv.* sophistically; *n.* sophist, sophisticalness.

Narcissism: when one grows too old to believe in one's uniqueness, one falls in love with one's complexity—as if layers of lies could replace the green illusion; or the sophistries of failure, the stench of success.   —John Fowles, *Daniel Martin*

soriasmus [*sôr"ē·az'məs*] *n.*   See MINGLE-MANGLE.

sorites [*sə·rī'tēz*] *n.*   An argument that is a series of sequentially related propositions, with the predicate of one becoming the subject of the next, and the conclusion tying back with the original subject; concatenation of syllogisms, e.g., "Writers are readers; readers are adventurers; adventurers are unpredictable; hence writers are unpredictable." *Adj.* soritical, soritic.

sound and fury   Intense or strident language that is fundamentally meaningless; empty words; bombast.

Pick up any magazine or newspaper and you will find many of the articles devoted to sound and fury from politicians, editors, leaders of industry, and diplomats.   —Stuart Chase, *The Tyranny of Words*

sounding *adj. British*   More impressive in sound than in truth or sense; high-toned.

sounding *n.*   See SIGNIFYING.

source book   An original, authoritative chronicle, document, etc., of importance as a basis or inspiration for subsequent writings and scholarship.

source-mining *n.*   J. H. Hexter's term for drawing on evidence or supportive quotations to bolster one's case while disregarding or mitigating contrary evidence; biased use of supporting facts; loaded or tendentious research.

sous-entendu [*soo·zän·tän·dü*] *n.* Something implied, understood, or insinuated; subtext or nuance.

sparsim [*spär'sim*]   Here and there; passim.

spatchcock *v. British*   To insert into a text as an afterthought or hurriedly; patch in; interpolate (from term for fowl prepared and cooked in haste).

In *The* (London) *Times* of April 8, 1974, it was said that certain students of international affairs "thought it . . . irregular that Mr. Callaghan, the Foreign Secretary, should have *spatchcocked* in his formal statement to the Council of Ministers on the terms of membership of the EEC a long quotation from the Labour Party's election manifesto."   —Norman Schur, *English English*

special pleading   The proferring of new material or information to counter an opponent's allegations instead of denying them; any deceptive argument that emphasizes only a particular or favorable aspect of an issue, situation, thing, etc.; cajolery or hype with a particular motive.

We are alerted that what is to follow is "amazing," "mind-boggling," "profound" or "staggering." Those prepared to overlook this special pleading and hyperbole will find informative descriptions of how the principles of quantum mechanics have affected the scientific world view.   —Timothy Ferris, *The New York Times*

specious *adj.*   Deceptive in appearing sound, persuasive, or genuine; seemingly true but false; fallacious; sophistical. *Adv.* speciously; *n.* speciousness.

"How infinite," wrote a master of the specious art of political doubletalk, "is the debt owed to metaphors by politicians who want to speak strongly but are not sure what they are going to say."
                   —Philip Howard, *Words Fail Me*

speech *n.*   The faculty of uttering sounds or words, or the power of articulation; the vocal aspects of language; nature or manner of speaking; talk or conversational interchange; instance of vocal expression by one person; individual statement or formal public address; lengthy statement; particular language, dialect, idiom, or style of expression.

I hazard that the King James Bible, the rhetoric of the store-front church, something ironic and violent and perpetually understated in Negro speech—and something of Dickens' love for bravura—have something to do with me today; but I wouldn't stake my life on it.
—James Baldwin, *Notes of a Native Son*

speechcraft *n.* Skill in speaking, as by command of rhetoric.

speech disorder Any of various chronic or pathological disabilities affecting human utterance or reading ability.

Terms for these conditions include acataphasia, agrammatism, alexia, allolalia, ambolalia, anepia, aphemia, apraxia, asemasia, asomotognosia, barbaralalia, baryphony, bradyarthria, coprolalia, cyclogy, dolichologia, dysarthria, dyslalia, dyslexia, dyslogia, dysphasia, dysphemia, dysphrasia, dysprosody, gammacism, halophobia, hemiplegia, heterophasia, idiolalla, lallation, lambdacism, laloplegia, monoideism, neolalia, palilalia, paraphasia, parolalia, pseudolalia, rhotacism, schizothemia, sigmatism, tachylalia, tachyphrasia, and traulism. See also APHASIA, ECHOLALIA, GLOSSOLALIA.

speechify *v.* To hold forth or harangue, esp. in a perfunctorily verbose or predictable manner.

In the chateau, where Virginie conscientiously tends the hearth, the harem-master—Seigneur—is a noble, enigmatic swell in ivory-colored breeches whose speechifying (tediously) spells out the novel's theme.   —James Wolcott, *New York Review of Books*

speech tag An attributive phrase for reported utterance, e.g., "he said," such as is used with quotations or dialogue.

speechway *n. (usually pl.)* A manner or tendency of speech in a particular group, region, or culture; style of talk.

Only an inch or so below the level of Harvard and Groton, English speechways are regarded as preposterous, and even as a shade indecent.   —H. L. Mencken, *The American Language*

speechwriting *n.* The writing of speeches, esp. as a profession for hired specialists. *N.* speechwriter.

"Actually, speechwriting is the reverse of newspaper writing," he says. "You put the important things near the end in a speech."
—Anthony Dolan, quoted by Francis X. Clines, *The New York Times*

spelling *n.* The representation of words by specific letters in a prescribed sequence; orthography; letters with which a word is written; ability to write words correctly. *V.* spell.

Now, instead of just telling me how to spell it, the teachers would always say, angrily, too, "Don't be lazy, David Brenner! Look the word up in the dictionary!"
  Teachers are really stupid! In order to look a word up in a dictionary you have to know how to spell it!
                    —David Brenner, *Soft Pretzels with Mustard*

spellword *n.*   A word used to cast a spell.

spiel *n.*   A voluble speech, esp. a glib presentation intended to persuade or sell; harangue; pitch. *V.* spiel.

The magistrate took off his glasses, and told Cora she was charged with the murder of Nick Papadikis. . . . It was a long spiel, and you could hear them coughing before he got done.
                    —James M. Cain, *The Postman Always Rings Twice*

spinach *n.*   Something undesirable or repellent; substance of expression that is unnecessary or irrelevant; nonsense, excrescence.

He has, in recent weeks, told so many readers of so many magazines so much about himself and the various meanings of his new novel and why the reviewers aren't going to like it or him that the book itself— quite a good one, incidentally—all but snores under a pile of symbolic spinach.   —John Leonard, *The New York Times*

spirit writing   See AUTOMATIC WRITING.

splendide mendax   [*splen'də·dā" men'däks*]   Honorably untruthful; lying, but for a good purpose.

split infinitive   An infinitive expressed with a modifier separating the "to" from its verb complement.

He dined at half-past seven on some soup, and haricot-beans with butter, and a baked apple. Meanwhile he counted the split infinitives in the day's *Pall Mall Gazette.*
                    —Frederick William Rolfe (Frederick Baron Corvo),
                                              Hadrian the Seventh

sponge word   C. Wright Mills's term for a word so overused and misused that its meaning is variable and questionable, as in the case of many sociological terms and political clichés, e.g., "freedom," "liberal." See also COVERING WORD.

spoof *n.*   A light and good-natured parody or debunking; gentle satire or burlesque; prank or hoax. *N.* spoofer; *v.* spoof.

It has been many years since that droll Centurion, the late and revered Richard Rovere, invented the phrase "American establishment" as a spoof, and the fact that platitudinarians now solemnly employ it to express their envy gives the final edge to his jest.
—George W. Ball, letter to *The New York Times*

spoonerism *n.*   In speech, the confusion or transposition of the initial letters or sounds of two words, e.g., "Hoobert Heever" for Herbert Hoover. Also MARROWSKY.

The true spoonerism has to form other words. And this kind of pun is perhaps more interesting because more oral. . . . *May I sew you to another sheet?* does more than a mere malapropism, then, for it spoonerizes inebriation.   —Geoffrey Wagner, *On the Wisdom of Words*

sportspeak *n.*   Robert Lipsyte's term for the colloquial, metaphorical jargon typical of many newspaper sports pages, characterized by breezy but generally clichéd terminology, awestruck description or tone, greatly varied verbs (elegant variations), humorous sobriquets, colorfully slangy or illiterate quotes from athletes, and a general tendency to enliven or inflate the routine facts and results of games; sportsese.

William Safire, the discoverer of the English language, devoted his weekly essay Sunday to the sort of colloquialisms that Bob Lipsyte long ago christened sportspeak. . . . Outside of the fact that sportspeak is used by too many who know nothing of sports, there is nothing objectionable about this subdivision of language.
—Red Smith, *The New York Times*

spot news   Current or immediate news; up-to-date, firsthand news reported from the scene.

spot-plague *n.*   H. W. and F. G. Fowler's term for a prose style that uses too many periods (rather than occasional conjuctions, semicolons, colons, etc.), as in a faux naïf journalistic style.

Simplification is therefore desirable. But journalists now and then, and writers with more literary ambition than ability generally, overdo the thing till it becomes an affectation; it is then little different from Victor Hugo's device of making every sentence a paragraph, and our last state is worse than our first. Patronizing archness, sham ingenuousness, spasmodic interruption, scrappy argument, dry monotony, are some of the resulting impressions.
—H. W. Fowler and F. G. Fowler, *The King's English*

Sprachgefühl [*shpräkh'gə·fül"*] *n.*   A feeling for language, or a sense of what is established usage, idiomatic, or euphonious.

Men of genius may take great liberties with their mother tongue without offense; but let them once run counter to its characteristic tendencies, let them violate the English *Sprachgefühl*, and their mannerism becomes, as it were, a foreign language.
— James B. Greenough and George L. Kittredge,
Words and Their Ways in English Speech

spread-eagle oratory   Boastful patriotic speech; jingoistic language; flag waving.

Threats, boasts, and bluffs, rising to spread-eagle oratory and chauvinistic epithets, serve similar contradictory functions; like a cat's bristling and arching her back, they try to obviate conflict by scaring off an enemy.   — Robert M. Adams, *Bad Mouth*

squabash [*skwô'bash"*] *v.*   To criticize crushingly.

squelch, squelcher *n.*   An effectively silencing remark; trenchantly crushing rebuke; put-down.

squib *n.*   A short, written anecdote or sketch, esp. a witty or satirical one; brief news filler. *Adj.* squibbish; *n.* squibbery; *v.* squib.

It is only in later years that some have succumbed to the disease of sensationalism to such an extent that this writer is told on good authority, by persons who should know, that it is more and more difficult to convince certain journalists that there are facts which either should be suppressed or should, if necessity absolutely demands it, be placed in a small "squib" on one of the rear pages.
— John P. Marquand, *The Late George Apley*

squinting *adj.*   Phrased so as to confuse referents or antecedents, that is, involving ambiguous syntax or sentence misplacement whereby it is unclear which part of the sentence a word, phrase, or clause is related to, e.g., "I decided when we got there we'd take a rest" (in which it is unclear what "when we got there" modifies). See also AMPHIBOLOGY.

staccato *adj.*   Terse and emphatic in speech or prose style, such as a passage of short, broken sentences or abrupt, rapid-fire dialogue for dramatic effect.

For example, Cal Leonard, the protagonist of "Jazz Beau," is described as "a pair of Mack Truck shoulders, a grinning mouth, and wild, flame-blue eyes." I suppose there was a body linking these goodies together, but the pace is so staccato that the author neglects to mention it.   —S. J. Perelman, "Swing Out, Sweet Chariot"

staircase wit   See ESPRIT DE L'ESCALIER.

Standard English   Proper or official English, as contrasted with English that is dialectical, slangy, obsolete, etc.

Are you wondering what happened to the bearded and bright-eyed radical teachers who graduated in the late sixties and marched out to save the world from the boredom of grammar and the snobbery of Standard English?   —Arn Tibbets and Charlene Tibbets, *What's Happening to American English?*

statement *n.*   The act of presenting, declaring, or articulating; informative expression; a spoken or written communication setting forth facts, policy, or opinion; single or particular utterance or sentence; public or official response or explanation; message or import of an artistic work or of an action. *V.* state.

If Monty Bodkin had been, like his loved one's cousin Ambrose Tennyson, an artist in words, he would probably have supplemented his bald statement that Mr Ivor Llewellyn was talking to a female with the adjective "earnestly," or even some such sentence as "I should imagine upon matters of rather urgent importance, for the dullest eye could discern that the man is deeply moved."
    —P. G. Wodehouse, *The Luck of the Bodkins*

stemwinder *n.*   A rousing speech that works up a crowd; powerful orator.

A few years ago, in a church basement in an upstate New York river town, I heard John Gardner give a revival sermon that was a stemwinder. Actually, the sermon was one of his short stories, and the church was a university chapel, but the reading had all the intensity of Jonathan Edwards railing away at sinners in the hands of an angry God.   —David W. McCullough, *People, Books & Book People*

stentorian *adj.*   Forceful of voice; very loud.

From below they heard the sound of George's stentorian monologue: "Mr. and Mrs. Torrington Bligh, Mr. and Mrs. Mitchell Magraw . . . Mr. Ladew, Miss Laura Ladew. . . ."
    —Edith Wharton, "After Holbein"

step head   See special entry NEWSROOM HEADLINE JARGON, p. 386.

stet Let it stand: editorial indication to leave copy or text as it is, ignoring previously noted changes or corrections.

stilted *adj.* Describing language that is so formal or lofty as to be stiff and unnatural; pretentiously wooden; artificial. *Adv.* stiltedly.

> It is a noisy, hollow replay of the Jimmy Hoffa story, written in stilted prose and presented in third-person present tense so that it emerges more as an attenuated screen treatment than as a novel.
> —Stanley Ellin, *The New York Times*

stinger See KICKER under special entry NEWSROOM HEADLINE JARGON, p. 386.

stinky-pinky See special entry WORD-GAME WORDS, p. 397.

stock *adj.* All too common and unoriginal; convenient and typical; perpetually heard or repeated; trite.

> Hollis tells the tale of Crace saying to Blair, "Things can't go on like this. Either you or I will have to go." "I'm afraid it will have to be you, Sir," answered the boy. King-Farlow doubts very much if this is true. Others had heard the tale, but it is, again, a stock tale both in schools and in the armed forces.   —Bernard Crick, *George Orwell*

stonewall *v.* To resort to debate or other parliamentary tactics to prolong, obstruct, or delay business at hand; filibuster; use obfuscation, misleading information, etc., to conceal wrongdoing or to thwart inquiry.

stop *v. British* To punctuate.

straight-A illiteracy James Degnan's term for academic gobbledygook or graduate school jargon of whatever variety.

streamer See BANNER under special entry NEWSROOM HEADLINE JARGON, p. 385.

stream of consciousness The continuous process or experience of individual consciousness as evoked in literature, usually in a first-person, run-on prose style; articulation or verbalization of a person's or character's continuous thoughts and feelings.

> If later writers were above a certain level, they turned aside and engaged in a respectable research of their own. Instead of trying to find out where humanity was going, they tried to find out what humanity was. They refused to make any attempt to find a prose equivalent for the soliloquy, which should expose the essentials of a man or woman in pregnant but selective phrases. They wanted the whole of their men and women down on the page, and selection means

exclusion. So they evolved the "stream of consciousness" method, they set about spinning "the interior monologue," which should give an account of the day-to-day, hour-to-hour, moment-to-moment impressions life made on their subjects.

—Rebecca West, *Rebecca West: A Celebration*

stretcher *n. British* An exaggerated account or story; yarn; lie.

We—George, Harris, and myself—took a "raw'un" up with us once last season, and we plied him with the customary stretchers about the wonderful things we had done all the way up.

We gave him all the regular ones—the time-honored lies that have done duty up the river with every boating man for years past—and added seven entirely original ones that we had invented for ourselves.

—Jerome J. Jerome, *Three Men in a Boat*

stricture *n.* A rigorous, usually severe criticism; censorious comment.

The strictures of "Q" and the other English critics were based in a misunderstanding of Mencken's thesis, which was about *language,* not the literature that might one day grow from it.

—Alistair Cooke, *On Mencken*

Strine *n.* Australian English, or the humorous, homophonic transliteration of Australian speech pronunciations, e.g., "garbler mince" (couple of minutes), "Letty Mare fit" (let him have it).

stringer *n.* A part-time local or regional consultant-contributor for a newspaper, magazine, news agency, etc., usually on retainer as an ad hoc reporter, writer, or source of information for news in his or her home area.

stultiloquence [*stul·til'ə·kwəns*] *n.* Foolish talk; babble. *Adj.* stultiloquent, stultiloquential.

studhorse type See SECOND COMING TYPE under special entry NEWSROOM HEADLINE JARGON, p. 386.

stump word See CLIPPED WORD.

style *n.* Manner of writing or speaking, as shown by degree of formality, choice and simplicity of words, phrasing, use of metaphor and other figures of speech, and tone and directness; prose craftsmanship and rhetoric; characteristic diction and syntax; informing presence and flavor of a school of writing or a particular writer's prose; distinctive or personal idiom. *Adj.* stylistic; *adv.* stylistically; *n.* stylist; *v.* style.

His was that fumbling for exactitude, the exact word and phrase within the limited scope of a vocabulary controlled and even repressed by what was in him almost a fetish of simplicity, to milk them both dry, to seek always to penetrate to thought's uttermost end. He worked so hard at this that it finally became just style: an end instead of a means: so that he presently came to believe that, provided he kept the style pure and intact and unchanged and inviolate, what the style contained would have to be first rate: it couldn't help but be first rate, and therefore himself too.

—William Faulkner, *Essays, Speeches & Public Letters*

stylebook *n.*   A reference guide for consistent treatment of copy at a publication, setting forth preferred stylistic, grammatical, spelling, and typographic practice.

On the other hand, the stylebook may be a compilation of exceptions, additions, and expansions of dictionary rulings.

—William Bridgwater, in *Editors on Editing*

stylized *adj.*   Expressed or represented in a conspicuously formalized or artistic manner rather than naturally; conventionalized; patterned and artificial, sometimes self-consciously; mannered. *N.* stylization; *v.* stylize.

Beginning as a *New Yorker* staff man from Ohio, who learned sophistication from E. B. White, like boys smoking corn silk in back of the barn, and staying pretty much within the stylized limits of that magazine, he stumbled upon a vision of man, woman, and dog that even an Eskimo (perhaps especially an Eskimo) would recognize and run from.   —Wilfrid Sheed, *The Good Word and Other Words*

subarticulation *n.*   A tentative or exclamatory utterance (or its rendering in writing), whether of surprise, agreement, disapproval, etc., that is expressive but not a standard word, e.g., "uh-huh," "aw."

subaudition [*sub"ô·dish'ən*] *n.*   The understanding or supplying of something not expressed or implicit; that which is so understood or supplied (subauditor).

I suspect that the original source of both is the language of the New York streets, with subauditions of a Yiddish idiom.

—Eric Partridge and John W. Clark,
British and American English Since 1900

sub-editing *n. British*   Copy editing (or copy reading). *Adj.* subeditorial.

. . . Every Sunday there was this sift and silt of newsprint in the domestic interiors of England. Big money lay in and behind it. In their brief elevation into objects of national curiosity these inconsiderable criminals and furtive amorists were sought out by vast organizations, groomed, glamourized and sub-edited in cliff-like buildings, multiplied and distributed with miraculous speed by powerful machines.   —Michael Innes, *Appleby's End*

sub finem [*sub fē'nəm*]   Toward the end (of a chapter, etc.).

subhead   See special entry NEWSROOM HEADLINE JARGON, p. 387.

subintelligitur [*sub"in·tə·lij'i·tər*] *n.*   A meaning or signification implied rather than expressed.

subjunctive   See special entry GRAMMAR ADJECTIVES, p. 400.

sublanguage *n.*   A minor or special language or idiom; dialect or jargon.

subreption [*sə·brep'shən*] *n.*   Deliberate misrepresentation or fraud, as through withholding of certain facts; false inference. *Adj.* subreptitious; *adv.* subreptitiously.

substantive   See special entry GRAMMAR ADJECTIVES, p. 400.

subtext *n.*   An underlying but implicit story or theme in a work, or an emotional or dramatic undercurrent in a speech or conversation; the unspoken; an anagogic interpretation.

And unless I'm reading in what isn't there, a symbolic subtext underlies the new book that wasn't present in the earlier one. For Part I of "A Company of Women" closes with a highly allusive scene beside a well that is difficult not to associate with the Genesis story of Jacob's first meeting with Rachel.
                    —Christopher Lehmann-Haupt, *The New York Times*

succès de scandale [*sōōk·sā' də skän·däl'*]   Commercial or artistic notoriety, as because of a work's impious or scandalous theme; a spectacularly shocking work or presentation.

The *succès de scandale* of 1926 could not possibly explain the rapidity and assurance with which *The Sun Also Rises* became, as it has remained, one of the genuine classics of modern American fiction.
                    —Carlos Baker, *Hemingway*

succès d'estime [*sōōk·sā' des·tēm'*]   A gaining of the esteem of reputable professional critics; an artistic work critically acclaimed but not necessarily having broad appeal or commercial success.

A somewhat larger number will get *succès d'estime* and with that the kind of well-paid journalism which *succès d'estime* carries with it in the United States and which is unlike anything else in the world.

—C. P. Snow, in *Writing in America*

succès fou [*sook·sā' foo*]   A crazy and startling success; overnight triumph or hit.

succinct *adj.*   Clearly and briefly expressed; compactly stated. *Adv.* succinctly; *n.* succinctness.

Death was the waxen effigy in the coffin when he was six and Great-grandfather passed away, looking like a great fallen vulture in his casket, silent, withdrawn, no more to tell him how to be a good boy, no more to comment succinctly on politics.

—Ray Bradbury, *Dandelion Wine*

sucker headline   See SCAREHEAD under special entry NEWSROOM HEADLINE JARGON, p. 386.

suggestio falsi [*sə(g)·jes'chee·ō" fôl'sī'*]   An intimation of something false: a statement that, though not specifically false, leads the questioner or listener to a conclusion that is, as by not explicitly denying a rumor or by feigning discretion (when none is needed); planting a false inference; maliciously pregnant evasiveness (contrasted with suppressio veri).

sui generis [*soo'ī jen'ər·is*] *adj.*   Of its own kind; alone and special; unique.

She was wearing bell-bottomed jeans, a pale terracotta-coloured shirt beneath a kind of loose woollen cardigan-cum-coat, too long to be one, too short to be the other, that she had often worn on their forays from the ship. It was unashamedly *sui generis,* and managed to hit, more than anything else she wore, that blend in its owner between the ancient blue-stocking's indifference to clothes and a contradictory, but not altogether casual, respect for how personality is conveyed through choice of them.   —John Fowles, *Daniel Martin*

summa *n.*   An extensive and comprehensive treatise, sometimes in many volumes, covering a field of learning, as by a medieval scholastic or by a theologian; a synthesizing masterwork; epitome.

And yet even that line can be crossed. He rather liked *Easy Rider,* the *summa* of self-pity.

—Wilfrid Sheed, *The Good Word and Other Words*

sumpsimus [*sump'si·məs*] *n.* Use of a strictly correct word, expression, quotation, etc., instead of a popular, long-standing erroneous or corrupt form, e.g., "You can't eat your cake and have it too," which became "You can't have your cake and eat it too"; a purist (contrasted with mumpsimus).

The struggle between sumpsimus and mumpsimus may be viewed as the struggle between *language* as a social institution and *speech* as individual usage.   —Noah Jacobs, *Naming-Day in Eden*

superfluous attribution See special entry JOURNALISTIC ATTRIBUTION AND EVASION, p. 380.

superlative *n.* A word, esp. an adjective or adverb, denoting the highest or most extreme degree of a trait or quality, usually in a positive sense; *usually pl.* term of unqualified praise.

Two-page ads in the *New York Times* are studded with hearty albeit shopworn superlatives, and the lines outside theaters where the film is playing look as if a bank were giving away—in the current, detestable pleonasm—free gifts.   —John Simon, *Reverse Angle*

suppressio veri [*sə·pres'ē·ō" ver'ī*] The suppression of something true: intentional withholding of a fact or pertinent piece of information so as to affect a decision or response; deliberate omission (contrasted with suggestio falsi).

There had perhaps been one case of *suppressio veri*. Tim had never told Guy about Daisy.   —Iris Murdoch, *Nuns and Soldiers*

surrealistic *adj.* Describing writing that uses random, incongruous elements of the unreal, imaginary, or fantastic, however disparate and free of sequence or causality, as a means of evoking the illogical world of the unconscious, dreams, or hallucination, and often employing stream of consciousness and Freudian imagery. *Adj.* surreal, surrealist; *adv.* surrealistically; *n.* surrealism, surrealist.

Thus, Heller will never use comedy for its own sake; each joke has a wider significance in the intricate pattern, so that laughter becomes a prologue for some grotesque revelation. This gives the reader an effect of surrealistic dislocation, intensified by a weird, rather flat, impersonal style, full of complicated reversals, swift transitions, abrupt shifts in chronological time, and manipulated identities. . . .
                       —Robert Brustein, in *The Critic as Artist*

swearword *n.*   An impolite or vulgar word used to express disgust or execration; an obscenity or blasphemy.

> While he followed Welch next door, wondering whether the subject for debate was the sheet, or his dismissal, or the sheet and his dismissal, Dixon reeled off a long string of swearwords in a mumbling undertone, so that he'd be in credit, as it were, for the first few minutes of the interview.   —Kingsley Amis, *Lucky Jim*

sweet talk   Flattering or coaxing, conciliatory talk, blandishments; cajolery. *V.*sweet-talk.

> He declared it was unsafe for a pregnant woman to drive. He thought she must at least get a driver's license. She said if a state trooper stopped her, she could sweet-talk him.   —Saul Bellow, *Herzog*

swiped chiché title   Mario Pei's term for a book title adapted from the phrasing of another, familiar title or titles, e.g., S.J. Perelman's *Eastward Ha!* from Charles Kingsley's *Westward Ho!*

syllabatim [*sil″ə·bā′tim*] *adv.*   Syllable by syllable.

syllepsis *n.*   Compressed phrasing, properly grammatical but with a surprising shift in sense, in which one word functions with two subsequent words, e.g., "He drinks with a silver flask and a local harlot." *Pl.* syllepses; *adj.* sylleptic, sylleptical; *adv.* sylleptically. See also ZEUGMA.

> It will be "a sad and despondent loss for anyone who misses it," which might look like a kind of syllepsis—a rhetorical device of which Reed, we may assume, has never heard—but is actually a case of simple ignorance of the meaning of despondent, which can apply only to people.   —John Simon, *Paradigms Lost*

syllogism *n.*   A reasoned three-part deduction, consisting of a major premise, a minor premise, and a conclusion, and presented either as a logical truth or demonstrative hypothesis; method or practice of deductive reasoning; subtle reasoning that is suspect or specious. *Adj.* syllogistic, syllogistical; *adv.* syllogistically; *n.* syllogistic, syllogistics, syllogization; *v.* syllogize.

> Groucho . . . uses strings of unlikely words to construct false analogies and false syllogisms, in that way showing how easy it is to bedevil the most innocent statements.   —Peter Farb, *Word Play*

symbol *n.*   A visible or palpable thing that represents something else because of resemblance, integral connection, association, or convention, esp. a discrete being, object, or emblem identified with a general intangible or abstract quality; special sign or character having a function or meaning in a specific field, such as mathematics or music; sensory thing, image, color, or the like used in a literary work to bear or betoken a signal meaning; thing or likeness indicative or suggestive of something else, or having a cultural or emotional significance; epitomizing example. *Adj.* symbolic, symbolical; *adv.* symbolically; *n.* symbolicalness, symbolization, symbolist; *v.* symbolize.

symbolism *n.* The use of visible or palpable things as specific signs or tokens to represent things, forces, qualities, universal truths, etc.; signification through real or sensory objects or occurrences; the imaginative use in art or literature of animate or inanimate phenomena for meanings beyond the real or immediate world; invested or latent meaning. *Adj.* symbolist, symbolistic; *adv.* symbolistically.

Literary symbolism is centrifugal and flees from the object, the event, into the incorporeal distance, where concepts are taken for substance and floating ideas and archtypes assume a hieratic authority.
—Mary McCarthy, *On the Contrary*

synchysis See special entry RHETORIC TERMS, p. 404.

syncopation See LETTER DELETION under special entry WORD-GAME WORDS, p. 396.

syncope [*sing′kə·pē*] *n.* Loss or omission of a sound, letter, or syllable in the middle of a word, e.g., "ne'er" (never). *Adj.* syncopated; *v.* syncopate.

In the matter of personal names, attention has been called to what a linguist would style syncopated forms now current in feminine first names: Barbra Streisand, Marlyn Mason, Ann-Margret.
—Mario Pei, *Double-Speak in America*

synecdoche [*si·nek′də·kē*] *n.* The figurative device of using a part for the whole, the whole for a part, or generally any use of a subcategory for a category or vice versa, e.g., "head" for a cow. *Adj.* synecdochic, synecdochical; *adv.* synecdochically; *n.* synecdochism.

Unhappily, there is no way in the English of Shakespeare, Milton, Pope, and Faulkner, to get rid of the synecdoche "man," which, as in "mankind," means man and woman.
—William F. Buckley, Jr., *A Hymnal*

synesis [*sin′ə·sis*] *n.* See CONSTRUCTIO AD SENSUM.

synesthesia, synaesthesia [*sin″əs·thē′zhə*]   Sensory mixing or verbal impressionism: a subjective sensation or impression of one sense evoked through another sense, for example, the color blue being visualized because of hearing a part of a symphony; hence a term applicable to certain metaphors in language, e.g., "If only you could taste words!" (advertisement), "noise pollution," "toothsome girl." *Adj.* synesthetic, synaesthetic.

synonym *n.*   A word having the same or almost the same meaning as a given word. *Adj.* synonymous, synonymic, synonymical; *adv.* synonymously; *n.* synonymity, synonymousness; *v.* synonymize.

He had an elegant vocabulary. He knew eighteen synonyms for sin, half of them very long and impressive, and the others very short and explosive and minatory—minatory being one of his best words, constantly useful in terrifying the as yet imaginary horde of sinners gathered before him.   —Sinclair Lewis, *Elmer Gantry*

synonymicon *n.*   A lexicon of synonyms.

synonymomania *n.*   Theodore Bernstein's term for the fear of using the same word twice "within three lines," and thus for the errant inclination to overload with synonyms (or elegant variations), which instead of adding variety or color to the prose are mannered and distracting in effect, e.g., the strained use of dialogue verbs such as "averred," "declared," "responded," etc., instead of the simple "said." Also MONOLOGOPHOBIA.

synonymy *n.*   The study or grouping of synonyms; a listing of synonyms, esp. one noting connotations that differentiate them; a scientific nomenclature, such as a record of various taxonomic names for the same species; the quality of being like or identical in meaning. *N.* synonymist.

The embattled (not yet besieged) attorney general, recognizing the attention to synonymy given his words, answered a question from Senator Richard Lugar of Indiana in this inclusive way: "No, I haven't had a discussion, a conversation, or an exchange about that."
—William Safire, *What's the Good Word?*

synopsis *n.*   A concise statement or passage that provides a general summary of a treatise, speech, etc.; condensation or abstract; outline of a story, play, or plot. *Pl.* synopses; *adj.* synoptic, synoptical; *adv.* synoptically; *v.* synopsize.

It was an authentic crisis because the programs contained a synopsis of the opera's plot, and Breen was afraid that without this guide the audience would have difficulty following the action.
—Truman Capote, "The Muses Are Heard"

syntagmatic *adj.* Determining the meaning of a word by considering it in the context of the sentence (contrasted with paradigmatic).

syntax *n.* The part of grammar concerning the way in which words, phrases, sentences, and clauses are arranged; prose cohesiveness; coherent train of thought in phrasing and sentence structure. *Adj.* syntactic, syntactical; *adv.* syntactically.

High in my glassed-in cubbyhole on the twentieth floor of the McGraw-Hill Building—an architecturally impressive but spiritually enervating green tower on West Forty-second Street—I leveled the scorn that could only be mustered by one who had just finished reading *Seven Types of Ambiguity* upon these sad outpourings piled high on my desk, all of them so freighted with hope and clubfooted syntax.
—William Styron, *Sophie's Choice*

systrophe See special entry RHETORIC TERMS, p. 405.

T

table talk Literary biography in the form of a well-known individual's day-to-day sayings and opinions; obiter dicta; informal conversation at the table or elsewhere, esp. that led by an eminent person. Also DEIPNOSOPHY.

> This passage is in the table-talk tradition and has the hit-or-miss charm of the dessert course, when all the diners feel self-confident, knowledgeable and uncritical.
> —Robert Graves and Alan Hodge, *The Reader over Your Shoulder*

tabloid *n.* A smaller-page format (usually without a fold), condensed newspaper featuring many photographs and usually sensational in style and content; digest. *Adj.* tabloid.

> Here is where they are trying to find a new life style, trying to find it in the only places they know to look; the movies and the newspapers. The case of Lucille Marie Maxwell Miller is a tabloid monument to that new life style. —Joan Didion, *Slouching Towards Bethlehem*

taboo word A word deemed vulgar or offensive because of inhibiting social or cultural mores, such as a profanity or distasteful sexual term; forbidden term, or one avoided because of its uncomfortable or negative onus.

> In the case of Lenny Bruce, it required a nation riding on a frenzy of iconoclasm, where grownups, sitting around a bar, felt a sense of liberation on hearing taboo words spoken out loud, smuttily, leeringly, by a "comedian," —William F. Buckley, Jr., *Execution Eve*

tacenda [*tä·ken′də*] *n., pl.* Things that are better left unmentioned.

tachygraphy [*ta·kig′rə·fē*] *n.* Shorthand or speed-writing. *Adj.* tachygraphic, tachygraphical; *adv.* tachygraphically; *n.* tachygraph.

taffeta phrases Florid or ornate phrases; euphemisms; fustian.

tag *n.* A signal quotation that explains, ornaments, or emphasizes a theme, such as a classical literary line or allusion; sententious line or motto; slogan; hackneyed saying or cliché; author's characteristic and recurrent expression or verbal mannerism; word or phrase appended to the posing of a question; label or epithet; cue or catchword; functionally useful word or phrase, such as certain adverbs or connective phrases; tagline.

Packer, who pushes me towards oblivion with tags of Biblical quotation, the gross impertinence of which he is unable to appreciate, religious illiterate that he is!   —Robertson Davies, *Fifth Business*

tag line   A climactic line, such as one that clinches an argument, adds a dramatic note, or ends a joke; identifying line or stock comment; watchword or slogan; signature line or key thematic phrase used at the bottom of an advertisement.

I had not been in any sense a godly-minded creature, and the Scriptures were always largely a literary convenience, supplying me with allusions and tag lines for the characters in my novel, one or two of whom had evolved into pious turds.
                                        —William Styron, *Sophie's Choice*

takeoff *n.*   A comic imitation or mocking of a work, whether as a parody, burlesque, caricature, or satire; spoof. *V.* take off.

tale *n.*   A narrative of events or story, and as a fictional prose composition similar to the short story but usually distinctive for the simple, speechlike tone of its presentation or its personal point of view; interesting or imaginative account or plot; recital or report of true, imagined, or legendary events; questionable story or piece of gossip; falsehood.

For a year he had been devoting all of his odd moments to the reading of books and now some tale he had read concerning life in old world towns of the middle ages came sharply back to his mind so that he stumbled forward with the curious feeling of one revisiting a place that had been a part of some former existence.
                                        —Sherwood Anderson, *Winesburg, Ohio*

talk *n.*   Vocal expression; speech; joint discourse or conversation; occasion of interchanging thoughts or feelings, or a personal discussion or chat; public speech or informal address; report, rumor, or gossip; inconclusive or empty utterance or discussion; verbiage. *Pl.* a conference or negotiation; *n.* talker; *v.* talk.

Then a woman made an announcement. He listened for some quaver of theatricality in the voice that would give her away, reveal her as the "nurse" in a different role. Talk always sounded like talk, never like a speech. Something read aloud or memorized or even willfully

extemporaneous could never pass for the flat, halting, intimate flow
of unmanaged monologue or conversation.

—Stanley Elkin, *The Living End*

talkee-talkee *n.* Broken or corrupted speech, as spoken by a
poorly educated island populace; lingua franca; incessant chatter; prattle.

talky *adj.* Talkative or verbose; having too much discussion or
dialogue, as a novel or play lacking action.

tall tale A humorous tale of extravagantly impossible happenings
or superhuman characters but told in a straightforwardly literal,
realistic style, such as the American frontier tales of Paul Bun-
yan and Davy Crockett; patently incredible story or account.

tall talk Extravagantly grand and inventive language, esp. irrepressible and colorful American idiom with sesquipedalian
words and boisterous superlatives; imaginative exaggeration.

Tall talk described the penumbra of the familiar. It blurred the edges
of fact and fiction. Discovered and established by urgent need and
quick consent, tall talk was a language without inhibitions. . . . It was
needed because the Old World notion of exaggeration had itself become inadequate. It was an explicit popular form of what later found
expression in stream-of-consciousness literature: "to depict the emotional and mental reactions of characters to external events, rather
than the events themselves." —Daniel Boorstin, *The Americans*

tapinosis [*tap"i·nō'sis*] *n.* Derogation of a person in the form of
scurrilous inanimate epithets; any undignified style or name-
calling to degrade another.

Synecdoche degenerates into tapinosis when an invidious or repug-
nant personal trait is made conspicuous by comparing a person to
some base inanimate object which is calculated to detract from his
dignity, as: *highbrow, egghead, sap, screwball, tightwad, battleax,
ham, heel, scab, deadpan, wallflower.*

—Noah Jacobs, *Naming-Day in Eden*

taradiddle, tarradiddle *n.* A falsehood or fiction, such as a spurious tale; petty lie; pretentious claptrap.

"I invite a trial of your ingenuity: if he knew Yeager was dead, either
because he had killed him or otherwise, why did he come here with
that tarradiddle?" —Rex Trout, *Too Many Clients*

tattle *n.* Gossip or tale-telling; hearsay. *Chiefly British,* idle or
trifling talk; chatter. *N.* tattler; *v.* tattle.

He worshipped his mother, and she was fond of him. But she was dignified and reticent, and pathos, like tattle, was disgusting to her.

       —E. M. Forster, *The Longest Journey*

tautegory [*tô'tǝ·gôr″ē*] *n.* Expressing something in different words. *Adj.* tautegorical.

tautology *n.* The needless repetition of an idea in different words immediately or contiguously; a pointlessly circular, self-fulfilling statement; reiteration or redundancy. *Adj.* tautological, tautologic, tautologous; *adv.* tautologically, tautologously.

The first indication of anything queer comes with the *shield of the German aegis;* but although this gives us pause for a moment, we immediately reassure ourselves by concluding that Mr. Davies surely knows that a shield is an aegis, and has allowed himself the little tautology . . . as a mere rhetorical flourish.

       —Edmund Wilson, *Classics and Commercials*

tautonym See special entry WORD-GAME WORDS, p. 397.

teaser See KICKER under special entry NEWSROOM HEADLINE JARGON, p. 386.

teaser campaign A series of advance advertisements, each purposely withholding certain information, intended to arouse the public's curiosity, esp. one to evoke interest in a coming motion picture or book.

technical term A term from a particular field or profession, such as science, diplomacy, or literary criticism, or that is unfamiliar to the general public or used by lay people in a different or less restrictive way; special and uncommon word. Also TERM OF ART.

I, however, remained censorious and subsequent glimpses of Sebastian, driving in a hansom cab and dining at the George in false whiskers, did not soften me, although Collins, who was reading Freud, had a number of technical terms to cover everything.

       —Evelyn Waugh, *Brideshead Revisited*

telegraphese *n.* See CABLESE.

telegraphic style See CABLESE.

telescope word See BLEND WORD.

tendentious *adj.* Written or spoken with an evident tendency or purpose and thus not impartial; deliberate in design or tone; biased. *Adv.* tendentiously; *n.* tendentiousness.

My father was skinny, nervous, selfish, unreliable, full of hot radical
passion; insolent in his faith, loyal to Marxism-Leninism, rude-eyed
and tendentious.   —E. L. Doctorow, *The Book of Daniel*

tendenz [*ten·dents'*] *n.* A definite, dominating purpose, viewpoint, or philosophy implicit in a literary work or publication.
Pl. tendenzen. See also DONNÉE.

tenor *n.* The general feeling, purport, or drift of something written or spoken; sensed "message" or tone.

tenth muse See special entry BOOKISH APPELLATIONS, p. 407.

terminal deletion See special entry WORD-GAME WORDS, p. 397.

terminological inexactitude Winston Churchill's term, now a jocose euphemism, for a distorted report or virtual falsehood; lie.

Or one may call a lie by another name—a fib for one told in jest, a
white lie for a serious falsehood where no harm is meant, a terminological inexactitude to spare one's parliamentary colleagues, or dancing on the edge of the truth, as one advertising man describes what
he does "for dramatic effect."
                    —Dwight Bolinger, *Language—The Loaded Weapon*

terminology *n.* The particular or characteristic vocabulary of a
science, art, or discipline; technical language; jargon. *Adj.* terminological; *adv.* terminologically.

De Tocqueville's idea of modern man lost "in the solitude of his own
heart" has been brought forward into our time in such terminology as
alienation (Marx), *anomie* (Durkheim), the *mass man* (Ortega y Gas-
set), and *the lonely crowd* (Riesman).
                    —Tom Wolfe, *Mauve Gloves & Madmen, Clutter & Vine*

term of art See TECHNICAL TERM.

terse *adj.* Finely concise and unsuperfluous; crisply economical
in style. *Adv.* tersely; *n.* terseness.

It is commonly believed that French is a terse language, and compared with its cousins, Italian and Spanish, it actually is, but compared with English it is garrulous, for it takes 36,000 syllables to say
what English says in 29,000.
                    —H. L. Mencken, *The American Language*

tertium quid [*tûr'shē·əm kwid'*] A "third something" that does
not fit either of two opposite categories, that eludes a dichotomy; something anomalous, ambiguous, or intermediate. See
also JE NE SAIS QUOI.

tertius gaudens   See special entry BOOKISH APPELLATIONS, p. 407.

testimonial   See special entry PROPAGANDA DEVICES, p. 381.

Teutonicism *n.*   See GERMANISM.

text *n.*   The actual wording of a written or printed work, or the transcript of a speech; the original words of an author, as opposed to a condensation or translation, etc.; specific printed version of a literary work, such as an authoritative recension of Scripture; main body of a book, as contrasted with notes, marginalia, etc.; a passage, esp. of Scripture, chosen as a sermon theme or reference for discussion; topic or lesson; a textbook. *Adj.* textual; *adv.* textually.

> It begins, "When Caesar noticed that the enemy was remaining for several days at the camp fortified by a swamp and by the nature of the terrain, he sent a letter to Trebonius instructing him"—"instructing him" isn't actually in the text but it's understood; you know about that.   —John Knowles, *A Separate Peace*

thanatopsis *n.*   A reflecting or meditation on death.

thersitical *adj.*   Loudly and violently abusive in speech; scurrilous.

thesaurus *n.*   A book containing categorized words, esp. an alphabetical or indexed word reference arranged according to concepts or subjects, synonyms, and antonyms; comprehensive word store or source of information; word-hoard; treasury. *Pl.* thesauri, thesauruses.

> All the synonyms in all the thesauri have been exhausted by historians, in their efforts to avoid an explanation form they distrust but have not been able to discard.
> —David Hackett Fischer, *Historians' Fallacies*

thesis *n.*   A proposition put forth or defended in argument or debate; purport of a book, article, or treatise; case; academic dissertation. *Pl.* theses.

> Mrs. Hrdy's arguments for this thesis are so clear that she ought to adapt them for wider circulation.
> —Paul A. Colinvaux, *The New York Times*

thesis novel   A novel that articulates or persuades of a point of view or cause, such as a fictionalized exposé of a corrupt government or a realistic portrayal of the exploitation of factory workers. Also ROMAN À THÈSE.

think piece   An article that includes background material along with both general and personal comments, analyses, or conjecture, as contrasted with the conventional factual news story.

> . . . It would be invidious for me to remark (even if I knew what I was talking about) that Eric Bentley is probably the best dramatic critic in the U.S. . . . The rest of the boys are just think-piece writers whose subject happens to be plays.
> —Raymond Chandler, *Raymond Chandler Speaking*

third tongue   See special entry BOOKISH APPELLATIONS, p. 407.

thought-cliché *n.*   Jacques Barzun's term for a simplistically erroneous notion popularly accepted and difficult to dislodge, e.g., that Darwin discovered the theory of evolution while voyaging on the *Beagle,* or that intellect is a bar to success in business and politics. See also BEN TROVATO, RECEIVED IDEA.

threnos   See special entry RHETORIC TERMS, p. 405.

throwaway *n.*   Free circular or leaflet, esp. an advertising or propagandistic handbill; anything rejected or worthy of throwing away; a statement or observation made casually or dismissively; abrupt comment. *Adj.* throwaway.

> . . . an utterly arcane and incomprehensible throwaway like pianist Charles Rosen's review of three hard-to-get books on music and meter, complete with musical scores. . . .
> —Philip Nobile, *Intellectual Skywriting*

thumbsucker *n.*   A political story that is speculative or analytical and only lightly researched; relatively shallow and inoffensive news story or feature.

> The collection is weakened by thumbsuckers on the Bicentennial, feminism and travel books that didn't absolutely require exhumation from the magazines in which they originally appeared.
> —Walter Clemons, *Newsweek*

tickler *n.*   A written reminder or notepad, schedule, etc., for future reference. *British,* a question or matter that is puzzling or delicate.

tick-tock *n.*   A feature story detailing the sequence of events leading up to a notable event or official announcement; background chronology.

tie-back *n.*   The part of a news story providing background material.

tie-in See special entry BOOK PUBLISHING TERMS, p. 363.

time copy Newspaper term for copy that can be used anytime, since it is not hard news. See also PORK.

time depth The period of time over which a language, language group, or culture evolves.

Timestyle, Time-ese *n.* The characteristically heady and melodramatically compressed prose style of *Time* magazine, with particular reference to its zesty verbs, marshaled characterizing adjectives and hyphenated compound words, clever coinages and puns, and above all (formerly) the frequent use of verbs at the beginnings of sentences and hence inverted syntax.

Brain child of joke-making, china-dog-collecting, cordovan-shoe-wearing Briton Hadden more than of *Time* co-founding, beetle-browed, baggy-britched Henry Luce was Timestyle. Wrote Wolcott Gibbs in a *New Yorker* profile of Luce: "Backward ran sentences until reeled the mind. Where it will all end, knows God!" Ended has inversion since Godwent Luce.

—John B. Bremner, *Words on Words*

tin ear Tone deafness, or in language a lack of feeling for the beauty and cadences of words; verbal unnaturalness or obtuseness, whether in speaking or listening. See also SPRACHGE-FÜHL.

Cohan is one of those unfortunate stylists whose tin ear directs him to refer to a person's face as a "visage." Characters are always "discerning," and nobody tears anything up when they can "rend" it. —Marilyn Stasio, *Penthouse*

tirade *n.* An impassioned, drawn-out speech that is critical and intemperate in language; angry harangue.

His malicious wit and fulminating tirades blazed a trail for English drama. —John Lahr, *The New York Times*

title page See special entry PARTS OF A BOOK, p. 364.

tittle-tattle *n.* Trifling, fatuous talk, esp. gossip about scandal. *Adj.* tittle-tattle; *v.* tittle-tattle.

Given that her subject is no more sharply defined than "fashionable life and literature from 1814 to 1840," it follows that the reader is quickly in danger of feeling cut off from the world of experience beyond that of Regency and early Victorian fictional tittle-tattle.

—Donald A. Low, *Times Literary Supplement*

tmesis *n.*   Dividing a word in two, or the inserting into a standard word or phrase of another word or expression, sometimes for irreverent or humorous effect, e.g., "which way soever"; diacope. See also INFIX.

tolutiloquence [*tol"yə·til'ə·kwəns*] *n.*   Speech that moves briskly along; breezy discourse.

Elements of emotional sentiment and archaic conventionalism rendered their opinions well nigh worthless. They were tolutiloquent in expressing horror at the impiety of mob-rule which had deprived them of the right to military salutes ordained by the Concordat.
—Frederick William Rolfe (Frederick Baron Corvo),
Hadrian the Seventh

tombstones   See special entry NEWSROOM HEADLINE JARGON, p. 387.

tommyrot *n. British*   Utter nonsense; foolishness.

"Oh, what a lot of tommy-rot," said Tilliard. "Can't a man and woman get engaged?"   —E. M. Forster, *The Longest Journey*

Tom Swiftie   See special entry WORD-GAME WORDS, p. 397.

tone *n.*   The pitch, intonation, or inflection of uttered speech; overall attitudinal or emotional cast or tenor of something written that derives from its style and diction; personal coloring or authorial attitude; implicit mood or feeling.

Tone cannot be defined except negatively, when it is bad. Anyone can tell when a writer is talking down—that is the condescending tone. But there is also the pompous, the chattering, the precious, the chummy, the toplofty, the cynical and sneering, the vulgar out of the corner of the mouth: the varieties of bad tones are infinite, for they correspond to the many possible mixtures of human emotions.
—Jacques Barzun and Henry F. Graff, *The Modern Researcher*

tongue *n.*   A language, dialect, or mode of speech; verbal manner or style; glib talk or back talk; capacity to speak; utterance.

. . . "Are you *mad*?" she would ask when I would disclose my suspicions of a particular gentleman or lad, "Why, he's a boy," or "Don't you know he's *repulsive* to me," which she always said in her best London voice, five years of Catholic schooling in England contributing much to the patrician parts of her American tongue.
—Norman Mailer, *An American Dream*

tongue twister   A word, phrase, or sentence difficult to pronounce, usually because it has a dense alliterative cluster of similar consonants dissimilar enough to confuse articulation.

Tattersall tried his hand at a few tongue twisters himself. "Vile Vernon Vogelsang violently vomited vast—" Stumped for a noun at a crucial juncture, he switched to another initial. "Poor Peter Plunkett puked putridly putrescent portions . . ."
—Peter De Vries, *The Cat's Pajamas*

tootle   *n.*   Feeble or verbose writing or speech; nonsense. V. tootle.

Topic A   A top news story receiving continued front-page coverage in newspapers; the front-running issue or story (originated by the New York *Herald Tribune*).

topical   *adj.*   Constituting a news or cultural topic of the day and aptly current in importance or popular interest; relevant or in vogue; involving or arranged by topics or subjects. *Adv.* topically; *n.* topicality.

For the apparent sake of topicality alone, a lot of unilluminating talk is devoted to Stengel's father-son relationship with Billy Martin.
—Frank Rich, *The New York Times*

toponym   *n.*   A place name, or one indicating a geographical derivation or origin. *Adj.* toponymic, toponymical; *n.* toponymy.

topos   *n.*   A stock rhetorical theme; commonplace idea or stereotyped expression.

Where the word of the poet ceases, a great light begins. This *topos*, with its historical antecedents in neo-Platonic and Gnostic doctrine, gives to Dante's *Paradiso* its principal motion of spirit.
—George Steiner, *Language and Silence*

tosh   *n. British*   Nonsense or rubbish.

totidem verbis   [*tō'ti·dem" wer'bēs*]   In so many words.

tour de force   A feat of strength, skill, or craftsmanship; a notably well-executed work or production, sometimes one that is an exercise in technique or showmanship at the expense of other qualities. Pl. tours de force.

John Steinbeck and Saul Bellow became my special heroes a little later, as I decided I wanted to be a writer; and each, I notice now,

chose to write a slapstick tour de force about a slaughter of the innocents in which the innocents were frogs.

—Edward Hoagland, *The New York Times*

tournure [*tōor·n(y)ōor'*] *n.* A turn of phrase.

tract *n.* A doctrinal pamphlet on a specific topic, usually a philosophical, political, or religious exhortation; book arguing a
belief or point of view.

Burroughs takes himself with a complete, owlish seriousness; indeed,
in his opening section he seems, as far as one can make out through
the pea-soup fog of his prose, to be offering the book as some kind of
tract against drug addiction.   —John Wain, in *The Critic as Artist*

trade book   See special entry BOOK PUBLISHING TERMS, p. 363.

trade-last   A heard flattering remark withheld by one person until
his listener offers a reciprocal reported word of praise; held-in-
reserve compliment.

An offer by B to report a compliment someone paid to A if A will first
report a compliment someone paid to B. If A has not heard a compliment paid to B by a third party, a personal compliment by A (who is
not required to be sincere but only to pretend to be) will usually do in
place of a third-person report. The child is father and mother of the
devious adult.   —John Ciardi, *A Second Browser's Dictionary*

trade paperback   See special entry BOOK PUBLISHING TERMS,
p. 363.

traduttori traditori [*trä·dōo·tō'rē trä·dē·tō'rē*]   Translators are
traitors.

tralatitious [*tral"ə·tish'əs*] adj.   Metaphorical or figurative; traditional or handed down; gossipy or from mouth to mouth. *Adv.*
tralatitiously.

transaddition   See special entry WORD-GAME WORDS, p. 397.

transatlanticism *n.*   A word or expression in use in both the
United States and Great Britain. *Adj.* transatlantic.

transcript *n.*   Something transferred into writing, typewriting,
print, or particular symbols; copy or duplicate, esp. an official
reproduction or record. *N.* transcriber; *v.* transcribe.

Except for a few excerpts released after the war, the trial transcript
of three thousand pages of testimony and legal argument remained a
classified government document until 1960.

—Eugene Rachlis, *They Came to Kill*

transcription *n*.   The process of copying or transferring in writing; written copy or record, such as a handwritten or typewritten version of something dictated or a complete text from shorthand notes; translated facsimile. *Adj*. transcriptional; *adv*. transcriptionally; *n*. transcript; *v*. transcribe.

I was exactly what they were looking for, they explained, as they were in the process of transcribing the Kaballah on parchment and had run out of blood.   —Woody Allen, *Side Effects*

transdeletion   See special entry WORD-GAME WORDS, p. 397.

transfer   See special entry PROPAGANDA DEVICES, p. 381.

transferred epithet   See HYPALLAGE.

translation *n*.   The rendering of something, and its meaning, from one language into another; a word, phrase, passage, or work transmitted from one language into another; a text not in its original language; rephrasing in simpler terms; clarification. *Adj*. translational, translative; *adv*. translationally; *n*. translator; *v*. translate.

With his vaudevillian's feel for legend and landscape (A Chaplin, I said of Lonoff in my senior paper, who seized upon just the right prop to bring an entire society and its outlook to life); with his "translated" English to lend a mildly ironic flavor to even the most commonplace expression; with his cryptic, muted, dreamy resonance, the sense given by such little stories of saying so much—well, I had proclaimed, who in American literature was like him?
                          —Philip Roth, *The Ghost Writer*

transliteration *n*.   The rendering of a letter or word from one language in the alphabet of another. *V*. transliterate. Also META-GRAPHY.

Kellogg's Rice Krispies transliterate their "SNAP! CRACKLE! POP!" to "POKS! RIKS! RAKS!" in Finland, to "PIM! PUM! PAM!" in Mexico, and to the Afrikaans-like "KNAP! KNAETTER! KNAK!" in South Africa.
                          —Geoffrey Wagner, *On the Wisdom of Words*

transposition, transposal   See special entry WORD-GAME WORDS, p. 397.

transverbation *n*.   Translating word for word.

trash *n.*   Worthless or pointless literature, esp. inferior commercial or formulaic fiction; transparently contrived, poor, or hack writing; rubbish; schlock. *Adj.* trashy; *n.* trashiness.

A political speech may be, and sometimes is, literature; a sonnet to the moon may be, and often is, trash. Style is what distinguishes literature from trash.   —Evelyn Waugh, *A Little Order*

travesty *n.*   Literary or dramatic ridicule of a serious or lofty subject through grotesquely frivolous, often coarse and farcical treatment or style, or an example of this; irreverent or uproarious burlesque; artistic debasement; a work that is blatantly inferior or a failure as an imitation; a regrettable mockery. *V.* travesty.

treacle *n.*   Something overly sweet or sentimental; saccharine drama or melodrama; cloying language. *Adj.* treacly.

Charles Brackett, a devoted admirer, described him in one of his novels as "a competent old horror with a style that combined clear treacle and pure black bile," while Harpo Marx spoke of his idol considered sheerly as an artist.   —Wolcott Gibbs, *More in Sorrow*

treatise *n.*   A formal or serious written treatment of a subject, systematically explaining or arguing pertinent facts, principles, and possible conclusions; comprehensive expository discussion.

She arranged the furniture—and was pleased when she found, in a household treatise, that "it is permissible to separate a pair of sofa commodes and their companion lamps."
                                                       —Vladimir Nabokov, *Lolita*

triad *n.*   See TRIPLET.

tricolon *n.*   See TRIPLET.

trim size   See special entry PARTS OF A BOOK, p. 364.

tripe *n.*   Something plainly worthless; trashy writing; rubbish.

You see this silver scar left by a bullet, right up here under my hair? I got that the night I said that any well-told story was worth the telling. An eighth of an inch nearer the temple, and I wouldn't be sitting here doing this sort of tripe.
                                —Dorothy Parker, *The Portable Dorothy Parker*

triplet *n.*   An arrangement of single words or phrases in a group of three. Also TRIAD, TRICOLON.

One doesn't often come across the simple phrase "a marvellous novel" nowadays: the fashion is for triads of adjectives ("exact, piquant and comical," "rich, mysterious and energetic"). . . .
—Mary-Kay Wilmers, *The State of the Language*

tristiloquy [*tris·til'ə·kwē*] *n.*   A dull, gloomy, mournful speech.

trite *adj.*   Inescapably obvious or unoriginal; hackneyed in language or thought; stale. *Adv.* tritely; *n.* triteness.

Most men and women are capable of feeling passion, but not of expressing it; their love letters . . . are either tritely flat or tritely bombastic.   —Aldous Huxley, *Collected Essays*

triticism [*trit'ə·siz"əm*] *n.*   A banal and obvious remark or observation; facile commonplace or catchphrase; cliché.

trivialize *n.*   To construe as or reduce to something trivial, as through cursory mention, superficial treatment, or flippancy; make unimportant or dismissible; dilute or debase in meaning or significance; cheapen. *N.* trivialization.

Mr. Vonnegut, by contrast, is always turning aside (as again, he confesses) to pop a quick joke, from what seems faint-heartedness, or else will bring himself up short with one of his trivializing signature phrases: "Hi-Ho," "Peace" or "So it goes."
—Edward Hoagland, *The New York Times*

Trollope ploy   Replying, in a series of communications, to an earlier message of an interlocutor or adversary rather than to the latest message, as for ulterior political motives (from Anthony Trollope's novels in which a heroine will willfully or deliberately misinterpret a man's squeezing of her hand as a marriage proposal).

trope *n.*   A rhetorical device or figure of speech, often one viewed pejoratively as being hackneyed or empty.

I wrote a novel in which a character says, "Ah well, as one door shuts another closes" and this was silently corrected to a statement that made sense. Naturally, I unsilently uncorrected it. Eric had learnt these ludic tropes and others like them in the army.
—Anthony Burgess, in *Eric Partridge in His Own Words*

tropology [*trō·pol'ə·jē*] *n.*   Figurative speech or writing or an example thereof; metaphorical expression; treatise on tropes. *Adj.* tropological, tropologic; *adv.* tropologically.

trot *n.* A summary, outline, or translation published as an aid to students; scholastic précis.

> I remember from my youth a series of trots which were advertised as containing two parallel translations, "the one literal, the other *correct.*"   —Jacques Barzun, *On Writing, Editing, and Publishing*

truism *n.* A sham statement in which the predicate expresses nothing that is not already implicit in the subject as it is defined; self-evident assertion; obvious truth. *Adj.* truistic, truistical.

> Now that the confessional genre has been appropriated by every other divorcee, adulterer, and successfully therapized individual, there is no end in sight to the number of truisms published as striking revelation, to the prurience parading as sociology.
> —R. D. Rosen, *Psychobabble*

trumpery *n.* Showy nonsense; fraudulent rubbish. *Adj.* trumpery.

tuism [*t(y)ōo'iz"əm*] *n.* Use of "you" in prose, as in an apostrophe. *N.* tuist. See also ILLEISM, NOSISM.

> The basis of my pet system was celibacy. I don't mean the mere state of being a bachelor. I mean celibacy of the soul—egoism, in fact. You have converted me from that. I am now a confirmed tuist.
> —Max Beerbohm, *Zuleika Dobson*

tu quoque [*t(y)ōo kwō' kwē*] *n.* A retort that one's adversary or detractor in fact is or does that which he criticizes; "you-too" counter-charge. *N.* tuquoqueism.

> . . . I felt my blood rising in temperature as I reflected on the malevolent inanity of his introductory observation, and then the resolution evolved that I would hit him back hard with a *tu quoque* involving *Myra Breckinridge*—which I had not then read. . . .
> —William F. Buckley, Jr., *The Governor Listeth*

turgid *adj.* Inflated in language, affecting grandeur but overblown and unclear; bombastic. *Adv.* turgidly; *n.* turgidity, turgidness.

> Was this the only history of the times, a mood blared by trumpets, trombones, saxophones and drums, a song with turgid, inadequate words?   —Ralph Ellison, *Invisible Man*

turnaround *n.* William Safire's term for political phrasemaking by reversal of familiar sayings, e.g., President James Buchanan after a loss at the polls: "We have met the enemy and we are theirs" (reversing "We have met the enemy and they are ours"). See also TWISTED PROVERB.

turn of phrase   Choice of phrasing, as for singularity or effect; particular wording; idiom or metaphor.

A writer on style, summarizing a valuable essay by the novelist George Orwell, tells the aspiring author never to use a cliché but always to "invent his own turn of phrase." The advice is good for training or retraining purposes. But it is not wholly practicable; it is an exaggeration: the adviser himself did not invent *turn of phrase*. He found the locution ready-made, and although it is not precisely a cliché, it is an old metaphor and quite indispensable.
—Jacques Barzun, *Simple & Direct*

tushery *n.*   Writing that uses affected, archaic words, as in a conventional romantic novel (coined by Robert Louis Stevenson).

twaddle *n.*   Silly or fatuous speech or writing; absurd gabble. *Adj.* twaddling; *v.* twaddle.

Love is not only the cardinal fact in the individual life, but the most important concern of the community; after all, the way in which the young people of this generation pair off determines the fate of the nation; all the other affairs of the State are subsidiary to that. And we leave it to flushed and blundering youth to stumble on its own significance, with nothing to guide it but shocked looks and sentimental twaddle and base whisperings and cant-smeared examples.
—H. G. Wells, *Tono-Bungay*

twee *adj. British*   Affectedly sentimental or quaint; arty; cute.

Canadians have tried *chaquet,* derived from *chaque,* implying equal but separate parts of a whole: it seems too twee, too boring, too Canadian.   —Philip Howard, *Words Fail Me*

twisted proverb   A humorous variation or inversion of a familiar proverb, maxim, slogan, etc., e.g., "Nothing exceeds like excess" (from "Nothing succeeds like success"). See also ECHO PHRASE.

Many of the best jokes of the sixties were twisted proverbs.
—Donna Cross, *Word Abuse*

typewriter word   See special entry WORD-GAME WORDS, p. 397.

typo *n.*   A typographical or printing error; misprint.

In the professional dreams that especially obsessed me when I worked on my earliest fiction . . . I might see for example that I was correcting galley proofs but that somehow (the great "somehow" of dreams!) the book had already come out, had come out literally, being proffered to me by a human hand from the wastepaper basket in its perfect, and dreadfully imperfect, stage—with a typo on every page, such as the snide "bitterly" instead of "butterfly" and the meaningless "nuclear" instead of "unclear."   —Vladimir Nabokov, *Ada*

typography *n.*   The art or process of printing from type; selection or arrangement of typefaces and characters; visual appearance or style of printed matter. *Adj.* typographical, typographic; *adv.* typographically; *n.* typographer.

Once the tone and the ante, however, have been pumped up to this awful frenzy, it becomes hard—even in reviewing Ms. Kael's work —to write in any other way; or, in the typographic clamor, to detect and follow a genuine critical argument.
                                    —Renata Adler, *New York Review of Books*

typomania *n.*   A writer's mania for publication.

U

U *adj.* Upper-class: characteristic of or appropriate to the speech and manners of the (usually) British upper class; using educated or prestigious language.

As the new book demonstrates, however, distinctions between U and non-U in language are getting fuzzier, what with the non-U people trying to sound U, and the U ones, out of reverse snobbery, espousing non-U terminology.   —John Simon, *Paradigms Lost*

ultracrepidarian [*ul″trə·krep″ə·dâr′ē·ən*] *adj.* Going beyond one's province or ken; judgmentally presumptuous, esp. as applied to a critic. *N.* ultracrepidarian, ultracrepidarianism; *v.* ultracrepidate.

unauthorized biography See special entry BOOK PUBLISHING TERMS, p. 363.

unconscious pun A word that becomes an inadvertently detracting, often comical pun because of the terminology or context of the sentence, e.g., "Mr. Schuster, who was killed in a highway accident after the play's cast party, had reportedly realized that the critics found him a theatrical turnoff." Also ACCIDENTAL PUN.

uncriticism *n.* Uncritical criticism.

underline See CUTLINE under special entry NEWSROOM HEADLINE JARGON, p. 386.

understatement *n.* Restrained or less than forthright expression, sometimes subtracting from full truth or the actual case but often an intentional style for dramatic or ironic effect; a comment that is incomplete, elliptical, or muted; avoidance of the direct or the exaggerated. *Adj.* understated; *v.* understate.

. . . the doctor has long since learned to withdraw his emotions from the plight of the patient and has replaced his own ability to imagine them and empathize with them, with a formula language—the social lie and the understatement—usually delivered with the off jocularity common to all gloomy professions.
—Diane Johnson, in *The State of the Language*

undertone *n.*   Low or subdued speech; an underlying quality or feeling, esp. an emotional undercurrent or tinge; note.

> She felt far from him. The undertone of his words repelled her and she withdrew her adoration for the Divers from the profanity of his bitterness.   —F. Scott Fitzgerald, *Tender Is the Night*

unfinished comparative   See AGENCY COMPARATIVE.

univocalic   See special entry WORD-GAME WORDS, p. 397.

unparliamentary language *British*   Coarse or obscene language; swearing.

unprintable *adj.*   So offensive or taboo as to be better left unmentioned or inexplicit; prohibitively vulgar or obscene.

> . . . he had a lingerie salesman's fondness for smoking-car anecdotes, the lower the better. About once a month a specimen would turn up which would usually not only be unprintable in any magazine not intended exclusively for the United States Marines but would also be drearily familiar to all worldly editors.
>   —Wolcott Gibbs, *More in Sorrow*

untranslatableness *n.*   The quality of not being closely renderable in another language or idiom; peerlessly true or apt expression, often considered the infallible test of good prose style; unexceptionable wording. *Adj.* untranslatable; *adv.* untranslatably.

upside-down pyramid   See INVERTED PYRAMID.

up style   Editorial style that favors capitalizing words rather than lower-casing them (contrasted with down style).

usage *n.*   The way in which words are used in everyday or particular situations, or language in actual practice; demonstrable or customary idiom; an instance of word choice.

> And it is only through complete, unswerving devotion to the perfect blending of form and substance; it is only through an unremitting never-discouraged care for the shape and ring of sentences that an approach can be made to plasticity, to color, and that the light of magic suggestiveness may be brought to play for an evanescent instant over the commonplace surface of words; of the old, old words, worn thin, defaced by ages of careless usage.
>   —Joseph Conrad, *The Nigger of the "Narcissus"*

usus loquendi [*yōo′səs lô·kwen′dē*]   Usage in speaking: usage of the day.

utterance *n.*   The act of or an instance of vocal speech; oral or written expression; something uttered or stated, such as a cry or a word or words. *N.* utterer; *v.* utter.

As always when he spoke, he sounded so plausible. Other people might call his utterances treachery but, to Scarlett, they always rang with common sense and truth.

—Margaret Mitchell, *Gone With the Wind*

V

vade mecum [*vā′dē mē′kəm*]   Go with me: anything, esp. a book, that is carried as a constant companion; handy and indispensable reference or guidebook. *Pl.* vade mecums.

> "I don't know," said Denis truthfully. He looked at the title page; the book was called *The Stock Breeder's Vade Mecum.*
> —Aldous Huxley, *Crome Yellow*

vagary *n.*   An occasional, unusual, or capricious action or notion; erratic or arbitrary fancy; idiosyncrasy. *Adj.* vagarious; *adv.* vagariously.

> The most troublesome part of an editor's job is the review of a manuscript in search of grammatical and rhetorical vagaries.
> —William Bridgwater, in *Editors on Editing*

value judgment   An explicit judgment of something or somebody, esp. a subjective one (based on the individual's personal values) in a factual, objective context; writer's or speaker's personal opinion or conclusion.

> Confident analysis conducted in psychological and sociological terms, accompanied by an odd reluctance to use what the social scientists call value judgments, is a striking feature of commentaries on Jonestown.   —David Reid, in *The State of the Language*

vanity press   See special entry BOOK PUBLISHING TERMS, p. 363.

vaporings *n. pl.*   Extravagant, inconsequential, or boastful talk or actions; self-important language; bombast. *Adj.* vaporing; *v.* vapor.

> He was frighted even to the marrow, and was minded to give order for your instant enlargement, and that you be clothed in fine raiment and lodged as befitted one so great; but then came Merlin and spoiled all; for he persuaded the king that you are mad, and know not wherof you speak; and said your threat is but foolishness and idle vaporing.
> —Mark Twain, *A Connecticut Yankee in King Arthur's Court*

Varietyese *n.*   The colorfully abbreviated, emphatic slang idiom of the show-business trade publication *Variety,* and especially of its headlines, typically a jargon using clipped words, inventive coinages, and often alliteration and rhyme, e.g., the words "pix" (pictures), "ankled" (quit), and "payola" (bribery), and the headline "Hip Nip In Hub" (Japanese jazz performer in Boston).

variorum See special entry SCHOLARLY (BIBLIOGRAPHIC) TERMS, p. 402.

venereal noun Any of specific collective nouns, each meaning "group" or "gathering," applied in a phrase to various animals (venery or hunting), as well as many such words coined facetiously for humorous double-meanings, e.g., "an exaltation of larks." Also NOUNS OF ASSEMBLAGE, COMPANY TERMS.

Actors and actresses come in *companies, casts, troupes,* and even *entrances* (in the Middle Ages a troupe was called a *cry*). Musicians are collected in *bands* and angels in *hosts.* But what are assemblages of writers called? I've heard of *schools, staffs, tribes, teams, strings, stables,* and *slates* of writers, but these aren't very good terms of venery. A *brood* or *concentration* of philosophic writers, a *column* of journalists, a *frown* of critics, a *fraid* of ghostwriters? Applying collective nouns designed for other animals might help. An *exaltation* (larks) of poets? A *murder* (crows) of mystery writers? A *stud* (horses) of pornographers? A *tidings* (magpies) of greeting-card writers? A *charm* (finches) of stylists? A *shrewdness* (apes) of publishers? A *watch* (nightingales) of editors? A *wickedness* (ravens) or *clowder* (cats) of critics? A *culture* (bacteria) or *brood* (hens) of bibliophiles? A *pitying* (turtledoves) of lonely-hearts columnists? A *barren* (mules) or *mute* (hounds) of blocked writers?
— Robert Hendrickson, *The Literary Life*

verbal *adj.* Of or pertaining to words; involving expression or wording per se, rather than meaning, thought, substance, or action; verbatim or literal; spoken rather than written; articulate or outspoken. *Adv.* verbally.

Just as cats and dogs like to be stroked, so do some human beings like to be verbally stroked at fairly regular intervals; it is a form of rudimentary sensual gratification.
— S. I. Hayakawa, *Language in Thought and Action*

verbal fallacy An error in reasoning due to improper use of language or ambiguity of terminology (contrasted with formal fallacy and material fallacy).

verbalism *n.* A verbal expression, esp. an empty or wordy locution; use of words with little regard to substance or realities.

There is no assurance in all the "findings," all the knowingness of the psychologist and the advertiser and the educationist, whose verbalisms cover and conceal the gaping holes in their empiric arts.
—Jacques Barzun, *The House of Intellect*

verbalist *n.* A skillful user of words; linguist or articulator; one giving too much attention to words at the expense of content, facts, or ideas. *Adj.* verbalistic.

verbalize *v.* To communicate through words; articulate; express in a wordy way. *N.* verbalization, verbalizer.

verbatim *adv.* Word for word; as an exact record of speech. *Adj.* verbatim.

It was this belief, and his desire to acquaint himself with the quantitative laws of religious phenomena, that had, in fact, led him to the roadside zoo where, as materialistic as his attitude toward stars might be, he did not hesitate to enter verbatim in his notebook Amanda's assertion, "Stars are merely projections of the human psyche—they are pimples of consciousness—but they are at the same time quite real."   —Tom Robbins, *Another Roadside Attraction*

verbiage *n.* Excess in verbal expression; needless or superfluous words or wording; wordiness.

Then one day he stood in a rented cap and gown among others and received the tightly-rolled parchment scroll no larger than a rolled calendar yet which, like the calendar, contained those three years— the spurned cleat-blurred white lines, the nights on the tireless horse, the other nights while he had sat in the overcoat and with only the lamp for heat, above spread turning pages of dead verbiage.
—William Faulkner, *The Hamlet*

verbicide *n.* Destruction or depreciation of word meaning, as through misuse, overuse, or emotional nuance superseding the word's original or objective sense.

Back in 1858 Oliver Wendell Holmes coined the word *verbicide.* He used it to describe the "violent treatment of a word with fatal results to its legitimate meaning, which is its life."
—Gyles Brandreth, *The Joy of Lex*

verbigerate [*vûr·bij′ə·rāt″*] *v.* To repeat stereotyped words, phrases, or sentences meaninglessly, as in some forms of mental illness. *N.* verbigeration.

verbile See special entry BOOKISH APPELLATIONS, p. 407.

verbocrap *n. British* See GOBBLEDYGOOK.

verbomaniac See special entry BOOKISH APPELLATIONS, p. 407.

verbose *adj.* Wordy. *Adv.* verbosely; *n.* verbosity, verboseness.

His influences? Sir Thomas Browne, de Quincey, Ecclesiastes, Henry James, Emily Brontë, Stevenson, Poe, Traherne. And, in later life, Julian Green perhaps? His style? It is his stories. At the very beginning, he was fond, I think, of a rather flowery verbosity; he used a lot of clichés, but they were always the right ones.
—Dylan Thomas, "Walter De La Mare as a Prose Writer"

verb sap (verbum sapienti) A word to the wise (suffices), or enough said: a discreet warning.

veriloquence [və·ril'ə·kwəns] n. Truth-speaking. *Adj.* veriloquent.

verisimilitude *n.* The quality or semblance of being true or real, as that of a novel that is convincing in its recreation of a social milieu; likeness; aesthetic believability; probability. *Adj.* verisimilar, verisimilous; *adv.* verisimilarly.

The novelist is ill-advised to be too technical. The practice, which came into fashion in the nineties, of using a multitude of cant terms is tiresome. It should be possible to give verisimilitude without that, and atmosphere is dearly bought at the price of tediousness.
—W. Somerset Maugham, *The Summing Up*

verismo [ve·rēz'mō] *n.* Emphasis in art and literature on everyday actuality, including the sordid and vulgar aspects of life, and hence an aesthetic or literary movement of extreme realism. *Adj.* verist, veristic.

Curiously, the evil gangsters struck me as more interesting and even more sympathetic than the protagonists. They were just trying to do their job, after all, and they spoke with a pleasingly low-key *verismo* that seemed more lifelike than the Rowlands-Adames [*sic*] rhapsodies of feeling.   —Andrew Sarris, *Village Voice*

vernacular *n.* Native or regional idiom, or nonstandard or substandard language, as opposed to the established, cultured language of a society; spoken, as opposed to literary, usage; everyday speech; a lingo. *Adj.* vernacular; *adv.* vernacularly; *n.* vernacularity.

When old Jack tells his stories . . . David Bradley renders Jack's speech in a country vernacular that is different from either Southern or ghetto dialect but no less colorful . . .
—Vance Bourjailly, *The New York Times*

verso   See special entry PARTS OF A BOOK, p. 364.

vice versa   With this order (of two terms or statements) being reversed; transposing the preceding; conversely.

It is apparently all right to have a young husband if you are an old woman in Palm Beach, but not vice versa; in fact, the vice versa is one of the few things the columnists in the *Social Pictorial* get really upset about.   —Nora Ephron, *Scribble Scribble*

vieux jeu [*vyoe zhoe*] *adj.*   Old game: describing a subject, topic, approach, etc. no longer of interest; old-fashioned or out-of-date.

I heard you laughing at the pride which certain of our connections take in the family tree, and I could almost have laughed with you, although this is a Boston joke that was *vieux jeu* even in my day.
                                         —John P. Marquand, *The Late George Apley*

vignette *n.*   A literary sketch, episode, or brief portrayal, esp. one that is appealingly personal and illuminating in its description.

The Captain shrugged and finished his drink. He had fabricated any number of ridiculous anecdotes about Alison and Anacleto, and they had all gone the rounds of the post with great success. The composition and sharpening of these scandalous vignettes afforded the Captain much pleasure.
                                         —Carson McCullers, *Reflections in a Golden Eye*

violent words   Jacques Barzun's term for "action" words as overused by hack writers to lard their prose with apparent vitality, esp. dramatic, "hard-hitting" verbs, e.g., "The telephone smashed the silence of the room," "Then we hit a little burg; the bus shuddered to a halt." See also WOW WORDS.

violin *n.*   Formerly, a news article written in purple prose; now a cover or lead story in a daily or weekly publication.

vis-à-vis [*vē"zə·vē'*] *prep.*   Face to face with; opposite to; compared with or in relation to. *Adv.* vis-à-vis; *n.* vis-à-vis.

And what about that conceivably greatest of English losses vis-à-vis the other European languages; the loss of the personal pronoun's second person singular form—the absence of "thou," except, perhaps, in talking to God?   —John Simon, *Paradigms Lost*

vituperation *n.*   Reviling or fault-finding in the form of abusive language; invective or railing. *Adj.* vituperative; *adv.* vituperatively; *n.* vituperator; *v.* vituperate.

Once Daisy, in a rage, had thrust a rose which he had given her, long thorny stem and all, down the back of his shirt, and that sharp pricking pain all the way down his spine came back to him during those vituperative monologues. —Iris Murdoch, *Nuns and Soldiers*

vocable *n.* A word, esp. a spoken or written term regarded as a sequence of sounds or letters rather than for its meaning; pronounceable sound or word. *Adj.* vocable; *adv.* vocably.

During its composition I would pace my cell distractedly, uttering soft meaningless vocables to the air as I struggled with the prose rhythms, and fighting back the desolate urge to masturbate that for some reason always accompanied this task.

—William Styron, *Sophie's Choice*

vocabulary *n.* A list of words, usually defined and alphabetized, as in a dictionary or specialized glossary; complete word stock of a language; sum corpus of words used in a sublanguage or by a group, class, or individual; scope of diction; command of words or range of expression.

A friend has told me of attending a party for writers and artists at which she introduced a painter to Marianne by saying, "Miss Moore has the most interesting vocabulary of anyone I know." Marianne showed signs of pleasure at this, and within a minute offhandedly but accurately used in a sentence a word I no longer remember that means an addiction, in animals, to licking the luminous numbers off the dials of clocks and watches. —Elizabeth Bishop, *Vanity Fair*

vocal *adj.* Involving or produced by the voice; uttered or spoken; possessing a voice or capable of speech; resounding with voices; inclined to or showing no hesitation in speaking out or criticizing; outspoken; vociferous. *Adv.* vocally; *n.* vocalness.

vociferation *n.* Earnestly vehement or loud outcry or speaking up, esp. in protest; outspoken insistence, clamorous talk. *Adj.* vociferous; *adv.* vociferously; *n.* vociferator; *v.* vociferate.

The Warden placed his own landau at the disposal of the illustrious young exile, who therein was driven to the station, followed by a long, vociferous procession of undergraduates in cabs.

—Max Beerbohm, *Zuleika Dobson*

vogue word A currently fashionable word, not necessarily new and often altered from its original sense by overuse; trendy term.

After four centuries of blameless and boring life with a precise denotation, the respectable abstract noun *credibility* has recently been picked up as a shameless vogue word. It has accordingly become skittish in its old age, broken out of its narrow semantic home, and started to trespass in the territories of other words. It is now widely used to mean credit, credence, the ability to persuade or impress others, the qualifications to make people believe what you say, and Heaven knows what else . . .   —Philip Howard, *Weasel Words*

voice *n.*   Vocal sound; utterance, or the ability to articulate or express; agency or medium for expression; the right to be heard; expression of thought, opinion, or feeling; particular or distinctive mode of speaking of a writer or of one of his or her characters; authorial persona; in grammar, the type of subject-verb agency, or the form of a verb with respect to the subject in a sentence, either as the performer (active voice) or the receiver (passive voice) of the action. *N.* voicer; *v.* voice.

This other person—this sometimes smugly omniscient, sometimes sophomorically philosophical, always disembodied voice that speaks directly to the reader—is only one of the many dismaying "other people" . . . in this short, bitter book.
                                          —Evan Hunter, *The New York Times*

volte-face [*volt·fäs*] *n.*   About-face: a complete change or turn-about of one's opinion, attitude, or policy. *V.* volte-face.

No motion-picture magnate is ever troubled by the *volte-face*.
                                          —P.G. Wodehouse, *The Luck of the Bodkins*

voluble *adj.*   Showing consistent ease and smoothness in speaking; continuously talkative; fluent. *Adv.* volubly; *n.* volubility, volubleness.

It was a habit with him to tell her all these matters, and he continued to do it even now, talking for long spells at dinner, as though by the volubility of words he could conceal from himself the ache in his heart.   —John Galsworthy, *The Man of Property*

vox et praeterea nihil [*voks' et prī·ter'ā·ə ni'hil*]   A voice and nothing more: sound without sense, or vanishing in translation: referring to a word or expression that does not lend itself to another language, such as a particular pun.

In a sane world I should be a great man; as things are, in this curious establishment, I am nothing at all; to all intents and purposes I don't exist. I am just *Vox et praeterea nihil.*
                                          —Aldous Huxley, *Crome Yellow*

vox nihili [*voks ni'hi·lē*]   See GHOST WORD.

vox populi, vox pop [*voks pop'yə·lē*]   The voice of the people; public sentiment. *Pl.* vox populis.

Outside, an ice cream van jingled its Greensleeves way down the road and Gavin wondered fleetingly whether this was tremendously unfair to Vaughan Williams, or whether he would have regarded it—ruefully —as some kind of accolade—vox populi to the chime.
—Elizabeth Jane Howard, *Getting It Right*

vulgarism *n.*   A nonstandard or illiterate word or expression, esp. but not necessarily one that is coarse, e.g., "an invite" for "an invitation"; a crude or demeaning usage.

My voice suddenly turned icy. Incorporeal, insubstantial, even ecto-plasmic these revenants may be, but I consider the term "ghost" a vulgarism and impermissible.   —S. J. Perelman, *The Last Laugh*

vulgate *n.*   Unrefined and often colorful colloquial English, either spoken or based on a spoken idiom and slang; vernacular.

American words express economic and social realities attractive to the young in England, to the hitherto underprivileged, and these words are becoming part of the dream life and vulgate of the post-war English scene.   —George Steiner, *Language and Silence*

W

waffle *v.* To speak in a wordy, vague, or evasive way, often as a hesitant response; hedge or equivocate; talk foolishly or vapidly. *N.* waffle, waffler.

They got drunk at a sportswriters' bar on Tenth Street and waffled on until three in the morning about Indians, street brawls, gunfights, and boxing. —David Black, *Like Father*

walla-walla *n.* Unintelligible sounds from many people talking at once (in the theater, a word that extras repeat in crowd scenes). See also RHUBARB.

Wardour Street English *British* Pseudo-quaint or pseudo-genteel English (from the London street formerly famous for its fake-antique shops).

Joyce gives us specimens of all kinds of puffed-up language, from provincial newspaper reportage to Wardour Street English, taking in also technical jargon, monstrous but vacuous catalogues, rituals from which the life has gone, and the sesquipedalian evasiveness of parliamentary answers. —Anthony Burgess, *Joysprick*

wart *n.* Journalist's term for a somewhat unflattering, discrediting, but "humanizing" observation, incident, anecdote, foible, etc., added to a profile of a person to make it more believable.

Amplification, for Ruark, is made up of an account of the subject's present-day doings and achievements: the appearance of a new book, the flat in London's Mayfair district, the hunting lodge in Africa, the villa in Spain, the contract for a new movie script. This section is relatively easy to write. But there is a problem. It may become so upbeat, so bushy-tailed that the story begins to lose credibility. Nobody can be *that* good, the readers begin to say to themselves. To allay this growing skepticism Ruark introduces a new element that he terms "the Nosepicker" or, to employ the word used by many magazine editors, "the Wart." This consists of an incident or anecdote that, in Ruark's words, "reflects discredit, in a nice way, on the subject." Sometimes, if the subject has been very naughty, the Wart may not be presented in such a nice way. In Ruark's profile the incident might concern his heavy drinking, someone wrongfully abused in his column, or the treatment of Virginia, his wife of twenty-four years.   —J. T. W. Hubbard, *Magazine Editing*

Washington Choctaw   See GOBBLEDYGOOK.

watchword *n.*   A password or code word by which members of a class or group recognize and accept one another; shibboleth; rallying cry or motto.

water haul   A fruitless effort: in journalism, unsuccessful research, interviewing, or writing.

weasel word   A word that neutralizes or "sucks the life" (like a weasel attacking an egg) from a connected word: any equivocal, inconclusive, or cosmetic term making the meaning or honesty of a statement shifty or empty and hence used to cover up or mislead, esp. as used in the language of publicity, advertising, or politics; wording to suggest implicitly what cannot be claimed literally or legally. *Adj.* weasel-worded. See special entry ADVERTISING WEASEL WORDS, p. 383.

They are insane. Jeremy will take her like the Angel itself, in his joyless, weasel-worded comealong, and Roger will be forgotten, an amusing maniac, but with no place in the rationalized power-ritual that will be the coming peace.
                    —Thomas Pynchon, *Gravity's Rainbow*

wegotism *n.*   Excessive use of the first person plural.

Wellerism *n.*   A facetious remark or comparison, expressed as a well-known quotation or saw followed by an incongruously irreverent or deflating clincher. Also QUOTH PROVERB.

Wellerisms antedate Dickens. They poured in full splash from Simon Spatterdash, in the comedy "The Boarding House; or, Five Hours at Brighton," by Samuel Beazley, which was a hit in London in 1811. Some of Simon's pure Wellerisms are:
    "I'm down upon you, as the extinguisher said to the rushlight." (In plays set in that period, we may still see footmen bringing a poled extinguisher down over the lights.)
    "Sharp work for the eyes, as the devil said when the broad-wheeled waggon went over his nose."
    "I'm all over in a perspiration, as the mutton chop said to the gridiron."
    Such aspects of humor became very popular. One of the favorite profferers of the tidbits was the comedian Samuel Vale, whose name, some have suggested, Dickens expanded into Weller.
                    —Joseph Shipley, *Playing with Words*

Westernism *n.*   A word or expression used in the American West, including frontier and cowboy slang words and Spanish corruptions, e.g., "buckaroo," "git," "varmint."

wheeze *n.*   A stock entertainer's joke; tiresome, trite saying or hackneyed old gag.

> To be judged capable of turning out: "Waiter, do you serve crabs?" "Yes, what'll you have?"—to be regarded as just the man to beg, borrow, steal or fabricate a wheeze like that every day—filled me with rage.   —Peter De Vries, *The Tents of Wickedness*

when-did-you-stop-beating-your-wife   question.   An   accusingly loaded question so worded, or implicitly ensnaring, that any reply that accepts the terms of the question will reflect unfavorably on the person answering. See also QUESTION-BEGGING.

whereas *n.*   A statement introduced by a "whereas," or a formal, legalistic preliminary declaration; qualifying explanatory clause or preamble.

> The resolutions, probably concocted by Everett himself or by one of his collaborators on the *North American,* began with long satirical whereases directed at the English reviewers, and proceeded to deplore the corruption of the language in the Motherland. . . .
> —H. L. Mencken, *The American Language*

which-mire *n.*   James Thurber's term for a regrettable sentence congested with proliferating "which" clauses.

> The relative pronoun "which" can cause more trouble than any other word, if recklessly used. Foolhardy persons sometimes get lost in which-clauses and are never heard of again. My distinguished contemporary, Fowler, cites several tragic cases, of which the following is one: "It was rumoured that Beaconsfield intended opening the Conference with a speech in French, his pronunciation of which language leaving everything to be desired. . . ." That's as much as Mr. Fowler quotes because, at his age, he was afraid to go any farther. The young man who originally got into that sentence was never found. His fate, however, was not as terrible as that of another adventurer who became involved in a remarkable which-mire. Fowler has followed his devious course as far as he safely could on foot: "Surely what applies to games should also apply to racing, the leaders of which being the very people from whom an example might well be looked for. . . ." Not even Henry James could have successfully emerged from a sentence with "which," "whom," and "being" in it.

The safest way to avoid such things is to follow in the path of the American author, Ernest Hemingway. In his youth he was trapped in a which-clause one time and barely escaped with his mind. He was going along on solid ground until he got into this: "It was the one thing of which, being very much afraid—for whom has not been warned to fear such things—he . . ." Being a young and powerfully built man, Hemingway was able to fight his way back to where he had started, and begin again. This time he skirted the treacherous morass in this way: "He was afraid of one thing. This was the one thing. He had been warned to fear such things. Everybody has been warned to fear such things." Today Hemingway is alive and well, and many happy writers are following along the trail he blazed.

—James Thurber, *The Owl in the Attic*

whispering campaign   The deliberate spreading of rumor or innuendo damaging to a person, cause, etc., esp. as a political tactic; word-of-mouth smear.

. . . it has been charged that many Washington whispering campaigns are based on terms which no one really understands. A Senator, for instance, is charged with being a "shameless extrovert." Another is a "former thespian"; or, before he was married, he practised "celibacy." This, coupled with vague accusations of things like "nepotism," very often finds the mark with unwary and uninstructed listeners.   —Mario Pei, *The Story of the English Language*

Whitehallese *n. British*   See GOBBLEDYGOOK.

white paper   A formal governmental publication setting forth the official findings and position on an issue.

The political dialects to be found in pamphlets, leading articles, manifestos, White Papers and the speeches of under-secretaries do, of course, vary from party to party, but they are all alike in that one almost never finds in them a fresh, vivid, home-made turn of speech.

—George Orwell, "Politics and the English Language"

whitewash *n.*   A glossing over or attempting to put in a favorable light that which is reprehensible or scandalous; a palliating of negative revelations; cover-up report. *V.* whitewash.

They'll accuse you of whitewashing Richard: "whitewashing" has a derogatory sound that "rehabilitation" hasn't, so they'll call it whitewashing.   —Josephine Tey, *The Daughter of Time*

white writing   See ZERO DEGREE WRITING.

who, what, when, where, how, and why   See FIVE W'S.

wienie *n.* In advertising, a word, gimmick, or "angle" that makes a product sound scientifically or exotically special; pseudo-scientific or pseudo-technical red herring.

What all admen are looking for is the "wienie"—the angle, the gimmick, the something that need not be different as long as it sounds different.   —Donna Cross, *Word Abuse*

Winchellism *n.* As popularized by columnist Walter Winchell, a coinage from respelling, shortening, or telescoping two words into one, often as a form of pun, for a snappy or humorous effect, e.g., "Age of Chiselry," "Girlesque," "infanticipating"; a journalistic wordplay.

It must have been at about the time that the country tilted into the Great Depression that I first saw "celebrity" shortened to "celeb." The truncation occurred, naturally, in a Walter Winchell newspaper column. "Celeb" is one of the few Winchell neologisms that have endured. Many were only respellings or distortions of familiar words: "That's the sitchee-ay-shun," or "What producer gave his squaw a swelegant black orb after He Found Her Out?" or "Oakie's sensayuma is de-voon."   —Willard R. Espy, *Words at Play*

windyfoggery *n.* Theodore Bernstein's term for any pretentiously turgid speech or writing.

In nature wind and fog do not normally coexist. In language, however, they sometimes do, and the greater the wind the more impenetrable the fog. This linguistic condition may be thought of as *windyfoggery* It embraces gobbledygook, that wordy, involved, and often unintelligible language usually associated with bureaucracy and big business. But it also includes the self-important circumlocution of ordinary orators, the pretentious pseudoscientific jargon of the pseudosciences, and the monumental unintelligibility of some criticism of those arts that do not readily accept the bridle of plain words
                                      —Theodore Bernstein, *The Careful Writer*

winged words Words that quickly and effectively express their message; eloquent language.

And now my mind was in a whirl: for I knew that this was my chance for speaking unwingèd words, which should lie and germinate and bear fruit there where I flung them.
—Frederick William Rolfe (Frederick Baron Corvo), *Don Tarquinio*

wisecrack *n.* A witty remark, esp. one that is teasing or sarcastic; flippant aside; gibe. *N.* wisecracker; *v.* wisecrack, crack wise.

Gwen's dizzy, bombed-out wisecracks arrive from behind an ill-disguised haze of almost tragic psychological disorientation.
—Frank Rich, *The New York Times*

wit *n.* A keen, astute sense of the connections and associations between ideas and words and an aptness for expressing such perceptions in a pleasing, amusing, or often brilliantly satirical way; lucidly penetrating and compelling observation; evident intelligence and understanding; delightfully insightful expression; clever language, esp. entertainingly epigrammatic or ironic comment or repartee. *Adj.* witty; *adv.* wittily; *n.* wittiness.

Though there is a murder in "Sheiks and Adders," most of the shooting is at language, and this raises questions about the role of wit in mystery novels. Is wit an escape, or just another reminder that we must grin and bear the world? Will the punch line replace the punch in the jaw? Is wit fun to curl up with? Is it suspenseful?
—Anatole Broyard, *The New York Times*

witling See special entry BOOKISH APPELLATIONS, p. 407.

witter *v. British* To ramble on.

witticism *n.* A witty remark or observation; clever saying or conceit.

Among the dozen or so screenwriters on the assembly line, which included Flotsam and Jetsam, a team that wrote several gangster classics, was one Winston Finston, a scholarly, withdrawn chap with a hearing aid, whose deafness, mercifully, shielded him from our boisterous witticisms. —S. J. Perelman, *The Last Laugh*

Witzelsucht [*vit′səl·zoō̆kht″*] *n.* Wit-mania: an obsession to joke, pun, or tell pointless stories.

wooden head See DEADHEAD under special entry NEWSROOM HEADLINE JARGON, p. 386.

woofing *n.* See SIGNIFYING.

woolly, wooly *n. British* Unclear in thought or expression; vague; confused or incoherent. *N.* woolliness.

"There are professors who have told me they would not dare to speak as simply as I do," said Philosopher Karl R. Popper, "though our constant endeavor is to distinguish between what is true and what is false. How impossible does it become if we speak in a woolly way!"
—Israel Shenker, *Words and Their Masters*

word *n.*   A distinct or identifiable sound, form of utterance, or unit of meaning or its presentation in characters; standard pronounceable or spellable linguistic form; moment for conversation; remark or comment. *Pl.* understandable expression, or discourse or communication; text; explicit command or directive; pledge or promise; news or information; rumor; open disagreement; accusations or criticisms; a holy message or gospel. *V.* word.

Was she simply a nexus of literary cross-references scribbled in the margins of a minor poem? And had my love dissolved her in this strange fashion, or was it simply the literature I had tried to make out of her? Words, the acid-bath of words!   —Lawrence Durrell, *Clea*

wordage *n.*   Amount of words or literary length, without regard to quality; words collectively; characters as a unit of prose measurement.

I have waded through some dull wordage in my day, but if there is anything as trying as an article on mothproofing a vest, I prefer to remain in the dark about it.
                    —S. J. Perelman, "Wholly Cleaning and Dyeing"

word deletion   See special entry WORD-GAME WORDS, p. 398.

wordfact *n.*   John Kenneth Galbraith's term for the self-fulfilling prophecy whereby a word or label, however misused, creates its own "truth" by classifying, or the tendency of specific terms to shape their own reality, e.g., constant reference to a group of people as "outcasts."

Self-fulfilling prophecy in which saying that something exists becomes a substitute for its existence, as when we label a child "dull" or "retarded" and actually cause him to become such. Scientist Loren Eisley warned us about the peril of wordfact when he said our most dangerous gift is our ability to define ourselves through words.
                    —William Lambdin, *Doublespeak Dictionary*

word-for-word *adv.*   In precisely the same words; verbatim; meticulously literal. *Adj.* word-for-word.

David Dalby of the London School of Oriental and African Studies has, on the other hand, pointed out that many Black American expressions like *be with it, do your thing,* and *bad mouth* (talk badly about someone) are word-for-word translations of phrases used widely in West African languages.
                    —Albert Marckwardt, *American English*

word-hoard *n.*   A vocabulary or command of words.

. . . in many a text the writer seems hardly to care who's who or what is at stake so long as he has an excuse to unload a big, hard-hitting word-hoard. This is especially true of news reports of sporting events in the American tradition, where the story pounds its way forward. . . . —Huntington Brown, *Prose Styles*

word jobber A hack writer.

wordmonger *n.* A writer who uses words ostentatiously or without much regard for meaning; any writer. *N.* word-mongering, word-mongery.

We like to imagine that we, just plain folks, are somehow, deep down where it really counts, superior to those pointy-headed word-mongers with all their hereinafters.
—Richard Mitchell, *Less Than Words Can Say*

wordplay *n.* Speech or writing in which words (and their meanings) are used with wit or clever ambiguity, as in repartee or punning; verbal sportiveness; a play on words.

Nor is "word play"—which usually refers to riddles, puns, jokes, wise sayings, verbal dueling, and so forth—a trivial pastime.
—Peter Farb, *Word Play*

wordsmith *n.* One skilled in using words or in literary craftsmanship; veteran professional writer; hack ghostwriter.

"Feisty" is to with-it wordsmiths as "perceived" is to academics, "luminous" is to theater reviewers, "asymmetric" is to SALT sellers, "trenchant" is to book blurbers, and "abrasive" used to be to political writers before Bella Abzug left the scene.
—William Safire, *On Language*

word-watcher *n.* A person keenly vigilant about words and language, such as a lexicographer or a writer of a language column.

wordy *adj.* Having or using too many words; verbose. *Adv.* wordily; *n.* wordiness.

Like John Barth's *Giles Goat-Boy*, *A Bloodsmoor Romance* is deliberately wordy and antique, a stony artifice carpeted with plastic moss.
—James Wolcott, *Harper's*

working and stylish words H. W. Fowler's differentiation between the simple word and the grander synonym, and between the acceptable (working) use of a word in one sense and its stuffy (stylish) misuse in another sense; natural versus affected idiom.

wow words   William Lambdin's term for "breathtaking" dramatic words overused by journalists, advertising writers, etc., to create a contrived excitement, e.g., "shocking," "drastic," "crucial," "crushing"; racy hyperbole. See also VIOLENT WORDS.

writer's cramp   Uncomfortable or painful muscle cramping in the fingers and hand because of the continuous manual effort in writing. Also GRAPHOSPASM, MOGIGRAPHIA.

In commenting on monographs, Moses' very hand rebelled. Five minutes at a letter and he got writer's cramp.   —Saul Bellow, *Herzog*

xenoepist   See special entry BOOKISH APPELLATIONS, p. 407.

xenoglossophilia   A love of using foreign or otherwise strange words.

xenoglossy [*zen'ə·glos″ē*] *n.*   Trancelike language, ostensibly alien or unknown to the speaker under normal circumstances.

Y

yammer *v.* To talk with urgent persistence, esp. in a frantic whining or complaining way. *N.* yammerer.

yarn *n.* A tale; a long, elaborate, and often hard-to-believe story (or one not requiring belief), esp. a personal narrative of remarkable events or adventures; drawn-out recitation; tall tale.

They made the king tell his yarn, and they made the old gentleman tell his'n; and anybody but a lot of prejudiced chuckleheads would 'a' *seen* that the old gentleman was spinning truth and t'other one lies.
—Mark Twain, *The Adventures of Huckleberry Finn*

yea-saying *n.* Affirmation or support; a response of approval rather than of disapproval; endorsement; ballyhooing. *Adj.* yea-saying; *n.* yea-sayer; *v.* yea-say.

Inarguably, most of what is produced in any art, particularly the audience arts of theatre and film, is junk; and obviously the nay-saying is a reaction against the most persistent yea-saying of the mass circulation press.   —Stanley Kauffmann, *The New Republic*

yellowback *n. British*   A cheap, sensational novel.

yellow journalism   Wildly irresponsible, sensational news reporting that exaggerates, distorts, or exploits to attract readers, as do many tabloids.

Oh, everything! The telegraph and society papers and interviewing and America and yellow journalism . . . and all those family memoirs and diaries and autobiographies and Court scandals. . . . They produce a new kind of public, a public which craves for personalities rather than information.   —Norman Douglas, *South Wind*

yellow press *Chiefly British*   Exploitive, sensational newspapers and periodicals.

There were times that I flirted with the notion of making some tepidly aggressive move myself, but banner headlines in the yellow press formed in my mind and I shrank from any action.
—Woody Allen, *Side Effects*

Yiddishism *n.* A Yiddish word or expression, e.g., "mensh," "yenta."

So lame is the writing that Miss Nanus must finally rely on . . . trashy sound effects to signify terror and a chorus of extras to fill in factual information. For humor, there's the expected sprinkling of Yiddishisms.   —Frank Rich, *The New York Times*

Yinglish *n.* English that is salted with Yiddish words.

you-too-ism *n.* See TU QUOQUE.

Z

zed *n. British* The letter *z*.

zero degree writing A fictional style, influenced by certain modern French novelists and literary theorists, intended to be rigorously dispassionate or "colorless" in its eschewing of metaphor, characterization, and other conventional humanistic or individualistic qualities of traditional novels. Also WHITE WRITING.

Pynchon's use of physics is exhilarating and as an artist he appears to be gaining more energy than he is losing. Unlike the zero writers, he is usually at the boil. —Gore Vidal, *Matters of Fact and Fiction*

zeugma [zōog′mə] *n.* A "yoking" or abbreviated construction, sometimes not strictly grammatical, in which a predicate or modifier is made to do double duty, i.e., "Her hair is blonde, her eyes [are] brown," "No amount of money or [number of] people can influence me." *Adj.* zeugmatic; *adv.* zeugmatically. See also SYLLEPSIS.

"You 'committed,' as you put it, a zeugma—or, more properly, a syllepsis. Should I suspend operations so I can congratulate you?"
—William F. Buckley, Jr., *Stained Glass*

zinger *n.* An exciting, startling line; sharply personal critical remark, esp. a mordant insult.

If he had been wooing old Republicans up to now with sure-fire vulcanized one-line zingers, he could hardly be unaware that millions of Independents, some of them young, were also watching.
—Norman Mailer, *Miami and the Siege of Chicago*

Zoilus See special entry BOOKISH APPELLATIONS, p. 407.

Part II

SPECIAL
ENTRIES

Book Publishing Terms

active title   An in-print book that a publisher considers to be selling well.

adaptation   A work converted from one artistic medium into another, such as a screenplay based on a novel.

authorized biography   A biography researched and written with the approval and cooperation of its subject or subject's family, heirs, or executors.

backlist   A publisher's steadily selling titles currently in print, as distinct from its most recent books; titles kept in print year after year, such as classics or reference books.

bestseller   A book ranking among those selling the best nationally (or locally) over a given period of time, esp. (in the United States) one so noted by *The New York Times*.

blockbuster   A book that is immediately an enormous success.

brand-name author   A renowned, successful writer whose name alone virtually assures that his or her latest book will sell well.

coffee-table book   A large-format, heavily illustrated book for casual browsing, usually expensive and appealing to readers chiefly for its visual richness.

commercial fiction   Novels published solely on the basis of probable popular appeal and anticipated high sales and which are usually unremarkable as works of enduring literary quality.

dual edition   The publication of a book in simultaneous hardcover and paperback editions.

fair copy   A neat, legible copy of a draft or proof made after corrections or revision. Also CLEAN COPY.

flap copy   The promotional, descriptive written material appearing on the inside folds of a book's dust jacket, sometimes including a laudatory quote or quotes and a capsule biography of the author.

foul copy   A draft or proof marked up with corrections.

frontlist   A publisher's newest books, or those of its current season.

gift book   A book published with only seasonal appeal and sales in mind, such as an expensive, illustrated, large-format children's or fine-arts volume, esp. a book published to capitalize on Christmas sales.

handle   An editor's succinct descriptive statement about a book for use by the publisher's sales staff to extol its virtues or distinctiveness.

imprint   A publisher's subdesignation on a title page or book cover identifying a book as special in some way, such as a name for a line or series or indicating that it is an acquisition of a particular (esteemed) editor ("A____Book").

instant book   A book (usually a paperback) opportunely rushed into print, usually following an event of great public interest. Also EXTRA, QUICKIE.

line   A publisher's continuing series of books that are similar or interrelated, such as historical-romance paperbacks.

managed text   A textbook whose "author" (or authors), usually a professor, only oversees and reviews its writing, which is done by freelancers and/or graduate students.

mass-market paperback   A widely distributed commercial paperback book in conventional, more or less pocket-sized format, including popular novels, thrillers, celebrity biographies, and sold not only in bookstores but in supermarkets and drugstores.

over the transom   Unsolicited (manuscript), that is, not requested by the publisher or sent in by a writer's agent; slush pile.

package   A book provided to a publishing house in complete, final form by a "packager," who has found its author and overseen its (freelance) editing, illustration, photographic and art layout, and typesetting.

paperback original   A book published initially as a mass-market or trade paperback, as contrasted with a paperback version following a hardcover edition.

penalty book   A second book contracted, reluctantly, by a publisher as part of an author's conditions for selling to that house the book the publisher wants to acquire.

query   A specific question, comment of doubt, or request for information or factual clarification noted on a manuscript or galley by an editor, copy editor, or proofreader.

reading line   A descriptive sentence on the front jacket of a book (but not on the title page), and a term used when the description is too long to be considered a subtitle.

remainder   A book sold at a low sale price and stocked in great quantity by a bookstore, often originally published (at normal price) with such later-stage sales in mind.

reprint A book, originally hardcover, republished by the same or a different house (for the most part unchanged) in paperback or hardcover.

trade book A hardcover book intended for sale to a general readership through retail bookstores, as contrasted with an academic or college treatise or textbook.

trade paperback A large-format paperback (or one of the general size of the usual hardcover book), sometimes aimed at a special or limited market, as contrasted with the smaller, mass-market paperpack, and usually sold only in bookstores. Also QUALITY PAPERBACK.

shelf life The estimated period of a book's salable display in bookstores.

slush pile Unsolicited manuscripts received by a publisher.

tie-in The issuing or reissuing of a book concomitantly with a film, television mini-series, related book, etc., as a timely sales strategy, or sometimes the novelization of a screenplay for publication coincident with the movie's release.

unauthorized biography A biography written without consultation with its subject or against his or her wishes (and often so advertised for selling appeal).

vanity press Collectively, publishers who offer to print a book at the author's expense, usually with minimal advertising of the resulting volume and no profit to the author.

Parts of a Book

acknowledgments Expression of personal gratitude by the author, sometimes included in the preface.

back matter All the printed matter (pages) following a book's actual text. Also END MATTER.

colophon A publisher's identifying device, symbol, or logo.

copyright page A page indicating the book's copyright © notice as well as library cataloguing data (with the International Standard Book Number), permissions, dates of previous printings or editions, and sometimes the publisher's mailing address.

dedication An authorial notice of tribute to or esteem for a person or persons, usually appearing on its own page.

end paper   The folded leaf, at the book's front or back, half of which is an inside-cover backing. Also END LEAF, END SHEET.

epigraph   An apposite quotation or quotations chosen by the author, sometimes appearing alone on a preliminary page. (See entry in main text.)

flyleaf   A blank page at the front or back of the book, the "free" half of the paper glued to the inside cover.

folio   Page number.

foreword   A preface, esp. one written by somebody other than the author (in which case it precedes the author's preface).

frontispiece   An illustration page facing a book's title page.

half title   A page, before the title page, showing only the book's title, not the author or publisher. Also BASTARD TITLE.

introduction   An introductory general, often explanatory, discourse or overview pertinent to a book's subject (as opposed to its purpose, scope, etc.) and tantamount to a preliminary chapter (usually paginated as part of the main text).

preface   Preliminary remarks or commentary about the book, as about how or why it came to be written and mentioning helpful sources.

recto   A right-hand page (with an odd number).

title page   A page indicating the book's title, author, and publisher (and its offices, geographically), and, when appropriate, its subtitle, editor, or translator.

trim size   The size of a complete page, including margins, in a book when it is finally published.

verso   A left-hand page (with an even number).

Footnote Abbreviations

abr. Abridged.
anon. Anonymous.
app. Appendix.
ca. (circa). About, approximately.
cf. (confer). Compare.
col. Column.
ed. Editor.

e.g. (exempli gratia). For example.
esp. Especially.
et al. (et alii). And others.
etc. (et cetera). And so forth.
et seq. (et sequentes). And the following.

f. And the following page.

ff. And the following pages.

fl. (floruit). Flourished.

ibid. (ibidem). In the same place.

id. (idem). The same (author).

i.e. (id est). That is.

inf. (infra). Below.

loc. cit. (loco citato). In the place cited.

m.m. (mutatis mutandis). The necessary changes being made.

MS or ms. (manuscriptum). Manuscript.

MSS or mss. (manuscripta). Manuscripts.

N.B. (nota bene). Take careful or special note of.

n.d. No date.

n.s. New series.

op. cit (opere citato). In the work cited.

o.s. Old series.

p. Page.

par. Paragraph.

pass. (passim). Throughout; here and there.

pl. Plate.

pp. Pages.

pt. Part.

pub. Publisher; published.

q.v. (quod vide). Which see.

qq.v. (quae vide). Which (plural) see.

r. Reigned.

repr. Reprinted.

ser. Series.

sup. (supra). Above.

supp. or suppl. Supplement.

s.v. (sub verbo). (To be found) under the word.

trans. Translation (by).

vide or v. See.

viz (videlicet). Namely.

vol. or v. Volume.

Accent and Symbol Terms

'	acute accent *(résumé)*
&	ampersand, ipseand (and)
⟨ ⟩	angle brackets (enclosing symbol)
*	asterisk (reference symbol)
˘	breve *(bŏŏk: book)*
●	bullet (used before itemized paragraphs)
∧	caret (insertion mark)
،	cedilla *(aperçu)*
·	center dot, center point, space dot (syl·la·ble)
ˆ	circumflex (raison d'être)
†	dagger, obelisk (reference symbol)
⌦	dele, deleatur (deletion mark)
¨	dieresis (or diaeresis) (naïve)
‡	double dagger (reference symbol)
ß	es-zet (German double *s*)
☞	index, fist (ornamental indicator)
« »	guillemets (French quotation marks)

`	grave accent *(à la carte)*
'	hamza, homzah (Arabic glottal stop)
fl,œ,æ	ligature, digraph (old spellings)
¯	macron *(brīd: bride)*
¶	pilcrow, blind, paragraph mark (phonetic symbol)
ə	schwa (phonetic symbol)
§	section mark (reference symbol)
~	swung dash (abbr. for understood word)
˜	tilde *(mañana)*
¨	umlaut *(Gemütlichkeit)*
°	volle, Swedish *a* *(Anders Ångstrom)*
ˇ	wing, wedge, hăcek, inverted circumflex *(Karel Čapek)*
/	virgule, slash, oblique slant, solidus, separatrix, diagonal (word or line division)

Libel

When the choice or misuse of words goes beyond matters of grammar or diction and involves possible damage to another's reputation, the question of libel, or slander in print, is raised.

The legal complexities of libel are many and vary from state to state. With this borne in mind, the following excerpts from Faustin F. Jehle's "Libel: An American Business Press Practical Guide," may help clarify some of the principles involved in the issue of libel—a word much heard and seen in our litigious society but, in detail, little understood by the layperson. Mr. Jehle wrote the pamphlet to provide a "ready reference" for reporters, editors, publishers, and authors.

Definition

Libel can be defined, generally, as calumny in print. If you *speak* in a manner that tends to injure another person's good name, you may have *slandered* him or her. If you commit the same words to print and publish them—or beam them out over the airwaves—you may be guilty of *libel*.

Libel law is continually being refined to reflect changing customs and life styles, but the basic concepts remain approximately the same. There is obviously a common thread running through the following definitions, derived from the case law of several states:

"*The fundamental rule* that lies at the basis of the entire law of libel is that no person may charge or infer that any other person is guilty of degrading, infamous, or criminal action *without justification or excuse,* which tends to expose him to public contempt, scorn, obloquy, ridicule, shame or disgrace, or tends to induce an evil opinion of him in the minds of right-thinking persons, or injures him in his reputation, trade, business, or profession, whatever the intention of the writer may be.''

"A written or printed statement or article, published of or concerning a person, which is false and tends to injure his reputation, expose him to hatred, contempt, scorn, obloquy, or shame, or harms his reputation so as to lower him in the estimation of the community, or deters third persons from associating or dealing with him, or specifically imputes to him guilt of any crime, fraud, immorality, vice, lack of honor, or dishonesty, or suggests or states that he is suffering from an infectious disease, or which has a tendency to injure or actually injures him in his trade, business, or profession, is libelous per se.''

"A writing is defamatory if it induces an evil or unsavory opinion of the plaintiff in the minds of a substantial number of the community, or deprives him of their friendly intercourse in society, even though such writing imputes no moral turpitude to him.''

"A written statement is libelous per se if it exposes a person to public scorn, contempt, obloquy, ridicule, or shame, by indirect and adroit methods as well as by crude and direct accusations.''

The general thrust is clear enough. Most people do not like to be portrayed in a bad light, and the Courts have provided them with some very specific remedies for those times when it does happen.

Essential Elements

1. A false statement in writing;
2. Communicated to a third person;
3. Accusing one of a crime; or
4. That one suffers from a loathsome disease; or
5. That tends to lower one in the esteem of society or hold one up to ridicule; or
6. Tends to injure a person in his or her trade, business or profession.

Note: Malice is *not* an essential element of libel. Libel per se, or by innuendo, can occur innocently and without intent.

Dangerous Words

1. All accusations of crime or imputation of crime

Abortionist	Blackmailer	Drug dealer
Arsonist	Con man	Embezzler
Bigamist	Crook	Extortionist

False swearing   Racketeer   Swindler
  (perjury)   Rigs or fixes games   Tax evader
Forger   Shady   Thief
Grafter   Skimmer   Treason
Guilty of fraud   Smuggler   User of false weights

2. Tending to injure trade, business, or profession

Ambulance chaser   Faker   Partnership with or
Bankrupt   Gouger   backed by known
Betrays confidence   Heavily in debt   criminals
Charlatan   Hypocrite   Plagiarist
Deadbeat   Insolvent   Pseudo-scientist
Delinquent—   Lacking credit   Quack
  unworthy of credit   Lacks integrity   Scab or strike breaker
Discharged for   Malpractice   Sells influence
  inefficiency   Never pays bills   Shyster
Disgrace to his   On payroll of   Unsanitary or
  profession   racketeers   dangerous products
Dishonest   Operates a "Boiler   Unprofessional
Drunkard   Room"   conduct
Engaged in unlawful   Paid for his job
  business or restraints
  of trade

3. Other

Adulterer   Homosexual   Quisling
A peeping Tom   Illegitimate   Receiver of kickbacks
A stool pigeon   Imbecile   Runs a brothel
Benedict Arnold   Incompetent   Scandalmonger
Corrupt   Insane   Unfaithful to wife
Dishonorably   Lack of chastity   Venality
  discharged   Loathsome disease   Wife or child abuser
Drug addict   Mental disorder

Reprinted by permission of American Business Press, Inc.

Fair Use

When is it legally permissible for an author to use excerpts from another writer's copyrighted work without having to obtain formal permission? How long may such a passage borrowed for quotation be? Must express mention of or credit to the source of the quote always be given?

The realm of fair use continues to be a gray one legally. But for most professional writers (and their publishers), particularly nonfiction writers, there is no escaping having to know something about it, or about the sometimes fine line between required permission and modest and just free, or "fair," use.

The following basics regarding fair use are gratefully excerpted from *The Writer's Lawyer*, by Ronald L. Goldfarb and Gail E. Ross (Times Books, 1989). Permission to quote from Mr. Goldfarb and Ms. Ross, please note, was required.

Fair Use

The notion of fair use, as one court stated, originally was developed by the courts "in order to balance the exclusive rights of the copyright owner and the public's interest in the dissemination of information affecting cases of universal concern such as art, science, history or industry."

Fair use allows a limited amount of exact copying and is considered a defense to an infringement claim. How much copying is allowed? Contrary to the widely held belief that fair use can be quantified to a number of words or lines, there is no such quantitative test. An often-quoted commentator once remarked that the best fair-use test a writer can use is to put yourself in the other person's shoes and decide at what point you would feel that you had been unfairly taken advantage of. When you reach that point you have ventured beyond the bounds of fair use. In 1961 the U.S. Copyright Office published a list of permitted fair-use practices:

- quotation of excerpts in a review or criticism for purposes of illustration or comment
- quotation of short passages in a scholarly or technical work, for illustration or clarification of the author's observations
- use in a parody of some of the content of the work parodied
- summary of an address or an article, with brief quotations, in a news report
- reproduction by a library of a portion of a work to replace part of a damaged copy
- reproduction by a teacher of a small part of a work to illustrate a lesson
- reproduction of a work in legislative or judicial proceedings or reports
- incidental and fortuitous reproduction, in a newsreel or broadcast, of a work located on the scene of an event being reported

The concept of fair use was later codified by Congress in the 1976 Copyright Act. According to the Copyright Act, the fair use of a copyrighted work for such purposes as criticism, comment, news reporting, teaching, scholarship, or research is not an infringement of copyright.

The new statute lists four factors for determining what is or is not fair use:

1. the purpose and character of the use, including whether such use is of a commercial nature or is for nonprofit educational purposes
2. the nature of the copyrighted work
3. the amount and substantiality of the portion used in relation to the copyrighted work as a whole
4. the effect of the use upon the potential market for or value of the copyrighted work

According to the legislative history of the act, Congress failed to provide more definitive fair-use guidelines because it found the doctrine to be an equitable rule of reason, with no generally applicable scientific definition. Thus, each case raises unique questions and must be decided on its own facts.

While the purpose of an allegedly infringing use is highly relevant, the fact that a book is intended to make a profit for its author does not preclude the application of the doctrine. Many of the purposes cited in the act, such as criticism and news reporting, are commercial endeavors that also educate the public. Nor does writing a book for educational purposes or for a nonprofit organization mean that the author has an unfettered right to take from someone else's work. The commercial or nonprofit character of an activity, while not conclusive, must be weighed along with the other factors in making fair-use decisions. If the nature of use is strictly a noncommercial, educational one, more copying is likely to be allowed and the use is more likely to be considered fair.

The third criterion, the amount and substantiality of the portion that is being used in relation to the overall copyrighted work, can often be an elusive standard. Obviously, the more you take from another's work, the more likely a court would find infringement and not fair use. But what if the copyrighted work is three hundred pages long and you copy or even paraphrase only fifteen pages? Is that fair use? This is when the "substantiality" of the short portion must be considered.

Blurb Adjectives

"To blurb," it has been said, "is to make a sound like a publisher."

Many adjectives—none of them derogatory—can be used for marketing purposes to describe a freshly published book. Among the more common clamorous descriptives drawn upon by publicists for flap copy or print ads are those listed below. They might well be considered overused superlatives, but continuing resort to them for successful book sales may suggest rather a kind of superlative overuse. The reader or the weekly critic may use any of them aptly, but should do so judiciously and in groups of less than four.

absorbing	extraordinary	penetrating
action-packed	fascinating	poignant
amazing	glittering	powerful
astounding	gripping	previously
beguiling	hair-raising	unpublished
beloved	haunting	profound
bewitching	heart-stopping	prophetic
bittersweet	hilarious	provocative
bold	hysterical	racy
breathtaking	illuminating	radiant
brilliant	immortal	relevant
captivating	impressive	remarkable
carefully re-	incendiary	required reading
searched	incomparable	rib-tickling
celebrated	indispensable	rich
chilling	informative	ripping
classic	insightful	riveting
compelling	inspiring	rousing
controversial	intriguing	scathing
convincing	invaluable	scintillating
courageous	irresistible	scorching
dazzling	long-awaited	searing
defiant	lusty	sensational
deft	lyrical	shattering
definitive	magnificent	shocking
delightful	major	sound
devastating	marvelous	spellbinding
distinguished	masterful	spine-tingling
disturbing	memorable	splendid
electrifying	mighty	standard
emotional	monumental	stark
enchanting	more than	steamy
engaging	moving	stirring
engrossing	much-needed	stormy
enjoyable	naughty	stunning
entertaining	nerve-shattering	superb
enthralling	nerve-tingling	suspenseful
epic	original	sweeping
epoch-making	outrageous	tantalizing
evocative	outspoken	tempestuous
exciting	outstanding	terrifying
explosive	overwhelming	thoughtful

thrilling	true	vivid
timeless	unflinching	witty
torrid	unforgettable	wonderful
touching	unprecedented	zesty
towering	unputdownable	
triumphant	uproarious	

Prose-Descriptive Adjectives

Along with countless adjectives in English that describe—and sensationalize—books and reading experiences, there are those that characterize writing itself. Collected here are some of the most commonly heard (or read) modifiers useful for describing the coherence, effectiveness, pace, originality, and readability of prose style.

awkward	florid	opaque	sloppy
baroque	flowery	ornate	smooth
bombastic	flowing	outworn	snappy
breezy	fluid	overblown	solipsistic
chatty	frothy	overdrawn	sonorous
choppy	garbled	overstated	spare
clichéd	glib	overwritten	sparkling
clipped	gushy	painterly	staccato
concise	hackneyed	pedestrian	stiff
convoluted	heavy-handed	pithy	stilted
crackling	idiosyncratic	plodding	succinct
crisp	illiterate	polished	supple
dazzling	incisive	ponderous	taut
deathless	inflated	powerful	tendentious
desultory	journalistic	precious	terse
discursive	labored	purple	tight
disjointed	laconic	quirky	tortured
dry	lapidary	racy	trashy
dull	leaden	rapturous	trenchant
economical	lean	rhapsodic	trite
elegant	limpid	rich	turgid
elliptical	literate	rolling	unadorned
euphonious	lively	seamless	understated
facile	long-winded	sententious	uneven
felicitous	lucid	serpentine	unreadable
flabby	lush	serviceable	wooden
flashy	mannered	sharply drawn	wordy
flat	masterly	shopworn	
flawless	meandering	sledgehammer	

Authorial Adjectives

It is the fortune, or fate, of some artists to become not only enduring figures of history but also adjectives—adjectives, moreover, that are applied to the work of other writers and thinkers.

If John Smith's works have longevity or a special quality, erudite critics and college freshmen will begin using the word "Smithian" or "Smithesque" allusively. Euphony, as well as genius, may be a factor in Smith's name becoming a literary descriptive. What if his name were Doe? Thus Dickensian, Kafkaesque, and Byronic are familiar to most of us, but we hear little of Ionescoesque or Cowardian drama or Twainian humor—or would it be Clemensian humor? Why are adjectives from such major writers as Austen, Cervantes, Fielding, London, Poe, and Waugh not more established in our language?

The following authorial adjectives are some of the most common encountered in literary contexts, and particularly in literary criticism. Although the focus of this book is prose writing, many of these adjectives come from the names of poets and dramatists, and a few from classical philosophers; they are included because they are so frequently seen in writing about writing, that is, in prose. To define such adjectives would be a difficult if not questionable task. The adjectives seem to endure. Meanwhile, certain present-day writers are slowly but surely, but not yet quite conclusively, becoming modish modifiers.

Addisonian   Joseph Addison (1672–1719)

Aristotelian   Aristotle (384–322 B.C.)

Balzacian   Honoré de Balzac (1799–1850)

Beckettian   Samuel Beckett (1906–1989)

Biercean   Ambrose (Gwinnett) Bierce (1842–1914?)

Blakean   William Blake (1757–1827)

Brechtian   Bertolt Brecht (1898–1956)

Brontëan   Charlotte Brontë (1816–1855), Emily Brontë (1818–1848)

Burnsian   Robert Burns (1759–1796)

Byronic   George Gordon (Noel), Lord Byron (1788–1824)

Carlylean, Carlylian   Thomas Carlyle (1795–1881)

Carrollian   Lewis Carroll, pen name of Charles Lutwidge Dodgson (1832–1898)

Chattertonian   Thomas Chatterton (1752–1770)

Chaucerian   Geoffrey Chaucer (c. 1340?–1400)

Chekhovian   Anton (Pavlovich) Chekhov (1860–1904)

Chestertonian   G(ilbert) K(eith) Chesterton (1874–1936)

Churchillian   Winston (Leonard Spencer) Churchill (1874–1965)

Ciceronian   Marcus Tullius Cicero (106–43 B.C.)

Coleridgean, Coleridgian   Samuel Taylor Coleridge (1772–1834)

Conradian   Joseph Conrad (1857–1924)

Dantean, Dantescan, Dantesque   Dante Alighieri (1265–1321)

Dickensian   Charles (John Huffam) Dickens (1812–1870)

Donnean, Donnian   John Donne (1572–1631)

Dostoevskian   Fëdor Mikhailovich Dostoevski (1821–1881)

Drydenian   John Dryden (1631–1700)

Eliotic   T(homas) S(tearns) Eliot (1888–1965)

Emersonian   Ralph Waldo Emerson (1803–1882)

Faulknerian   William Faulkner (1897–1962)

Flaubertian   Gustave Flaubert (1821–1880)

Forsterian   E(dward) M(organ) Forster (1879–1970)

Frostian   Robert (Lee) Frost (1874–1963)

Gibbonesque   Edward Gibbon (1737–1794)

Goethean   Johann Wolfgang von Goethe (1749–1832)

Gogolesque, Gogolian   Nikolai Vasilievich Gogol (1809–1852)

Hawthornesque, Hawthornian   Nathaniel Hawthorne (1804–1864)

Hemingwayesque   Ernest (Miller) Hemingway (1899–1961)

Homeric   Homer (fl. 850 B.C.)

Horatian   Horace (Quintus Horatius Flaccus) (65–8 B.C.)

Hugoesque   Victor (Marie) Hugo (1802–1885)

Huxleian, Huxleyan   Aldous (Leonard) Huxley (1894–1963)

Ibsenian   Henrik (Johan) Ibsen (1828–1906)

Jamesian   Henry James (Jr.) (1843–1916)

Jeffersonian   Thomas Jefferson (1743–1826)

Johnsonian   Samuel Johnson (1709–1784)

Jonsonian   Ben Jonson (1573?–1637)

Joycean   James Joyce (1882–1941)

Juvenalian   Decimus Junius Juvenalis (A.D. 60?–140?)

Kafkan, Kafkaesque   Franz Kafka (1883–1924)

Keatsian   John Keats (1795–1821)

Kiplingesque   Rudyard Kipling (1865–1936)

Laurentian, Lawrencian D(avid) H(erbert) Lawrence (1885–1930)

McLuhanesque (Herbert) Marshall McLuhan (1911–1980)

Marlovian Christopher Marlowe (1564–1593)

Melvillean Herman Melville (1819–1891)

Menckenesque, Menckenian H(enry) L(ouis) Mencken (1880–1956)

Meredithean George Meredith (1828–1909)

Miltonian, Miltonic John Milton (1608–1674)

Nabokovian Vladimir Nabokov (1899–1977)

Orwellian George Orwell, pen name of Eric Blair (1903–1950)

Ossianic "Ossian," or James Macpherson (1736–1796)

Ovidian Ovid (Publius Ovidius Naso) (43 B.C.–A.D. 17?)

Pepysian Samuel Pepys (1633–1703)

Petrarchan Francesco Petrarch or Petrarca (1304–1374)

Petronian Petronius (Gaius Petronius) (1st Century A.D.)

Pinterian Harold Pinter (1930–   )

Pirandellian Luigi Pirandello (1867–1936)

Platonic Plato (427?–347 B.C.)

Plautine Plautus (Titus Maccius Plautus) (254?–184 B.C.)

Popian, Popean Alexander Pope (1688–1744)

Proustian Marcel Proust (1871–1922)

Pushkinian Aleksander Sergeevich Pushkin (1799–1837)

Rabelaisian François Rabelais (1494?–1553)

Richardsonian Samuel Richardson (1689–1761)

Runyonesque (Alfred) Damon Runyon (1884–1946)

Ruskinian John Ruskin (1819–1900)

Saroyanesque William Saroyan (1908–1981)

Shakespearean, Shakespearian William Shakespeare (1564–1616)

Shavian George Bernard Shaw (1856–1950)

Shelleyan, Shelleyesque Percy Bysshe Shelley (1792–1822)

Skeltonic John Skelton (1460?–1529)

Spenserian Edmund Spenser (1552?–1599)

Stendhalian Stendhal, pen name of Marie Henri Beyle (1783–1842)

Strindbergian (Johan) August Strindberg (1849–1912)

Swiftian Jonathan Swift (1667–1745)

Swinburnian Algernon Charles Swinburne (1837–1909)

Tennysonian Alfred, Lord Tennyson (1809–1892)

Thackerayan   William Makepeace Thackeray (1811–1863)

Thoreauvian   Henry David Thoreau (1817–1862)

Thurberesque   James (Grover) Thurber (1894–1961)

Tolstoyan, Tolstoian   Lev Nikolaevich Tolstoy or Tolstoi (1828–1910)

Trollopian   Anthony Trollope (1815–1882)

Voltairean, Voltairian   Voltaire, pen name of François Marie Arouet
    (1694–1778)

Wellsian   H(erbert) G(eorge) Wells (1866–1946)

Whitmanesque, Whitmanian   Walt(er) Whitman (1819–1892)

Wildean   Oscar (Fingal O'Flahertie Wills) Wilde (1854–1900)

Wordsworthian   William Wordsworth (1770–1850)

Yeatsian   William Butler Yeats (1865–1939)

Zolaesque   Emile Zola (1840–1902)

Dialogue Verbs

Many of us wish to achieve simplicity in writing, and the suggestion to "just say what you want to say" is proverbial. "Just say 'say,' " similarly, can be equally wise counsel as to which verbs to use in presenting dialogue. That artless verb—simply—does the job. Moreover, many of the best contemporary fiction writers and reporters (taking a page from the format of play writing, perhaps) go a step further by eliminating speech-tag verbs altogether whenever possible in presenting conversation on paper.

But variety in utterance verbs remains the stock in trade of many writers, particularly novelists and often, unparticularly, pulp novelists. The question here is how much, or how ill-advised, the variety. A lacing of dialogue with averreds and respondeds and insisteds—or so-called elegant variations—suggests the cheap hallmarks of both journalese and souped-up potboilers.

"Facial verbs" can be an even more infectious mannerism. These are verbs denoting facial expressions or emotional reactions that indicate no act of speaking but are airily welded to utterances: " 'Absolutely not,' she frowned"; " 'Gladly,' he chuckled"; " 'Let's do it!' they beamed." These word-in-cheek stylings—we might also call them ventriloverbs—are essentially shanghaied nouns forced into being colorful (and space-saving) verbs. Their use is indeed economy of "expression."

Sometimes the line between a valid verb of utterance and one belonging to physiognomy-speak is debatable. Journalism professor and usage consultant Roy Copperud, who calls the transgressions "manufactured verbs," points out (citing H. W. Fowler) that the idiosyncrasy goes back at least as far as novelist George Meredith, who used "husked," "fluted," "defended," and "surrendered" to introduce direct speech. "This appears to be a variation of what Ruskin described as the pathetic fallacy—ascribing lifelike acts to inanimate things, such as having the sun smile. Fowler also criticized some words that come closer to indicating utterance, such as *scorned* and *denied*." Nonetheless facial verbs have become so prevalent in writing today that we can only blush our acceptance or wink our reservations.

Meanwhile, there is nothing to be said against genuine verbs of utterance, which are as old as literature. When used with care and moderation they swiftly convey character reactions and traits and add drama and vividness to a well-wrought scene. The dialogue verbs below are offered as a helpful word-hoard for quotation-taggers, with the caveat never to say die to that simple "say."

acknowledged	ejaculated	observed
added	emphasized	offered
admitted	exclaimed	ordered
advised	explained	piped
allowed	expostulated	pleaded
admonished	gasped	pronounced
announced	gibbered	protested
answered	groaned	purred
argued	howled	quipped
asked	inquired	reasoned
asserted	insisted	remarked
averred	instructed	remonstrated
barked	interceded	replied
begged	interjected	reported
began	interposed	responded
blathered	interrupted	resumed
blurted	intoned	retorted
called	jabbered	said
cajoled	jeered	scoffed
cautioned	joked	screamed
commented	lied	shouted
complained	maintained	shrieked
conceded	managed	snapped
concluded	moaned	sobbed
confessed	mumbled	spluttered
continued	murmured	spoke up
cried	muttered	sputtered
demanded	noted	stammered
dithered	objected	stated

stressed	urged	went on
stuttered	uttered	whimpered
suggested	ventured	whooped
taunted	vouched	yammered
teased	wailed	yelled
told	warned	

Journalistic Attribution and Evasion

Responsible journalism requires accuracy, but the facts on which reporting thrives are often secondhand. The reporter doesn't see the arsonist dousing tenement stairs with gasoline but is told about this by witnesses or fire officials. The reporter doesn't sit in on the congressional committee caucus where a deal is made on a bill; he learns of it from Representatives or their aides.

For this reason, attribution is essential. By noting who provided information or comment, the bearer of the news is being fair with the readership and, in the process, guarding against professional embarrassment over misinformation or, worse, libel suits—should the material be questionable or wrong. The source need not, and often cannot, be identified and is often referred to only as "a source." Yet it is important that the reporter, through attribution, be specific in presenting information as known or stated by others. This separates that material from the facts known by the reporter.

Overcautiousness and excessive reliance on attribution are a different matter. Formulary and often ludicrous self-protective, "distancing" phrasing can be seen or heard in news reporting every day—evasive modifiers, tediously repeated referents, and misuse and overuse of the passive voice and of such words as "suspect" and "alleged." The result is stultifyingly faceless reportage.

A century ago, the excesses of such reportorial disclaiming of responsibility were compactly satirized by Mark Twain: "A woman giving the name of Mrs. James Jones, who is reported to be one of the society leaders of the city, is said to have given what purported to be a party yesterday to a number of alleged ladies. The hostess claims to be the wife of a reputed attorney."

The reporter can also err in going to the other extreme: by using biased or loaded phraseology, largely through "color" verbs that have a slanted or emotional tinge.

The following groupings of words and phrases exemplify some of the traps into which journalists can fall: expressions we see or hear every day that may, when not used responsibly or meaningfully, tell us less—or more—than serves objectivity.

Cloaked Attribution   Sometimes justifiable, but sometimes no more than a discreet way of ducking responsibility.

observers say	allegedly	has learned that
reportedly	was identified as	evidently
is expected to	is believed to be	seemingly
reputed, reputedly	informed sources say	it is anticipated that
apparently		is seen as

Journalese Attributives   Supposed synonyms for "said," or elegant variations, which can be used inappropriately, inexactly, and merely for variety's sake.

stated	opined	related
remarked	averred	replied
stressed	reported	observed
declared	argued	agreed
claimed	added	affirmed
emphasized	maintained	commented
advised	announced	
asserted	concluded	

Loaded Attribution   Verbs that imply the reporter's agreement or disagreement with what is said, acceptance of information as fact, or approval or disapproval by the publication—that is, that editorialize, evoking a judgmental response in the reader or listener.

conceded	cited the fact that	disclosed
complained	denounced	snapped
explained	revealed	pleaded
noted	pointed out	raged
admitted	insinuated	stammered
brought up the fact that	ranted	choked
	whined	sobbed
confessed	confirmed	
uncovered	sputtered	

Needless Quotation Marks   Where statements clearly come from a source other than the writer, and where the words so enclosed are so ordinary as not to deserve quote marks or so wordy as to make paraphrasing preferable.

A three-alarmer, described as "big" by the fire captain . . .

He was praised for what authorities said was "exceptional and un-called-for bravery. . . ."

He referred to the so-called "domino" theory.

Superfluous Attribution   Repeated or redundant attributives, where an occasional reminder suffices.

Police say an alleged burglar . . .
the alleged suspect
She was indicted for allegedly . . .
Police say. . . . According to police . . .
Witnesses say a reported purse-snatcher . . .
self-confessed

Propaganda Devices

Propaganda has a long history as a means of appealing to human emotions at the expense of clear, rational thinking and full truth. The erstwhile Institute for Propaganda Analysis, founded at the outset of World War II out of concern that Americans might be too easily manipulated by propaganda, devoted considerable attention to the methodology of persuasion and formulated seven basic "devices" used by propagandists. These devices were widely taught in American high schools in the 1940s and 1950s. Still relevant today not only to politics but to the media of publicity and advertising, they may be defined as follows:

bandwagon   The device of appealing to people's readiness to "jump on the bandwagon," that is, identify themselves with the most popular cause, the best-selling product, etc.; appeal to conformity.

card-stacking   The device of loading an argument with evidence for one side while suppressing evidence to the contrary; bias through selected facts or statistics.

glittering generalities   The device of using glowingly idealistic abstractions, catchwords, or euphemisms to make a cause attractive, or dressing up an argument grandiloquently but unspecifically; lofty or patriotic blandishments.

name-calling   The device of arguing or campaigning by abusively labeling the opposition in speech or in print, rather than by substantively arguing one's own case, and often by using terms having strongly negative associations; resorting to personal accusations and epithets as a vilifying tactic.

plain folks   The device of characterizing a candidate (or product)—and the audience or public—as simple and down-to-earth and hence a humble, kindred person; persuasion through grass-roots image and folksy language.

testimonial The device of using praise or advocacy of something by a well-known person as proof of its worthiness, or appeal through endorsement; a declaration attesting to the value, quality, or character of somebody or something.

transfer The device of exploiting a favorable popular attitude toward one thing by surrounding something else with its aura, that is, enhancing the latter's appeal by association; persuasion by cloaking something in the attractive but irrelevant aspect of something else.

The following material is excerpted from the second bulletin issued by the Institute for Propaganda Analysis—in November 1937. More than fifty years later, the devices are still useful as watchdog terms for methods of persuasion.

How to Detect Propaganda

We are fooled by propaganda chiefly because we don't recognize it when we see it. It may be fun to be fooled but, as the cigarette ads used to say, it is more fun to know. We can more easily recognize propaganda when we see it if we are familiar with the seven common propaganda devices. These are:

1. The Name Calling Device
2. The Glittering Generalities Device
3. The Transfer Device
4. The Testimonial Device
5. The Plain Folks Device
6. The Card Stacking Device
7. The Band Wagon Device

Why are we fooled by these devices? Because they appeal to our emotions rather than to our reason. They make us believe and do something we would not believe or do if we thought about it calmly, dispassionately. In examining these devices, note that they work most effectively at those times when we are too lazy to think for ourselves; also, they tie into emotions which sway us to be "for" or "against" nations, races, religions, ideals, economic and political policies and practices, and so on through automobiles, cigarettes, radios, toothpastes, presidents, and wars. With our emotions stirred, it may be fun to be fooled by these propaganda devices, but it is more fun and infinitely more to our own interests to know how they work.

Name Calling "Name Calling" is a device to make us form a judgment without examining the evidence on which it should be based. Here the propagandist appeals to our hate and fear. He does this by giving "bad names" to those individuals, groups, nations, races, policies, practices, beliefs, and ideals which he would have us condemn and reject. For centuries the name "heretic" was bad. Thousands were oppressed, tortured, or put to death as heretics. Anybody who dissented from popular or group belief or practice was in danger of being called a heretic.

Use of "bad names" without presentation of their essential meaning, without all their pertinent implications, comprises perhaps the most common of all propaganda devices.

Glittering Generalities "Glittering Generalities" is a device by which the propagandist identifies his program with virtue by use of "virtue words." Here he appeals to our emotions of love, generosity, and brotherhood. He uses words like truth, freedom, honor, liberty, social justice, public service, the right to work, loyalty, progress, democracy, the American way, Constitution defender. These words suggest shining ideals. All persons of good will believe in these ideals. Hence the propagandist, by identifying his individual group, nation, race, policy, practice, or belief with such ideals, seeks to win us to his cause. As Name Calling is a device to make us form a judgment to *reject and condemn,* without examining the evidence, Glittering Generalities is a device to make us *accept and approve,* without examining the evidence.

Transfer "Transfer" is a device by which the propagandist carries over the authority, sanction, and prestige of something we respect and revere to something he would have us accept. For example, most of us respect and revere our church and our nation. If the propagandist succeeds in getting church or nation to approve a campaign in behalf of some program, he thereby transfers its authority, sanction, and prestige to that program. Thus we may accept something which otherwise we might reject.

In the Transfer device, symbols are constantly used. The cross represents the Christian Church. The flag represents the nation. Cartoons like Uncle Sam represent a consensus of public opinion. Those symbols stir emotions. At their very sight, with the speed of light, is aroused the whole complex of feelings we have with respect to church or nation.

Testimonial The "Testimonial" is a device to make us accept anything from a patent medicine or a cigarette to a program of national policy. In this device the propagandist makes use of testimonials. This device works in reverse also; counter-testimonials may be employed. Seldom are these used against commercial products like patent medicines and cigarettes, but they are constantly employed in social, economic, and political issues.

Plain Folks "Plain Folks" is a device used by politicians, labor leaders, business men, and even by ministers and educators to win our confidence by appearing to be people like ourselves—"just plain folks among the neighbors." In election years especially do candidates show their devotion to little children and the common, homey things of life. They have front porch campaigns. For the newspaper men they raid the kitchen cupboard, finding there some of the good wife's apple pie. They go to country picnics; they attend service at the old frame church; they pitch hay and go fishing; they show their belief in home and mother. In short, they would win our votes by showing that they're just as common as the rest of us—"just plain folks"—and, therefore, wise and good.

Card Stacking "Card Stacking" is a device in which the propagandist employs all the arts of deception to win our support for himself, his group, nation, race, policy, practice, belief or ideal. He stacks the cards against the truth. He uses under-emphasis and over-emphasis to dodge issues and evade facts. He resorts to lies, censorship, and distortion. He omits facts. He offers false testimony. He creates a smoke-screen of clamor by raising a new issue when he wants an embarrassing matter forgotten. He draws a red herring across the trail to confuse and divert those in quest of facts he does not want revealed. He makes the unreal appear real and the real appear unreal. He lets half-truth masquerade as truth. By the Card Stacking device, a mediocre candidate, through the "build-up," is made to appear an intellectual titan; an ordinary prize fighter a probable world champion; a worthless patent medicine a beneficent cure. Card Stacking employs sham, hypocrisy, effrontery.

The Band Wagon The "Band Wagon" is a device to make us follow the crowd, to accept the propagandist's program en masse. Here his theme is: "Everybody's doing it." His techniques range from those of medicine show to dramatic spectacle. He hires a hall, fills a great stadium, marches a million men in parade. He employs symbols, colors, music, movement, all the dramatic arts. He appeals to the desire, common to most of us, to "follow the crowd." Because he wants us to "follow the crowd" in masses, he directs his appeal to groups held together by common ties of nationality, religion, race, environment, sex, vocation. All the artifices of flattery are used to harness the fears and hatreds, prejudices, and biases, convictions and ideals common to the group; thus emotion is made to push and pull the group on to the Band Wagon.

Advertising Weasel Words

Weasel words neutralize, contradict, or divert from the meaning of words that they accompany, thereby making statements glibly equivocal or meaningless—usually intentionally, with waffling or profit aforethought. They are semantic additives or subtractives that, as Donna Cross says in *Word Abuse,* "make you hear things that aren't being said and thereby make you believe things that simply aren't true." Likewise, there are weasel phrases.

Though the term comes from the notion—a fallacy, according to John Ciardi—that the weasel sucks out the content of an egg and leaves the shell empty and intact, it is doubly apt because of the other associations we make with "weaseling." No word, of course, is per se a hedging qualifier. It becomes one only by contrived use to "eviscerate" or draw attention away from accompanying words.

"Weasel word" was coined in 1900 by Steward Chaplin in an article in *Century Magazine*. But it was Theodore Roosevelt who popularized it, sixteen years later, in a speech in St. Louis criticizing President Woodrow Wilson's advocating of "universal voluntary training." Roosevelt said, "You can have universal training or you can have voluntary training, but when you use *voluntary* to qualify *universal,* you are using a weasel word; it has sucked all the meaning out of universal. The two words flatly contradict each other."

Weaselly writing often involves using two words where one will do. In a word (or more than one word), distracting periphrasis.

Today the term is sometimes loosely applied to any expression that is hollow, fraudulent, or purely cosmetic—to vogue words, counterwords, glittering generalities, "agency" comparatives, or any other form of semantic bamboozling. But the Rooseveltian sense seems worth keeping in the shell: the word or phrase that appears to be a supportive or innocuous companion but is in fact compromising or sweetening truth and meaning. Whether its use is Machiavellian or pusillanimous, the weasel word—along with specious logic, euphemism, and the loaded word—is the agent of evasion and half-truth.

Weaselisms can be found in political rhetoric, court proceedings, bureaucratic memoranda—and possibly a difficult personal letter you wrote last week. Advertising, especially—if by no means all advertising—abounds in weasel words. On Madison Avenue they take the form of chummy subversive phrases tacked on to verbs, impressive-sounding but hollow adverbs, bogus superlatives, "and more"—to borrow a weasel phrase. Their purpose is sleight of speech: to suggest what cannot literally be stated or may not legally be claimed, to at once hint, evade, and reassure:

> authentic replica (or a genuine fake)
> ersatz (or imitation, useful in advertising to the less educated)
> placebo (or imaginary, and like "ersatz" a safely unfamiliar word for admitting the noneffectiveness of certain "health" products and "aphrodisiacs")
> new larger package (but not the contents)
> has more than (something minimal, or not much more than)
> has less than (something maximal, or not much less than)
> the major ingredient of (possibly a quite common ingredient, and maybe very little of it)

acts to (but may not improve, remove, help, or cure)
can be (but may not usually be)
as much as (but not necessarily or usually that much)
helps to (but doesn't effectively or conclusively)
has the look of (but is not the real thing)
almost like (but is not)
new (but possibly inferior to or less than the old)
guards against (but doesn't exactly prevent)
award-winning (award from whom?)
popularly priced (popular with whom?)
gift offer (or gift only with a purchase)
and more (more what?)
fortified with (possibly something not at all fortifying)
up to (but ordinarily less than)
the original (but perhaps now the inferior and unimproved)

Sometimes the function of a weasel word is not so much to subtract from meaning and truth as to distract—to be a verbal buffer or red herring preceding the unexceptional or uncommendable truth (in the form of a noun). Adjectives and adverbs often serve this purpose:

all	greatest	one and only	super
biggest	handy	one of a kind	timely
classic	ideal	only	top
colossal	incredible	perfectly	top-of-the-line
delicious	invaluable	practically	unbelievable
deluxe	jumbo	prestigious	uniquely
discount	just	quality	
exclusively	largest	real	
fabulous	latest	remarkably	
fancy	long-awaited	revolutionary	
fantastic	natural	simply	
fashionable	now	smoother	
genuine	nutritious	spectacular	

Newsroom Headline Jargon

bank   The lower line or section of a headline, generally of a smaller type size than the line above it, as in an "upside-down pyramid" head. Also DECK.

banner   A single headline, in large type, extending above all the columns on the front page. Also STREAMER.

barker   A kicker in type larger than the headlines beneath it. Also HAM-MER, REVERSE KICKER.

bikini head   A headline highlighting a particular aspect of a story.

binder line   An inside-page headline in large type above a lengthy story or series of stories. Also BLANKET HEAD.

broken head   A headline whose lines have different widths.

bumping heads   Headlines that abut in any way.

circus makeup   Layout using eye-catchingly varied kinds and sizes of type.

crossline   A middle line of a multisection headline (each section usually in a different-size type).

cutline   An explanatory line beneath a picture. Also CAPTION, LEGEND, UNDERLINE.

deadhead   An uninterestingly unspecific or abstract headline. Also CRIN-OLINE HEAD, FLAT HEAD, WOODEN HEAD.

drophead   A headline beneath a banner (or special use of a bank), referring to the same story. Also HANGER, READ OUT.

jump head   An abbreviated headline noting the continuation of a story from an earlier page, and giving a sense of the original head.

kicker   A short, smaller-type line above a headline to provoke interest. Also EYEBROW, HIGHLINE, STINGER, TEASER.

label head   A nonverb head used for texts, glossaries, etc.

overline   A headline above a picture.

ribbon   A one-line head of more than one-column width and smaller in type size than a banner.

rocket head   A display-type or boldface headline quoting words from the news story.

scarehead   A sensationalizing headline dramatizing something ostensibly alarming. Also SUCKER HEADLINE.

screamer   A large, boldface banner headline.

second coming type   The largest, blackest headline type. Also STUD-HORSE TYPE.

skyline head   A banner headline at the very top of the front page, above the newspaper masthead (flag or nameplate). Also OVER-THE-ROOF HEAD.

step head   Successively indented lines making up a multiline headline (one with "hanging indents"). Also DECK HEAD, DROPLINE.

stock head   A standing, or reserve, head that can be used as needed, e.g., "Book Review."

subhead   A smaller or minor headline within the body of a story.

tombstones   Two similar headlines side by side. Also BUMPING HEADS.

Mixed Metaphors

The mixed metaphor continues to flourish, not only in colloquial speech but also in reputable books and journalism, to say nothing of political oratory. It is perhaps distinctive as a grammatical fault in being both an incurable tendency in otherwise literate writers and a rich source of humor.

The term is at best imprecise or debatable. What are called mixed metaphors are often actually confused catchphrases or idioms. Moreover, metaphors cannot only be mixed, they can also be mischosen, fused, or malapropized—or all of these in a confounding combination. Eighty years ago, in *The King's English*, H. W. and F. G. Fowler saw fit to discuss not only mixed metaphors and malapropisms but also "maltreated idioms," or unwittingly fused expressions. More recent terms coined for types of metaphorical confusion include "curdled cliché," "malaphor," "skewed metaphor," "boniprop," "metafive," "doubletake," "knock-kneed metaphor," and "mixaphor."

Metaphor, according to Theodore Bernstein in *The Careful Writer*, "is a useful adornment of writing: useful because it permits communication of a complex thought in small compass, an adornment because it introduces color and imagery into what might be a commonplace statement.

"If, however, the writer does not stick to the image he has set up, he is in danger of creating a mixed metaphor, known here for short as a *mixaphor*. In that event he has vitiated the usefulness of the figure by confusing the reader through a jumble of pictures, and has spoiled the adornment by shattering it. If, for example, he writes, 'She is a tigress with her antennae on the alert for the grasping hand that might undermine the keystone of her existence,' we get no picture of anything and are left with a sense of absurdity. This does not mean that a writer may not include two different pictures in a single sentence or a single passage; they must, however, be distinctly separate and it must be clear that the writer knows what he is about."

In their *Dictionary of Contemporary American Usage*, Bergen and Cornelia Evans liken the use of metaphors to splashes of stones: "The fault in what is usually recognized as a mixed metaphor is that the mixture is bad. The effect of a metaphor has been compared to that of a stone dropped into a large body of water. As the first splash of the stone sets up an ever widening series of concentric circles, so the primary comparison of the metaphor sets up a series of associative comparisons, widening out into other aspects and qualities of the things compared. And if any of these are grossly inapplicable to the primary comparison the effect may be ludicrous. . . ."

The Fowlers note also that an important factor in deciding when metaphors are mixed and when not is whether they are both "live" metaphors, or palpable and literal as images. "If only one of the metaphors is a live one, the confusion is not a confusion for practical purposes."

When is something a mixed metaphor? When is it not exactly a mixed metaphor but, say, a malapropism, or two fused metaphors? The following. six categories—fused metaphor, malapropism, "malonym," mistaken metaphor, "mixaprop," and mixed metaphor—capsule some of the varieties of figurative confusion encountered every day in conversation or writing. See also the alphabetical entries MÖBIUS MOT and MONDEGREEN, and the special entry IRISH BULLS, p. 392.

Mixed Metaphor   The use of two or more clashing metaphors within one sentence or brief passage. "When you're up the creek without a paddle, I won't pull your irons out of the fire" (up the creek without a paddle, pull your irons out of the fire); "The chairman backs him to the hilt every time he shoots from the hip" (back to the hilt, shoot from the hip); "Obviously, whether he wanted to go on playing dirty pool in a tank of sharks remained up in the air" (play dirty pool, tank of sharks, up in the air).

Fused Metaphor   The unwitting dovetailing of two metaphors. "I'm not going to bail out his chestnuts" (bail him out, pull his chestnuts out of the fire); "Ms. Wilson, whom she chose to be her partner, turned out to be her cross around the neck" (cross to bear, albatross or millstone around the neck); "They were definitely treading on thin waters" (treading on dangerous ground, on thin ice, in dangerous waters).

Malapropism   The use of a similar but ludicrously wrong word. "The tense situation mitigated against rash action" (instead of militate); "By saying no, she was burning her britches behind her" (instead of bridges); "It's a fragment of your imagination—don't be in such high dungeon" (instead of figment, instead of dudgeon).

Malonym   A single metaphor, cliché, or catchphrase but with a homonym or homophone mistake. "She made it quite clear I had to tow the line" (instead of toe); "For Carol to give Jim a six-pack was like carrying colds to Newcastle" (instead of coals); "The reporter on the *Chronicle* was cutting that story out of hole cloth" (instead of whole).

Mistaken Metaphor   A misuse of a single metaphor, confusing it but not fusing it with another. "Her acting ran the gauntlet from A to Z" (run the gauntlet instead of run the gamut); "The suspense had the whole audience on hooks and crooks" (by hook or crook instead of on tenterhooks); "There's more than one way to grind an ax" (an ax to grind instead of more than one way to skin a cat).

Mixaprop   A mixed metaphor along with a malapropism. "You can't dance up a storm when you have too many cooks spilling the broth" (dance up a storm, too many cooks spoil the broth, spilling the beans); "She was sailing under more false promises than you could shake a leg at" (sailing under false colors, false premise, shake a stick at, shake a leg); "I knew they were giving me the bum's rush by denying me excess to the club" (getting the bum's rush, deny access to).

The Language of Comic Double-talk

Comic double-talk, sometimes called framis, is not the pure nonsense of Lewis Carroll's jabberwocky. Rather, it is a weaving of made-up words into otherwise normal, intelligible speech. One of its greatest practitioners was the entertainer Al Kelly (1896–1966), who was born Abraham Kalish.

Kelly, who was introduced straight-facedly as a guest lecturer or expert at countless professional conferences around the United States, noted two other curious things about double-talk. It has the same "hysterical" effect on the high and the low, or the educated and the uneducated; and the oftener one hears it, the funnier it becomes.

Kelly knew whereof he double-spoke. Among the hundreds of organization memberships he was hired to victimize were those of the American Medical Association, the American Newspaper Guild, B'nai Brith, the Boy Scouts Association, Chase Manhattan Bank, General Motors Corporation, and athletes at West Point Military Academy.

Kelly didn't invent this medium of convincing-seeming noncommunication. But he made it into an art by realizing quickly that buildup and subtlety were important to the overall flummoxing effect: beginning a speech to, say, a convention of brain surgeons with perfectly normal English sentences and only gradually working in nonsense words, which "prolongs the agony" for the intently listening audience. The more earnest and emphatic the delivery—as with forceful gesticulations for emphases—the better.

Possibly the most interesting phenomenon with regard to nonsense English, however, is the fact that many people put on in this way either remain unaware of its meaninglessness or respond—to save face, indeed to save face with themselves?—as if it is all perfectly clear to them. On one occasion Kelly was introduced (and double-spoke) as Assistant Secretary of the Navy to famed World War II admiral William ("Bull") Halsey at a lunch club. He later learned that Halsey was indignant, first, because the government had been stupid enough to put a man like Kelly in charge; and, second, because Halsey had not been consulted about the appointment.

Can you make up the sort of words used by such double-talkers as Kelly, and weave such verbal fakery into sentences and more that will sound only gradually questionable in sense?

Kelly included no transcripts of his routines in his autobiography, *Al Kelly's Double Life,* to show us samples of his nonsense in action. But he did include a "dictionary" of some six hundred of his double-talk words, complete with "definitions." Yiddish, his dictionary reveals, was unquestionably one of Kelly's influences in making up his lunatic locutions. Many of the words ("bilingal," "feminal," "iamic") are just a hair off genuine words. Some ("hegeera," "justis," "macak," "objestion") are like slight respellings. And others ("rufous," "wahoo") have counterparts that are genuine words. The similarity of his "nompothetic" ("to enact laws not hitherto drivenated") to the rare legal word "nomothetic" suggests that Kelly did some leafing through legitimate dictionaries for verbal material to mangle.

Here is a sampling from Kelly's glossary, followed by a brief passage, "Condersation," that offers at least a glimpse of his double-talk style.

aclivoter A climber who dreźd better pidents.

aggreging Stremping a better hylemick.

albicate Turning color klemz in dark nooms.

aquapooltim Astronomical drayn in a goym.

aximen Sign of lowering a lempel.

babmion A species of Gogs on limpets.

bilingal Use of two or more guanages.

biezen A lem hickter generally oyzgeblot.

bucel A live leem sometimes under nepts.

caride A juicy hidge cut by zenz.

caladisterate To rurl the hair in twit mids.

camira A fleedle used in dretch.

carblem Not otherwise hopt on semets.

dactimogrophy Relating to dactimagraphinetical yoymz.

direnicious A child born to an aged tlenx.

donick Used for negelisical undim.

eavel Edge, hall lobi or ebid.

ebrazitate Minus abraz or tate equally divided.

Eciptic A circle of speerz angular zodacs.

enkapel A porodore containing seddled nobes.

facimorm A stickle resembling a blintz.

feminal To become womanish or chamber maid.

ferboric Heat or larmth on a hot nigel.

gamanometric A device showing heat ciperoid twangs.

glekle A tinkle bell found in hyzer.

grayser A tall crumpig.

greckin A smallgreck lamipoyted in creel.

halexy An explosive colchar loosed on mo.

iamic Pertaining to iams differing from ickies.

impistle Painting walls sterelated with premz.

izedis Same as izedoss or izzedem.

jinbal A swivel gun mounted on a kleptel.

justis As soon as possible to reloyn.

kyvaus To find out morter naylem.

latvick From litvick closer to Galitz and further aldo.

linkel Anything closed tuftly.

madefrication The act of madifaying a kloomit.

masaket A botanius woolp.

nabmar A large vesticulated hittel worn in clod sips.

nompothetic To enact laws not hitherto drivenated.

ondel A small cryg left with a relative.

ozodemetry Ozodemit rios flabed inred grooz.

parabibel A pair of biblech who loveretenye.

pegamor A sharklike fish that destroys the mogen.

picotet A botanic carnation worn at umbrils.

quolfure Hairy arrangements left untished.

quotham Indeed, savoray or indescriptible

rabbib mouth Denoting excavatory films in trept yize.

ribatatel Fatherly advice distused bu relative.

rufous Reddish brown color lendelated crozmy.

sadaron   An instrument that krips mayndels.

sald   A salted bidtid used in geromics.

somabulatic   A latic who soms or not.

takeh   Same as avada, alzo and vosden.

telebende   A village crompot who dizzles constantly.

tilgrab   Robbing the box while ringing the till.

umglick   An unlucky myer who loses in tarate.

ungemootchet   To bother someone hastily but good.

volenter   To offer to velil indirationally.

wahoo   A clarion blass heard further than bild.

washberd   Cleaning a whigle with scizorless teds.

xanocrotic   A frothy noolp made with xan.

xeroticik   To feel better after using a delm.

yumpet   Nightly fobers who lug mifniks.

zepesary   To brew a coke in a nessel.

zorgnit   Not to worry or dyge in public.

zymopilious   The art of peeling a zymo neculously.

Condersation

The room descends the couch of trid making a hockery of all that mepts is it not a breze beneath a coyl which pleeds and harnasses vory meens let all who are froom degate apathy not like others pertinding swob the seas of above may yet dimay what in our hearts falls effercense.

Irish Bulls

A bull, when not promulgated by a pope, is a verbal blunder. The so-called Irish bull is a statement in which the choice of words or combination of idioms is curiously, not to say unforgettably, incongruous. But while its ideas or metaphors are incongruous and often contradictory—surreally oxymoronic—they have an apparent congruity. This often results in a piece of spontaneous illogic with appealing possibilities. It has been defensively described as "always pregnant."

Why "Irish" bull? According to Roy Copperud in his *American Usage and Style, the Consensus,* the term perhaps "arose from the tendency of the British to ridicule the people they could not keep down, or perhaps from the ignorance and consequent mistakes of uneducated Irish immigrants to America. But who is to say the Irish were any more ignorant, or any more prone to errors in diction, than any other uneducated immigrants, including the English?''

For Americans, the unwitting wit of Irish bulls is best preserved in the treasured remarks of the Hollywood mogul Samuel Goldwyn; indeed, Irish bulls are often called Goldwynisms, although many of Goldwyn's ecorded comments are more accurately mixed metaphors or malapropısms. Irish Mr. Goldwyn was not.

The flavor of the Irish bull is captured rather quantitatively by C. C. Bombaugh in his 1905 book *Oddities and Curiosities of Words and Litrature,* in a letter purportedly by "an Irish member of Parliament":

We are in a pretty mess; can get nothing to eat, nor wine to drink, except whiskey; and when we sit down to dinner, we are obliged to keep both hands armed. Whilst I write this, I hold a pistol in each hand and a sword in the other. I concluded in the beginning that this would be the end of it; and I see I was right, for it is not half over yet. At present there are such goings on that every thing is at a stand still. I should have answered your letter a fortnight ago, but I did not receive it till this morning. Indeed, hardly a mail arrives safe without being robbed. No longer ago than yesterday the coach with the mails from Dublin was robbed near this town; the bags had been judiciously left behind for fear of accident, and by good luck there was nobody in it but two outside passengers who had nothing for thieves to take. Last Thursday notice was given that a gang of rebels were advancing here under the French standard; but they had no colors, nor any drums except bagpipes. Immediately every man in the place, including women and children, ran out to meet them.

For more recent examples of Irish bulls, we have only to consult the words of certain politicians, the term papers of certain high school and college students, and the utterances of Yogi Berra. Or the countless pronouncements of Mr. Goldwyn—many of which, it is said, may have been devised by his press agents. The following memorials to his fractured insights à la Irish bull suggest that confused expression can be a form of expressive confusion.

An oral contract isn't worth the paper it's written on.
Include me out.
Our comedies are not to be laughed at.
Well, she's colossal in a small way.
He worked his way up from nothing, that kid. In fact, he was born in an orphan asylum.
This new atom bomb is dynamite.
Didn't you hear me keeping still?

We have to get some fresh platitudes.

I read part of it all the way through.

We're overpaying him but he's worth it.

If Roosevelt were alive he'd turn over in his grave.

I'll give you a definite maybe.

Anybody who goes to see a psychiatrist ought to have his head examined.

In two words, impossible!

Yes, my wife's hands are very beautiful. I'm going to have a bust made of them.

A bachelor's life is no life for a single man.

Going to call him "William"? What kind of a name is that? Every Tom, Dick, and Harry's called William.

It's more than magnificent—it's mediocre.

Tell me, how did you love my picture?

Goldwynisms! Don't talk to me about Goldwynisms, f'Chrissake. You want to hear some Goldwynisms go talk to Jesse Lasky!

Word-Game Words

For many, words (and single letters and symbols) provide endless puzzles, ratiocinations, and fascinations in their own right. The rapidly growing avocation of logology, or "recreational linguistics," has its own curious lexicon for antic verbal exercises both prosaic and poetic. Several of the prosaic, or non-verse-form, terms for such alphabetic ingenuities are presented here.

acrostic   A verse or arrangement of paragraphs in which certain initial, final, or conspicuous letters together (often vertically) spell out a word or message.

alternade   The writing of a word or words on two lines so that the separate lines yield different words, e.g.,

"calliopes" as C L I P S
              A   L O E

"truancies" as T U N I S
               R A C E

anagram   A transposal resulting in a word that is apposite to or synonymous with the given word, e.g., "villainousness" into "an evil soul's sin."

antigram   A transposal of letters in a word or words that produces a reversal of meaning; hence, an antonymous anagram, e.g., "the Waldorf" into "dwarf hotel."

beheadment   The eliminating of an initial letter from a word to leave another, legitimate word, e.g., of the "p" from "pirate" to leave "irate." Also APHERESIS, DECAPITATION.

charade   The dividing of a word, without changing the letter order, into other words semantically unrelated (that is, not the evident parts of a compound word), e.g., of "amiable together" into "am I able to get her," "significant" into "sign if I can't."

charitable word   (Willard Espy) A word that, if any one of its letters is omitted, remains a word, although a different one, e.g., "seat" (eat, sat, set, sea).

chronogram   A word, name, or inscription (as on certain Renaissance coins, books, and church memorials) containing capital letters that can be deciphered as the Roman numerals of a specific date, e.g., a line commemorating the death of Queen Elizabeth: *"My Day Is Closed In Immortality"* (1603)—C. C. Bombaugh.

croaker   (Williard Espy) A Tom Swiftie with a punning verb rather than a punning adverb, e.g., " 'Get out of that tree!' he barked."

curtailment   The cutting off of the last letter of a word to leave a different word, e.g., of the "e" from "paste" to leave "past." Also APOCOPE, PARAGOGE.

echo   The repeating of the end of a question, or responding with a close rhyme, that serves as an answer, e.g., answering "What did you do when the king left Parliament?" with "Lament," or answering "Would you give it your best endeavor?" with "Ever."

head-to-tail shift   A transposing of the first letter of a word to the end to form a new word, e.g., changing "trap" to "rapt."

hospitable word   (Willard Espy) A word that becomes a different word when a single letter is added to it, e.g., "hear" becoming "heart," "rap" becoming (variously) "trap," "reap," "ramp," or "rapt."

isomorph   One of two or more words that have the same sequential pattern of letters, as indicated by numbers, e.g., "barbarian" and "murmurous" (pattern: 123123425).

kangaroo word   A word carrying within it (without transposing any letters) a synonym of itself, e.g., "encourage" ("urge"), "evacuate" ("vacate"). Also MARSUPIAL.

letter change   The changing of one letter in a word to form another word, e.g., changing "avenge" to "avenue."

letter deletion   The removing of a letter within a word to leave a different word, e.g., of the "s" from "resign" to leave "reign." Also ELISION, SYNCOPATION.

letter insertion   The adding of a letter to a ("hospitable") word to produce another word (that is not a mere inflection), e.g., adding "f" to "scar" to make "scarf."

letter rebus   A rebus composed only of letters, with no symbols or pictures, e.g., "B" meaning abalone ("a B alone"), "ST$_M$ING" meaning misunderstanding ("M is under ST and ING").

linkade   The pairing of two words whereby a one-letter overlap will yield a different word, e.g., "for" and "reign" to produce "foreign."

lipogram   A composition or book written entirely without using a particular letter of the alphabet, e.g., the 50,000-word 1939 novel *Gadsby*, by California musician Ernest Vincent Wright, which nowhere uses the letter "e."

metallege   A pair of words differing only in the transposition of two letters, e.g., "causal" and "casual," "nuclear" and "unclear," "float" and "aloft," "milestone" and "limestone." Also META-THESIS.

nonpattern word   A word that uses no letter more than one time, e.g., "postneuralgic." Also ISOGRAM.

pair isogram   A word in which each letter appears the same number of times, e.g., "intestines."

palindrome   A word or words that when read backwards, from right to left, form the same word or words (or sequence of letters), e.g., "madam," "level," "draw pupil's lip upward." (There are also vertical palindromes—to be turned upside down—and mirror palindromes.)

pangram   A phrase, sentence, motto, verse, etc., containing all 26 letters of the alphabet (ideally, repeating as few letters as possible), e.g., "I, quartz pyx, who fling muck beds" (Willard Espy).

piano word   A word, all of its letters (a, b, c, d, e, f, or g) notes in a musical octave, that can be played on the piano, e.g., "cabbaged."

rebus   A visual riddle of pictures and/or symbols (sometimes with parts of words) that must be verbalized or read aloud for the meaning to be deciphered, e.g.,

Hill
John = John Underhill, Andover, Mass.
Mass

      B

fault man quarrels wife fault = Be above quarrels between man and wife; there are faults on both sides.

YYURYYUBICURYY4 me = Too wise you are, too wise you be, I see you are too wise for me.

reversal A word or words that when read backward produces a different word, e.g., "devil" ("lived").

rhopalic An expression or sentence in which each word has one more letter (or syllable) than the preceding one, e.g., "I do not know where family doctors acquired illegally perplexing handwriting."

stinky-pinky A noun coupled with a rhyming adjective, e.g., "plain Jane," "lacquered placard."

tautonym A word or name made up of two identical parts or repeated words, e.g., "so-so," "Pago Pago," "tomtom," "twenty-twenty."

terminal deletion The eliminating of the first and last letters of a word that results in a new word, e.g., from "flown" making "low," from "magenta" making "agent."

Tom Swiftie A sentence with a concocted quotation and a following punning adverb, e.g., " 'Please get your front tire off my ankle,' he said lamely."

transaddition The adding of a letter to a word along with rearrangement of the original letters to make a new word, e.g., making from "sham" (and adding "s") "smash."

transdeletion The removal of a letter from a word along with rearrangement of the remaining letters, resulting in a new word, e.g., making from "toothpaste" (less a "t") "osteopath," from "undergo" (less an "o") "gerund." Also TRANSADDITION.

transposition. A new word made by rearranging the letters of another word, e.g., "canoe" from "ocean," "enumeration" from "mountaineer." Also TRANSPOSAL.

typewriter word A word that can be typed on a single row of typewriter keys, e.g. (the top row), "typewriter," "proprietor."

univocalic A sentence, book, verse, etc. that uses only one of the five vowels in English, e.g., "Men were never perfect; yet the three brethren . . . " (Willard Espy).

word deletion   The removal of a word concealed within a word to leave a third word, e.g., removing "spa" from "trespass" to leave "tress," "tie" from "patient" to leave "pant."

Grammar Adjectives

Technical but descriptively useful adjectives for the various functions of words withing sentences. As the examples indicate, some words fall under more than one category.

accusative   Indicating a direct object (or noun or pronoun predicated on a direct object) or certain adverbial complements, e.g., "She wrote a book," "He imagined my sister to be her," "I waited one week."

adversative   Indicating opposition or contrasting of two things, e.g., the conjunctions "yet," "still," the phrase "all the same."

appositive   Indicating close, adjacent, or equivalent relation, such as a following noun that further describes or specifies, e.g., "It's near Chat's Last Stand, the fast food place."

attributive   Indicating modifying of a noun (usually preceding it); not following a copulative verb, e.g., "the imposing woman."

causative   Indicating causation by the sentence subject, e.g., "He sets them down," "They felled two trees," the suffix "-en" in "widen."

collective   Indicating a group or aggregate of persons or things, e.g., the nouns "herd" and "grove."

conjunctive   Indicating joining or connecting, or functioning as a conjunction by linking sentences or clauses, e.g., the adverbs "accordingly," "yet," "consequently."

coordinate   Indicating connection involving parallel thoughts or equivalence in importance, emphasis, rank, etc., e.g., "We'll do it by hard work and by sheer persistence."

copulative   Indicating linking or predication of words, phrases, or clauses, e.g., the verb "is."

correlative   Indicating combined or reciprocal function but not adjacency in the sentence, e.g., the conjunctions "not only" and "but," "neither" and "nor," the phrases "on the one hand" and "on the other hand."

dative Indicating indirect object (action or feeling toward) or the object of certain prepositions, e.g., "He gave me the leftovers," "The scarf is for her."

declarative Constituting a statement or assertion that may be either true or false, e.g., "Language must continually change."

defective Indicating lack of a customary grammatical (or inflectional) form or forms, or used in only one form, e.g., "quoth," "wend," "behooves."

demonstrative Indicating something pointed out or singled out, e.g., the pronouns "this" and "these."

determinative Indicating the pointing forward to a subsequent phrase or clause that explains or completes, e.g., "such words as . . . ," "the one that. . . ."

disjunctive Indicating contrast, difference, alternatives, etc., between words, phrases, or clauses, e.g., the conjunctions "but," "or," "though."

distributive Indicating reference to a particular thing or to every member of a group, e.g., the pronouns "each" and "none."

effective Indicating (with a verb) the final stage or point or the result of an action.

factitive Indicating completion of a predicate, or the need of a transitive verb of calling, making, thinking, etc., for not only an object but also an object complement, e.g., "It turned the sea red," "They named her Cynthia."

frequentative Indicating repeated action or recurrent state or situation, e.g., "Raindrops are falling." Also ITERATIVE, REDUPLICATIVE.

genitive Indicating close and exclusive relationship, as by denoting possession, a characteristic or trait, or source, e.g., "the building's shadow," "the woman's touch."

imperative Indicating explicit request, supplication, prohibition, warning, command, etc., e.g., "Stop!" "Do let's be serious."

imperfective Indicating action that is incomplete and continuing, e.g., "She is still dancing." Also ATELIC, DURATIVE.

indicative Indicating the usual form of a verb: simple assertion or interrogation, or expression in terms of what is a fact or is clearly related to reality, e.g., "The book is on the table."

ingressive Indicating the beginning of an action, state, etc., e.g., the verbs "get," "set out," "awaken." Also INCEPTIVE, INCHOATIVE.

intensive   Indicating appositional (or adjacent) use for emphasis, e.g. "I myself," "the word itself."

interrogative   Indicating a question, e.g., "What's the word for that?"

nominative   Indicating the subject of a verb (or predicate after a copulative verb), or direct address, e.g., "She eats too much," "He is my uncle."

partitive   Indicating restricting, setting off, or only a part of, e.g., "a scrap of food," "one of your friends."

prepositive   Placed before another word or words, or prefixed, e.g., "most foul murder."

postpositive   Placed after another word or words, or suffixed, e.g., "murder most foul."

privative   Indicating lack or loss of, absence of, or negation, e.g., the prefixes "un-," "a-," "non-," the suffix "-less."

reflexive   Indicating an action of the agent or grammatical subject upon itself, that is, with the subject and object being the same person or thing, e.g., "She feeds herself" or (implicitly reflexive) "She keeps in shape."

relative   Indicating reference to or dependence on an antecedent word, phrase, or clause, or introducing a subordinate clause, e.g., "which," "who," "whatever."

subjunctive   Indicating expression of something not actual or real but rather a desire, demand, plan, doubt, requirement, conception, etc., e.g., "Were I your sister . . ."

substantive   Indicating a noun or a word or phrase functioning as a noun, e.g., "running away."

Scholarly (Bibliographic) Terms

ancilla   An aid or guide to understanding, appreciating, or mastering something that is difficult. *Pl.* ancillae.

apparatus criticus   Supplementary background or critical material provided in a scholarly edition, such as variant versions of the text or pertinent glossaries. *Pl.* apparatus critici.

catalogue raisonné   A detailed and systematic descriptive classification of books, works of art, etc., arranged by subjects and with informative or critical notes; thematic, annotated bibliography. *Pl.* catalogues raisonnés.

codex An ancient unbound manuscript, as of scriptures or a classical work in Greek or Latin. *Pl.* codices.

collate To compare and examine critically (different texts, etc.) in order to determine (or present for readers) likenesses or discrepancies and to synthesize; to see that all parts of a book are present and properly arranged.

conspectus A general survey or overview; synopsis or summary. *Pl.* conspectuses.

corrigendum An error needing correction, esp. as noted (too late) by an inserted page in a book or pamphlet; a listing of errors along with the corrections; errata. *Pl.* corrigenda.

editio princeps The earliest printed edition of a work, esp. of one previously circulated in manuscript form; first edition. *Pl.* editiones principes.

exordium The beginning or introductory part of a discourse or treatise. *Pl.* exordiums, exordia.

facsimile edition An edition of a book that is a page-by-page photographic reproduction of an older or original edition.

fascicle A section of a book being issued in installments before its publication as a complete work.

Festschrift A collection of writings on various subjects by different people for a special occasion or year, esp. a literary anniversary tribute to a scholar. *Pl.* Festschriften, Festschrifts.

florilegium A collection of excerpts or writings; anthology. *Pl.* florilegia.

holograph A manuscript, letter, etc., in the handwriting of its author.

incunabula Books printed before the year 1501, valuable as records of early typography and as the first typeset versions of numerous classical, medieval, and Renaissance works. *Sing.* incunabulum. Also CRADLE BOOKS, FIFTEENERS.

interlinear Written or inserted between the lines; printed in differing, alternate lines, such as a text offered in two languages.

lection A particular version of a passage in a text, or a variant reading.

Literaturwissenschaft Literature as a scholarly study based on historical and philological principles.

prolegomenon A preliminary or introductory essay; foreword. *Pl.* prolegomena.

pseudepigrapha   Works ascribed (usually with conscious falsehood or pious fraud) to another author; spurious works purportedly by biblical prophets.

scholium   A scholar's explanatory remark or comment in the margin. *Pl.* scholia, scholiums.

variorum   An edition or version of a book including notes and comments by several scholars and/or textual variations. Pl. variorums.

Rhetoric Terms

With the exception of "hyperbole," "litotes," "periphrasis," and a few others, rhetoric (and grammatical) terms remain rare and literally Greek to the eye. Yet many of these classical figure-of-speech words can still be found in the pages of unabridged English and American dictionaries—often with confusingly differing definitions. They constitute an intricate and difficult lexicon. But despite their complexity and intimidating, almost medical look and sound, they are among the most precise descriptive words we can draw from to denote fine points of style and persuasive devices in language; in fact, the distinctions in meaning between many rhetorical terms are often so minute—or overlapping—as to be frustrating to the layperson seeking the proper word.

The fifty terms presented here are only some of the hundreds of such technical oratorical-stylistic terms, most of them as applicable to language today as they were two millennia ago in the ancient world.

accismus   Pretended refusal or disclaiming; hypocritical modesty.

adynaton   Magnifying or exaggerating an actual event by reference to something impossible.

aenos   Use of erudite words or allusions to appeal to the learned.

amblysia   Phrasing in such a way as to forewarn or to cushion a dire announcement, but sometimes thereby alarming in itself.

anadiplosis   Repeating the final word or words of a phrase or clause as the beginning of the ensuing phrase.

anthimeria   The using of one part of speech for another for a striking effect (and hence a type of enallage).

apaetesis   The angry putting aside of a matter to be taken up later.

apocrisis   Replying to one's own arguments.

apomnemonysis   Quoting an approved authority.

apophasis Seeming to be denying something while really affirming it; mentioning by denying mention.

asphalia Emphatic guaranteeing of what one is saying, as by assuring others, wagering about the truth of something, etc.

autoclesis Introducing an idea or subject by seeming to refuse discussion of it, thereby arousing interest.

auxesis An ordering of thoughts expressed in a sequence of ascending importance; also, high-sounding language or hyperbole.

bdelygmia A litany of abuse; string of execrations.

catacosmesis An ordering of words in descending order of importance; anticlimactic sequence in phrasing.

commoratio Dwelling on a point by repeating it in different words.

comprobatio Complimenting one's judges or audience to gain their favor.

diallage Concentration of several separate arguments upon a single point.

dialysis Rational disposing of reasons for or against something; "dismembering" or reasoning away.

diasyrm Arch disparagement, as by mocking praise.

diatyposis Vivid presentation by means of exciting language.

dichaeologia A defense of failure or disgrace, as by blaming extenuating circumstances, inadequate help, or betrayal by friends.

effictio Personal description, as a head-to-foot catalogue of one's outward appearance.

effiguration Elaborate, detailed description of an object or event.

epanorthosis Correcting or retracting a statement even while making it, or thinking better of what one has begun to say.

epicrisis Praising or disparaging by paraphrasing or citing somebody else.

epiplexis Asking a question as a form of reproach, or arguing that a sensible person must surely see the truth.

epitrope Conceding a point in an argument in such a qualified or ironic way as to make it seem unimportant or injurious to one's opponent, or to make one's opponent the butt of ridicule.

eucharistia Profuse praise as an expression of gratitude and confused emotion.

exergasia   Repeating a point by using different figures of speech to give the impression of saying something new.

expeditio   Quickly rejecting or passing over minor points to come to the main point.

gradatio   A progressive sequence of statements that are linked by words or clauses repeated; repeated anadiplosis.

heterogenium   Answering irrelevantly to distract attention from a sensitive or difficult point.

hypocrisis   Mockery through exaggeration of an opponent's mannerisms or speech habits.

irmus   A long sentence that culminates with a dramatic or emphatic close.

medela   Apology for a friend's undeniable misconduct or faults.

mempsis   An impassioned but somewhat caustic supplication in which a pointed complaint is implied.

metabasis   A brief noting of what has already been said and what is to follow.

metastasis   Casual mention of a subject as if it were unimportant; responding to a person's criticism or insult with a riposte that uses or plays on his or her words.

orismus   Defining something by rejecting things that are similar, that is, by specifying what it is not.

paradigma   Referring to something similar and its qualities or fate as an example to press a point.

philophronesis   Resorting to gentle speech or humble submission in order to mitigate anger or to mollify.

praecisio   Withholding of words, as to express contentment or contempt; deliberate silence.

pseudomenos   An argument forcing an adversary to lie.

pysma   Asking a series of brief questions, requiring different answers, for dramatic effect.

scesis onamaton   Omission of a verb or verbs from an expressed thought; sentence fragment.

significatio   Implying more than one says.

synchisis   Deliberately jumbled word order to indicate a confused state of mind.

systrophe A congeries of descriptive phrases expressing various aspects of one thing.

threnos Lamentation; emphasizing or dramatizing one's hardships or difficult situation; a rhetorical "misery loves company."

Bookish Appellations

From archaisms, obscure slang terms, pedanticisms, foreign expressions, and literary characters, English has a large store of labels literary and lingual for people, including the following examples of bookish name-calling.

analphabet An illiterate.

anonymuncule A petty or shifty writer hiding behind anonymity.

Aolist One who claims to be inspired.

aristarch A severe but just critic; rigorous scholar or grammarian.

asinus ad lyram An ass at the lyre: one lacking artistic talent or appreciation.

barbae tenus sapientes Wise men with thin beards: men who purport knowledge they do not possess.

bel esprit One with a gifted mind or fine sense of wit.

bibliobibuli People who read too much, oblivious of the real world.

biblioclast A destroyer of books.

bibliolater, bibliolatrist A book worshiper; intense bookworm.

bibliophile One who loves books, esp. a collector interested in beautiful or rare bindings, formats, etc.

bibliotaph One who hides or hoards books.

Boanerges A fiery, ranting orator or preacher.

Boeotian One who objects to or is hostile to works of art or literature because he or she does not understand them.

Bombastes Furioso One who talks big.

borborygmite A user of foul language.

breathseller A hired speaker.

cacograph A bad writer or speller.

colporteur   A peddler of religious tracts or books.

comstock   A literary prude or morally censorious person.

dentiloquist   One who speaks with clenched teeth.

diaskeuast   An editor.

dryasdust   A dull antiquary or pedant lacking imagination.

flaneur   An intellectual trifler.

gobemouche   One who swallows flies: a credulous gossip or dupe for any rumor.

grammaticaster   A petty or pedantic grammarian.

great cham   (Smollett's term for Samuel Johnson) An authoritative, dominant literary personage or critic; literary arbiter.

harmless drudge   A lexicographer.

hierophant   A high priest or religious interpreter; avowed spokesperson or elucidator for an idea, policy, occult group, etc.

homme moyen sensuel   Middling instinctual man, or the average reader.

homo unius libri   A person versed in only one book or point of view; author known chiefly for a single book.

Latinotaster   A person having only a smattering of Latin.

lexicomane   A lover of dictionaries.

lirripoop   A learned, academic fool.

logogogue   A self-styled authority on words.

logophag, autologophag   One who eats his or her own words.

logophile   A word lover.

makebate, breedbate   One who provokes quarrels and contention.

mome   A carping critic.

mumjummer   A bureaucrat adept at speaking or writing gobbledygook.

mystagogue   A teacher of or trafficker in mystical doctrines.

onomatomaniac   One who is obsessed with words, names, or the sounds of words.

penster   One who writes petty or hackneyed things.

perpilocutionist   A person who talks through his or her hat; dissembler or hypocrite.

philodox One enamored of his or her own opinions.

philosophaster A shallow philosophical dabbler or poseur; pseudo-thinker.

précieuse An affected, self-styled literary woman.

proneur One given to excessive praise or flattery.

pseudologue A pathological liar.

quibberdick A nasty, venomous quibbler.

quidnunc, claver A rabid, nosy gossip.

sculler A teacher compelled to do scholarly writing and publishing in order to earn his or her livelihood.

sedulous ape A slavish imitator.

sillograph A skeptical satirist or debunker of a particular school of thought or philosophy.

tenth muse A notable female poet or writer.

tertius gaudens A third party who revels in or profits by a dispute between two others.

third tongue A slanderer.

verbile One whose mental imagery is largely one of visualized words.

verbomaniac A person obsessed with words.

witling A would-be wit of limited intelligence.

xenoepist One who speaks with a foreign accent.

Zoilus A carping, hairsplitting pedant or critic.

Readability: The Fog Index

People who strongly disagree about the informativeness, literacy, or probable longevity of a piece of prose will often be in more agreement about its readability.

If readability is no certification of literary quality, it is always a communicational virtue: a quality in writing, whatever its content or lack thereof, that induces the reader to move from sentence to sentence. The readable writer may not be a lucid thinker, much less a profound one. He or she may possess nothing more than the natural ability to write in a conversational way or the hard-earned skill of arranging words without stylistic kinks, puzzles, or reverses that betray the reader. Fluid and understandable prose is perhaps a matter less of eloquence than of avoiding what confuses and what overtaxes attention.

Can readability be measured? If it can, is the key to it the use chiefly of short words? The number of hard words? The length of the sentences? The complexity of the ideas discussed?

Along with the Yardstick Formula of Rudolf Flesch, one of the best-known formulas devised in recent years to "measure" readability is that of Robert Gunning, who was a crusader against jargon and a writing consultant to newspapers and magazines. Gunning's formula is called the Fog Index.

Gunning is careful to emphasize that the Fog Index is not a tool for becoming a great writer but is useful rather for measuring complexity in prose and determining whether writing is gauged to its audience. *"Use the yardstick as a guide after you have written, but not as a pattern before you write,"* he cautions. "Good writing must be alive; don't kill it with system." Thus the Fog Index is probably most useful as a measuring stick for turgidity in writing—in short, for confirming longwindedness or obfuscating jargon. In a column about Gunning, Russell Baker observed that the Fog Index serves well for "writing the gobbledygook out of official prose." It may be of particular use to teachers and business people in "objectifying" criticism that they need to make of the writing of students or subordinates.

Gunning also suggests that use of the index can soothe one's conscience about avoiding certain "must" reading matter. "Most of us have a pile of material we have laid aside to read later. We feel guilty for not getting at it. Usually a Fog Index check will show that this laid-aside matter is more complexly written than it should be or need be."

Below are Gunning's instructions for determining the Fog Index of a passage of writing. The resulting number or "score" represents not intelligence level but school grade level. For example, Gunning found the Fog Index of Margaret Mitchell's *Gone With the Wind* to be 8, or eighth-grade reading level, and those for various national magazines to range from 9 to 12. For a more comprehensive discussion of the Fog Index and questions of readability, see Robert Gunning's *The Technique of Clear Writing*.

To find the Fog Index of a passage, then, take these three simple steps:

One: Jot down the number of words in successive sentences. If the piece is long, you may wish to take several samples of 100 words, spaced evenly through it. If you do, stop the sentence count with the sentence which ends nearest the 100-word total. Divide the total number of words in the passage by the number of sentences. This gives the average sentence length of the passage.

Two: Count the number of words of three syllables or more per 100 words. Don't count the words (1) that are proper names, (2) that are combinations of short easy words (like "bookkeeper" and "manpower"), (3) that are verb forms made three syllables by adding -*ed* or -*es* (like "created" or "trespasses"). This gives you the percentage of hard words in the passage.

Three: To get the Fog Index, total the two factors just counted and multiply by .4.

Let us apply this yardstick to a few sentences from *The Summing Up* by W. Somerset Maugham:

> I have never had much patience with the writers who claim from the reader an effort to *understand* their meaning. You have only to go to the great *philosophers* to see that it is *possible* to express with *lucidity* the most subtle *reflections*. You may find it *difficult* to *understand* the thought of Hume, and if you have no *philosophical* training its *implications* will doubtless escape you; but no one with any *education* at all can fail to *understand exactly* what the meaning of each sentence is. Few people have written English with more grace than Berkeley. There are two sorts of *obscurity* you will find in writers. One is due to *negligence* and the other to *willfulness*.

The number of words in the sentences of this passage is as follows: 20—23—11—13—20—10—11—10. (Note that the third sentence is actually three complete thoughts linked by a comma, in one instance, and a semicolon in the other. These should be counted as separate sentences.) The total number of words in the passage is 118. This figure divided by 8 (the number of sentences) gives the average sentence length—14.5 words.

The words of three syllables or more are italicized in the above passage. There are 15 of them, or 12.7 percent.

Adding the average sentence length and percentage of polysyllables gives 27.2. And this multiplied by .4 results in the Fog Index of 10.9, about the level of *Harper's*.

Use this yardstick often as a quick check to see if your writing is in step with other writing that has proved easy to read and understand. If your copy tests 13 or more, you are beyond the danger line of reading difficulty. You are writing on the college level of complexity and your reader is likely to find it heavy going even though he is paying close attention. Copy with a Fog Index of 13 or more runs the danger of being ignored or misunderstood.

Some Additional Literary Terms

Most of the terms in this addendum are unquestionably rare, if not archaic, but a few have currency in modern linguistics. Mere curiosities or

not, here they are—in the interest of completeness—as a minor complement to the generally more useful terminology of the main text. They
remind us that our English language possesses many words with remark-
ably specific literary meanings.

ab absurdo   From absurdity: falsely argued because of being absurd.

ablaut *n.*   A pattern of inflectional vowel change in a root or affix, e.g.,
"give, gave, given." Also APOPHANY, GRADATION.

acroamatic *adj.*   Told orally only to chosen followers or disciples; esoteric. *Adj.* acroamatical; *n.* acroama.

acrophony *n.*   The designating of an alphabetic letter by a word having
the same initial sound, e.g., "Fox" for "F" in radio code. Also AC-
ROLOGY.

acyrology *n.*   Incorrect language. *Adj.* acyrological; *adv.* acyrologically.

adnominal *adj.*   Modifying a noun.

adnoun *n.*   An adjective used as a noun.

agent noun   A noun denoting a doer or effecter of an action, e.g.,
"writer" or "cook."

aisling *n.*   A vision described in an evocatively dramatic or poetic way.

aition *n.*   A tale meant to explain a religious experience.

alloquial *adj.*   Involving or pertaining to addressing other people. *N.*
alloquialism, alloquy.

annomination *n.*   Playing on words; paronomasia; adnomination.

apograph *n.*   A reproduction, copy, or transcript. *Pl.* apographa.

appraisive *adj.*   Constituting an evaluation or judgment, as a review or
critical essay.

bahuvrihi *n.*   A two-element term whose first element specifies (the type
of) the second element, e.g., "redneck," "show window," "light-
headed," or the class of such words; an adjectival-nominal compound.

balaam *n.*   Newspaper or magazine filler or otherwise unimportant
copy.

belettered *adj.*   Having after one's name abbreviations or letters of academic or official attainment.

Bellerophontic letter *n.*   An itemized listing or memorandum, as of numerous documents.

breviary *n.* A summary, abridgment, abstract, or brief version of something. Also BREVIATE

brocard *n.* A simple rule or principle; maxim.

catalecta *n.* Additional short pieces or fragments by an author

cataphasia *n.* Verbigeration.

catchcry *n.* An expression or word used as a rallying cry.

categorematic *adj.* In logic, having meaning (as a word or expression) by itself, without other words (contrasted with syncategorematic). *Adv.* categorematically; *n.* categorem.

choke pear *n.* A retort that succeeds in silencing another; withering rebuke or sarcasm.

chresmology *n.* Oracular prophesying; soothsaying.

chrysostomic, chrysostomatical *adj.* Golden-mouthed (used of admired orators).

collocutor *n.* The person to whom or with whom one is speaking.

company terms Venereal nouns.

constative *adj.* Being or making a statement categorizable as either true or false (contrasted with performative). *N.* constative.

congener *n.* A cognate word.

coruscation *n.* A flash of brilliant intellectual playfulness or wit.

costumbrista *n.* The literary or artistic describing of local scenes, folkways, characters, etc.

count noun A noun used in such a way that it can be quantified, or pluralized by a numeral, indefinite article, or pronoun such as "many," e.g., "book" or "needle" (contrasted with mass noun).

credenda *n.* *pl.* Articles of belief or faith. *Sing.* credendum.

cruciverbalist *n.* A crossword-puzzle lover.

curiologic *adj.* Pictorial rather than symbolic, as hieroglyphic characters.

delectus *n.* A selection of instructive passages in Latin or Greek; classical chrestomathy.

diacope *n.* Tmesis.

diglot, diglottic *adj.* Bilingual. *N.* diglot.

epimyth *n.* A story's or fable's moral.

empurpled *adj.*   Having purple passages, lushly overwritten

enchiridion, encheiridion *n*   A manual or handbook

epiphonema *n.*   A dramatic concluding summary or exclamatory comment.

ergasy *n.*   A literary production; treatise

euphonym *n.*   A euphonious synonym.

exaration *n.*   An act of writing, or its product; composition.

explicandum *n.*   Philosophically, a term whose meaning is to be explained.

explicans *n.*   Philosophically, the meaning of a term.

ex silentio, e silentio   From silence: from the fact of a lack of specific evidence, as an improvised argument.

flat *adj.*   Having no inflectional suffix, e.g., an adverb without a "-y" or "-ly" ending ("to run swift").

gentilic *adj.*   Being or involving an adjective or noun indicating ethnic or racial affiliation.

gradus *n.*   A book of phrases, exercises, etc., for learning an art, technique, or craft; originally, a pupil's handbook for learning Greek or Latin prosody.

grimoire *n.*   A sorcerer's incantatory manual.

homiliary *n.*   A collection of homilies.

homoeoteleuton *n.*   The occurring in writing of the same or similar endings close together, whether accidentally or intentionally. *Adj.* homoeoteleutic.

hydronymy *n.*   The naming or names of bodies of water.

hypozeugma *n.*   The combining of several subjects with a single verb.

idiasm *n.*   An individual stylistic or other mannerism.

imsonic *adj.*   Onomatopoeic.

incult *adj.*   Crude, disjointed, or unpolished in literary style.

index verborum   A book's glossary of terms used or discussed.

inedita *n.*   Writing that is unpublished.

insititious *adj.*   Inserted or interpolated.

inter alios   Among other persons.

interjaculatory *adj.*   Uttered or thrown in parenthetically.

isagogue *n.* A scholarly introduction to a particular field of study *Adj* isagogic, isagogical

kinesics *n.* The study of nonlinguistic or paralinguistic communication, as of facial expressions, gestures, and shrugs; body language as a science. *Adj.* kinesic; *adv.* kinesically

kyriolexy *n.* The habit of using literal expressions

logopedics *n.* The treatment of speech defects

mantissa *n.* A relatively unimportant addition to a work, speech, etc.

mass noun A noun used generally or abstractly such that it cannot be quantified or used in the plural, e.g., "bread" or "resilience" (contrasted with count noun).

metalepsis *n.* Metonymy used in place of a word already (just) used figuratively, e.g., "That *yacht* will not be the answer to his voyage (figurative) to self-discovery."

monitory *n.* A letter containing a warning, esp. an episcopal letter.

monoliteral *adj.* Consisting of a single letter; in cryptography, monographic, or using single letters in a cipher.

mononym *n.* A one-word term.

nitigram *n.* Epigram.

noctuary *n.* A chronicle or journal of nighttime activities or incidents.

nominatim *adv.* By name: openly or expressly.

onomasiology *n.* The study of words and expressions that can be considered related, as of terminology for a region or for a profession; the ways in which a given concept can be expressed. *Adj.* onomasiologic.

opera omnia A writer's complete works.

optative *adj.* (Of a sentence) Expressing a desire or hope.

orthology *n.* The art of using words correctly.

pandect *n.* A comprehensive, exhaustive treatise or digest.

paradiplomatic *adj.* Deriving from evidence that is not authoritatively textual.

parapraxia, parapraxis *n.* A slip or lapse, as a slip of the tongue; lapsus linguae.

pararthria *n.* Incoherent speech.

paregmenon *n.* A two-word expression in which one of the terms is derived from the other, e.g., "sense and sensibility."

parisology *n.*   Ambiguous wording; equivocation.

paromologia *n.*   Conceding something in order to strengthen one's own case.

pasquil *n.*   Pasquinade.

performative *adj.*   Being an utterance that in itself performs an act, so to speak; for example, an admission of guilt (contrasted with constative). *N.* performative.

perseverate *v.*   To repeat, or battologize, esp. compulsively; go back over to reassess. *Adj.* perserverative; *n.* perseveration.

philosophism *n.*   Sophistry.

pithanology *n.*   Specious or rhetorically seductive speech.

poecilonym *n.*   A synonym. *N.* poecilonymy.

polymythy *n.*   Narrative use in one work of several stories, plots, etc.

postface *n.*   A brief note appearing at the end of a publication.

precative *adj.*   (Of a sentence) Expressing a beseeching or a request.

probouleutic *adj.*   Pertaining to preliminary discussion.

promptuary *n.*   A handy reference book.

prorrhesis *n.*   A preliminary statement.

pseudolalia *n.*   Nonsensical or meaningless speech sounds.

quillet *n.*   A quibble, or a minor or subtle distinction.

reddition *n.*   Explanation, esp. through a comparison.

retroversion *n.*   Translation back, or retranslation, into the original language.

rifacimento *n.*   An adaptation of a literary work.

satisdiction *n.*   Saying enough.

screeve *Chiefly British. n.*   A begging letter.

scrivener *n.*   An unknown or minor writer.

scrivener's palsy *n.*   Writer's cramp.

semelfactive *adj.*   Denoting a verb that expresses action as occurring singly or instantly, without continuation or repetition, e.g., "arrive."

sermuncle *n.*   A brief sermon. Also SERMONET, SERMONETTE.

sillabub *n.*   Florid language

sloan *n*   A putting-down or snub

spadish *adj.* Bluntly direct or candid.

spicilege *n.* An anthology.

stigmeology *n.* The art of punctuation.

sublineation *n.* Underlining.

subliterature *n.* Writing or works inferior to those deemed worthy as literature. *Adj.* subliterary.

subvocal *adj.* Conceiving or ordering speech, or sentences, mentally, apart from or before articulating such thoughts.

sylloge *n.* A summary, collection, or compendium.

syncategorematic *adj.* In logic, not able (as a word or expression) to stand alone to have meaning, or expressive only in conjunction with another or other words, e.g., "are" or "few"; not an independent term (contrasted with categorematic). *Adv.* syncategorematically; *n.* syncategoreme. Also CONSIGNIFICANT.

synorthographic *adj.* Spelled alike.

tapinophoby *n.* Dislike of the low in literature.

textus receptus The standard or generally accepted (as genuine or authoritative) text of a work.

theophoric *adj.* Bearing or deriving from the name of a deity.

tractate *n.* An essay, treatise, or dissertation.

tractatule *n.* A minor tractate.

transumption *n.* The making of a copy or duplicate. *N.* transumpt.

transumptive *adj.* Metaphorical.

unicum *n.* A one-of-a-kind or sole example, as a singular piece of writing.

tralation *n.* Metaphor.

varia *n.* A literary miscellany.

verbid *n.* An infinitive or participle.

wiredrawn *adj.* Lengthily or finely drawn out, as an analogy; intricately spun.

word-catcher *n.* A person who is fussy or difficult about words; word lover.

writation *n.* Bad writing.